PI
AN

Petronius' *Satyricon*, long regarded as the first novel of the western tradition, has always sparked controversy. It has been puzzled over as a strikingly modernist riddle, elevated as a work of exemplary comic realism, condemned as obscene and repackaged as a morality tale. This innovative reading of the surviving portions of the work shows how the *Satyricon* fuses the anarchic and the classic, the comic and the disturbing, and presents readers with a labyrinth of narratorial viewpoints. Victoria Rimell argues that the surviving fragments are connected by an imagery of disintegration, focused on a pervasive Neronian metaphor of the literary text as a human or animal body. Throughout, she discusses the limits of dominant twentieth-century views of the *Satyricon* as bawdy pantomime, and challenges prevailing restrictions of Petronian corporeality to material or non-metaphorical realms. This 'novel' emerges as both very Roman and very satirical in its 'intestinal' view of reality.

VICTORIA RIMELL is a lecturer in classics at Girton College, Cambridge, and was previously a junior research fellow at University College, Oxford. She studied at Cambridge and London and has taught at the Universities of London, Oxford and Cambridge and at the Open University. She also worked as a journalist for two years. Her published work so far has dealt with Roman elegy and satire.

PETRONIUS AND THE ANATOMY OF FICTION

VICTORIA RIMELL

Girton College, Cambridge

CAMBRIDGE
UNIVERSITY PRESS

CAMBRIDGE UNIVERSITY PRESS
Cambridge, New York, Melbourne, Madrid, Cape Town, Singapore, São Paulo

Cambridge University Press
The Edinburgh Building, Cambridge CB2 8RU, UK

Published in the United States of America by Cambridge University Press, New York

www.cambridge.org
Information on this title: www.cambridge.org/9780521815864

First published 2002
This digitally printed version 2007

A catalogue record for this publication is available from the British Library

Library of Congress Cataloguing in Publication data

Rimell, Victoria.
Petronius and the anatomy of fiction / Victoria Rimell.
p. cm.
Includes bibliographical references and index.
ISBN 0 521 81586 X
1. Petronius Arbiter. Satyricon. 2. Satire, Latin – History and criticism.
3. Petronius Arbiter – Technique. 4. Rome – In literature.
5. Fiction – Technique. 6. Narration (Rhetoric) I. Title.
PA6559.R495 2002
873′.01 – dc21 2002067382

ISBN 978-0-521-81586-4 hardback
ISBN 978-0-521-03701-3 paperback

Contents

Acknowledgments

It is a pleasure to thank the Department of Classics at King's College, London, in particular Alessandro Schiesaro and Michael Silk, for their generous support, open minds and wit. I am grateful also to the King's College London Association for the scholarship which let me work and play in London for two years, and to University College, Oxford (especially my guru, Chris Pelling) for the fellowship which gave me space to write and rewrite. John Henderson has always made me think harder and offered buzzing comments on various drafts of this book, so many and heartfelt thanks are due to him. I am indebted, too, to Philip Hardie and Rhiannon Ash, and to my eagle-eyed readers at Cambridge University Press. Finally, I would like to thank Michael Sharp, along with the other members of staff at the press, for their guidance and expertise, and last but not least my parents, for everything and more.

Abbreviations

AClass	*Acta Classica*
AJP	*American Journal of Philology*
ANRW	H. Temporini, *Aufstieg und Niedergang der Römischen Welt*, Berlin 1972
ASNP	*Annali della Scuola Normale Superiore di Pisa*
BICS	*Bulletin of the Institute of Classical Studies*
CA	*Classical Antiquity*
C&M	*Classica et Mediaevalia*
CJ	*Classical Journal*
CP	*Classical Philology*
CQ	*Classical Quarterly*
CR	*Classical Review*
CW	*Classical World*
G&R	*Greece and Rome*
HSCP	*Harvard Studies in Classical Philology*
ICS	*Illinois Classical Studies*
JDAI	*Jahrbuch des Deutschen Archäologischen Instituts*
JHS	*Journal of Hellenic Studies*
JRS	*Journal of Roman Studies*
LCM	*Liverpool Classical Monthly*
MD	*Materiali e Discussioni per l'Analisi dei Testi Classici*
MH	*Museum Helveticum*
PCPhS	*Proceedings of the Cambridge Philological Society*
PSN	*Petronian Society Newsletter*
REL	*Revue des Etudes Latines*
RhM	*Rheinisches Museum*
TAPhA	*Transactions of the American Philological Association*

TLL	*Thesaurus Linguae Latinae*, Leipzig, 1900–
WJA	*Würtzburger Jahrbücher für die Altertumswissenschaft*
WS	*Wiener Studien*

I have used K. Müller's 1995 edition of Petronius throughout unless otherwise stated. All translations are my own.

Introduction
Corporealities

At the beginning of the twenty-first century, a critically aware reader approaching Petronius' *Satyricon* for the first time might well feel as if she is queuing to see an overhyped film, the kind of provocative Hollywood flick designed to bait media and consumers alike with wild expectations, reactions and predefinitions. Critics have claimed repeatedly that the *Satyricon* is 'singularly uninterpretable',[1] that it 'presents more puzzles than any other ancient text'[2] or that it stands as 'the most controversial text in all of classical literature',[3] an exotic 'hothouse plant displaying all the qualities of overstimulated growth'.[4] And although it is generally safe to say that we have moved on from times when 'the scabrous nature of some of the episodes made a scholarly interest in the work eccentric or suspect',[5] the sexual 'shock factor' is undeniably part and parcel of the way we (are taught to) read the *Satyricon*, and remains an important facet of its 'enigma' as well as of its appeal.[6] We cannot study Petronius without at some point coming across Fellini's whorish adaptation and Polidoro's soft porn,[7] or hearing about the cryptic 1960s publication entitled *New York expurgated: A moral guide for the jaded, tired, evil, non-conforming, corrupt, condemned and the curious – humans and otherwise – to underground Manhattan*

1 Slater (1990) 250. 2 Sullivan (1968a) 21.
3 Rudich (1997) 186. 4 Quinn (1979) 249.
5 Sullivan (1986) 254. See Rose (1966b) for an account of such readings.
6 As Josipovici argues (1982: 20), 'the ultimate play with the reader still involves curiosity, [and] that curiosity is still sexual, if we are prepared to recognise that the domain of sex is as large as Freud suggested – that is, that what is at stake is the desire to discover the meaning of one's body'. As Connors reminds us (1998: 8), each manuscript source for the *Satyricon* is in part a document of reception, a striking example of which is the O family of manuscripts, which cut out all obscene detail to transform Encolpius into a more respectable *pedagogus*.
7 This film was made in 1969, the same year as Fellini's *Satyricon*. It is said to 'capitalise on the public's imagination of orgies under the emperor Nero' and to be 'unmemorable' (Schmeling 1994a: 151). Also in 1969, notes Schmeling, 'the Stratford (Ontario) Festival produced a musical-comedy version of the *Satyricon*, which focused on the *Cena* and a portrait of Trimalchio and his friends in modern-day dress as boorish millionaires in the worst American tradition' (151).

(Grove Press, New York, 1966), penned by (who else?) 'Petronius'.[8] It is tempting to conclude that the relative silence of British classicists on the *Satyricon* may still have more than a little to do with its 'inappropriateness', the very quality that inspired the Bloomsbury Group to extol Petronius as *the* antidote to English Victorian morality.[9] In short, we continue to be embarrassed, critically or otherwise, by a text which by all accounts 'will neither explain itself nor go away'.[10]

Needless to say, the *Satyricon* comes with its own idiosyncratic baggage of dilemmas and obstacles to comprehension and conceptualisation. Rudich plots a five-point list of the odds stacked against its modern readers, which also neatly illustrates the polarisation of organising critical rhetoric and rambling Petronianese:

> First is the fragmentary condition of the extant text which appears to represent (although the scholarly debate on the matter still continues) about one sixteenth of its original length. Nor can it be said with full confidence that the order of the episodes that we now possess corresponds with their progression as designed by the author. It must also be stated at the outset that the extant text is bound to contain numerous allusions whose meaning is entirely lost to us... Finally, the major difficulty derives from the author's chosen mode of discourse – a first person account placed in the mouth of a picaresque character, an 'unreliable narrator' *par excellence* who is the subject of mockery and ridicule, and thus apparently unfit to champion any genuine authorial opinions... The difficulties only multiply if one inquires into what could be taken for the political dimension of the novel: of its writer's dissident insights and sensibilities, if any, as traceable in the parts of the text we possess. Under scrutiny, the matter becomes increasingly elusive: there hardly seems to exist a single passage that yields an unequivocal political message.[11]

Not only has the *Satyricon* come to us perforated with (possible) holes and tears, or even shrunk down to a fraction of its original size,[12] but

[8] See Schmeling (1994: 151). According to Schmeling, no explanation is given for the author's (or authors') *nom de plume*.

[9] E.g. Letter of Lytton Strachey to Virginia Woolf, November 8, 1912: 'Is it prejudice, do you think, that makes us hate the Victorians, or is it the truth of the case? They seem to me a set of mouthing, bungling hypocrites... I would like to live for another 200 years (to be modest). The literature of the future will, I see clearly, be amazing... To live in those days, when books will pour out of the press reeking with all the filth of Petronius'. Quoted in Schmeling (1994a) 166.

[10] Slater (1990) 1.

[11] Rudich (1997) 186–7.

[12] Sullivan (1968a: 34–8) suggests that the original text may have stretched to 400,000 words, between sixteen and twenty-four books. See further debate in Walsh (1970: 73–6) and Reeve (1983). Also see Gowers (1994) on the idea that Neronian literature sees itself as concentrated or boiled down, *decoctus*. Or perhaps this is an amputated, castrated or mutilated text, constantly performing its status as bad (i.e. impotent) literature (*ut corpus orationis enervaretur et caderet* / 'so that

it also seems to have been 'undertaken with the deliberate intention of defeating the expectations of an audience accustomed to an organizing literary form'.[13]

Yet it is interesting that for many critics, the idea that the *Satyricon* cannot be read like, or compared to, other texts, has proved strangely liberating. Despite the 'moralist' standpoint of post-war critics such as Arrowsmith, Bacon and Highet, who saw in the *Satyricon* 'a deep searching analysis of the death throes of classical *Romanitas*', preached from an Epicurean pulpit,[14] Petronius has remained for most a 'fun' author, whose 'topsy-turvy world'[15] can never be taken too seriously. In many ways, the *Satyricon*'s very 'uniqueness' has represented a welcome relief from the detective-work grind of classification and elucidation:[16] in his undergraduate edition of the *Cena*, for instance, Gilbert Lawall reassures that the text as a whole 'remains one of the few works of ancient Roman literature that one reads simply for pleasure'.[17] Similarly Auerbach, for whom the *Satyricon* marks the 'ultimate realism attained in antiquity', calls the *Cena* 'a purely comic work', dictating that 'it must not be treated on any other level except the comic, which admits no problematic probing';[18] Quinn comments 'It is refreshing to read Latin so simple and direct',[19] while Sullivan's influential 1968 book defines Petronius as a 'literary opportunist', a view taken up by Wright and Walsh, who are similarly convinced of the irresponsible, often cynical and invariably comic intentions of the work.

the body of your speech is emasculated and dies,' *Sat.* 2.2): Most (1992) gives a full account of Neronian literature's obsession with dismemberment, in particular the role of dismemberment in a conceptual vocabulary for analysing texts and parts of texts.

13 Zeitlin (1971a) 635.

14 Arrowsmith (1966) 325. Like T. S. Eliot, whose *Wasteland* was inspired by what was seen as Petronius' bleak vision of spiritual desolation, Arrowsmith, Highet and Bacon all see contemporary concerns about a disintegrating society and immoral urban living mirrored in the *Satyricon*. However, Arrowsmith (1959: xi) also finds room for light entertainment: 'the effect of the *Satyricon* is neither scorn nor indignation, but the laughter appropriate to good satire enlarged by the final gaiety of comedy; the comic completes the satire and gives the whole randy work that effortless rightness of natural gaiety that makes it so improbably wholesome'. Cf. Highet (1941: 181): 'manners, education, aesthetics: in these three fields Petronius had a serious intention to correct or chastise, but there is always something comic about the way he does it'.

15 Holzberg (1995) 63.

16 Sullivan notes (1967: 78), 'the principle of uniqueness is a tempting one to invoke for a work that is so manifestly different from the rest of Latin literature. Certainly the adjective "unique" occurs frequently in critical comment on the *Satyricon*'.

17 Lawall (1995) iv. 18 Auerbach (1953) 31.

19 Quinn (1979) 252. Cf. Schmeling (1994a: 144): 'A great virtue of Petronius, it seems to me, is his ability to say everything simply, which makes his language seem healthy and in touch with the living, spoken language. The *Satyricon* is marked by casual simplicity or off-hand stylishness which we envy because it appears to have cost nothing to achieve.'

Walsh in particular argues for a reading of the *Satyricon* as 'bawdy entertainment' and dismisses more uneasy reactions as exaggerated or unfounded ('I do not believe that the variety of literary tone reflects an anarchic view of life. I prefer to see it as a virtuosity in which the author and the reader take pleasure').[20] Slater's 1990 study, much influenced by reader-response criticism, propounds a more subtle version of the well-established 'anti-moralist' standpoint, in which Petronius is imaged as a tricky nihilist whose ultimate goal was pure entertainment. Slater's vision is frustratingly dead-ended, suggesting that the *Satyricon*'s preoccupation with critical failures supports the notion that the text itself is intentionally unintelligible, 'critically unreadable':[21] the idea that this is a 'comic text' is already taken for granted in his conclusion that its 'primary source of comedy' is the ongoing strategy by which 'a reader's expectation of decoding meaning through ordinary procedures of reading can be aroused only to be frustrated'.[22] Throughout, a generalised post-structuralist emphasis on the 'ludic' nature of texts and reading processes is misappropriated to demonstrate both that this unusually complex literary work is by definition a 'comedy', and also that all meaning in such a text is perpetually elusive.

Here, and in all the approaches to the *Satyricon* as 'pure entertainment', there lurk tones of self-exculpation and denial: in each analysis the 'comic' is made to efface the 'serious', the political, and the problematic, as if laughter were always a barometer of pleasure, not pain, or as if there were never such a thing as a bad, ugly joke, or jokes on *you*. It is no coincidence that such perspectives are often accompanied by constructions of critical distance or aloofness, which conspicuously sidestep complicity. Conte, for example, deciphers the difficult relationship between, or doubling of, Petronius the author and Encolpius the narrator, by dividing loyalties: the 'rogue' narrator is funny because we, like the intellectually sophisticated author, can look down on and mock him from a position of objectivity and superiority 'outside' the text. Thus:

The reader cannot help advocating the '*bona mens*', that common sense which is so often invoked in the *Satyricon* as the significant missing element. Petronius as 'hidden author' creates an 'implied self-image', and the ideal reader, by

[20] Walsh (1974) 189–90. [21] Slater (1990) 3.

[22] Slater (1990) 237. In his preface, Slater appears already to have decided that Petronius is a 'writer of comedy' (249) (and that he himself is developing as a critic of comedy) by stressing that *Reading Petronius* is an extension of his previous work *Plautus in Performance*, which analysed how performance criticism could inform us about styles of humour. The rather misleading rhetorical strategy of setting Petronius and Plautus side by side on the first page frames expectations and sets unquestioned agendas for the whole book.

> forming exactly this image of the author, takes shape in the text as a set of values in opposition to those of Encolpius and closer to normality. By making faces, as it were, behind the narration of Encolpius, the author first ensures that the protagonist and narrator reveals himself and his own naïveté and then leaves him without the protective illusions that the narrator has constructed for himself: in this way he secures for himself the reader's conniving response.[23]

Conte is much influenced by Auerbach, who forges similar perspectives: 'Petronius looks from above at the world he depicts. The vulgarity of language is not designed to arouse laughter in a large crowd but is rather the piquant condiment for the palate of a social and literary elite accustomed to viewing things from above with Epicurean composure.'[24] He is echoed by Sullivan, who claims of Petronius, 'his self-conscious sophistication may be seen in the careful dissociation of author from narrator, who is constantly made the butt of the author's ridicule and satire'.[25] Even Slater, who elsewhere talks of 'reader participation',[26] goes on to class himself clear-headedly as an 'observer'.[27]

Critics have rarely wanted to get *involved* in reading the *Satyricon*, not simply because, in different ways, they do not support the concept and implications of 'participatory' reading, but because this is a threatening text whose gritty, low-life universe can seem dangerously infectious if viewed up close. The approaches I have just outlined, which all rely on interpreting the *Satyricon* as comedy or flimsy entertainment viewed from on high by objective, if frustrated spectators, are reactions not only to uncertainty surrounding the state of the text, but also to the problematic implications of *not* reading the *Satyricon* from a distance – implications which, I will argue, are continually negotiated in the text itself. It is all too easy to erase difficulties and contradictions by summing them up as entertainment, or by pleading the academic equivalent of insanity – non-comprehension.[28] If a text is so disjointed and ultimately superficial, it can never have the power to move, upset or change its readers: if in doubt, we can always laugh. The risk of finding anything more complex

[23] Conte (1996) 22. [24] Auerbach (1953) 47. [25] Sullivan (1968a) 258.

[26] Slater (1990) 14ff.: 'Yet reading is a far from passive process. It is just as participatory, though in different ways, as watching a performance in a theatre' (14). Goffman (1974: 130) takes this one step further: 'The theatre-goer is the stage actor's opposite number . . . He collaborates in the unreality onstage. He sympathetically and vicariously participates in the unreal world generated by the dramatic interplay of the scripted characters. He gives himself over. He is raised (or lowered) to the cultural level of the playwright's characters or themes.'

[27] Slater (1990) 242.

[28] I refer in particular to Slater's conclusion (1990: 249): 'The *Satyricon* consumes itself completely in the process of reading, leaving no hidden message behind, no secret structure suddenly revealed, only a reader simultaneously more capable of detecting fraudulent meaning and more hungry for an elusive "real" meaning.'

than intellectual hyperactivity in the *Satyricon* is limited by the idea that a fragmented, anti-narrative text necessitates fragmented reading: very few critics have attempted, on paper, to read the work as a 'whole' or to analyse points of contact between points A, B or Z, because it is already taken for granted that the *Satyricon*'s schizophrenic aesthetic splinters continuity, and that narrative teleology is the only formula for coherence.

Moreover, the use of 'novel' as a means of definition frequently does not help to unpack the difference or intricacy of the *Satyricon*.[29] All too often, 'novel' also anaesthetises engagement by packaging or relabelling problems of interpretation which have yet to be fully analysed. Frequently too, Bakhtin's extensive work on the history of the novel provides a convenient board of authority on which to pin definitions of the *Satyricon* as *novelistic* which in fact fudge the real issues at stake. Let us look, for example, at Slater's concluding remarks on the prickly topic of 'genre':

> By evoking Bakhtin's concepts of parody and heteroglossia of language systems, we have virtually assured our answer to the question of how to categorise the *Satyricon*. The answer is one few today would find serious fault with: the *Satyricon* is a novel. For Bakhtin the novel is not a genre, and so we have both answered and denied the generic question: no other generic description (neither simple parody nor satire) will do, and yet it is not enough to say we have simply the absence of genre, for the careful and deliberate juxtaposition of language systems within the continuities of narrative shows that we have more than a miscellany. Thus if 'novel' is not a genre, it nonetheless gives us a certain frame of expectations.[30]

Slater seems to have all bases covered, yet his argument is less reassuring than circular: 'novel' rehearses, rather than answers, our questions, and tells us next to nothing about what and how the *Satyricon* means. Depending on which passages of Bakhtin's œuvre are singled out for 'application', 'novel' either pretends to define (and thus resolve) the *Satyricon*'s incorporation of a mass of literary styles and forms, or proclaims the work's difference and uniqueness (its novelty), oversimplifying multiplicity as a 'displacement' of a range of 'models' rather than as a more ambitious engagement with the concept of intertextuality.[31]

[29] Barchiesi (1996: 192) rightly qualifies his use of theories of the novel in discussing Petronius with the proviso: 'la parola moderna porta con sé implicazioni pericolose'.

[30] Slater (1990) 233–4.

[31] See for example McGlathery (1998), whose reading of the widow of Ephesus story (*Sat.* 111–12) 'applies' a combination of Bakhtin's theory of the carnivalesque and his thesis that Petronius' story epitomises the novelistic world view. Despite some initial reservations, the authoritative Bakhtinian opposition of the 'valorized absolute past of the Roman national epic' and the 'sordid present' of the novel (327) is ultimately reiterated. This article is discussed in detail in chapter 8. I understand intertextuality (like Fowler 2000: 118 *et passim*) as a 'property of the literary system'

I propose to start, therefore, by reevaluating the crucial questions and definitions repeatedly proposed or uncritically implied in readings of Petronius: in what ways, exactly, is the *Satyricon* 'funny', and for whom? Is it possible to separate author and narrator, and to maintain a critical 'distance' from Encolpius, who offers the *only* perspective on and experience of this fiction? Similarly, can we claim that Encolpius is simply stupid (and therefore 'inferior') and not ever or always self-consciously posing as a clown, empowered by ironic self-mockery and by his audience's necessary inability to tell when they are being manipulated or fooled? It is a real challenge to take in this hefty text at once, especially when it looks so disordered, but what happens when we try?[32] Is it as crazy and surrealist as it seems, do the parts make a whole, and how scripted is the appearance of fragmentation? Why do we assume it does not 'make sense' simply because it erodes standard terms of definition, and are there other ways, apart from plot and narrative, in which a text can trace patterns, make a point?

My analysis will suggest that we should not underestimate just how crafted, organised or contradictory the *Satyricon* is, or to what extent those contradictions are framed as a threat to reader objectivity as well as to critical hierarchies and rhetorics of categorisation. My approach is influenced and framed by the subtle insights and challenges of two classicists in particular, whose work stands out in Petronian criticism: Connors' 1998 study *Petronius the Poet* examines representations of poetic performances and other overt uses of poetic structures in the *Satyricon*, looking at how verse and prose are staged as rival structures of representation which interact and overlap; in questioning the prevailing view of the *Satyricon's* multiple voices as 'literary chaos', Connors argues that 'there is more to hear than cacophony'.[33] She is much influenced by Zeitlin's 1971 article on the two buttressing poems of the *Satyricon*, the *Troiae Halosis* and the *Bellum Civile*. In sharp contrast to her contemporaries, Zeitlin argued that

which primarily 'involves a recognition that interpreting [and, too, writing] an individual text involves reading [writing] it against a background of the many other texts that constitute the literary system'.

32 I am not suggesting a work of criticism can ever capture or replicate the totality of a work of fiction; as Connors warns, each interpretation inevitably 'fragments and reassembles its object of study' (1998: 147).

33 Connors (1998) 1–2. Beck (1973) to some extent reflects and extends this idea, framing the *Satyricon* as a 'well-wrought, sophisticated and self-consistent work of narrative fiction' (43). However, Beck is concerned here only with proving the consistency of Encolpius' character in an argument which, as I will suggest below, is overly rigid and limiting. A brief argument for the 'coherence' and 'unity' of the *Satyricon* is also necessary to Arrowsmith's packaging of the work (1966) as 'fundamentally serious, even moral; a sophisticated Epicurean satire'.

the poems demand not to be read as detachable fragments, as dictated by preconceptions of the *Satyricon* as disjointed and episodic, but are dependent for their meaning both on each other and on their prose contexts. Her article is ambitious in stressing 'community of theme', 'coherence' and 'unity'.[34] However, as Zeitlin clarifies at length in a different article of the same year, entitled 'Petronius as paradox: anarchy and artistic integrity', a 'coherence of underlying themes and symbols'[35] is coexistent with Petronius' anarchic 'vision of disintegration', the 'fundamental disorder' of a work which 'exhibits no rigid unity of tone, no stylistic purity or simplicity, no concentration on a single emotion and probably not a single plot or theme'.[36]

In reasoning now for coherence, now for disjunction, Zeitlin touches on the core dilemma of the *Satyricon*, one which, as I see it, is not simply a function of the state of the text and the uncertainty of our own knowledge or ignorance about it, but is a dynamic and strategy played out consistently throughout the work. The *Satyricon* constantly performs its 'radically anti-classical world view'[37] as a paradox, one which swings neurotically between structure and disjunction, between the building of boundaries and their dissolution. While it undeniably enacts a 'subversion and rejection of classical aesthetic criteria'[38] (linearity, causality, teleology...), the *Satyricon*'s chaotic perspectives are *organised* as such (for how could they not be?), which is not to infer that they are not, after all, chaotic. This is a text that continually offers and demands new ways of seeing. Ironically, it rewards readers who start from the 'beginning' and work right through to the 'end', not with a coherent narrative but with repetitions of words, phrases and images which dye each 'episode' with colours and tones from surrounding passages.

Throughout this book, I will be arguing that the *Satyricon* enacts, through concatenations of images and metaphors, the difficulties and double binds implicit in reading (this text). The *Satyricon* is a theatrical, prismatic and highly metaphorical piece of writing in which viewing, imagining and picturing things are a rich, as well as unpredictable, mode of expression. This is a text in which metaphor is a kind of hallucination, the result of fuzzy vision, recovered memory, seeing too much, or imagining too hard. From the beginning, the processes of reading, writing and learning literature are sucked seductively into this image-system in

[34] Zeitlin (1971b) 57–8, 81–2. [35] Ibid. 81.
[36] Zeitlin (1971a) 635. The subtlety of this idea is more fully understood by reading the two articles side by side.
[37] Ibid. 634. [38] Ibid.

which all abstracts and absolutes are brought to life:[39] animated, energized, but at the same time invested with vital qualities of ephemerality and transformability. As we will see in close-up as we proceed, literature in the *Satyricon* is no longer just written, static and containable, but is imaged as a live body, a flesh or food ingested in the process of learning and spewed out from bodies in performance: inside the consumer, it is a volatile force transmuted in the process of digestion which may also gnaw away its host from within. This disruption of civilising hierarchies between eater and eaten evokes a graphic picture of the risks of eating (and therefore reading) *per se*. Yet in Petronius' universe, good scholars must not only face the horror of eating, they must stuff themselves to the point of nausea (as the ambitious freedmen do in the endless *cena*), for bloating is a precondition of writing.

In the *Satyricon*, everything lives and breathes, and the entire text grows out of the mischievous Latin pun of eating as being (*est* = he eats/he is).[40] Poems and speeches are living bodies which are fed, eaten, grow old, show signs of senility or are visibly afflicted by impotence; or they are contained in or written on human bodies as scars or tattoos. As we read the *Satyricon*, we continually face the idea that literature can affect our bodies and 'inner selves', and that reading may be influenced by (uncontrollable, unconscious) physical impulses, just as texts contain powerful, threatening 'insides' which are often best kept hidden. The dishes staged by Trimalchio as interpretative challenges are still alive and rumbling in his stomach, and animals served for dinner contain live intestines, while the (misinterpreted) wooden Trojan horse is pregnant with fighting men. Perhaps the most overt illustration of this tension between inside and outside bodies comes at *Sat.* 56, when Trimalchio implicitly compares the trials of being a money-lender or a doctor to the difficulty of a writing career: you have to be an expert to see what is lurking beneath a veneer of cleanliness and prosperity, but be warned, that knowledge leads you straight to the diseased and cheapened core of things:

[39] Compare Bramble's introductory remarks on Persius, who at this point is compared directly to Petronius (1974: 1): 'he [Persius] takes the concepts and metaphors of literary criticism back to their physical origins, so concretely dramatising an analysis of the causes of decadence in contemporary letters'.

[40] Or, as Brillat-Savarin said (and most diet magazines and nutrition handbooks have echoed since), 'Dis-moi ce que tu manges, je te dirai ce que tu es.' As Kilgour discusses (1990: 6), the aphorism 'You are what you eat' automatically breaks down the distinction between eater and eaten on which autonomous Western identity is based: hence it is also a model used for asserting cultural identity, and is the focus for standard terms of interracial abuse – to the English the French are 'frogs', while to the French the English are 'les rosbifs'.

'quod autem' inquit 'putamus secundum litteras difficillimum esse artificium? ego puto medicum aut nummularium: medicus, qui scit quid homunciones intra praecordia sua habent et quando febris veniat, etiam si illos odi pessime, quod mihi iubent saepe anetinam parari; nummularius, qui per argentum aes videt.' (56.1–4)

'But what' he said, 'do we reckon is the hardest profession after writing? I think the doctor's, or the money-changer's: the doctor's, because he knows what poor men have in their insides and when they'll get a fever – even though I hate doctors the most, because they're always ordering me a dose of duck; the money-changer's, because he sees the copper under the silver.'

The mass of narratives and scenes in the *Satyricon* stage and restage such crises of incorporation. Repeated visions of the consumption and ejection of literature evoke intellectual and bodily self-consciousness by dramatising a breakdown of the integral self, and an inversion or confusion of the distinctions between interiors and exteriors which constitute that self. Through metaphor, the *Satyricon* wants to get 'inside' its audience, to banish objectivity, or the distancing of reader from text. This disarming, even aggressive, strategy attacks a traditional construction of the citizen male (and the educated male reader) as an independent, impenetrable, self-contained stronghold, while the same force of metaphor dissects and infiltrates a canonic body of literature, often to transform it (almost) beyond recognition.[41] Freedom of speech, the brave young intellectual's axiom captured in the image of contemporary poetry as a gushing river pouring forth unfettered from the writer's heart, becomes also a potent symbol for physical vulnerability, for a lack of liberty and (self-)control, as well as for 'inside' wars, *intestina bella*. Likewise, the *Satyricon*'s repeated description of recitation as a penetration of solid physical boundaries not only connects episodes but also intrudes on the definability of poetry and prose *per se*, which melt into and devour one another apparently without control or distinction.

I will argue that it is precisely in constructing a unifying pattern of images that the *Satyricon* provokes a radical, chaotic world view: paradoxically, it demands to 'make sense' only in terms of a confusion and mutation of normative boundaries and binaries. Moreover, the basic dilemmas

[41] Young (1989: 153) sees narrative frames (prefaces, openings, endings, closings, codas) as embodiments of the self; cf. Ricoeur (1992: 140ff.) or Goffman (1974: 541): storytelling is a special instance of the social construction of the self in which 'what the individual presents is not himself but a story containing the protagonist who may also happen to be himself'. The unconventional form of the *Satyricon* can be said to enact a dissolution of the unified self. Hershkowitz (1998) deals with this ontological insecurity as a kind of 'madness'.

of reading this text are continually reflected and formulated in imagery: as we swallow down Encolpius' adventures, we can never get 'outside' the quandary of who our narrator really is, whether he is Petronius' foolish puppet, always silently mocked by a clever, detached author, or whether he is ever or always Petronius in disguise: ironic, satirical and double-edged. Being trapped in Encolpius' flawed, opaque, first-person account, as well as, paradoxically, having the whole text trapped inside us even as we read, is a problem and constraint (as well as a joke) that affects our interpretation of every line and scene.

Close examination of the *Satyricon*'s visuals, and their implications, I argue, renders constructs of the superior, distant author and critic commenting from high on the immorality and corporeality of the characters impossible to sustain. Body/text metaphors are geared to complicate the way we read the *Satyricon* by making (our) bodies complicit in that experience: they seem to say that reading cannot *not* be physical and visceral, motivated by pleasure and bodily responses, yet these ideas are expressed in narratives which spotlight how physical urges lead to misinterpretation, pain and a demeaning loss of self-control – anything, in fact, but satisfaction. The senses of taste and smell, our basic models for knowing, are no longer to be trusted: according to Encolpius, the otherworldly rhetorical schools, analogous to the make-believe 'reality' of Petronius' fiction in which we are immersed,[42] are full of know-all students who smell as if they have been working all their lives in a windowless kitchen (*qui haec nutriuntur, non magis sapere possunt quam bene olere qui in culina habitant* / 'People who are fed on this diet can no more have good taste than people who work in a kitchen can smell good', *Sat.* 2.1).[43] Being constantly reminded of the power and unreliability of bodily reactions, as well as of the physical vulnerability concomitant with literary knowledge, makes enjoying this work in any straightforward way extremely troublesome.

[42] *nunc et rerum tumore et sententiarum vanissimo strepitu hoc tantum proficiunt, ut cum in forum venerint, putent se in alium orbem terrarum delatos* / 'Now the only upshot of this bombastic stuff, this vapid din of talk, is that when students enter a forum, they think they've been beamed to another universe' (*Sat.* 1.2).

[43] This idea is explored in fragment XXXXII (Müller 1995), published in the codex Bellovacensis by Claude Binet in 1579: *fallunt nos oculi, vagique sensus / oppressa ratione mentiuntur. / . . . Hyblaeum refugit satur liquorem / et naris casiam frequenter odit. / hoc illo magis aut minus placere / non posset, nisi lite destinata / pugnarent dubio tenore sensus*: 'Our eyes deceive us, and our wandering senses squash down reason and tell us fibs . . . the full stomach shuns Hybla's honey, and the nose turns up, often, at the sniff of cinnamon. One thing couldn't taste better than another, unless the senses were meant to waver, and battle it out.' (This particular fragment was not given to Petronius in the MS, but Binet published it anyway, along with one other, on account of their strong resemblance to the tone and style of Petronius.)

Readers are continually encouraged to scrutinise their own performance and to question their inherited knowledge, suspicious of an elusive but ever-present author whose guidance and reassurance they desperately need but never hear.

It clearly goes without saying that the *Satyricon* is a text obsessed with pleasures (and displeasures) of the flesh, yet its 'corporeality' has been repeatedly packaged as an aspect of its purported vulgarity or lack of sophistication. Despite the fact that the description of literature and oratory as bodies is a familiar metaphor in the ancient world, and in Neronian literature especially,[44] critics have restricted their analyses of bodies and bodily functions in the *Satyricon* to material, literal realms. For Conte, such a position is bound up with his central thesis that the 'low life' epitomised by Encolpius is constantly opposed to the covert intellectual (that is, *bodiless*) presence of author and critic, who are further elevated by a condemnation and critique of the material:[45] thus, a 'tendency to exalt reality is constantly opposed to the unconquerable energy of a "low" world that knows only physical desires... the body, food, sex and money are the forces Petronius uses to demystify the false sublime in the *Satyricon*.'[46] Conte stresses:

> The Petronian narrative reduces the spiritual and the abstract to the same level as the physical and material, and it concentrates on the body and on natural functions to make this happen. By describing the processes of ingestion and sexual activity, it parades the active participation of the body in its material context. From this perspective, the satirical narrative reduces everything that might be heroic or noble to a common level of physical experience.[47]

He concludes, 'The reduction of the spiritual to the material ends up corresponding to the reduction of the metaphorical to the literal.'[48]

44 See Bramble (1974), Most (1992), Gowers (1993) especially 12–24 and 180–90 and Gowers (1994).

45 Gallop (1988) argues that Western European tradition has always sought to 'subjugate the secondary body to a disembodied consciousness': positions of power, traditionally colonised by the aristocratic male, are 'historically dependent on other classes, races and sexes to embody the body as well as care for the master's body so he would not have to be concerned with it, so he could consider himself disembodied, autonomous and free to will'. Ironically, Gallop argues, Barthes' concept of 'The Death of the Author' becomes a way of separating the text from any human who might have lived in a body, 'the last gesture of formalist autonomy defending against any body outside language, outside discourse', yet at the same time death is 'part of the bodily enigma, perhaps the most violent sign that we live in a nonsensical body which limits the powers of our will and consciousness' (19–20).

46 Conte (1996) 105. 47 Conte (1996) 114.

48 Ibid. 137–8. Conte takes the lead from Auerbach and Bakhtin, whose readings of the *Satyricon* emphasise the ultimate 'realism' of the work, its degradation of canonic literature (particularly the grand epics of Homer and Virgil) and its refreshing preference for the literal over the literary, the

Throughout, I will be arguing that the dichotomies proposed overtly or implicitly by Conte and others, between physical/intellectual, low/high worlds,[49] are blind to the *Satyricon*'s development of a series of striking metaphors which are themselves concerned with undermining or reordering such hierarchies. Indeed, bodies in the *Satyricon* are focal points for an all-encompassing exploration of the slippage between the real and the metaphorical, intangible or imagined. For the body, as the 'most potent metaphor of society',[50] also encapsulates the contradiction of metaphor itself.[51] While bodies appear to be integers of reality (they display age, gender, experience, status), they also work to dodge or transcend it – they are prime agents of disguise and transformation. On the one hand, the body has served across cultures and times as an icon for all things real, bounded and whole: the Roman citizen's body, grounded in a history of building walls within which an empire could be contained, was by definition impenetrable; the body language of the public-speaking citizen male in the Roman imagination ideally radiated the strength, stability and solidity of stone,[52] while the classic English stiff upper lip, the privileged man's ability to 'keep everything in' inherits all the most idealistic Roman definitions of, or metaphors for, manliness, governed by

down-to-earth over the ethereal or metaphorical. E.g. (Auerbach 1953: 30): 'Petronius' literary ambition, like that of the realists of modern times, is to imitate a random, everyday, contemporary milieu with its sociological background, and to have his characters speak their jargon without recourse to any form of stylization.' Or Bakhtin (1981: 222), discussing Petronius' widow of Ephesus tale: there are no 'metaphorical sublimations which might destroy the unity of the dryly realistic surface of the story . . . even symbolic features are missing, not a single element is exploited as metaphor. Everything occurs on the level of real life.' See my discussion in chapter eight.

49 These rationalising approaches inevitably reflect the age-old Cartesian dichotomy whereby desires of the body are subordinated to the reasons of the mind.

50 Turner (1984) 114.

51 As Kilgour observes, metaphor is identified with deceit and duplicity, yet 'from another angle, it also unites and brings about an apocalyptic ending of alienation and a remembering of an original unity. Detour of meaning leads to and even guarantees a total recovery of loss through an ascent to a higher level of meaning' (1990: 13), cf. Ricoeur (1976: 55). 'Body' is as elusive and as primal as metaphor: Derrida sketches this point as he tries to discuss it – 'I cannot *treat it* (en traiter) without *dealing with it* (sans traiter avec elle). I do not succeed in producing a *treatise* (un traité) on metaphor which is not *treated with* (traité avec) metaphor which suddenly appears *intractable* (intraitable)' (1998: 102–3).

52 See Sennett (1994) (especially 87–148) for discussion of how urban structures and spaces are imaged in terms of human bodies and vice versa. The architect Vitruvius in particular aimed to demonstrate how the body is structured according to geometric relations, and how the geometry of Roman space in turn disciplined bodily movement. E.g. Vitr. 1.2.4: *uti in hominis corpore e cubito, pede, palmo, digito ceterisque particulis symmetros est eurythmiae qualitas, sic est in operum perfectionibus* / 'As in the human body, from cubit, foot, palm, finger and other small parts comes the symmetric quality of eurhythmy; so it is in the completed building.'

architectural qualities of straightness and impenetrability.[53] Even the citizen's legal rights were grounded in the preservation of these boundaries, and as Kilgour discusses, the Latin concept of *persona* is a definition of the self based on solid distinctions between inside and outside, *meum* and *tuum*.[54]

Yet on the other hand, of course, this construction is transparently flawed (hence the anxious need continually to reaffirm it).[55] The daily violation of the body's metaphorical architecture is a biological fact: nobody is born solid, as the constipated Trimalchio puts it (*Sat.* 47.4).[56] The acts of eating, kissing, excreting, even talking, all evince the inevitable fluidity of the human physical 'structure', the necessities and vulnerabilities of incorporation, our final dependency and ephemerality.[57] It follows that we often experience embodiment as alienation: bodies can feel like clumsy and unstable appendages to the psyche as well as our most immediate and omnipresent experience of reality and its solidity.[58] Understanding this, that our own body is at once all flesh, a body like any other, and an aspect and container of the self, is indeed, as Paul Ricoeur has explored at length, 'a problem of vast proportions':[59] coming to terms with the contradictory status of one's own body, the idea that our

[53] See Shotter and Gergen (1989: 14–16) on the Western conception of the person as a 'bounded, unique, more or less integrated motivational and cognitive universe', and on how this idea is dismantled by both structuralist and post-structuralist theory. See Hershkowitz (1998: 190–2) for a summary of feminist deconstructions of integrated selfhood.

[54] See Kilgour (1990) 27: 'Petronius' dual or hidden identity as narrator overrides the boundaries of (poetic) *persona*: his body and voice are always potentially shared with Encolpius.'

[55] As Williams stresses (1999: 142 *et passim*, echoing Gleason 1995 and Davidson 1997), such hegemonic ideologies deal in extremes in order to make themselves seem absolute and unquestionable, and are inherently unstable: 'in the balancing act of masculinity, one stumble can ruin the entire performance'.

[56] Trimalchio's discussion of his toilet habits, in which he pictures bowel control as a torture (*tormentum*) and laxatives as a shortcut to freedom, is a pivotal point in the *Satyricon*'s problematisation of definitions of (physical) liberty: is 'bowel freedom' making a simple moral and philosophical point here (as Gowers argues in her discussion, 1993: 257, backed by Cic. *Fam.* 9.22.5 commenting on the Stoics' acceptance of farting and belching as prerequisites of personal freedom)? Or is this the twisted, unconsciously self-victimising rhetoric of a 'free(d)'man: the kind of 'freedom' any true, self-respecting citizen would snigger at? Yet *nobody* is born solid: maybe your socially superior toilet training is an even more pathetic version of *liberté* – *fake* self-control.

[57] Excretion, the bodily function that so fascinates Trimalchio in the *cena*, is at the core of Kristeva's notion of the 'abject', a bodily part or product that is both repulsive and a part of the self: 'It is no longer I who expel, "I" is expelled. The border has become an object. How can I be without border?' (1982: 3).

[58] Turner (1984: 7–8): 'we have bodies, but we are bodies'. The body 'is at once the most solid and the most elusive, illusory, concrete, metaphorical, ever present and ever distant thing'. Cf. Josipovici (1982: 1): 'our bodies are, in a sense, more familiar than our closest friends, and yet they are and will remain mysterious and unfamiliar'.

[59] Ricoeur (1992) 33.

body is (no more than) a 'mediator between the intimacy of the self and the externality of the world' might even be said to function as a prime dilemma and definition of human consciousness.[60]

The upsetting, culturally concealed truth of physical instability and vulnerability is itself often appropriated by metaphor. As Bartsch has recently summarised, fiction writers, poets, governments and historians alike have played upon extremes of physical violation in order to describe terrible suffering or times of cultural crisis, whether negative or positive. Ideological clashes and upheavals are told in the lacerated body of the soldier; in cultures worldwide, festivals and rites of passage are marked by (self-)mutilation; Bakhtin's carnivalesque is energised by a hyperbolic emphasis on bodily functions, which overturns a mind/body hierarchy. And Lucan's Civil War cuts to the heart of Rome to expose its foaming *viscera*.[61]

In the *Satyricon* there is no separating text and body, the literary and the literal, the abstract and the present, because the body encompasses and disorients those apparent dichotomies, continually breaching the material realm to which it appears to be confined. The *Satyricon* manipulates a familiar idiom of the metaphorical body to illustrate epistemic implications of deconstructing an integral, controlled self,[62] a process which is itself a metaphor for reconceptualising literature (or reading) as fluid and metamorphic rather than fixed and delimited.[63] Of course, the poised masculine self is by no means an uncontested ideal, especially in the Latin literature of first-century BCE Rome. The *Satyricon* is interwoven with the dissenting voices and fragmenting bodies of Roman elegy and satire, Senecan tragedy and post-Virgilian epic. In particular, I hope to show, Ovid's experiments with incorporation and flux in the *Metamorphoses* are central to the *Satyricon*, particularly in the journey to and scenes at Croton (*Sat.* 100–41), the home of Pythagoreanism (the

60 Ricoeur (1992) 33 *et passim* (see especially 30–5). Similar ideas are explored in Natanson (1970), e.g. 'the immediacy of my experience of corporeality should be understood as an indication of the interior perspective I occupy with respect of "my body". I am neither "in" my body not "attached to" it, it does not belong to me or go along with me. *I am my body*' (12).

61 See Bartsch (1998: 11–13) and Bakhtin (1968).

62 The image of the body as all things unified and bounded is always complicated and betrayed by (this) metaphor, the figure of speech which illustrates a subject via reference to something alien to that subject.

63 For colourful accounts of body metaphors in Latin literature, from the body politic (*unum esse rei publicae corpus*, Tac. *Ann.* 1.12) to Rome as *caput rerum* (Livy 2.22.8–12) see Gowers (1993), esp. 12–32. See Bramble (1974: 35–8) for the history of conceiving speeches or the discipline of oratory as a body (*oratio autem, sicut corpus hominis* Tac. *Dial.* 21). On this topic also see Most (1992) and Gunderson (1998).

philosophy of metamorphosis) in Ovid's epic. Both authors use images of eating and the exchange of bodies as models for encounters between people and texts. Yet in Petronius, metamorphosis, like literature, is all in the mind, a figment of the imagination or a product of fallible, creative memory: the *Satyricon* is a highly theatrical text in which characters and even spaces and objects are not visually transformed but are continually being reconceptualised, very often through metaphor. We are constantly challenged to decipher who is acting what role, what is an act, or not an act, so that difficulties of interpretation become self-conscious exercises in reading body language and in ploughing the depths of our own literary knowledge, which is often called into question or ultimately confused by characters' shifting, multiple identities.

The one thing we cannot do when we read (and imagine) Petronius, is what Slater advises in his introduction, where he addresses his audience as if they are guinea pigs in the hypnotist's chair:

> We begin, though, by forgetting – forgetting our previous experiences of Petronius' text, forgetting old questions and familiar controversies, even forgetting that there is a Petronius behind the speaking 'I' of the text. Like the souls in Plato's Republic, about to be reborn, let us drink the waters of Lethe and drown, at least for now, our memories of how we or others have read the *Satyricon* before.[64]

That there can be such an innocent, pure, first-time reading is a fantasy, for any text. Yet the impossibility and naivety of this ideal is precisely the point the *Satyricon* tries to make. However much we want this to be the 'first', the 'only' Roman novel, the work that single-handedly showcases the novelty of 'Novel', the *Satyricon* always constructs its 'difference' out of sameness: it does not supplant, succeed or ignore other texts, it obsessively incorporates them, imperialistically chews up the known world of literature until, ironically, it is itself fat and flaccid. Yet it demands the same of its readers. Unless you are stuffed to bursting point with literary knowledge, the *Satyricon* says, you are sure to look as foolish as Encolpius (contrives to look); yet the very act of consuming sufficient material to participate in the contemporary intellectual scene is fraught with risk.

For example, a starting point of discussions throughout this study is the image of characters in Quartilla's brothel being force fed Petronius' heady concoctions in the form of *satyrion*, so that from the outset it is hinted that reading *Satyricon* might send you whirling into Encolpius' head; this spiked drink becomes an aperitif for Trimalchio's similar dinner party in

64 Slater (1990) 23.

which the consumption of all kinds of logodaedalic creations threatens to tip the pleasure of reading well over into pain (see chapter three). In chapter four, I argue that the *Troiae Halosis* is performed as a physically threatening outburst of 'diseased' poetry from Eumolpus' belly, set in direct parallel to the exit of the Greek soldiers from the horse, and to the similarly fake guts spilling out from Daedalus' roast pig: the *Satyricon*'s poetaster assails his own audience (who swallow down his verse) 'from within', just as the Trojans are booby-trapped within their own walls. In chapter five, we see how Eumolpus' second tour-de-force, the *Bellum Civile*, dramatises precisely what happens when the saturated Neronian scholar overindulges in literature (and literary metaphors), pouring out the excess in the gut-wrenching poetics of civil war. In chapter six, discussion of the *Satyricon*'s overarching pseudo-epic plot of avenging Priapus must begin with another memorable performance of aggressive food-verse at *Sat.* 60, where priapic pastries shoot off into the guests' trespassing orifices.

Later, in Eumolpus' story of the widow of Ephesus, discussed in detail in chapter eight, we find out how eating Virgil's *Aeneid* IV in bite-sized chunks can be hypnotic at best, soul-destroying at worst, when the exemplary widow is made to prove that it is not only bad literature like this, or literature-gone-bad, which can make you (love-)sick. By the time we get to the poet's gruesome 'last moments' in *Sat.* 140–1, discussed in chapter ten, we discover that the prospect of eating the poet is made to sit uncomfortably alongside the experience of having read this fiction, a rank *satura* of meats smothered in spicy sauces. What does digestion do to literature, the *Satyricon* asks, and what does (this) literature do to your insides? Eating and reading are compulsive activities in this text, yet I argue that it is precisely this compulsion for massive ingestion that is seen to menace the containment and status of literary knowledge, with paradoxical consequences for writer's and readers' authority. Perhaps you cannot rely on memory, now a bodily function subject to movement and change, yet at the same time remembering (both past readings and previous scenes in the *Satyricon*) is exactly what counts. One thing is for sure, Petronius warns: If you drown your memories, you go down with them.

CHAPTER I

Rhetorical red herrings

We begin reading the *Satyricon in medias res*. How random a point of entry *Sat.* 1 is we cannot know; and neither can we choose not to privilege it as a beginning.[1] Yet accidental, constructed or not, our beginning of the *Satyricon* sets up key ideas and images which will penetrate the entire work: most importantly, the role of performance and body language in education and in public life, the repertoire of literary knowledge required to perform, read and understand, the slippage between fiction and reality, and the dynamic interdependency or confusion of orator/audience, author/narrator and narrator/reader.

The first thing we learn when we start reading the *Satyricon* is that we are always reading the narrator's account, Encolpius' words. Ironically, the plunge straight into direct speech means that we begin by acting Encolpius' act, performing his role as we read: *num alio genere furiarum declamatores inquietantur, qui clamant . . . ?* / 'Aren't the rhetoricians tortured by another tribe of Furies when they cry . . . ?' As Henderson reminds us, to experience the world according to Encolpius is always 'to be trapped in his performance, to wallow with him in bad taste and bad verse'.[2] Here, we are trapped not least because we cannot tell whether Encolpius' speech is meant to be self-mocking, whether its clumsiness cynically or unconsciously enacts the inadequacies of those it purports to attack, whether Encolpius is voicing his own opinions or is simply following a formula dictated to him by a teacher, who may or may not be Agamemnon. The environment of the rhetorical school, grounded as it is in the skills of deception and role-play, focuses our attention on the

[1] See Schmeling (1991) 352–3 and Sullivan (1968a) 38–80 for a history of attempts to construct the beginning and end of the *Satyricon*. In an argument echoed also in Masters' reading of the end of Lucan's *Pharsalia* (1992: 247–59), Schmeling concludes that the *Satyricon* is *intended* to appear structureless and open-ended: in this text, he argues, 'reality is just a continuation of epic crises', a view he associates with that of Zeitlin (1971a: 633 and 683), who writes 'Encolpius has no past and no future, no determination or purpose beyond passing pleasures' (683).

[2] Henderson (1998b).

core dilemma of the *Satyricon*: to what extent is Encolpius' voice his own, to what extent is he a split personality, an impenetrable act, a puppet for Petronius? How are we to read his narrative, or decipher his (Petronius') manipulation of our limited perspective?[3] As soon as we start reading the *Satyricon*, a text infamous, ironically, for its looseness, its rebellion against convention and the law of genre, we find ourselves caught inside the narrative and voice of Encolpius, a voice which we are bound to condemn as buffoonish, petty and naïve, even while we suspect both the power and sheer entertainment value of its self-conscious self-ridicule.[4] From the outset, 'getting into' this novel seems to problematise the crucial separation of Encolpius and Petronius, or of Encolpius and his audience, which many critics have emphasised in their readings of the *Satyricon*.[5]

As if to emphasise the point, Encolpius' apparent hypocrisy muddles the relationship between critic and criticised. In order to condemn the fantastic rhetoric of trainee orators, he has to act out their 'loud empty phrases' in direct speech (*haec vulnera pro libertate publica excepi* / 'I took these wounds for the sake of public freedom', 1.1). According to Encolpius, the young men who practise oratory these days are all fools (*et ideo ego adulescentulos existimo in scholis stultissimos fieri*, 1.3), yet he is interrupted by Agamemnon who proceeds to address him as '*adulescens*' (3.1). In Encolpius' world of fiction, the power of body language rules supreme: today's rhetoricians are Oscar-bidding actors prostituting themselves to

[3] The concept of Encolpius' split (or coherent) 'personality' has been the source of much debate in criticism of Petronius. Sullivan (1968a: 119) argues that Encolpius' character is disorganised and fragmentary, not because he is at odds with himself, but because he displays 'those traits which are appropriate responses to the demands of the particular episode'. Against this, Beck argues (1973) that Encolpius is two distinct personalities, the wise, retrospectively self-critical narrator and his former wild, idealistic, foolish self. In his later article (1975), Beck reaffirms this idea, stressing the need to 'disentangle' narrator from protagonist: Encolpius' foolishness is to be taken 'at face value', as is his distanced, knowing commentary on it. Compare the counter-argument from Veyne (1964: 303ff.) who sets out claims for Encolpius' 'fausse naïveté'. Yet the point is rather that we never can tell when Encolpius is telling it straight or pretending, is being naïve, or ironic, any more than we can tell (as Beck himself argues, 1982: 208) whether a line or passage in the *Satyricon* is 'authorially privileged'. The dilemma of Encolpius' 'personality' is by definition insoluble. Indeed as F. Jones points out (1987: 811), Beck's separation of narrator and protagonist is already shaky when examined on its own terms, as there are several instances in which our narrator gets 'so involved in his recollections that he loses his ironic distance'. Similarly, George (1966) finds that despite arguing that Petronius would never wish to identify himself with the effeminate, subtle-as-a-brick Encolpius, 'the dissociation between author and Encolpius is not complete' (355).

[4] Although an impulsive self-distancing from the character of Encolpius is necessarily part of our experience of reading the *Satyricon*, the text does not allow such objectivity to be sustained, and indeed turns such a critique against itself.

[5] As Laird stresses (1999: 210), a preoccupation with objectivity held by literary critics of the *Satyricon* has been motivated partly by the status of the text as discourse of evidence among historians.

a hungry audience (*hunc oculum pro vobis impendi... succisi poplites membra non sustinent* / 'I sacrificed this eye for you... my hamstrung knees cannot support my body', 1.1).[6] Yet Encolpius furnishes his own argument with a string of body metaphors: the affected speech of a school-taught orator is imaged as a castrated body (*ut corpus orationis enervaretur et caderet* / 'the body of the speech is emasculated and dies', 2.2); the schoolboy's style is diseased, bloated and flatulent (*maculosa... turgida... ventosa*, 2.6); the whole of art is a decrepit corpus fed on one bland, fast-food diet, lacking the vigour even to reach old age (*ac ne carmen quidem sani coloris enituit, sed omnia quasi eodem cibo pasta non potuerunt usque ad senectutem canescere*, 2.8).[7] Meanwhile the poor students are *confined* to set speeches (*declamationibus continebantur*, 2.3), ruined by the cloistered pedant (*umbraticus doctor*), and the school itself is a windowless kitchen whose cooks smell terrible, or implicitly, have lost the ability to detect their own stink (2.1).[8] Encolpius, on the other hand, stands in the open air outside the school (*in porticu*, 3.1), yet, again, this critique is a product of that same environment, and is designed to impress a teacher who has just completed a sweaty session *inside* the school (*in schola*, 3.1). Encolpius images his own entrapment, and that of his readers: his confusion of inside and outside, formulated now as fiction and reality, stuffy darkness and breezy daylight, mirrors a deconstruction of the reader's position as objective, non-participatory observer.[9] This speech lures us into a closed world of fiction, just as pupils who hear the bombastic strains of the rhetorician are transported 'into another world' (1.2). There is nothing of 'real life' in this culinary hothouse

[6] The display of wounds in oratorical performance is a well-documented tactic, the *locus classicus* of which is Marius in Sallust, *Iug.* 85.29, cf. Plutarch, *Mar.* 9. Also see Seneca, *Prov.* 4.4; Cicero, *de Or.* 2.124 and Quintilian, *Inst.* 6.1.21. For a detailed discussion of the politics of scar-display see Leigh (1995).

[7] Compare Quint. *Inst.* 2.4.5, where he compares the first steps in an education to a milk diet, progressing to the 'rich juice' of history, before the 'banquet' of classical literature, followed by the inferior but attractive food of the minor poets.

[8] This image of the rhetorical school as a dark place far removed from the bright light and real life of the forum is a common one. See e.g. Quintilian, *Inst.* 10.5.17; Tac. *Ann.* 14.53 (*in umbra educata* / 'brought up in the shadows') and Juv. *Sat.* 7.172–3 (*qui rhetorica descendit ab umbra* / 'who comes down from his rhetorical shade'). Generally, life in the shade is often associated with luxurious, self-indulgent living, e.g. Plaut. *Truc.* 608–11. Seneca (*Ep.* 122) violently attacks the *lucifugae* (those who shun the light), who live by night and sleep by day, spending the hours of darkness amid wine, perfumes and banquets.

[9] Indeed, unlike (for the most part) the entertainment on offer in the theatre or gladiatorial arena, oratory could be a participatory sport. As Kennedy explains (1978: 172): 'in Augustan times declamation became a social fad for adults as well as the basis for second century education... rhetoricians invited the public to hear the speeches of themselves and their students much as a modern citizenry might go to a school athletic event, except that visitors were invited to participate in the declaiming.' See also Kennedy (1994) 168–72.

of a text: we too are about to be treated to Encolpius' pet hates (those novelistic pirates and tyrants, oracles and sacrificed virgins), and there is not long to wait before Trimalchio will serve up those condemned words and acts sprinkled with poppy seed and sesame, for his very first course (*mellitos verborum globulos et omnia dicta factaque quasi papavere et sesamo sparsa* / 'honey balls of words, every phrase and act sprinkled with poppy-seed and sesame', 1.3; cf. *glires melle ac papavere sparsos* / 'there were even dormice rolled in honey and sprinkled with poppy-seed', 31.10).[10] What critics such as Slater have chosen to see in the *Satyricon*'s obvious complexity – the radical liberation of interpretability, the comedy of confusion – misinterprets Petronius' central joke of entrapment.[11] As Agamemnon comments, Encolpius' speech is *non publici saporis* / 'not of common flavour' (3.1): yet this is just the first taste of things to come.

The implications of this joke, however, are never as funny as the gag itself. Ensnared in Encolpius' narrow-minded narrative, are we too bound to lose our tastebuds, our grip on aesthetic value?[12] As its title partly suggests, the *Satyricon* is a *satura*, a satiric feast on a scale to match Trimalchio's.[13] As we see later in Quartilla's brothel, it is also to be imbibed as an aphrodisiac aperitif, as a *satyrion* (*omnes mihi videbantur satyrion bibisse* / 'they all looked to me like they'd been drinking satyrion', *Sat.* 8.4), resulting in a loosening of control and awareness all too reminiscent of Encolpius' caricature of dizzy students of rhetoric. This bloated fiction always threatens to stuff us so full that we no longer smell the difference between good and bad literature. While we are encouraged, here and throughout the *Satyricon*, to swallow an empowering metaphor of reading as eating, as incorporation, at the same time this text predicts a reading always determined by risk and constraint: we can so easily overeat, or be force-fed under the influence of Satyri_on. The first scene we have of the *Satyricon* suggests that readers are stuck in the *culina* of Encolpius'

[10] This line also reminds us of Horace's comparison at *Ars P.* 374–8 between an otherwise pleasant banquet at which poppy seeds in offensive Sardinian honey (*Sardo cum melle papaver*) are served and a poem which fails because of some small fault.

[11] Slater (1988: 165): 'we have finally reached the logical, New Critical conclusion that the *Satyricon* is an entirely self-contained literary game without any message whatsoever'. Slater (1990: 237) imagines the *Satyricon* as a cinematic farce, comparing its 'cross-wired' construction, 'designed to maximise the reader's frustration', to Harpo's trick switchboard in the Marx Brothers' film, which connects complaining callers with those they are most likely to annoy. 'This pattern,' he concludes, 'constitutes one of the primary sources of comedy in a text, which is precisely what I contend happens in the *Satyricon*.'

[12] The joke is of course sicker if we believe our Petronius is taking time out from his role as *Arbiter*.

[13] As Gowers suggests (1993: 116) in discussing satire's confusion of literature and food (*satura* means a mixed dish, whereas *satur* means 'full'), 'it is hard to believe that Petronius is not punning on the similarities in his title *Satyricon*'.

narrative, and that there is no escape, no room to step back. In effect, it says, we are constrained by the very thing we are meant to contain, within our own bodies.

Agamemnon's reply to Encolpius is similarly veiled and self-implicating. As Kennedy points out, it is important to note that he is not offended by Encolpius' remark that teachers have been the ruin of eloquence (*pace vestra liceat dixisse, primi omnium eloquentiam perdidistis* / 'Let me tell you, you teachers more than anyone have been the ruin of true eloquence', 2.2);[14] on the contrary he flatters and cajoles him: the object of the game here is not sincerity, but skill in role play and in seduction. Teachers must be just as sycophantic as their pupils, for unless they say exactly what the *adulescentuli* want to hear, they will be stranded, as Cicero warns, *soli in scholis* (alone in the schools). Teachers are like *ficti adulatores* (mock sycophants of comedy) sucking up to rich men for a free dinner: *nihil prius meditantur quam id quod putant gratissimum auditoribus fore (nec enim aliter impetrabunt quod petunt nisi quasdam insidias auribus fecerint)* / 'they think first about what they reckon will please an audience most (for they'll never get what they're after unless they lay traps for the ear)' (3.3). Professors of rhetoric bait their audience with food, in order that they themselves might eat at a rich man's table. The idea that literature is a currency that might be exchanged for a dinner, or that literary discourse, as in Plato's *Symposium*, might be conceived in the dining room alongside or in place of food itself, is a recognisable idea.[15] Yet Petronius complicates the metaphor by suggesting that, in using his most seductive writing to acquire a free dinner, the orator or author might end up devouring the fishy guests, who hang off his every baited word. For a master of oratory, Agamemnon continues, is like a fisherman hunting a tasty catch: *nisi tamquam piscator eam imposuerit hamis escam, quam scierit appetituros esse pisciculos, sine spe praedae moratur in scopulo* / 'If, just like a fisherman, he doesn't bait his hook with food he knows the little tiddlers will go for, he'll be left stuck on the cliff with no hope of a catch' (3.4).[16] Meanwhile the little fish thrust prematurely into the law courts are raw (*cruda*, 4.2), ready for ripening by the power-hungry pedant.

In the literary world (or the world of fiction), Agamemnon suggests, each participant is situated within a hierarchy of incorporation, but one which constantly threatens to consume the consumer: in order to get fed

[14] Kennedy (1978) 171 8. [15] See Gowers (1993) 40 9.
[16] Persius also uses *esca*, 'titbit', in his famous phrase at 1.22: *auriculis alienis colligis escas*? / 'Do you collect titbits for other people's ears?'

by a larger hand, the fisherman devours his catch, which in turn contains the already eaten bait: the orator must eat his own words, becoming in his performance a walking, talking oration served up at dinner to another ravenous audience.[17] What appears to be, in Agamemnon's formulation, a slick hierarchy of eater over eaten, can easily transform into a complicated vicious circle in which, as the Encolpius–Agamemnon exchange itself shows, it is very difficult to distinguish between the roles of fisherman and fish, teacher and pupil, orator and audience.[18] Agamemnon may be (posing as) Encolpius' teacher but, as Kennedy concludes, it is Encolpius who is 'dangling his literary line and Agamemnon (who is) dancing on the end of it'.[19]

Importantly, we can see this fishpond metaphor of learning and performance rephrased at salient points throughout the *Satyricon*: for example, at the end of the *Cena*, which has been obsessed with characters learning how to interpret food 'fed' to them by the authoritative Trimalchio and has presented its readers with a series of puzzles about how to read food in literature, the after-dinner bath becomes a fishpond: *coniciamus nos in balneum* / 'let's jump into a bath' urges Trimalchio at 72.3, but Ascyltos and Encolpius proceed to fall into a fishpond (*piscinam*, 72.7) as cold and threatening as the river Styx: Encolpius falls into the same abyss (*in eundem gurgitem*) and is only saved when the porter (*atriensis*) pacifies the

[17] Fish is a seductive food, the sycophant's dish of choice: according to Juvenal, mullets were often used as 'bait' by legacy-hunters (*Sat.* 5.97–8, 6.38–40); in *Sat.* 4, Crispinus' fishy gift to Domitian is the grossest flattery of all. Courtney (1980: 198) suggests that it was traditional to make presents of large fish to monarchs: see e.g. Martial 13.91; Suet. *Tib.* 60; Sen. *Ep.* 95.42.

[18] In the zodiac dish in Trimalchio's *cena*, fish (*piscis*) also stands for people who are rhetoricians and chefs (*in piscibus obsonatores et rhetores* 39.13), that is, those who catch and cook fish. Cf. Martial 10.31, where Calliodorus sells a slave to buy a fish for dinner, which makes him a bit like a cannibal. Also see Juv. *Sat.* 4.25–6: Crispinus could have bought the fisherman for the price he paid for the turbot (*potuit fortasse minoris / piscator quam piscis emi*). When in lines 67–8 he offers the fish to Domitian, he says, *propera stomachum laxare sagina, / et tua servatum consume in saecula rhombum* / 'Hurry up and fill your belly with fodder, and devour a turbot saved to grace your reign'; yet as Braund observes (1996: 250), *sagina* means 'animal fodder' (Var. *Rust.* 3.17.7; Pliny, *HN* 9.14) and is the smaller fry on which bigger fish feed. Yet *sagina* is not as incongruous as Braund suggests here: the point is that, in this mischievous and subversive confusion of eater and eaten, fisherman and fish, Domitian ends up being the biggest fish of all. For discussion of Juv. *Sat.* 4 see also Gowers (1993: 202ff.), Freudenburg (2001: 258–64) and Rimell (forthcoming).

[19] Kennedy (1978) 178. Cicero uses the same idea of the teacher of rhetoric as a 'feeder': see *De Or.* 2.39.162: 'for my part, if I now wanted a complete novice trained up for oratory, I'd prefer to hand him over to these assiduous types who hammer away day and night on the same anvil at the same job; they'd only put into his mouth the choicest morsels, anything chewed up really small, just like nurses feeding baby boys.' Baiting an audience with food is imaged in Plautus, *Men.* 77–95: Panayotakis (1995: 7) discusses this 'stock theatrical figure of the parasite'. Fishing is also a metaphor for aggressive seduction in Prop. 4.1.143–4, where the poet-lover struggles to remove the hook stuck in his chin.

Cerberus-like guard dog by throwing food into its barking jaws.[20] The hellish whirlpool, like the rhetorical school fishpond, is a metaphor for stirring up literature's images of epic underworlds, and more generally for the process of engaging with, or being swamped by, a mass of literary material. At *Sat.* 42.1–2, before he tells the guests about a funeral he has just attended, Seleucus had already warned them about the dangers of bathing: '*ego' inquit 'non cotidie lavor; baliscus enim fullo est, aqua dentes habet, et cor nostrum cotidie liquescit*' / '"I for one," he said, "don't wash every day, because the bath is like a fuller, the water has teeth, and your heart melts away daily."' Water is an aggressive animal that wants to eat you alive, from inside.

Later on, when Lichas' ship sinks and the crew jump overboard, the men are prey not to fish, which is Lichas' fate (*piscibus beluisque expositus es, Sat.* 115.13) but to fishermen (*procurrere piscatores parvulis expediti navigiis ad praedam rapiendam* / 'Some fishermen in handy little boats rushed to seize their prey', *Sat.* 114.14). Of course, the idea that fishermen on the shores of Croton are likely to be aggressive cannibals *as well as* unscrupulous legacy-hunters is made all the more pertinent as the narrative continues, culminating, in the text as we have it, in the inhabitants' willingness to eat Eumolpus' flesh as if it were ready cash. When Lichas' body is washed up by a wave, Encolpius remarks, *en homo quemadmodum natat* / 'Look how the man floats' (115.10), *natat* being a curious verb to use of a dead body, but not of a fish.[21] Eumolpus, still composing the last lines of what we presume is the forthcoming *Bellum Civile* as the ship goes down, is taken (as if) to safety in a fisherman's hut (*hoc opere tandem elaborato casam piscatoriam subimus maerentes, Sat.* 115.6). As Encolpius comments in 115.16, *ubique naufragium est* ('shipwreck is everywhere').[22] The idea that to learn about literature you have to swim in it, and that in order to learn or simply to be entertained you take the author's bait and so risk getting

[20] Petronius' *atriensis* is Virgil's *portitor* Charon: instead of helping the hero cross the waves and whirlpools of Acheron (*vastaque voragine gurges, Aen.* 6.296), he pulls him out of the murky water when he falls in. The distraction of the overtly fictional dog clearly recalls the doping of Cerberus in *Aen.* 6.417–23, yet in the *Satyricon* the barking dog is fed titbits *de cena*, which is perhaps why stuffed Encolpius is himself too doped up to walk straight (*nec non ego quoque ebrius* / 'I was also drunk', 72.7).

[21] E.g. *Sat.* 39.3: *pisces natare oportet* / 'a fish should have something to swim in'.

[22] As Connors discusses (1998: 76–83), Petronius plays on the Senecan metaphor of sea storms and shipwreck as representing the unpredictability of life (in contrast to the 'safe harbour' offered by philosophy): see Sen. *Dial.* 6.6.3; 6.15.4; 11.9.6–7; *Ep.* 99.9. However, here and throughout the *Satyricon*, the waves of fortune also illustrate the riskiness and unpredictability of reading and learning, both in general and in terms of this text (like Encolpius in the *Cena*, we can never tell what's coming next).

eaten, is colourfully evoked throughout the *Satyricon* and mirrored, we will see, in the reconceptualisation of other key hierarchies and binaries.

We first encounter the image of sea or water as a frame of reference for the learning and performance of literature later on in Agamemnon's speech;[23] in *Sat.* 4, he excuses himself from Encolpius' attack on teachers by blaming the schoolboy's parents, who drive him like an unripe or indigestible foodstuff into the voracious forum. If only, he muses, boys could be left to paddle of their own accord in some serious reading (*ut studiosi iuvenes lectione severa irrigarentur*, 4.3). To make his point about loosening up the learning process, Agamemnon switches into a more 'fluid' medium, improvised verse, which he intends to be a parody of Lucilius, whose poetry is characterised by Horace as an offensively un-Callimachean torrent, a muddy river of verse:[24] if you intend to make a success of the serious arts, he suggests, the first thing to do is to get out of the fishpond: don't flatter tyrants in the hope of getting a free meal, don't extinguish your mental energy with wine at banquets (*nec . . . obruat vino / mentis calorem*), and don't pay good money to be entertained by an actor (*Sat.* 5 vv. 4–8). Yet in avoiding the dangerous seas of oratorical performance, Agamemnon's student will follow an altogether more watery path: first he should give his youth to the study of poetry and drink of Homer's font (*Maeoniumque bibat felici pectore fontem*); only when he is full up (*plenus*) of the Socratic school can he really loosen the reins and shake the weapons of Demosthenes like a free man (*liber*). Then he can let Roman writers pour around him (*circumfluat . . . suffusa*). Outside the walls of the forum his pages will gush free (*det pagina cursum*) to sing of feasts and wars (*epulae et bella*); eventually he will be so stuffed that words will pour out from his chest like a deep river (*sic flumine largo / plenus Pierio defundes pectore verba*). The idea is reminiscent of the fonts of Callimachean inspiration, echoed, for example, in Horace, *Carm.* 4.2,[25] and also of Cicero's *De Oratore*, where knowledge flows from wisdom like rivers from the Apennines, pouring out philosophers into the safe harbours of the Greek Mediterranean and orators into the rocky seas of Tuscany, 'in which even Ulysses himself wandered'.[26]

23 See Sochatoff (1970) on images of the sea throughout the *Satyricon*.

24 *Sat.* 1.4.11: *cum flueret lutulentus, erat quod tollere velles* / 'There was much that needed dredging from his muddy stream'.

25 4.2.5–8: Horace praises Pindar, whose deep-toned voice is like a swollen river surging down a mountain (*monte decurrens velut amnis, imbres / quem super notas aluere ripas / fervet*). For similar imagery also see Quint. *Inst.* 9.4.61; 10.1.61.

26 Cicero *De Or.* 3.19.69, cf. 2.62.

The imaging of Roman literature as a free, liquid energy which once read, learnt and consumed is barely confinable within the human body, reverberates at significant junctures throughout the *Satyricon*. Agamemnon's poem at *Sat.* 5 is echoed particularly in the use of the verb *fundere* ('to pour') and its cognates: *effundere* ('to pour out'), *perfundere* ('to drench or anoint'), *infundere* ('to pour on/in'), and so on, words used regularly to express the seepage or excretion of bodily fluids,[27] the fall of rain and the flowing of rivers or streams,[28] or the outpouring of words and sounds.[29] In *Sat.* 23, at the brothel of Quartilla, a *cinaedus* enters to offer his advice in verse to sodomites (*eiusmodi carmina effudit* / 'He poured out the poem as follows'), telling them to let their limbs run free and soft and highlighting again the idea that the 'pouring out' of liquidised words entails somehow the penetration of solid physical borders: the phrase *cursum addite* ('let 'em run, too') here runs in parallel to Agamemnon's advice in *Sat.* 5, v. 17: *det pagina cursum* ('Let the page run free'). At *Sat.* 108, when civil war is raging on Lichas' ship, Tryphaena interjects with a poem, the first line of which is a near repetition of Lucan 1.8 ('*quis furor*' *exclamat* '*pacem convertit in arma*?' / ' "What madness," she exclaimed, is turning peace into war?" '). When she has attempted to calm destruction among the waves, warning, *ne vincite pontum / gurgitibusque feris alios immittite fluctus* / 'Don't try to conquer the sea and pile more waves on savage floods' (reminding us of the *gurges* engulfing Encolpius at 72), the narrator adds, *haec ut turbato clamore mulier effudit* / 'The woman poured this out hysterically, at full volume'.[30] The fighting is calmed by a feast and by some recreational fishing, which, we are to remember, dramatised the rhetorical construction of artificial hierarchy in *Sat.* 4: *alius exultantes quaerebat fuscina pisces, alius hamis blandientibus convellebat praedem repugnantem* / 'One man started to hunt the leaping fish with a spear, another pulled in his struggling prey on seductive hooks' (109.6) – hooks which have already been suggestively baited with Agamemnon's metaphor in *Sat.* 3.4.

[27] E.g. *Aen.* 2.532; Ov. *Met.* 2.610, 8.417; Sen. *Ph.* 552; Lucan 7.536.

[28] E.g. Ov. *Met.* 15.282; Livy 6.8.7; 6.32.6; Ov. *Pont.* 2.1.26.

[29] E.g. Ter. *Ad.* 769; Ov. *Met.* 7.248; 12.469; 14.429; Cat. 64.125 and 321; Verg. *Aen.* 3.344; Hor. *Epist.* 2.1.146.

[30] As Connors observes (1998: 77), the mini civil war on board Lichas' ship of poetry is also a 'storm' which forecasts the shipwreck, while shipwreck *is* civil war (poetry). Tryphaena may be calming the dispute, but in another sense she is stirring up the sea for the *real* storm: *turbatus* can be used of roughening waves, *clamor* of thunder, while *effudit* can be used in connection with pouring rain. Similarly, when the storm does begin in *Sat.* 114.1, Encolpius' conversation (*dum haec taliaque iactamus* / 'we mulled over this and other matters') echoes the association of Aeneas' speech before the storm (*talia iactanti*, *Aen.* 1.102) with Virgil's description of the 'storm-tossed' hero (*iactatus*, *Aen.* 1.3): implicitly it is the crew's use of words that tempts or causes the storm.

The largest poem of the *Satyricon* ('a big chunk of undigested epic')[31] is Eumolpus' *Bellum Civile*, which like the *Troiae Halosis* is preceded and introduced by a chunk of moralising on modern art.[32] In *Sat.* 118, Eumolpus states that those who are tired of poetry often take refuge in poetry's harbour (*portum feliciorem* / 'a happier port'); yet writing poetry is more difficult than you think, as the poet has to be flooded by a huge river of literature (*ingenti flumine litterarum inundata*) especially if he aims to handle the chaotic subject of civil war, which also threatens to drown him (*ecce belli civilis ingens opus quisquis attigerit nisi plenus litteris, sub onere labetur* / 'for instance anyone who tackles the huge theme of civil war will sink under the pressure unless he is full of literature', 118.6).[33] In the *Bellum Civile* itself, as civil war erupts, mangling the cultural heart of Rome and stirring up obscene divisions (brother against brother, father against son), so the *fundere* compounds begin to flow: *Iulius ingratam* ***perfudit*** *sanguine Romam* / 'Julius drenched ungrateful Rome in blood', 64; *Cocyti* ***perfusus*** *aqua* / 'soaked in the water of Cocytus', 69; *spiritus, extra / qui furit* ***effusus*** / 'the air which rages as it pours out', 69–70; *iam pridem nullo* ***perfundimus*** *ora cruore* / 'It's been a long time since my lips dripped with gore', 96; *tunc Fortuna levi* ***defudit*** *pectore voces* / 'Then Fortune poured out these words from her fickle heart', 102; *iam classes fluitare mari totasque per Alpes / fervere Germano* ***perfusas*** *sanguine turmas* / 'Now ships sweep the sea and the cavalry soaked in German blood seethe over Alpine ranges', 213–14. And as Encolpius tells it: *cum haec Eumolpus ingenti volubilitate verborum* ***effudisset*** / 'When Eumolpus had poured out these lines with immense fluency'. Eumolpus' account of the fall of Rome, as we will explore later, must constantly swallow up the *Troiae Halosis* and the story of the fall of Troy, the defining, haunting moment of which, here and in the *Aeneid*, is the pouring out of Greek soldiers from the belly of the horse (***effundunt*** *viros*, *Sat.* 89. v. 57).[34] Finally, Encolpius starts to spurt poetry himself in 132.11, with similar passion (*haec ut iratus* ***effudi*** / 'He angrily poured out these words').

The use of *fundere* in connection with the *Satyricon*'s poetry seems to hint that the verse passages signify a quickening of pace and a loosening of constraints, that we might almost see poetry as prose running away with

31 Connors (1998) 100.

32 The speech at 88 also uses water as a metaphor for knowledge (*philosophiae fons* / 'philosophy's font', 88.7).

33 Which is exactly what happens to Lichas.

34 For all other uses of *fundere* compounds, which are not explicitly connected with pouring out words/poetry in the *Satyricon*, see Appendix I.

itself, breaking the boundaries of its context. For Connors, the poetry passages embody poetic memory, functioning as cues to look 'outside' the text to recall the sources it incorporates. Yet the idea that poetry is associated with liberation and expansiveness is by no means obvious: poetry is, after all, contained and predicted by the rigid patterns of metre. Indeed Connors sets the scene rather in terms of a juxtaposition of stylized, traditional structures of poetry and the fluid inventiveness of prose fiction.[35] Petronius' imaging of free-flowing verse is therefore not a straightforward one, and it does not make sense to oppose 'free' verse and stolid prose, or vice versa.[36] Rather, I would argue, the metaphor of literature or the environment of its reception as a sea, river or fishpond, unified by the repetition of *fundere*, intrudes on the definability of poetry and prose *per se*. As I will explore in greater detail later, the intricate way in which the poems reflect, programme and reinterpret the larger prose narrative challenges the recognisability and function of literary form: could prose be poetry in disguise or, vice versa, is Petronius a poet pulling off a winning performance as novelist?[37] Poetry and prose do not merely stage rival structures of representation, as Connors argues:[38] in sharing the same space and resources, they call into question the writer's (and the critic's) ability to represent, to control and contextualise his work.

This is not a call for interpretative aporia, but rather a challenge to *look* closely at the representative structures of the *Satyricon*, to enter into the richly visual spirit of this work. When, at the end of his speech at *Sat.* 2.9, Encolpius says, 'the decadence in painting was no different, after the snooty Egyptians found a shortcut to this high art form', this is not (only) a throwaway generalisation which, argues Walsh, 'further undercuts any temptation to take Encolpius' lecture seriously'.[39] Rather, it points out that not only is the *Satyricon* theatrical (*like* a comedy, a mime, a Senecan

[35] Connors (1998) 1–2.

[36] Beck implicitly does this (1973: 57–60) by making Encolpius' verse in the final twenty chapters represent the flighty, uncontrolled sentiments of a protagonist 'in the thick of his adventures' alongside the contrasting 'prose realities of his real life'. See also Dronke (1994: 12).

[37] The question of whether prose could be poetry in disguise is broached by Tacitus in his *Annals*, where history is written to sound like poetry but look like prose. The collapse of boundaries between poetry and prose mirrors an ambiguity between history (or 'reality') and fiction, which is a constant concern of the *Satyricon* and is spotlit at *Sat.* 118.6: Eumolpus declares, *non enim res gestae versibus comprehendendae sunt, quod longe melius historici faciunt* / 'it is not just a question of recording actual events in verse, which historians can do far better', but he proceeds to recite a mini-epic about real events (civil war) which reflects in a complex way 'real' events that have happened to himself and his friends in the course of this novel.

[38] Connors (1998) 2. [39] Walsh (1996) 157.

tragedy...), but its very appearance, on the page as it were, is theatre: Petronius' writing is to be looked at, and we are to assess the meaning and appeal of its shape, colour and texture. Encolpius' banal, superficial comment, concluding an image-packed speech, is the first pointed hint that we must approach this novel with our eyes as well as our minds if we are to explore Petronius' fascination with what things look like, and with the influence and fatal deceptiveness of appearances.

Agamemnon's eccentric metaphor for the pressures and vulnerabilities faced by today's young orators and audiences, who struggle to keep afloat in a dangerous fishpond, sets up one of the *Satyricon*'s central images of literary repertoires or contexts as fluid seas, baths and rivers. This liquid metaphor, which we recognise again and again in the narrator's use of *fundere* compounds, becomes a way of describing all Latin literature, of which this experimental fiction is a cutting-edge example: as a free-flowing waterway gushing from the heart of the free man. Water becomes an obvious and powerful metaphor for freedom of thought and speech, for the creativity afforded by civilised, privileged urban living – the kind of lifestyle which, for Petronius' characters, is defined by endless baths and wine (*Liber*-ty in a glass).[40] Trimalchio promises his slaves will 'taste the water of freedom' (*aquam liberam gustabunt*, 71.1), and swimming, not sinking, is a metaphor in the *Cena* for manumission: in *Sat.* 57, one of the freedmen tells the story of the day he was freed (*enatavi* / 'I swam out') which, as Bodel notes, reminds us that newly freed slaves are said to have 'escaped the storm of servitude', and often shave their heads in the manner of shipwrecked sailors.[41] As Bodel also notes, in the picture of a shaven-headed Trimalchio at *Sat.* 29, he is described as *levatum mento* / 'held up by the chin', which recalls the phrase *supponere mento manum/digitum* ('to support the chin with the hand/finger') used twice metaphorically by Ovid and once literally by Propertius to describe the assistance offered to a drowning man.[42]

Yet it becomes increasingly clear that, like interpretative objectivity, this kind of freedom is illusional, founded in a hierarchical structure (outside–inside, free–trapped) whose boundaries are swamped by the

[40] Trimalchio adopts Liber as his patron and father (*Sat.* 41.8).

[41] See Bodel (1994: 251); also see Cic. *Tusc.* 5.87 on the idea of 'swimming' out of trouble.

[42] As Corbett suggests (1967: 260–1), discussed by Bodel (1994). See Prop. 3.7.69; Ov. *Pont.* 2.3.39; 2.6.14; cf. Pet. *Sat.* 43.4: *et quod illius mentem sustulit, hereditatem accepit* / 'the thing that made him hold up his chin was coming into an estate'. Bodel notes that the phrase *levatum mento* also recalls images of Alexander the Great with his head turned towards the stars like the god-kings of the Near East; equally, it echoes the erotic gesture famous from Greek vase painting in which an older lover caresses the chin of a youth between thumb and uplifted palm.

very metaphor that describes them. The *flumen largum* ('wide river') of sophisticated literature is an (anti-)Callimachean image representing inspiration that comes from within (*pectore*),[43] yet it is also a dark whirlpool in which the poet himself can drown (if, that is, he isn't caught for somebody else's lunch). Slater's account of the *Satyricon* as an interpretative void tries to get us off the hook, to let us bathe in perplexity: of course, if we decide that the point is to be confused, we can experience blissful release from the bind of critique. Yet as I have tried to show, and as I hope to explore in much greater detail, the kind of interpretative, moral and political freedom foregrounded in this text is discomfortingly double-edged: at any point, Petronius wants us to realise, that toe-curling bath could metamorphose into an icy, hook-infested sea.

Thus far, I have begun to sketch out the importance of Petronius' highly sensuous and metaphorical imagery as a device used to connect apparently disconnected episodes and scenes. We have begun to see that this complex tapestry of metaphor, based on the imagery of fluidity and slippage within hierarchies of incorporation, points not to fragmentation but rather to *metamorphosis* as the overriding principle at work. The *Satyricon* is not unified in the sense that it is always changing. Yet in appearing to melt fundamental hierarchies, metamorphosis, as it is dramatised in images of flux and incorporation, problematises the very concepts on which it seems to be based: free composition, free thought and speech, liberty itself. Incorporation in the *Satyricon* is imaged as that which we are always anxious to achieve, but can never completely preserve: the neat hierarchy of eater over eaten begins to disintegrate when literature is also imaged as a live, hungry body, devouring other literary material and continuing to eat away inside its educated host; boundaries begin to melt when the act of recitation, particularly of poetry, is described in terms of a liquid outpouring of bodily content: *effudit, effudisset*... This text's central theme of self-transformation is a paradox that builds as many limitations and walls as it demolishes, producing a readership that is not simply *free* to be confused but on the contrary is paranoid to react at all.

Moreover, the parallels we are meant to draw between the two oral activities, eating and speaking, consumption and performance, mean that we as readers and critics are made highly conscious of the notion that what comes out of our mouths is inevitably a product of what went in, a

[43] On the idea of water as a source of poetic inspiration in Callimachus and in later writers, see Crowther (1979), Knox (1985) and Cameron (1995: 363–6).

concept frequently referred to in the rhetorical handbooks.[44] Quintilian, for example, argues that care of the voice, the physical tool which can make or break an orator, begins with good eating habits (11.3.23): poor food will emasculate speech and diminish authority. Yet the good orator, as Gunderson discusses, is a *vir bonus* defined by his innate essence rather than by his function (by what he *is*, rather than by what he eats or says).[45] In its appropriation of the language and imagery of rhetorical handbooks, the *Satyricon* explores precisely this paradox surrounding the meaning or interpretability of the oratorical body: a body which is so manifestly (solidly) good and virile, but at the same time is always on the verge of failing because of what it allows inside itself, be it bad advice or junk food.[46] Throughout the *Satyricon*, the idea that we say what we eat, that we *are* what we eat, is a highly dramatic metaphor for undermining hierarchies – between eater and eaten, between text and context, text and reader, author and narrator – and also for questioning concepts of self-sufficiency and originality. The idea that all speech has an external source that has already been (unconsciously) internalised and the twist that the narrative you feel entrapped by is actually trapped *in you*, is the central concept that underpins the *Satyricon* as a radically anti-classical work.[47]

[44] The clearest example of this idea in the *Satyricon* is Phileros' euphemism at *Sat.* 43: *de re tamen verum dicam, qui linguam caninam comedi* / 'I'm actually going to tell the truth on this one, seeing as I've eaten dog-tongue.'

[45] Gunderson (1998) 169.

[46] Gunderson (ibid.: 174) argues that rhetorical handbooks rely and prey on the fallibility of the orator's body: 'the rhetorical handbook then becomes a necessary prop for male subjectivity'.

[47] The phrase used by Zeitlin (1971b).

CHAPTER 2

Behind the scenes

In reading the opening scenes of the *Satyricon*, we are reminded that acting is endemic in the learning, writing and performance of literary works. As many critics have recently explored, much of the challenge of learning (how to perform) literature in ancient Rome consists in walking the tightrope between the stages of orator and actor, figures at opposite ends of the social spectrum whose roles overlap in strategies of bodily masquerade for the entertainment of an audience. The rhetorical theorists, motivated to fuel their readers with doubts about the legibility of body language, continually flirt with comparing and contrasting orator and actor.[1] As a privileged, educated young scholar, therefore, Encolpius is necessarily the consummate performer, and lives his 'real life' as a fiction. Yet his behaviour frequently lapses into pure novelistic theatre: at *Sat.*17.4, Quartilla is moved to ask, *quaenam est haec audacia, aut ubi fabulas etiam antecessura latrocinia didicistis?* / 'What is this cheek? And where did you learn to rival the robbers of romance?' The *Satyricon* as a whole, it almost goes without saying, is a highly theatrical text. As Panayotakis' exhaustive study has shown, it is not only preoccupied in general terms with the entertainment of pretence and masquerade, but also articulates

[1] In *Inst.* 1.11.2–3, and 1.12.18, Quintilian advises his pupils not to adopt the gestures and movements of an actor, and to rigorously avoid 'staginess' of any sort lest it corrupt the mind. Yet in 2.10.13, he states that the ideal oratorical discourse is based on that of the comic actor (neither common nor artificial), and in 2.12.1–2 he explicitly compares orators to other stage performers such as gladiators and wrestlers. Cicero in his *De Oratore* suggests that orators should study actors as anti-models (*ne mala consuetudine ad aliquam deformitatem pravitatemque veniamus* / 'so that bad practice does not lead to some coarse or ugly habit', 1.34.156–7), but continues to set the two professions in parallel, if only to differentiate them (*qui actor imitanda, quam orator suscipienda veritate iucundior?* / 'What actor gives greater pleasure by his imitation of real life than your orator affords in taking on some real case?' 2.8.34). Quintilian writes that impersonation is the most difficult task for the young orator to master (*Inst.* 3.8.49), and that many speeches are composed (like actors' scripts) for others to deliver, with the character and position of the speaker in mind. See Gleason (1995) for discussion of rhetorical education as a 'calisthetics of manhood' in which one's adequacy as a man was always under suspicion.

its core scenes as if they were designed for the stage.[2] Yet, as the preliminary exchange between Encolpius and Agamemnon shows, acting in the *Satyricon* is perhaps more disruptive than entertaining. The process of acting is transformative and is in many ways analogous to metamorphosis: it performs our unnerving human ability to transcend and subvert the boundaries of the corporeal self, making kings of beggars, intellectuals of idiots, women of men, animals of people, or the old of the young, potentially confounding principles of hierarchy that define social liberty and its antitheses. In taking on the role of somebody else, in this case an old-fashioned *senex*, Encolpius exposes the instability or multiplicity of his own identity, which overshadows the entire text: is he Petronius in disguise, the author often defined and defended as the moral and intellectual opposite of Encolpius the rogue? To what extent do author and narrator act each other? And in appearing as an actor, as Encolpius, to what extent can Petronius exculpate himself physically from the narrative and its telling?

Petronius is both absent and present in this narrative, which is precisely how Worthen defines the actor's positioning in his eye-opening study: 'onstage, the actor is both there and not there for us. He is present as an actor, strutting his stagey stuff, but he is also absent, negated by the dramatic illusion he creates'; the actor is engaged in a 'double effort' that 'reveals him as an actor while it conceals him within his dramatic role'.[3] The difference here, of course, is that whereas we (usually) know an actor is acting, in the *Satyricon* the distinction, and ability to distinguish, between what is and what is not an act are posed to readers as a central dilemma, while the prevalence of theatrical paradigms and the visual impact of language in this fiction help engineer the construction of its readership as reactive participants in a Neronian stage show. As Bartsch discusses, Nero's rule sees the theatre transformed into an anxious site for the reversal of actor–audience relations which is reflected throughout public life,[4] an idea made explicit at *Sat.* 45, where Trimalchio's guests look forward to a show hosted by Titus in which the performing gladiators are freedmen, just like the audience, who will themselves perform a spectacle to rival that of the arena: *et ecce habituri sumus munus excellente in triduo die festa; familia non lanisticia, sed plurimi liberti* / 'and look, we're soon to get a superb three-day show for the festivity: and not just your average troop of gladiators – many of them are freedmen' (45.4); *videbis*

[2] Panayotakis (1995). [3] Worthen (1984) 3. [4] Bartsch (1994) 1–35.

populi rixam inter zelotypos et amasiunculos / 'You'll see public quarrels in the crowd, between lovers and jealous husbands' (45.7). These are exciting times: as Worthen writes, 'One could argue that the stage becomes fully dramatic only when its performers can excite the histrionic sensibility of their audience'.[5]

As well as being highly theatrical, the narratives of the *Satyricon* are also preoccupied with concealment, in particular with covering up the body in cloaks or darkness. This emphasis on camouflage is especially salient in *Sat.* 6–26, the episodes leading up to Trimalchio's *cena*. From the time they leave the *porticus*, Encolpius and Ascyltos are lured into dark, deceptive places which recall the steamy confines of Encolpius' metaphorical *culina* (*Sat.* 2.1): an old woman disguised as a prophetess traps Encolpius in a *locum secretiorem* ('more discreet location') which turns out to be a brothel in *Sat.* 7.2; he covers his head to disguise himself as he escapes (*caput operui*, 2.4). Meanwhile Ascyltos was led down dark turnings (*anfractus obscurissimos*, 8.3) by a man who proceeds to offer him money for sex. When Encolpius finally spots Giton in *Sat.* 9.1 it is *quasi per caliginem* ('almost through complete darkness'), and on finding out about his 'brother's' adultery, denounces Ascyltos as a *nocturne percussor* ('a night-assassin'). Still in perpetual semi-darkness (*deficiente iam die* / 'it was already dusk') at *Sat.* 12.1, the gang visit the local market, where there is a great deal of junk on sale, made to look far more expensive than it really is by the veil of twilight (*sed tamen quarum fidem male ambulantem obscuritas temporis facillime tegeret*). Encouraged by the undercover atmosphere, the gang steal a cloak (*pallium*), itself a dramatic token for concealment, which they then partly cover in order to display only the bright corner of fabric to prospective purchasers (12.2). Yet in the process of selling the cloak, they spot a man wearing a shirt they recently lost, which conceals their savings in gold pieces inside its seams (*Sat.* 12–13). Hiding their relief like accomplished actors, they attempt to buy back the shirt, but are stopped in their tracks by a veiled woman (*mulier operto capite*, 14.5) who recognises the stolen cloak. The situation collapses into farce as the three pull at the shirt, a treasure trove which looks like a dirty rag, while the disguised woman tugs at the expensive cloak, which they now don't need to sell: an audience has gathered round (14.7) to watch a performance which in fact is about nothing more than performance (that is, *disguise*) itself. The savings are eventually recovered when a policeman on night-duty (*advocatus nocturnus*, 15.2) lets them off, and the illusion that

[5] Worthen (1984) 3.

appearance is a true indicator of the nature or content of a thing is maintained before the audience inside this narrative. Petronius' readers, however, have been alerted to the imagery of concealment and have had their eyes opened to the trickiness of visual representation.[6]

Yet even clever readers in (or of) the *Satyricon*, the market-traders like Ascyltos who can spot a hidden fortune in a second-hand shirt, rarely escape falling victim to deception. In *Sat.* 16, the gang are just sitting down to supper when another veiled woman (*mulier operto capite*) knocks at the door, to ask, *me derisisse vos putabatis?* / 'Did you think you had me fooled?' (16.3). It is Quartilla's maid, announcing that they have intruded on *nocturnas religiones* in honour of Priapus in her secret chapel. By the time she removes the cloak from her head (*retexit superbum pallio caput*, 17.3), they are trapped. Quartilla and her maid Psyche move in for the kill, and all Ascyltos can do in response is to bury his head in his cloak (*operuerat Ascyltos pallio caput*, 20.3).[7] The pre-dinner torture begins, and all three are pummeled by a snappily-dressed sodomite (*Sat.* 21); when the first session is over, the victims of their own mastery of disguise decide to keep this terrible secret concealed forever (21.3).

Much of the *Satyricon* is staged in darkness. After the twilight scenes at the market, the drama of Quartilla's brothel continues into an evening which never ends: even after wrestling with the *cinaedus*, Encolpius reports at *Sat.* 21.5, *utcumque igitur lassitudine abiecta cenatoria repetimus* / 'And so the tiredness somehow vanished and we put on evening dress again'. When after several courses and gallons of Falernian wine they begin to drop off to sleep, Quartilla rouses them again: *etiam dormire vobis in mente est, cum sciatis Priapi genio pervigilium deberi?* / 'How can you even think of sleeping when you know full well it's your duty to devote a wakeful night to Priapus' genius?' (21.7). Once more the guests grow heavy-eyed, and the little remaining lamp oil spreads a thin, dying light. Yet in no time at all, the butler has woken up and refilled the lamps, and a girl enters the dining room crashing brass cymbals, with the result that *refectum igitur est convivium* / 'the dinner was therefore started again' (23.1). The rhythm of

6 Throughout the *Satyricon* clothing is the focus for a confusion between insides and outsides: e.g. at *Sat.* 41.12, a drink is 'as good as an overcoat' (*tamen calda potio vestiarius est*), or at *Sat.* 44.15, Ganymede 'eats his clothes' (*iam pannos meos comedi*), that is, he sells them to buy food. There may be a pun intended on *panis* (bread) here, as C. Connors has suggested to me.

7 The allegorical use of the veil, which as Ferber (1999: 222) argues 'leads us to the veil as a symbol of allegory itself', is especially common in the Bible: Paul interprets the veil as veiled speech, in contrast to the plain speech of the Christians. The Book of Revelation means literally 'lifting up the veil'. Ferber comments, 'Writers committed to revealing the truth often resort to veil imagery', citing Blake, Shelley and Schiller's poetry as post-classical examples.

the narrative mimics the confused movements of Encolpius as he loses his way at *Sat.* 6–7, always to return to the same spot:

itaque quocumque ieram, eodem revertebar, donec et cursu fatigatus et sudore iam madens accedo aniculam quandam, quae agreste holus vendebat, et 'rogo' inquam, 'mater, numquid scis ubi ego habitem?'

So wherever I went, I kept coming back to the same place, until, when I was tired out from walking and dripping with sweat, I went up to an old lady selling country vegetables and said, 'Can I just ask, ma'am, do you happen to know where I live?'

Trimalchio's *cena* is already a repetition of Quartilla's nocturnal celebrations, and this occasion too seems to be freed from the normal constraints of time, taking place through an artificially extended night which continues even after the cock has crowed (*'usque in lucem cenemus.' haec dicente eo gallus gallinaceus cantavit* / ' "Let's dine until dawn." Just as he was saying this a cock crowed', 73.6–74.1) and long after the guests have had their fill. Trimalchio even enters the dining room peering out from beneath a scarlet cloak (*pallio enim coccineo adrasum excluserat caput*, 32.2),[8] a key prop for his role as creative manipulator in this beguiling show.[9] Even when Encolpius and Giton escape in the morning, it is still dark, and Encolpius records 'it was now midnight' (79.1). Have we missed a bit? Has the dinner gone on through the day and into the next evening, or is Encolpius, as usual, confused, especially as he admits he is drunk at this point, and says that he would get lost even if it *was* daylight: *accedebat huc ebrietas et imprudentia locorum etiam interdiu obfutura* / 'we were drunk too, although our ignorance of the area would have left us confused even in the daytime' (79.2–3)? Has time become irrelevant in any case, so distorted by the *cena* as to become meaningless? Or is the darkness metaphorical, a clever narrative effect to be read alongside the references here to Theseus' blind escape from the labyrinth with the aid of white chalk marks, or to Oedipus' blindness, which we are reminded of in the image of the two men dragging their bleeding feet along the road? It is we as readers who are finally left in the dark.

Darkness is used overtly as a metaphor for deception or veiling at various points throughout the *Satyricon*: for example, at *Sat.* 95.3, the

[8] Covering the head here may be a reference to slaves' or freedmen's practice of covering the forehead to conceal marks branded or tattooed on them in servitude.

[9] The *Cena* is perhaps the most overtly theatrical section of the *Satyricon*. See Appendix 1 in Bartsch (1994): 'The *Cena Trimalchionis* as theater'. Compare Sandy (1974), Saylor (1987), Bryson (1990: 49), Jones (1991), Rosati (1999).

landlord of a block of flats accuses the fugitives of trying to leave in secret without paying for their room (*vos mehercules ne mercedem cellae daretis fugere nocte in publicum voluistis* / 'I bet you meant to run off down the street in the dark rather than pay for your room'). At 112.5, the soldier secretly carries food to the widow of Ephesus' tomb as soon as darkness falls (*prima statim nocte in monumentum ferebat*). Or on board Lichas' ship, Eumolpus disguises Giton and Encolpius as branded slaves under the cover of night (103–4). Moreover, before they decide on this particular escape plan, the stowaways rehearse their options for deception by playing precisely on the metaphor of cloaking or covering the head which we have seen several times before:

quomodo possumus egredi nave, ut non conspiciamur a cunctis? opertis capitibus, an nudis? opertis, et quis non dare manum languentibus volet? nudis, et quid erit aliud quam se ipsos proscribere? (101.11)

How can we get off the ship without everyone seeing us? Shall we cover our heads or bare them? If we cover them, everyone will want to do the poor sick men a favour. If we keep them uncovered, we'll basically be setting ourselves up!

Yet the final scenario of writing fake tattoos on their foreheads is a trick posing as an unveiling of the truth of slavery: the precedent of ex-slave Trimalchio's covered, shaven head seems to inspire the double-crossing connection between a tattooed brow and the very act of deception, so that Eumolpus' inky inscription is itself a shadow or veil: *ita eaedem litterae et suspicionem declinabunt quaerentium et vultus umbra supplicii tegent* / 'so the letters will deflect suspicions and at the same time cover your faces with the shadow of punishment' (103.2).

Whether something is or is not an act in the *Satyricon* is often staged as a dilemma concerning the perception of or distinction between what is inside and outside the (human or metaphorical) body. This text exploits the potential hypocrisy of rhetorical theory, which maintained the principle that physical appearance corresponded to and represented inner moral character[10] alongside the notion that the orator must master the techniques of acting or impersonation. Identities of characters in the *Satyricon* are never written all over their faces, and nothing is what it seems. As Trimalchio warns, 'A man who is ready to believe what is told him will never do well' (43.6).[11] Again, Encolpius' apparent and

[10] For examples of this principle see Cic. *Leg.* 1.27.

[11] *numquam autem recte faciet, qui cito credit*. However, even the character who makes a motto of guarding against gullibility is deceived by his own wife: *ad summam, mero meridie si dixerit illi tenebras esse, credet* / 'in fact, if she tells him it's dark at noon, he'll believe it', (37.5).

self-declared myopia means that we can never escape the joke that we are also blind to the most cunning of the *Satyricon*'s tricks, and nowhere is this visual incapacity more in evidence than in Trimalchio's *cena*.

It is important that the *cena* begins and ends with a visual representation: when the guests enter, they cannot help looking at the hallway walls, painted with an image of Trimalchio at a slave market (*Sat.* 29.3–8). The frieze portrays a detailed narrative of his career, which ends in apotheosis as Mercury whirls him up to his official throne in the sky (*in tribunal excelsum Mercurius rapiebat*, 29.5). Yet it is difficult for the *Satyricon*'s readers to picture this scene, in part because it is difficult to imagine such a detailed visual narrative from the brief description given, but importantly also because Encolpius seems to obscure the difference between what is actually happening and what is part of the two-dimensional mural: he says, *notavi etiam in porticu gregem cursorum cum magistro se exercentem* / 'I also noticed a troop of runners practising in the gallery with their coach' (29.7) and continues to describe the furniture, but it is not clear whether *in porticu* is intended to mean *on* the colonnade walls, or *within* them. We are then told that there are other pictures to see, illustrating the *Iliad*, the *Odyssey* and the gladiatorial show given by Laenas, yet we are kept in the dark as to what they look like and by this point in any case our vision is blurred. Like Encolpius, we cannot take it all in at once (*non licebat †multaciam†*[12] *considerare*, 30.1). We all begin reading the *Cena* in a frustrating state of sensory overdrive.

Then at the end of the meal, before the guests take baths, the *Cena* is framed by another representation engineered by Trimalchio: in *Sat.* 71.9–11, he gives instructions on the picture he wants painted on his tomb:

> te rogo, ut naves etiam [monumento mei] facias plenis velis euntes, et me in tribunali sedentem praetextatum cum anulis aureis quinque et nummos in publico de sacculo effundentem; scis enim, quod epulum dedi binos denarios. faciantur, si tibi videtur, et triclinia. facias ut totum populum sibi suaviter facientem. ad dexteram meam ponas statuam Fortunatae meae columbam tenentem: et catellam cingulo alligatam ducat: et cicaronem meum, et amphoras copiosas gypsatas, ne effluant vinum. at unam licet fractam sculpas, et super eam puerum plorantem. horologium in medio, ut quisquis horas inspiciet, velit nolit, nomen meum legat.

I want you to carve ships at full sail, and put me sitting in my toga on my official seat, wearing five gold rings and pouring out coins from a bag to the public; you know, don't you, that I gave a dinner worth two denarii a head. I'd like

[12] *multaciam* is corrupt, and various suggestions have been made: Bücheler has *multa iam*, Marbach *multa clam*, Heinsius *multa ad aciam*, Scheffer *multa etiam*.

you to make an image of a dining room set of couches, if you would, and also, picture everyone there having a great time. On my right, put a statue of my darling Fortunata holding a dove, and have her leading a little dog tied up with a waistband, and also my little boy, and large amphorae sealed with gypsum so the wine doesn't run out. Oh, and I want a broken urn with a boy weeping over it. Put a sundial in the centre, so that anyone who looks at the time will read my name whether he likes it or not.

Thus the dinner scenes vividly described by Encolpius, as if in a picture, are replayed in Trimalchio's description of an envisaged, as yet also unrealised image. Trimalchio is the real author of his *Cena*, the framing of which defines authorship as control of representation, the ability to manipulate an audience which on the surface at least must enjoy being deceived (*totum populum sibi suaviter facientem*, 71.10).[13] The guests' reaction to Trimalchio's morbid request testifies to the power of the *imagined* image:[14] everyone begins to weep, as if they had been invited to his funeral (*tamquam in funus rogata*, 72.1). Trimalchio has represented his death as a time of liberation (he's to set them free in his will, *Sat.* 71.1) yet the deceptiveness of the *Satyricon*'s water metaphor is revealed again as the guests, who have imagined that the time of death has come, are encouraged to jump into baths as hot as crematorium ovens (*sic calet tamquam furnus, Sat.* 72.3). Life and death, liberation and entrapment are fatally confused as Trimalchio urges, *cum sciamus nos morituros esse, quare non vivamus?* / 'Since we know we are to die, why don't we live a little?' (72.2) and Ascyltos fears, *ego enim si videro balneum, statim expirabo!* / 'If I so much as *see* a bath, I'll keel over on the spot!' (72.6). As we have noticed already, there is a fine line between a welcoming bath and Ascyltos' perilous fishpond (*in piscinam, Sat.* 72.7).

The dining room frolics are a feast for the eyes, for the dinner guests and for Petronius' readers alike (*novitas tamen omnium convertit oculos* / 'everyone turned and stared at the novelty', *Sat.* 35.2). Yet the inadequacy of Encolpius' description, which confuses static, two-dimensional pictures with the look of real things and events, solidified now in narrative,

[13] Just like Nero, we are tempted to say: Bartsch (1994: 199) summarises the most striking evocations of Nero in the passages starring Trimalchio: 'The acrobat who falls on Trimalchio during dinner (*Sat.* 54.1; Suet. *Ner.* 12.2); Trimalchio's carver called Carver (*Carpus, Sat.* 36.5–6; epigraphical evidence of P. Grimal, *Rev. Phil.* 15, 1941, 19–26); his golden bracelet (*Sat.* 34.4, 67.7; Suet. *Ner.* 6.4); the ceiling panels that open to let down gifts (*Sat.* 60.1–3; Suet. *Ner.* 31.2); the box in which he stores his first beard (*Sat.* 29.8; Suet. *Ner.* 12.2).'

[14] Pictures, it seems, can be more powerful if they are merely imagined, as they are in ekphrasis: Heffernan (1993: 1, 7) argues, 'ekphrasis evokes the power of the silent image even as it subjects that image to the rival power of language . . . to represent a painting or a sculpted figure in words is to evoke its power.'

infects us as readers with the very same myopia. The frustrating parallels engineered between the visual, or interpretative, ability of inside and outside audiences are made even more piquant by the *Satyricon*'s ongoing metaphor of literature as food to be consumed. In reading the *Satyricon*, the metaphor tells us, we are eating the *cena* which has already been devoured by the dinner guests; we participate in the tasting of a layered dish of the kind that graces Trimalchio's table – a boar containing an 'already eaten' flock of birds (*Sat.* 40), or an enormous pig stuffed with sausage intestines and black pudding guts (*Sat.* 49). Yet the infuriating irony of what we are clearly meant to identify as parallel consumptions of Trimalchio's *cena* is that it makes us think in terms of real events, which happen outside the text on one hand, and their fictional representation inside the text as constructed by Encolpius on the other. There is no such division, we must pinch ourselves to keep remembering, no outside text. Encolpius is a fictional character recalling fictional events, and it is Petronius who is pulling the strings, the 'hidden author'[15] who is also, in his manifestation as Encolpius, always *fictional*.

The elaborate dishes in the *cena* repeatedly enact the unpredictability of appearances. In *Sat.* 33.3, a wooden hen nested in straw is brought to the table in a basket. As the music gets louder, inviting suspense, slaves delve into the straw to pull out peahen's eggs. Trimalchio's idea was to put the exotic eggs under an ordinary hen, but he decides to double the trick by using a wooden (fake) hen instead. The eggs, which Trimalchio warns are probably inedible, because *iam concepti* ('already addled') are in fact made of fine meal (*farina pingui*). Encolpius is on the point of throwing his portion away when he sees a fellow diner poke through a shell and discover a fig-eater, a pre-cooked baby bird rolled up in spiced egg yolk. Even the core of this recipe for masquerade is defined by what it has eaten: the bird is obese (*pinguissima*) from pecking figs, just as Trimalchio, we imagine, is puffed up (*plenus*) in pulling off this highly sophisticated stunt. This is much more than just an egg, in more ways than one: there is no getting around, or *outside* it, for the whole world, says Trimalchio, is an *ovum*, containing a universe of blessings within her shell (*terra mater est in medio quasi ovum corrotundata, et omnia bona in se habet tamquam favus* / 'mother earth lies in the centre of the universe, as round as an egg, holding all her blessings inside her like a honeycomb', *Sat.* 39.15).[16] Similarly the compelling zodiac dish at *Sat.* 35 presents a world on a

[15] This is Conte's phrase, used in the title of his book (1996).

[16] This Hesiodic image of an all-containing mother earth reminds us that Greek foundation myths picture the genealogy of the gods as a hierarchy of incorporation (a succession of devouring

plate, each personality-food digested in the communal gut representing the free flow of social interaction in Trimalchio's dining room cosmos.

At *Sat.* 40, slaves are setting the stage for yet another spectacle by throwing blankets painted with hunting nets over the couches. Encolpius reports, *necdum sciebamus, <quo> mitteremus suspiciones nostras* / 'we still didn't know what to be suspicious of' (40.2). Each course has become a riddle to be solved in the eating. When a vast wild boar is brought in on a tray, dressed in a cap of freedom, with baskets of dry and fresh fruit hanging from its tusks and pastry piglets suckling its breast, Encolpius is ready for a challenge. The boar is cut open and birds fly out, while Trimalchio jokes, *etiam videte, quam porcus ille silvaticus lotam comederit glandem* / 'now you see what fine acorns the woodland boar has been eating' (40.7), further confusing the issue of what is really inside the pig by suggesting that the digested acorns have metamorphosed into live thrushes. Meanwhile Encolpius sneaks off into a corner to ponder another challenge, daring to ask a slave what he thinks (*Sat.* 41.1–3). The slave replies that there is no trick, no concealment: *sed res aperta* ('it's perfectly obvious', 41.4). The boar had appeared at the previous evening's meal and the guests had let it go, so it returns now as a freedman. Just as Trimalchio has lured his guests into perceiving everything as a riddle, now he tricks them with the obvious. Encolpius shows us that it is very easy to make a fool of yourself in interpreting Trimalchio's charades: searching frantically for complexities beneath the surface makes you miss the very thing that is staring you in the face (*damnavi ego stuporem meum et nihil amplius interrogavi, ne viderer numquam inter honestos cenasse* / 'I cursed my stupidity and asked no further questions for fear of looking like I'd never dined among decent folk', 41.5).

Yet Encolpius also shows us that it is very difficult not to enter into the spirit of interpretation. When a pig even bigger than the enormous boar is brought in (*Sat.* 49), he admits, *non potui me tenere* ('I just couldn't contain myself', 49.7).[17] Trimalchio manages to convince everyone that his slave has forgotten to gut the animal, and the audience is spellbound when sausages and black puddings flow out (*effusa sunt*, 49.10): like Agamemnon's poem in *Sat.* 5 (*defundes pectore*) or Eumolpus' *Bellum Civile* in *Sat.* 124.2 (*effudisset*), this sophisticated recipe composed by Trimalchio flows

fathers ending in Zeus) which is triggered by Earth's final inability to hold all the gods inside her. The cracking open of Trimalchio's eggs is the catalyst for a similar narrative of incorporation.

[17] The gag here is that Encolpius is about to embarrass himself by letting his own insides (his interpretation of the pig) burst out, alongside the belly of the pig, which is about to pour out its own clever rebuke.

straight from the belly of the pig, like free verse. This poetic creation is even more complicated than the boar, as even its contents are in disguise: *tomacula cum botulis* ('sausages and black puddings') posing as liver, lungs, intestines.

From this point on, our narrator begins to show signs of panicking whenever he senses a theatrical scene in the making. When Trimalchio pretends to be hurt by a clumsy slave, Encolpius remarks (*Sat.* 54.3): *pessime mihi erat, ne his precibus per <rid>iculum aliquid catastropha quaereretur. nec enim adhuc exciderat cocus ille qui oblitus fuerat porcum exinterare* / 'I was really scared that his begging routine was leading up to some comic twist. After all, the cook who had forgotten to gut the pig hadn't faded from my recollection.'[18] His reaction borders on paranoia; *itaque totum conspicere triclinium coepi, ne per parietem automatum aliquod exiret* / 'And so I started to scan the dining room, fearing that some clockwork contraption was about to jump out of the wall' (54.4). In *Sat.* 60.2 he hears a noise coming from the ceiling and is so startled he jumps from his seat (*consternatus ego exsurrexi et timui*). Yet despite having his suspicions permanently aroused, Encolpius continually fails to interpret Trimalchio's food-texts correctly. When he meets the culinary *pièce de resistance* at *Sat.* 69.9, he is so hooked on the theatrical theme that he boasts, *ego, scilicet homo prudentissimus, statim intellexi quid esset* / 'As for myself, being a pretty sharp chap I realised at once what it was.' The goose-like animal, he suspects, is bound to be made from wax or clay: wrong again, reveals Trimalchio, as the whole thing is made out of a pig (*Sat.* 70.1). Daedalus the chef can create a fish out of a sow's womb, a woodpigeon out of bacon, a turtledove out of a ham, and a chicken out of a knuckle of pork. The consummate craftsman can make animals metamorphose before your very eyes.

While dramatising the difficulty of interpreting the contents of dishes without tasting them first, Trimalchio also seeks to distinguish himself from the crowd by displaying his own privileged knowledge of interiors. In *Sat.* 38.5 we are told that every one of his cushions has purple or scarlet stuffing (*nulla non aut conchyliatum aut coccineum tomentum habet*), so that they look as luxurious on the inside as they do on the outside.[19] Like Superman with his all-penetrating gaze, Trimalchio likes to see

[18] Yet of course the cook didn't forget to gut the pig: has Encolpius forgotten that he didn't forget, or is this a trap which tries to catch out reader-memory, just as we began to take comfort in imagining the *Satyricon* as episodic anti-narrative, in which we never have to remember the previous scene in order to understand the next? See my discussion in chapter eleven.

[19] Although of course the point is that neither we nor the guests ever get to see inside the cushions, so have no way of knowing whether this is just more manipulative rhetoric.

insides, as if to pretend they are not always concealed: nobody and nothing can ever surprise him (*mihi nihil novi potest afferri* / 'no one can bring me anything new', 39.4). As the 'author' of this *cena*, he adopts the supercilious persona of the writer, doctor or money-lender, as extrapolated in *Sat.* 56.1–4: 'What do we reckon is the hardest profession after writing?' Like the prophetic *vates* seeing into the future, Trimalchio is privileged to reveal his inside information to entertain those less fortunate than himself: the canny money-lender pretends his copper coins are silver; for a fee, the doctor flatters his patient that his intestines are in good order; the writer veils the truth in his pursuit of mystery, suspense, drama, fiction *per se*. For example, in *Sat.* 39.3, he is privy to his guests' digestive systems when he advises them to drink lots of wine, because *pisces natare oportet* ('a fish must have something to swim in'). He kisses a slave boy in *Sat.* 75.4 not because the slave is pretty, but because, unlike some people, Trimalchio can appreciate what lies beneath good looks: *non propter formam, sed quia frugi est* / 'not on account of his beauty, but because he's talented'. He flaunts knowledge of his bowel movements (47) and employs astrologers to inform him about his own gut (*intestinas meas noverat; tantum quod mihi non dixerat quid pridie cenaveram* / 'he knew my own insides, and only stopped short of telling me what I'd had for dinner the night before', 76.11). Like the independent, virile body, the same inside and out, all Trimalchio's produce is apparently self-produced and self-contained: he is fully in control of what (he knows) comes from within (*omnia domi nascuntur: lana, citrea, piper, lacte gallinaceum si quaesieris, invenies* / 'everything is home-reared: wool, lemons, pepper – if you want hen's milk, we've got it', *Sat.* 38.1).

Yet, it transpires, like 'home-cooked' meals designed to attract the tourist to an 'Olde English' pub, Trimalchio's indigenous produce is imported in bulk:

> arietes a Tarento emit, et eos culavit in gregem. mel Atticum ut domi nasceretur, apes ab Athenis iussit afferri; obiter et vernaculae quae sunt, meliusculae a Graeculis fient. ecce intra hos dies scripsit, ut illi ex India semen boletorum mitteretur. (38.2–4)

> He bought rams from Tarentum and bummed them into his flock. He had bees brought from Athens, so that he could have 'home-made' Attic honey; incidentally, the Roman-born bees will be improved by the Greek ones. Within the last few days, even, he has written off for a cargo of mushroom spores from India.

There *is* no such thing as self-sufficiency, as the human demand for food proves; it always has to be faked, a point Trimalchio takes pride in flaunting at a higher level here. The fact that even the privileged and independent display their bodily sameness and dependency in the necessary processes of incorporation is precisely what Trimalchio lets slip again and again in the *cena*, while he attempts to show off his own knowledge of interiors by confusing his audience's visual ability and expectations of what lies beneath the surface. Between courses at *Sat.* 47, his superior self-revelation backfires when he doesn't seem to be any more in control of his own insides than the victimized guests: *nemo nostrum solide natus est* / 'nobody is born solid'.

We are entertained by the fact that the artists of the *cena*, Trimalchio and Encolpius, seem to be easily fooled. We laugh at Encolpius' failure to learn the language of Trimalchio's culinary representations because the alternative, his successful interpretation of each scene, would seem as inappropriate and unfunny as giving the correct answer to a joke. The comedy of the *Satyricon* relies on this fictional limitation of perspective,[20] and encourages readings of the text as 'pure entertainment', a jolly Neronian farce which is too silly to be serious, too superficial to be political. However most critics have continually chosen to ignore the fact that Encolpius the myopic fool is also our eyes and ears in this fiction: we must laugh with him, as well as at him, aware of the truth that we too simply cannot predict or articulate the relationship between insides and outsides in this text. Like the actors in Nero's audience, forced to participate in a pretence of entertainment, readers of the *Satyricon* are trapped in a theatre of paranoia in which it might well be preferable to convince oneself to sit back and enjoy rather than to contemplate the implications of what lies beneath the surface: as Trimalchio suggests in *Sat.* 56.2, the public really doesn't want to know the state of a poor man's gut (*quid intra praecordia sua habent*). Once you start thinking about it, like the freedman Hermeros, 'the worms will breed' (*in molle carne vermes nascuntur*, *Sat.* 57.3).

The difficulty of reading this fiction through the eyes of Encolpius is brought into focus by the representation of images in the highly visual but opaque narrative of the *Cena*. We saw how in *Sat.* 29, Encolpius does not recognise that Trimalchio has two of the most famous texts of the ancient world, the *Iliad* and the *Odyssey*, painted on the walls of his atrium (*interrogare ergo atriensem coepi, quas in medio picturas haberent. 'Iliada et Odyssian'*

[20] This fictional limitation of perspective is made explicit or even dramatised at crucial points, e.g. when Encolpius admits his memory is hazy (*sexcenta huiusmodi fuerunt, quae iam exciderunt memoriae meae* / 'There was a whole string of jokes like this, which have now escaped my memory', *Sat.* 56.10) or when he and Quartilla watch a performance through a tiny slit in the door (*in primis Quartilla per rimam improbe diductam applicuerat oculum curiosum*, *Sat.* 26.4).

inquit / 'I began to ask the doorman about the pictures they had in the centre. "It's the Iliad and the Odyssey" he said').[21] Now later on at *Sat.* 52.1, Trimalchio announces that he owns four-gallon cups engraved with the image of Cassandra killing her sons (*quemadmodum Cassandra occidit filios suos*), in which the sons are dead but are painted so realistically you would think they were still alive (*et pueri mortui iacent sic ut vivere putes*); he also has jugs on which you can see Daedalus shutting Niobe into the Trojan Horse (*ubi Daedalus Niobam in equum Troianum includit*, 52.2). And in *Sat.* 59.3–5, when performers act out a mythical story in Greek, Trimalchio reads out a translation from a book, saying,

'scitis' inquit 'quam fabulam agant? Diomedes et Ganymedes duo fratres fuerunt. horum soror erat Helena. Agamemnon illam rapuit et Dianae cervam subiecit. ita nunc Homeros dicit quemadmodum inter se pugnent Troiani et Parentini. vicit scilicet et Iphigeniam, filiam suam, Achilli dedit uxorem. ob eam rem Aiax insanit et statim argumentum explicabit.'

'So do you know' he asked 'what story they're doing? Diomede and Ganymede were brothers. Helen was their sister. Agamemnon kidnapped her and sacrificed a deer to Diana in her place. So here Homer is telling the tale of the war between Troy and Parentium. He won of course, and after that he married his daughter Iphigenia to Achilles, which drove Ajax bonkers – that bit's coming up in a second.'

The usual critical response to these representations of myth is one of amusement at Trimalchio's perversion of well-known, even sacred narratives. On *Sat.* 50–52, Smith comments, 'Petronius will unfold Trimalchio's absurd ignorance of history and mythology, as well as his pretensions to good taste'.[22] Slater emphasizes the 'dense comedy' of these 'typical Trimalchian confusions of mythology'.[23] On *Sat.* 59, Smith states the accepted view that, 'Trimalchio's wild version of the story is entertaining precisely because each detail distorts some identifiable part of the normal version':[24] thus he supplements Castor and Pollux with the Greek warrior Diomedes and the Trojan boy Ganymedes, whose names merely *look* related. Agamemnon replaces Paris as Helen's abductor, and Helen is crossed with Iphigenia when, as in the Iphigenia story we know, a deer is sacrificed in her place. The false promise that Iphigenia will marry Achilles if she comes to Aulis is realised in Trimalchio's version, but the

[21] Yet we are stuck when it comes to interpreting Encolpius' failure to recognise the paintings as Homeric epic: is it an indication of our narrator's (contrived?) ignorance, of the doorman's ignorance or desire to impress, or of Trimalchio's hype?

[22] Smith (1975) 134. [23] Slater (1988) 168. [24] Smith (1975) 165.

marriage occurs at the end of the war, not the beginning. Instead of being maddened when the arms of the dead Achilles were given to Ulysses rather than to himself, Ajax is enraged with sexual jealousy at Achilles' marriage, whether we are meant to imagine his lust fixated on Iphigenia or on Achilles himself. Of the pictures on Trimalchio's cups and jugs, Smith again expresses the critical consensus that, although Pausanias tells us that Cassandra had two sons who were murdered along with Agamemnon (2.16.7), 'it is obvious that Trimalchio simply confuses her with Medea, whose murder of her two children was a much more familiar story'.[25] There is similar confusion on the jug, as Trimalchio clumsily integrates three different myths: that of Daedalus, who constructed a wooden cow for Pasiphae, of Niobe, the grieving mother whose children were killed by Apollo and Artemis, and the story of the Trojan Horse (*Sat.* 52).

The first problem with assuming Trimalchio's buffoonish ignorance of myth and confusion of narratives is that the relationship between ekphrasis and image is never revealed. We know from the beginning of the *Cena* that Encolpius has trouble recognising and explaining pictures to his readers, or even taking them in at all (e.g. *Sat.* 30.1). We also know that this difficulty is negotiated throughout the *Cena* in the context of *acting*: it is problematic, for Encolpius (and hence for us as readers) to rely on images, which are misleading and function so as to veil interiors and obscure meaning, just as the actor puts up a deceptive front which conceals his real, non-acting self in the visually impacting environment of the theatre. So when Trimalchio, whose role throughout the *Cena* is to deceive through dramatic or visual representation, describes the pictures on his crockery, we cannot rely on Encolpius to confirm that the description is actually *representative*, or to decipher where description crosses over into interpretation. Similarly at *Sat.* 59, there is no comment from Encolpius to confirm or deny that what Trimalchio says he is reading from the book in Latin corresponds to the dining room drama that is being enacted in Greek.

Secondly, we might add that, if Trimalchio's apparent displays of ignorance are straightforward jokes, as critics have perceived, their comic potential is about as overwhelming as Trimalchio's pun on '*carpe*' in *Sat.* 36. They are so obviously out of synch with their Homeric originals that it is hardly original or clever to make an issue of their absurdity. Could this be Trimalchio taking his role as deceptive and manipulative 'author' of the

[25] Smith (1975) 139.

Cena to an extreme, rather than showing himself up as an ignoramus?[26] If so, then he could hardly have picked more appropriate mythical characters than Cassandra (the revealer of truth who is never believed, to whom Trimalchio compares Fortunata in *Sat.* 74), and Daedalus (the cunning architect of interpretative and, in the *Cena*, culinary labyrinths). Meanwhile Trimalchio's game of character-swapping in *Sat.* 59 (let's get Helen to play Iphigenia, Agamemnon would make a great Paris!) reflects the theme of acting as metamorphosis at work in the *Cena* and throughout the *Satyricon*: characters are either named after mythical characters (Agamemnon, Menelaus, Circe, Psyche, Ganymede, Bacchus, Dionysus, Philomela and so on)[27] or playact as them (Giton plays Ganymede and Ulysses in *Sat.* 92/97, Lichas is imagined as a Cyclops, Encolpius adopts the epithets of Odysseus in *Sat.* 127, Eumolpus is Aeneas reciting the fall of Troy as in *Aeneid* II in *Sat.* 89, and so on). What we see here is not (just) nonsense, but a dramatisation of acting and theatricality run wild:[28] when all the world's a stage, and when everyone's an actor, able instantly and convincingly to switch role and metamorphose, then who can tell who's really who?

Yet more than that, Trimalchio's apparent rewriting, or rereading of the Greek performance in Latin enacts more general strategies involved in writing the *Satyricon.* This text is not simply a bloated parasite, incorporating bits of its Greek and Latin predecessors into a messy and inconsistent whole. Throughout the *Satyricon*, eating is a catalyst for metamorphosis: as the consumed alters the consumer, as we become what we eat, so too Petronius' 'sources', be they solid, liquid or vaporous, are rewritten in the process of their incorporation. Through Trimalchio's alternative myths, intoned from a Latin book like the one we are reading, we see incorporation envisaged as a creative, transformative act which will unnerve as well as humour its readers, make them swallow new perspectives. The *Cena*'s spirit of loosening corporeal boundaries and letting

[26] I.e., is this just a performance of myth-in-action, demonstrating that myth (narrative) is never static but is continually re-created every time it is read or told?

[27] Slaves were often given mythological names, perhaps, as Fitzgerald suggests (2000: 5), because it 'allowed their masters to share in the civilized world of which Greek culture was the most precious fruit'. For Trimalchio, naming is always about creative control, about playing at being a (Greek) poet thinking up new names to fit his fictional worlds.

[28] And also, perhaps, of intertextuality run wild. As Fowler explores (2000: 119–20), all famous characters and celebrities are consciously or unconsciously intertextual (Clinton–Kennedy, Britney–Madonna–Marilyn, and so on). Such relationships, as Fowler reminds us, are 'not fixed but constantly available for reuse and negotiation by interpreters, including characters themselves'. Today, this social intertextuality is the essence of celebrity, or celebrity reporting, used to create titillating juxtapositions on glossy page after page.

it all hang out operates alongside an apparent liberation of language and narrative in the form of riddles, puns and warped myths.

On another level, however, the alternative to viewing these passages as displays of Trimalchio's ignorance is fairly tricky, and in doing so we risk exposing or confirming our own ignorance of the creative processes at work in the *Satyricon*. Instead of meaning nothing and simply representing absurdity, now it seems Trimalchio's myths could potentially mean anything at all. For modern readers, the joke is definitely on us as we struggle with gaps in the text and suspicions that a crucial passage might be clarified by a missing phrase or section of narrative. It might be just as well for us to join in with Encolpius in fudging the issue and maintaining an (all too telling) 'no comment' policy.[29]

[29] Note that this discomforting self-exposure is not quite the kind of entertainment envisaged in Slater's verdict of comic unreadability.

CHAPTER 3

The beast within

The *Satyricon* is a hybrid text, depicting a hybrid world. In this chapter, I aim to look in greater detail at the *Cena Trimalchionis* and surrounding scenes to explore how loosening corporeal boundaries in the spirit of metamorphosis is played out as a fusion or interaction of human and animal bodies. Arguably all extended texts, ancient and modern, concern themselves in some way with human/animal metaphorics,[1] and this familiar, organising imagery is undoubtedly one of the ways in which the *Satyricon* sets itself (mischievously or not) within recognisable frames for reading.[2] Yet I will argue that this fiction takes such idioms to an extreme to explore their deeply threatening implications (for reading), not least their disruption of civilised hierarchies between eater and eaten. In the *Cena* especially, a dramatic awareness and confusion of what eats and what in turn gets eaten is manifested in a vacillating characterisation of humans as animals, animals as humans.[3] Here, the myth that the consumption of food involves an aggression and hence the complete control of eater over eaten is repeatedly debunked by Petronius' unhealthy 'you are what you eat' mantra, which, we will see, gives rise to some beastly metaphors for digestion.

We first encounter such imagery in the programmatic speeches of Encolpius and Agamemnon: after the feeding frenzy of the rhetorical school described by Encolpius in *Sat.* 1, Agamemnon defends his role as purveyor of junk food by playing victim to his ravenous but faddy pupils, who will be fed only the finest canapés: they are fish he must bait from

[1] But satire and ancient prose fiction stand out for their hybridity, argues Gowers (forthcoming): *mille hominum species et rerum discolor usus* / 'Men come in 1,000 different forms, and human life is multicoloured' (*Pers.* 5.52) is Persius' philosophy.

[2] As Kristeva suggests (1982: 207), 'on close inspection, all literature is probably a version of the apocalypse that seems to me rooted, no matter what the socio-historical conditions might be, on the fragile border (borderline cases) where identities (subject/object etc.) do not exist or only barely so – double, fuzzy, heterogeneous, animal, metamorphosed, altered, abject'.

[3] This 'metamorphosis' is noted by Arrowsmith (1966: 315).

his lonely rock (*Sat.* 3.4). As we have already seen, the *Cena*, framed by baths which become fishponds, is an extensive play on this metaphor: Trimalchio is the fisherman who repeatedly hooks in his hungry guests by feeding them delicious titbits, and proceeds to trap them in his dark and labyrinthine home, just as Encolpius imagines pupils stifled in the smelly *culina* of the rhetorical school (*Sat.* 1). Agamemnon's poem at *Sat.* 5, which sets up the pervasive image of contemporary Latin literature as the effusion of imbibed literary sources, a wide river (*flumen largum*) pouring from the heart (*defundes pectore*), also evokes an important picture of the writing man which seems to connect human and animal: when his learning is complete, the young orator can 'loosen the reins' of his style (*mittat habenas liber*), suggesting that the skills of composition are comparable to the skills of horseriding demanded of a hunter or soldier. This is merely a suggestion, the vaguest hint in fact, yet this image of writing as horseriding, and of literary material as a horse you can learn to control and on which the author is eventually carried, gains strength and relevance as we continue reading.

The next time we encounter horseriding as an image is in Quartilla's brothel in *Sat.* 24. I have already noted the connection between Agamemnon's poem at *Sat.* 5 and the *cinaedus*' poem at *Sat.* 23: the introduction to this poem immediately recalls Agamemnon's earlier description of sophisticated verse in *Sat.* 5: *eiusmodi carmina* ***effudit*** / 'he poured out the poem as follows' (23.2). The four-line ditty that follows clearly attempts, at least, to be pacy and rhythmical, as free-flowing as Agamemnon has described and prescribed: the imperatives – *convenite, tendite, addite, convolate* ('gather round', 'stretch out', 'give a little', 'let fly') – slide over one another like bony but well lubricated limbs, the phrase *cursum addite*, as we saw in chapter one, instructing lithe bodies in the same way as Agamemnon advocated free-verse (*det pagina cursum*, 5. v.17).[4] When he has 'eaten' Agamemnon's words (*consumptis versibus, Sat.* 23.4), the slimy sodomite gets to work on Encolpius' groin (*super inguina mea diu multumque frustra moluit*, 23.5). But when the long-suffering Encolpius reminds Quartilla that Ascyltos is also present, she instructs the *cinaedus* to change partners, and he 'swops horse' (*equum mutavit*, 24.4):[5] the rider exchanges literary

[4] Williams (1999: 177) suggests that the lively metre and content of this poem indicate that the *cinaedus* is supposed to be a dancer, in line with the Greek etymology *kinaidos*, meaning an effeminate dancer who entertained audiences with a tympanum or tambourine and adopted a lascivious style (see Nonius 5.16–17M; Firmicus Maternus, *Math.* 6.31.39 cf. 8.20.8).

[5] On the metaphor of riding for sexual intercourse see Adams (1982: 165–6). The woman (or effeminate man) is usually depicted as the rider, the man as the horse (the verb describing the woman's position is *sedeo*, 'to sit', e.g. Martial 11.104.14), but according to Artemidorus (1.56; 4.40) a horse symbolised a woman.

material for a sexual partner.[6] Meanwhile Quartilla turns her attention to Giton (*mox manum etiam demisit in sinum et pertractato vasculo tam rudi* / 'next she slipped her hand down to his lap and got to work on his raw little tool') and says: *'haec' inquit 'belle cras in promulside libidinis nostrae militabit; hodie enim post asellum diaria non sumo'* / ' "This," she said, "will do its military service very nicely tomorrow, as a little hors-d'oeuvre for our lusts. I'd rather not take my daily ration today after that donkey-fish" ' (24.7). Quartilla and her sodomite are the first of many in this novel to use Petronius' characters as quasi-literary material, to be taken for a ride, while the creator of the *Satyricon* is just the kind of author Agamemnon is talking about in *Sat.* 5, loosening the reins and riding bareback through feasts (*epulae*) and wars (*bella*). Yet now the sexual pun on riding translates Agamemnon's consumption of literary resources as penetration: learning, like eating, is motivated by a voracious (sexual) hunger embodied in the naturally insatiable *cinaedus*, while the delicate act of keeping the balls of literary knowledge in the air is captured in the figure of the predatory, aggressive sodomite who is at the same time vulnerable, soft and penetrated.

The implication is always that if you loosen the reins you can so easily make an ass of yourself. In *Sat.* 31.9, antipasti are served to the guests from a bronze *asellus* ('donkey'). At *Sat.* 63.3, Trimalchio announces that his story-telling ability is like that of an *asinus* compared to Niceros.[7] In *Sat.* 64.3, Plocamus says he can't tell a story because his 'galloping days are over' (*quadrigae meae decucurrerunt*), a metaphor which perhaps inspires the image of Apuleius' prologue, in which the narrator refers to his style of writing as a *desultoria scientia* (the skill of a rider jumping from horse to horse). In *Sat.* 64.11–12, Trimalchio orders his dog-like slave Croesus to ride his back like a horse (*basiavit puerum ac iussit supra dorsum ascendere suum. non moratus ille usus <est> equo manuque plena scapulas eius subinde verberavit* / 'He kissed the boy and ordered him to get on his back. He mounted his horse without delay and slapped Trimalchio's shoulders with his open hand.') And in *Sat.* 134.2, Proselenos rants at the impotent Encolpius:[8] *mollis, debilis, lassus tamquam caballus in clivo, et operam et sudorem perdidisti* /

[6] Incidentally, when they are en route to the brothel via the marketplace at *Sat.* 6, Encolpius announces that he has forgotten where his *stabulum* is: the kind of guest house (or brothel) Encolpius frequents is no better than a stable designed for lowly beasts like cows and horses. For instances where *stabulum* means stable or the equivalent see e.g. Prop. 3.22.9; Virg. *G.* 3.352; *Ecl.* 3.80; Sen. *Ag.* 845.

[7] In Persius and Apuleius, as Gowers discusses (forthcoming), the ass represents the unsubtle reader or storyteller who stubbornly resists philosophical awakening. This is perhaps understood or echoed here.

[8] Note that Codex l and (in margin) codex Lambethanus indicate that the speaker here is the old woman Oenothea addressing Encolpius, not Proselenos as Müller thinks.

'You're soft, wimpish, and as knackered as a cab-horse on a hill. You've wasted your efforts and your sweat.' Practically everyone in the *Satyricon*, it seems, is horsing around, yet whenever we encounter the image of a man controlling or acting like an ass, we are always meant to recall the dynamics and manoeuvres of literary composition as evinced in the mirroring poems of Agamemnon (*Sat.* 5) and Quartilla's *cinaedus* (*Sat.* 23). As with all apparent hierarchies in the *Satyricon*, the opposition between the controlled horse and the controlling rider (author) is constantly confused, as we see in the examples at *Sat.* 63 and 64 (for Plocamus, the galloping storyteller is a metaphor for youthful wit, while for Trimalchio, being a four-legged narrator makes you a clumsy, unsophisticated creature). Likewise, we can never decide whether the *Satyricon* is being told by the asinine Encolpius or an author in complete control of the reins, and how far the Petronius we imagine in the saddle is also playing the ass.[9]

Let us turn now once more to the *Cena*, in which beastly puns and animal behaviour have been easily subsumed by critics in an overall picture of low-life slang and carnivorous indulgence. After the extensive appetisers and aperitifs, Trimalchio's feast begins to take off with the appearance of the spectacular zodiac dish in *Sat.* 35.[10] Heads turn at the sight of it (35.1). On a round plate are set the twelve signs of the zodiac in a circle, and on each sign the artist (*structor*) has placed a representative food: chick-peas, which look like tiny rams' heads, for Aries, beef for the Bull, testicles and kidneys for the Twins, and so on. As we have seen, this dish has a universal scope, as Trimalchio wants to suggest: the scene of its presentation serves as an introduction to the metaphors and images which dominate the *Cena* and to a large extent the whole of the *Satyricon*. The recipe explicitly associates people and personalities with foods to be eaten, as Trimalchio further explains in *Sat.* 39.5: he begins:

caelus hic, in quo duodecim dii habitant, in totidem se figuras convertit, et modo fit aries. itaque quisquis nascitur illo signo, multa pecora habet, multum lanae, caput praeterea durum, frontem expudoratam, cornum acutum. plurimi hoc signo scholastici nascuntur et arietilli.

[9] Apuleius goes on to make this idea the basis for his *Metamorphoses*, as Gowers discusses (2001), alongside Persius' similarly split personality, for which Varro's Menippean satires (with titles like Bimarcus = 'split Varro') had set a precedent. Gowers compares Persius' namesake as *semipaganus* (or 'half caste': see Hor. *Sat.* 1.7) and hybrid ass-eared image (*findor ut Arcadiae pecuaria rudere credas* / 'I'm splitting you'd think all the herds of Arcadia were braying!' Persius 3.9) to Apuleius' creative manoeuvring as donkey philosopher. 'Yet the joke in both authors is to inflict asinal form on their readers before they notice', i.e. as Persius sneers, *auriculas asini quis non habet?* / 'Who doesn't have asses' ears?' (1.121).

[10] All conspicuously part of the 'theatre', especially as Laberius wrote several mimes with titles like *Aries*, *Cancer* and *Gemelli*.

> The sky in which the twelve gods live turns into as many shapes, and at a certain point becomes a ram. So anyone born under that sign has plenty of flocks and wool, a hard head, a shameless forelock and sharp horns. Many scholars and young bucks are born under that sign.

He goes on to describe the personality traits connected with the other signs: for example, Geminis tend to sit on both sides of the fence (*utrosque parietes linunt*), Leos are masterful gluttons (*cataphagae et imperiosi*), Pisceans are born caterers and rhetoricians (*obsonatores et rhetores*) (39.6–13).[11]

Yet the zodiac dish suggests not only that we are what we eat but also, more graphically, that the guests are about to eat themselves. There is no such thing as simple consumption in Trimalchio's culinary theatre, no straightforward hierarchy of incorporation, despite all the multi-layered dishes. In the universe of food, it's 'dog eat dog', a gross transgression of the eater/eaten hierarchy that structures civilised society and implies an absolute rejection of barbaric cannibalism. In its universality, this horoscopic platter contains and predicts the gamut of foods that will be on offer throughout the *cena*, from cakes (*scriblita*) and kidneys (*rienes*) to goose (*anser*), fig (*ficus*) and fish (*pisciculus marinus / mulli*): once again, an apparently self-contained scene (or body) in the *Satyricon* overflows, and unlawful eating can run and run. We can also note that *pisciculus* is the same word used by Agamemnon in *Sat.* 3 to describe trainee orators (*quam scierit appetituros esse pisciculos* / 'which he knows the little fish will go for'). The dish prompts us to glance back to this imagery and forecasts that its foods shall forever be associated in the *Satyricon* with types of people. Trimalchio's guests, described at *Sat.* 38.7 as *valde suco[s]i*, or 'juicily rich', spend an endless night eating themselves, and more disturbingly, each other, in a theatrical arena which is as aggressive as it is narcissistic.[12] For the most startling feature of the dish, with only twelve food-symbols to go around, is that it contains the paranoid vision of a guest consuming his zodiacal rival, an incompatible personality which will transform and destroy him from within.[13]

Indeed, Trimalchio may be the brains behind the performance, but he is also an active participant: in *Sat.* 47, the amphibian Cancerian (*in cancro ego natus sum* / 'I was born under Cancer', *Sat.* 39.8)[14] is troubled by some indigestion and declares, *alioquin circa stomachum mihi sonat, putes taurum /*

[11] Calendars always evoke and dictate cultural identity: see Beard (1987).

[12] Eumolpus goes on to convince the legacy hunters of Croton that his flesh is 'tasty' because it will taste of cash.

[13] This is what we might call *real* character acting. Trimalchio wants everyone to be on his stage, at all costs.

[14] In *Sat.* 42.7, Seleucus describes an 'old love' as a *cancer*, when the zodiacal precedent is still echoing in the guests' ears: men are not only associated with animals, and with foods to be

'Something's rumbling in my tum; you'd think I had a bull in there.' Readers are tickled and haunted at once by the image of Trimalchio's gut attempting to contain not a hunk of beef, but a walking, talking Taurean. We are also reminded here of Quartilla's trope at *Sat.* 25.5–6 as she prepares the pre-pubescent Pannychis for her 'wedding':

nam et infans cum paribus inquinata sum, et subinde prodeuntibus annis maioribus me pueris applicui, donec ad [hanc] aetatem perveni. hinc etiam puto proverbium natum illud, [ut dicatur] posse taurum tollere, qui vitulum sustulerit.

As a child I was defiled by boys of my own size, and then as the years went by I applied myself to bigger, until I came of age. In fact I think that's where the proverb 'she can bear a bull that bore a calf' came from.

Again, I would argue, readers are encouraged to associate the act of eating with the penetration of physical boundaries and hence with the feminisation of the consumer. Trimalchio seems as innocent of the association as the young Pannychis is of the ritual about to begin. The parallels between the two figures are subtly evoked by mirror images: like Pannychis, her head veiled in scarlet in *Sat.* 26.1 (*puellae caput involverat flammeo*), Trimalchio enters the *cena* in *Sat.* 32 with his head covered by a scarlet cloak: (*pallio enim coccineo adrasum excluserat caput*).[15]

It is clear that this image of incorporating a bull, whether by eating or being penetrated, achieves its full impact only in the reader's connection of these two figures, Pannychis/Quartilla and Trimalchio. As critics have observed, the *Cena Trimalchionis* is often alluded to as a Cretan labyrinth: its culinary creator is named Daedalus, and in *Sat.* 79.4, the gang manages to escape only by following white chalk marks left by Giton (Pannychis' first lover, now acting as Theseus) on the way in. When we make the connection between the images of Pannychis and Trimalchio, it is tempting to picture Pannychis in the role of Europa, whose position early on in the narrative 'gives birth to' the image of Trimalchio as half-man half-bull, a minotaur in control of a labyrinth which has always mythologised our darkest fascinations with cannibalism and bestiality.[16] This is all fantasy, of course, yet I would suggest that the *Satyricon* constantly summons the disfiguring, anti-classical energy of Ovidian metamorphosis in its will to

consumed, but also with bad feelings, disease, emotions, that can get inside a man and worry him like a bad dinner.

15 Covering the head is characteristic of representations of brides or mourning women in antiquity.

16 For a full account of how Petronius suggests that Trimalchio's *cena* is a labyrinth or a Virgilian underworld see Courtney (1987), Bodel (1994) and Connors (1998: 35–6).

be read imaginatively, as a live, theatrical text whose fast-moving scenes equally demand the reader's rapidly shifting perspective.

Meanwhile the zodiac dish offering of Agamemnon's *pisciculus* (the food symbol for Scorpio at *Sat.* 35), alongside the mullets representing Pisces, the sign of rhetoricians and chefs (because they fish for pupils *and* for dinner) adds an interesting dimension to Trimalchio's exhortation in *Sat.* 39.2: *hoc vinum vos oportet suave faciatis. pisces natare oportet* / 'You must make this wine go down a treat. A fish should have something to swim in.' Which is the bigger fish, the Pisces or the *pisciculus*, and which watery star-sign is going to get to eat the other? Trimalchio's audience, hanging on his every dish, is always at risk of biting off much more than it can chew: for as we have seen, it is the guests who end up swimming at the end of the meal, not (or rather *like*) the fish.[17] In integrating people and food, the zodiac menu is a catalyst for inversion, for a constantly vacillating reversal of outside and in, inside and out.

Throughout the *Satyricon*, people are characterised in terms of their animal counterparts, especially when they are being abused: at *Sat.* 42.4, Seleucus declares, *minoris quam muscae sumus* / 'We're worth less than flies.' *quid rides, vervex?* / 'What d'you think you're laughing at, mutton head?' a freedman asks Ascyltos at *Sat.* 57.2, and then, *quid nunc stupes tanquam hircus in ervilia?* / 'Why are you looking at me dumb, like a goat in a field of vetch?' (57.11). In *Sat.* 58, the demure Giton is twice slandered as a *mus* ('mouse'), and at *Sat.* 74.10, Fortunata curses Trimalchio as a *canis* ('dog'). At *Sat.* 44.4, Ganymede condemns the cowardly excess of the upper classes and wishes, *o si haberemus illos leones, quos ego hic inveni, cum primum ex Asia veni* / 'If only we still had the lions I found when I first came from Asia.' He goes on to say that the town magistrate is not worth three figs, and that nowadays, *populus est domi leones, foras vulpes* / 'People are lions at home and foxes outdoors' (44.14). Ganymede's rant sounds like rhetoric made up for entertainment's sake: how can he complain about famine and poverty (*iam annum esuritio fuit*... *heu heu cotidie peius*... *si perseverat haec annona, casulas meas vendam*... / 'There's been a famine for a whole year now... God, things are worse by the day... if food prices keep up, I'm going to have to sell my cottage') when he is dining in luxury on a never-ending supply of delicacies? When Echion confronts his pessimism with the retort, *tu si aliubi fueris, dices hic porcos coctos ambulare* / 'If you were anywhere else, you'd say that roast pigs walked in

[17] And in *Sat.* 21.6 at the parallel dinner in Quartilla's brothel, Encolpius reports that *they* swam in wine (*vino etiam Falerno inundamur*).

the street' (45.4), the joke becomes all too real: in this desperate age of famine, Trimalchio's guests have become cannibalising beasts; where we see opulence, we should be seeing poverty, the excess of desperation. In this light, Trimalchio's culinary masquerade becomes a device to conceal the gruesome truth. Petronius' realism, like Seneca's tragedy, is felt in the gut, as we imagine the endless sickening consumption of human flesh.[18]

There is also no shortage of examples of animals being dressed up as humans, and in addition of cooked animals appearing onstage 'alive': at *Sat.* 40, the second main course of the *cena* is a wild boar, whose entrance is accompanied by all the paraphernalia of a hunt (that is, of a *live* animal).[19] There are mock nets, painted on blankets to be thrown over the couches, men lying in wait with spears, and even a pack of Spartan hounds. Meanwhile the boar appears dressed as a newly freed slave wearing a cap of liberty (*pilleatus*) and is 'killed' by Carver, who plunges a hunting knife deep into its side. The cap of freedom is given to the slave who impersonates Bacchus in the following chapter, thus continuing the connection between animal and human. As Encolpius' dinner companion explains, the dish of the human-boar may be more transparent than we at first assume (*non enim aenigma est, sed res aperta* / 'There's no riddle, it's obvious', *Sat.* 41.4): the boar turned up at yesterday's dinner but left without being eaten, so now he joins the feast for a second time, as a freedman.[20] We might wonder whether the freedmen dining today have also gained their liberty only to face death by being eaten on a future occasion. This is the kind of conclusion (or confusion) Encolpius jumps to when in *Sat.* 47.10 he mistakes three little pigs for a troupe of human jesters before Trimalchio asks, *quem ex eis vultis in cenam statim fieri?* / 'Which one of these would you like turned into dinner *tout de suite*?' Trimalchio's *cena*, it is now clear, is not only the dinner party to which Encolpius and his friends have been invited, but is also the actual dinner:

[18] I am thinking in particular of Seneca's *Thyestes*, where the inevitable perpetuation of tragedy is imaged in the 'pregnant' body of Thyestes, who has eaten his children as a punishment which replicates his own crime of penetration and who must now repeat the process by 'giving birth', or throwing up.

[19] For detailed discussion of similarities to staged hunts or *venationes* in this scene, see Jones (1991).

[20] As Fitzgerald (2000: 99–100) discusses, the domestic animal and slave both inhabit an ambiguous place in the ancient system of categories. In the Aristotelian scheme, animals inhabit the highest layer of the infrahuman category, next to slaves and barbarians who occupy the lowest layer of the human. Greek and Roman law emphasises a fluid boundary between the domestic animal and the human, whose living space is often shared. In Greek, slaves are referred to collectively as *andrapoda*, by analogy with *tetrapoda* (four-footed).

the guests form another edible stratum in Trimalchio's layered dishes, entering *in cenam*, into the food itself.[21]

Trimalchio's speech at *Sat.* 56.1–4 is crucial in illustrating how the *Satyricon*'s negotiation of insides and outsides, being and seeming, is expressed in terms of the dissection and incorporation of bodies. He asks the congregation: 'What do we reckon is the hardest profession after writing?' Before they can reply, he answers, 'I think the doctor's and the money-changer's: the doctor's, because he knows what poor men have in their insides... the money-changer's, because he sees the copper under the silver.' It is the role of the writer also, he implies, to have privileged knowledge about the inside of his material, which he must only reveal, like the doctor or money-changer, with great cunning. In fact, if he is anything like the doctor dealing with poor patients, or the accountant wanting to short-change his clients, he is more likely to disguise the hidden truth for personal gain.

Interestingly, however, Trimalchio now changes the angle of his discussion to talk about hardworking animals, as if to compare explicitly the difficulty of human and animal jobs:

nam mutae bestiae laboriosissimae boves et oves: boves, quorum beneficio panem manducamus; oves, quod lana illae nos gloriosos faciunt. et facinus indignum, aliquis ovillam est et tunicam habet.

You see, of all the dumb animals the hardest workers are cattle and sheep: the cattle, because thanks to them we get to eat bread; the sheep, because their wool clothes us in splendour. So it's a terrible act, when someone eats lamb and also wears a wool tunic.

Despite the carnivorous ethos of the meal, Trimalchio now seems outraged at the consumption of meat, admiring the animals that have graced his platters for their domestic roles as providers of bread and wool.[22] Trimalchio, who is sweating it out in the role of deceptive author privileged to see inside his guests' bellies, succeeds in fuddling the distinction between animal and human, between animals which constitute and provide food, between those who get eaten and those who eat. People who consume lamb also look like lambs because they wear their skins (*ovillam est et tunicam habet*): the use of the third person singular of *edo* here might also look, at a quick glance, as if it is the third person singular of *sum*,

[21] We are reminded that *cena* can be used to mean 'company at dinner', e.g. Juv. *Sat.* 2.120 (*cena sedet*) or Pliny, *HN*. 12.10.

[22] See below, chapter five, for discussion of the parallels between this and Pythagoras' speech preaching vegetarianism in *Met.* 15.

another hint at the fine line between eating and being eaten.[23] Trimalchio reveals that his guests, who like the sheepish *mutae bestiae* of *Sat.* 56 cannot get a word in edgeways whilst he is philosophising, have bellies full of guilt. In *Sat.* 26.7, they had in mind the *expectatio liberae cenae* ('the expectation of a *libera cena*')[24] but in Trimalchio's eyes there's no such thing as a free lunch.

In *Sat.* 61.2, Trimalchio accuses Niceros of being bestially dumb (*nescio quid nunc taces nec muttis* / 'I don't know why you're now silent and dumb'), and encourages him to tell stories (*narra illud quod tibi usu venit* / 'tell us about your adventure'). Niceros proceeds to enthrall his audience with a metamorphic tale of his love affair with the innkeeper's wife Melissa (a woman, he is careful to say, whose personality rather than looks he finds attractive). When her husband Tarentius dies on the estate, he and a soldier friend of his take to the road. They stop by some gravestones on the roadside, and the next thing Niceros knows, his friend has changed into a wolf (*et subito lupus factus est*, 62.6) and has run off howling into the woods; his discarded clothes have turned to stone. When Niceros finally reaches Melissa's house, she informs him that a slave has wounded a wolf which broke into the farm and killed the sheep like a butcher (*tamquam lanius sanguinem illis misit*, 62.11). At dawn, Niceros returns home to find the soldier lying in bed like an ox, with a wounded neck (*iacebat miles meus in lecto tamquam bovis, et collum illius medicus curabat*, 62.13). On realising that his friend is a werewolf, Niceros concludes, *nec postea cum illo panem gustare potui, non si me occidisses* / 'and afterwards I could never sit down to a meal with the guy, not if you had killed me first': by changing from a man to a wolf to an ox, and confusing the civilised boundaries between human and animal, butcher and beast, the soldier threatens the rituals of dining and forfeits his right to eat among men. As Niceros hints in the phrase *non si me occidisses*, the man who can metamorphose into an animal, or even be described as an animal (*tamquam bovis* / 'like an ox') endangers the stability of the eater/eaten hierarchy, a disruption which is thematised throughout Trimalchio's *cena*.

By *Sat.* 64.2, metamorphosis has taken hold and the creative dinner-table narratives are flowing, leading Encolpius to report, *totum triclinium esse mutatum* / 'the whole dining room was mutating'. At this point the guests are so full that conversation is beginning to replace food: like

[23] Especially with prodelision: *ovillam (e)st*.

[24] The joke here is that a *libera cena* (literally: 'free dinner') is the technical term for the last meal offered to prisoners or gladiators about to confront wild beasts in the arena (see Tert. *Apol.* 42.5). Are they going to eat, or be eaten?

Seleucus in *Sat.* 42, Habinnas, who has entered drunk, proceeds to tell everyone about a funeral feast he has just attended (a *cena* within a *cena* which mirrors the layered dishes that have been the focus of Trimalchio's feast) in a story which extends the previous story's anxiety surrounding eating (*et quid si non abstinax fuisset?* / 'and what would have happened if he hadn't tried fasting?' 42.5). At the centre of Scissa's table is a joint of bear (*ursinae frust[r]um, Sat.* 66.5), which Scintilla is rash enough to taste: she almost vomits up her insides (*paene intestina sua vomuit*), which reminds us of the role of bees in Trimalchio's vegetarian speech at *Sat.* 56 (*apes... mel vomunt* / 'bees... vomit honey'), especially as Scissa's guests have just dined on honey cakes (*saviunculum*), and an abundance of warm honey (*mel caldum... de melle me usque tetigi, Sat.* 66.3). Habinnas eats over a pound of bear flesh, thinking it tastes more like boar (*nam ipsum aprum sapiebat*, 66.6),[25] but proceeds to philosophise like Trimalchio's carnivorous nemesis: *et si, inquam, ursus homuncionem comest, quanto magis homuncio debet ursum comesse?* / 'and if, I say, a bear can eat a man, surely a poor man has much more of a right to eat a bear?' It is little wonder that Scintilla, a delicate creature, is made sick at the smallest taste of this dish: eating a bear which may contain the chewed up remains of some unlucky man is enough to make anyone's stomach turn, even *transform.* Habinnas' tale, which replays the anxieties of incorporation that dominate the telling of the *Cena* as a whole, leaves us in no doubt of the *Satyricon*'s morbid imaging of the vulnerability and horror of *intestina*, the slippage between insides and outsides which exposes the fragility of the individual as well as the subjectivity of the reader, reminded continually of the metaphorical act of 'eating' from Petronius' satirical plate.

[25] See Gowers' discussion (1993: 30): the confusion of boar and bear hints further at the ambiguity between human and animal intestines, from the fake guts of the boar in Trimalchio's feast to Scintilla's tripe-like insides pouring out in the other dinner, itself an inside 'layer' in *this cena*.

CHAPTER 4

From the horse's mouth

Encolpius and his gang escape the shady confines of the labyrinthine *cena* in complete darkness (*neque fax ulla in praesidio erat, quae iter aperiret errantibus, nec silentium noctis iam mediae promittebat occurrentium lumen* / 'There was no guiding light to show us the way as we wandered, nor did the midnight silence give us any hope of running into someone with a lamp', 79.1). As we saw in the marketplace scene at *Sat.* 12–15, darkness is a metaphorical device which sets the stage for obscurity and concealment. The *cena* has been a lengthy drama of misrecognition, imposture and disguise played out in the interactions of the characters but importantly also in the ongoing image of Trimalchio's house as a windowless kitchen, an underworld, a labyrinth, a dungeon permanently shrouded in darkness whatever the time of day. Moreover Trimalchio's party tricks of concealment and revelation are only sustained, it seems, because of the ongoing 'blindness' of our prime witness and narrator Encolpius: thus when he exits the dark *cena* and is still in darkness, his inability to see or find his way appears to be merely an externalisation of his intellectual myopia. Like a troop of stand-ins for the part of Oedipus, the ever-blind gourmands drag their bleeding feet over flints and broken pots they cannot see in the road (*per omnes scrupos gastrarumque eminentium fragmenta traxissemus cruentos pedes*, *Sat.* 79.3), before following Giton's chalk marks like mock-heroic Theseuses running from Trimalchio the minotaur. In the following chapter (*Sat.* 80), Encolpius cloaks himself for a 'Theban duel' with Ascyltos over Giton: they act now as Oedipus' sons and half-brothers, Eteocles and Polynices, competing for the throne of Thebes (*infelicissimus puer tangebat utriusque genua cum fletu petebatque suppliciter, ne Thebanum par humilis taberna spectaret neve sanguine mutuo pollueremus familiaritatis clarissimae sacra* / 'The poor boy touched our knees and begged us in tears not to let this humble inn be the site of a Theban duel, and not to let the sanctity of our friendship be polluted by our own blood', 80.3).

Having lost the battle, it is thus in the tragic role of blind exile that Encolpius reaches the site of his next visual challenge, in an episode which is pivotal in the *Satyricon*'s exploration of aesthetic awareness and the role or understanding of images as representations (or not) of invisible or interior truths. The gallery scene, of which we have already had a taste in the representations beginning and ending the *Cena*, leads up to, and cannot be dissociated from, one of the most significant verse passages of the *Satyricon*, Eumolpus' *Troiae Halosis* (*Sat.* 89). It is here that the *Satyricon*'s imaging of incorporation, as it relates to eating, drinking, learning and performance, is expressed in a poem which challenges us to envisage precisely how poetry is incorporated by prose or vice versa, how we are to interpret what Neronian poetry must 'contain', despite and because of its metamorphosing pretensions. The concept of incorporation, as evinced now in the *Troiae Halosis*, can no longer be taken as lightly as it can in the *Cena*, in which it is the focus of endless practical jokes: in a broader historical and political arena, this poem says, the *Satyricon* constantly replays a crisis of incorporation in which Troy was destroyed and Rome founded because of the mistaken literal interpretation of a body that turned out to be full of bodies. What has up till now been interpreted as mere 'horsing around', the hilarious confusion of human and animal bodies, is now rewritten and reimaged as the most formative misreading of all time: the acceptance of the pregnant wooden horse into the walls of Troy.

Encolpius is overwhelmingly impressed by the superficial, and by realistic images which claim to have nothing to hide. As he enters the gallery at *Sat.* 83,[1] he is in awe of the work of the famous Greek realistic painter Zeuxis, and the drawings of Protogenes, which seem to 'rival the truth of nature herself' (*et Protogenis rudimenta cum ipsius naturae veritate certantia non sine quodam horrore tractavi*). He positively worships Apelles (*etiam adoravi*) because his figures are defined with such accuracy, it is as if he had painted their souls (*ut crederes etiam animorum esse picturam*, 83.3).[2] Ironically, realism abolishes real-life distinctions between outsides and

[1] The most famous example of such a gallery is that evoked by the Elder Philostratus as the setting for the paintings which he describes in his two books of *Imagines*. Compare Lucian's description of an ideal house in *De Domo*, which ends in a series of ekphrases of mythical paintings in a gallery. Such galleries, especially in Rome, are frequently mentioned by Pliny, *HN* 35 and 36.

[2] In Pliny, *HN* 35.61, Zeuxis 'gave to the painter's brush . . . the full glory to which it aspired'; Apelles (35.79) 'excelled all painters who came before or after him'. Protogenes (35.80) was Apelles' 'equal or superior in everything', except in knowing when to stop working on a painting. Apelles' portraits (35.88) were such perfect likenesses that a physiognomist could tell from the paintings alone how long the sitter had lived or had to live. Also see Quint. *Inst.* 12.10.3-6. See Elsner (1993) for his suggestion that Encolpius' dumb, literalist attitude is written into his (unconscious?) punning in

insides, rendering all human complexities (souls) superficial. Yet it soon becomes clear that this first impression is illusional and naïve: in the first few lines of this passage, we are made to realise the instability of the paintings' apparent perfection: Zeuxis' work is 'not yet overcome by the defacement of old age' – its details are ephemeral like those of the human body itself, soon to wear away, we are tempted to think, to reveal its previously hidden and less appealing features. We are reminded here of Encolpius' initial speech on the history of literature and his visual impression of contemporary art's prematurely aging body (1.8). Secondly, when Encolpius then looks at other representations of myths in the gallery, including the rape of Ganymede, the struggle between Hylas and a naiad, the aftermath of Apollo's murder of Hyacinthus, it is clear to Petronius' readers, who are seeing these pictures in a literary text, that even so-called realistic images based on literary narratives suggest to the viewer far more than they show, or can show, in two dimensions.[3] Although the paintings only represent one scene in a mythical narrative, for example Apollo's guilt following the death of Hyacinthus (*damnabat Apollo noxias manus* / 'Apollo cursed his polluted hands'), Encolpius' emotional reaction is a response to the memory of a story triggered by an image which cannot possibly incorporate the complexities of the entire literary narrative. Encolpius also suggests that the narrative conjured up by the image overlaps with the narrative of the *Satyricon* within which it features: he says, *Apollo pueri umbram revocavit in florem; et omnes fabulae quoque habuerunt sine aemulo complexus. at ego in societatem recepi hospitem Lycurgo crudeliorem* / 'Apollo resurrected the boy as a flower; and all these figures enjoyed love's embraces without a rival. I, on the other hand, have picked a partner more cruel than Lycurgus' (83.5–6). Encolpius wants to see himself in Apollo, to rewrite the narrative he has just told in order to put himself, rather than Ascyltos, in the position of power over their lover Giton. It is implicitly only in the description, that is the reading, of pictures that their power and complexity are revealed. By his own commentary Encolpius rubbishes his interpretation of Apellian 'realism' as the pictorial equivalent of wearing your heart on your sleeve (*crederes etiam animorum esse picturam, Sat.* 83): even Apelles' paintings do not image what

the description of each artist, e.g. Apelles is so called because that's what the Greeks call him (*appellant*).

[3] This kind of ekphrasis, a description of a work of art itself based on a literary text, is the most fascinating and titillating of all. As Fowler argues (1991: 27), 'precisely because ekphrasis represents a pause at the level of narration and cannot be read functionally, the reader is possessed by a strong need to interpret . . . the way we approach ekphrasis is paradigmatic of attitudes to much wider issues of interpretation'.

they indeed *show*, as it is the reader who determines to a large extent what a picture incorporates, especially when the picture portrays a well-known narrative.[4] In retrospect the *extremitates praecisae* ('precise outlines') of Apelles' figures begin to look far more fuzzy as they strive in vain to maintain a neat divide between text and context. And of course, the idea that pictures and images in the *Satyricon* are difficult to interpret because of their actual and suggested narrative detail is always exacerbated by Encolpius' (staged or real?) myopia and short attention span.

When the poet Eumolpus enters the gallery to strike up conversation with Encolpius, he appears almost like another realist figure, a rather straightforward, cartoon stereotype of a poet who seems to come alive when you look at him:[5] there is no depth to Eumolpus, as he wears his identity in his appearance as well as his name (*cultu non proinde speciosus, ut facile appareret eum <ex> hac nota litteratorum esse* / 'He was shabbily dressed, so it was obvious from that sign alone that he was a man of letters', 83.7). The phrase *ex hac nota litteratorum esse*, as Connors notes, indicates that Eumolpus' learnedness is inscribed on his body almost as a written mark, for an audience to read like a book.[6] He declares who and what he is (*ego poeta sum* / 'I am a poet'), and repeats Encolpius' superficial assumption that his poor dress is a label for Poet, following this with a hexameter poem that explains how to recognise a man from what is conspicuous about him, whether it is his clothes or his wealth.[7]

In *Sat.* 85–7, Eumolpus tells a story which looks back to the gallery image of the rape of Ganymede in *Sat.* 83 and forward to the *Troiae Halosis*, itself a description of a picture. This tale is crucial to the *Satyricon*'s strategy of emphasising the continuity, as well as the distinction, between poetry and prose, between (descriptions of) images and straightforward

4 We might compare Zeitlin's observation on *Daphnis and Chloe* (1990: 432): 'Normally in the genre of romance, the spectators who come upon the spectacle of erotic paintings are themselves lovers, who react to the themes of the paintings they see out of a sense of their own subjective experience.' Elsner (1993: 33) suggests that the *Satyricon* mimics but subverts this by replacing heterosexual with homosexual love. He also suggests (34) that Encolpius' subjectivism subverts the Stoic notion, key to Roman ideas of artistic creativity, of phantasia. This argument challenges Slater (1990: 228–30) who tentatively proposes that Petronius may have held the Stoic doctrine of phantasia, or at least used it to attack simple views of mimesis.

5 This scene, in which a gallery viewer is moved by works of art and then begins a dialogue with another viewer who has entered, is typical of the Greek novel: Longus' *Daphnis and Chloe* and Achilles Tatius' *Leucippe and Clitophon* both begin with conversations struck up in the presence of a painting.

6 Connors (1998) 63–4.

7 As Connors suggests (1998: 63), this poem plays upon the traditional mode of satire, the *sermo* or conversation. It also recalls Horace, *Carm.* 1.1 and Tibullus 1.1: Eumolpus introduces himself as if he is beginning an anthology of poems.

narrative, between texts and contexts, insides and outsides. We are always reminded that at the beginning of the *Aeneid*, the rape of Ganymede is one of the key causes of Juno's anger, which is an endless source of grief to the Trojans: we are used to the idea that the fall of Troy is a consequence and revenge for 'the honours given ravished Ganymede' as Virgil puts it in Book I. Moreover, we should remember that we have been hearing the story of Ganymede throughout the *cena*, because Ganymede is one of Trimalchio's guests who participates in the dinner-table banter that goes on between courses. And at *Sat.* 59, Trimalchio recites from a written text his version of a Ganymede story in which the boy is the brother of Helen, another connection with the war at Troy. Later on, Eumolpus tries to seduce Giton, praising him as his Ganymede (92.3).[8]

Now, in the gallery scene, the picture of the rape of Ganymede, shepherd of Ilium (i.e. Troy), reminds us of the fuller narrative in which the abduction also involves a horse-gift (Zeus gives Ganymede's father horses as compensation for his lost son): importantly we have to look beyond the simplicity of the two-dimensional image to see this. Then, the story told by the realist Eumolpus is also about a love affair with a beautiful young boy from Pergamum (Troy), a real-life Ganymede also in his father's charge whom the god-like poet finally seduces by acting as his 'tutor' and pretending to promise him gifts, culminating in the offer of a thoroughbred horse (*cras puero asturconem Macedonicum optimum dabo* / 'Tomorrow, I plan to offer the boy a superb Macedonian thoroughbred', 86.4). Being a naïve Trojan who has already let the enemy into his own home, the boy falls for the trick, yet this gift is so extravagant that Eumolpus cannot provide it. The boy is left pleading, *domine, ubi est asturco?* / 'But Master, where's the thoroughbred?' (86.7), threatening to tell his father if his wish is not granted. And yet, according to Eumolpus, the boy is also addicted to his older lover and still wants to be seduced again and again (he's not even satisfied with repetition, Eumolpus comments), despite the fact he says he feels cheated and is laughed at by his classmates (87.4). The idea that Ganymede still wants to be wooed, that he is tricked again and again looks forward to the *Troiae Halosis*, an overtly repetitive poem which dramatises the (masochistic?) Roman appetite for endless rewritings of the sack of Troy: setting Eumolpus' tale and the poem in parallel focuses our attention on the seductiveness of repetition, or of rereading, itself.

[8] It is almost as if Eumolpus thinks he can win over Giton because he has given Encolpius the gift not of a horse, but of a poem about a horse, the *Troiae Halosis*.

Like Agamemnon's poem at *Sat.* 5, Eumolpus' *Troiae Halosis* is preceded by a piece of rhetorical moralising that actually seems to follow on directly from Encolpius' speech at *Sat.* 1–2 which ends, *pictura quoque non alium exitum fecit, postquam Aegyptiorum audacia tam magnae artis compendiariam invenit* / 'The decadence in painting was no different, after Egyptian cheek found a short-cut to this high art form' (2.9). At this point Encolpius was interrupted by Agamemnon and could not continue to talk about visual art. Now, whereas Encolpius seduced Agamemnon with a speech on the decadence in contemporary literature and rhetoric, so Eumolpus replies, as it were, with an equally trite set piece on decadence in painting.[9] Instead of remembering the high art of Plato and Demosthenes, Pindar and Homer, Thucydides and Hyperides, Eumolpus calls on the talents of Democritus and Eudoxus, Chrysippus and Lysippus, Myron, Apelles and Phidias.[10] He concludes, *noli ergo mirari, si pictura defecit, cum omnibus diis hominibus formosior videatur massa auri quam quicquid Apelles Phidiasque, Graeculi delirantes, fecerunt* / 'Don't be surprised then at the decadence in painting, when gods and men alike think that an ingot of gold is more beautiful than anything those crazy Greeks Apelles and Phidias ever did' (88.10–89.1).

So as well as casting our minds back to previous speeches in the *Satyricon* which talk about approaches to literature and artistic standards, this introduction to the poem spotlights in particular the cliché of a contemporary lack of aesthetic sensibility, an inability to see things for what they really are. It gets us thinking about the value of aesthetic appeal – is the look of something what really counts, or should we care more about what something is really worth? These debates are crucial when we come to view, second-hand, the painting of the fall of Troy, which retells the story of what happens when people take appearances for granted.[11]

At the beginning of *Sat.* 89, Encolpius, rather like Aeneas at the murals on Dido's temple at *Aen.* 1.494–5, is already entranced by the picture. Eumolpus notices his interest and announces: *itaque conabor opus versibus*

[9] The theme of decadence in the arts was cliché in Roman art-historical writing (compare Vitr. 7.5; Pliny, *HN* 35.2, 28).

[10] In this passage, Elsner suggests (1993: 39), Eumolpus seems to have got his facts backwards: according to Pliny (*HN* 34.37), Lysippus died rich after producing hundreds of statues, not after brooding over the lines of a single piece; and Myron's weakness was not giving enough 'expression to the feelings of the soul' (*HN* 34.58), not the other way around.

[11] A similar scenario was played out in the marketplace scene (*Sat.* 12ff.) where the gang come across a dirty cloak which looks worthless but in fact contains gold pieces in the lining. You just can't trust your eyes alone, as Ascyltos fears at *Sat.* 12.6. See my earlier discussion in chapter two.

pandere / 'and now, I will attempt to explain this work in verse'.[12] The use of the verb *pandere* (literally, 'to open up') is of course very interesting in the light of what Encolpius has told us about the gallery of artworks, which are meant to be obvious and to need no investigation, no scratching beneath the surface. It also reverberates with Virgil's image of the gates of Troy opening up for the Trojan Horse (*panduntur portae* / 'the gates were thrown open', *Aen.* 2.27; *dividimus muros et moenia pandimus urbis* / 'we breached the walls and laid open the buildings of the city', *Aen.* 2.234), which in turn forecasts the opening up of the belly of the horse (*laxat claustra, Aen.* 2.259, cf. *Danai relaxant claustra et effundunt viros* / 'The Greeks loosened the bolts and poured out their men', *TH* 57).[13] It is a highly ominous word to use, therefore, reminding us even before Eumolpus has started to perform of the potential implications of visual misinterpretation.

Now the *Troiae Halosis* itself, despite being written in iambic trimeters and in a style reminiscent of Senecan tragedy, clearly looks like a copy of the tragic narrative of the second book of Virgil's *Aeneid*.[14] Indeed, as a description of a picture, it is images rather than sounds and rhythms which we should perhaps privilege, despite the fact that, like the other ekphrases of the *Satyricon*, there is no way of knowing whether the poem actually describes the picture which we of course cannot see. We are blindfolded, and this, as ever, is precisely the point: our experiences are those of Encolpius, whose world, as we have seen, is perpetually shrouded in darkness. In his book, Slater concludes that the *Troiae Halosis* is meaningless as an interpretation of a work of art, that it amounts to a 'failure of interpretation'; Elsner echoes this statement of failure. Both critics argue that Eumolpus isn't in the end trying to describe a painting, and is merely 'churning out his own poetry'.[15] I would suggest that there are no grounds whatsoever for this conclusion: the assumption that Eumolpus isn't referring to the notional picture is gratuitous, a stab in

[12] Eumolpus' announcement that he will explain the picture in a poem recalls Lucretius, 1.55; Verg. *G.* 4.284; *Aen.* 6.723; Stat. *Silv.* 5.3.156.

[13] Mirrored later in the *Bellum Civile* when Fortuna commands the earth to open up (*pande, age, terrarum sitientia regna tuarum* / 'Open, then, the thirsty realms of your dominion' v. 116); this mirroring helps play on the notion of the earth as primal mother lustful, fertile and dangerously creative.

[14] Walsh (1968) notes distinctive elements of Senecan style throughout the poem; for example, the use of *iam* to begin lines (1, 15, 50, 54); the repetition of words such as *sacer, manus* and *metus*; and 'jingles' with *iubar* and *iubare* (39, 54, 60), cf. Sen. *Med.* 436ff. Zeitlin (1971b) stresses that the language and the sequence of ideas and action are predominantly Virgilian. However the poem could equally refer to Lucan's lost *Iliacon*, or to an epic on the fall of Troy penned by Nero himself (referred to by Suetonius in *Ner.* 38 as *Halosis Ilii*). See Erskine (1998) for an overview of literature about the fall of Troy from the third century BC onwards.

[15] Slater (1990) 244. Elsner (1993: 40) argues that the poem 'fails to make any contact with the work of art it purports to describe'.

the dark. We simply cannot tell how one art form translates into another. Moreover, our inability to perceive the relationship between image and the reading of an image (which as I stressed above is always potentially complicated) is precisely what reading the *Satyricon*'s image-packed and highly metaphorical narrative and seeing the world through the eyes of Encolpius has been about from the very beginning.[16]

In reading the *Troiae Halosis*, however, the point is further that there is a great deal at stake in not being able to tell what kind of representation or fabrication this poem is: readers of this poem are doomed like the hapless Trojans to be blind to the negotiation of this double level between surface image and hidden contents. The fall of Troy might be, as Walsh says, 'the most hackneyed of hackneyed themes',[17] but Petronius' brilliant strategy repeats the old Greek trick of making his audience blind to what is before their very eyes (on the page) with the result that we experience the fall of Troy as if for the first time, through the eyes of the Trojans. Indeed, as critics have suggested, the poem itself looks very much like an eyewitness account, of the kind told by a messenger in a Senecan play:[18] it can be read as a fresh narration of a scene that has only just happened. Perhaps Petronius has managed to write the first original Troy poem, against all odds. This strategy, which plays again on the limitation of our perspective, could be seen to have the impetus of a Senecan tragedy, in which the reader's frustration of knowing what is going to happen is matched only by the fear of not quite knowing *how* it is going to happen, by the sheer emotional impact of hyperbolic repetition. Thus we are reminded that on one level the *Satyricon* constantly tempts us to ditch sophisticated and scholarly insight in favour of an entertaining romp through Encolpius' adventures (indeed sometimes, as I have suggested, there seems little option but to go with the flow as we are trapped in Encolpius' world and cannot see out). Yet in the *Troiae Halosis*, we get to experience first hand the price of reading the *Satyricon* as pure entertainment when our inability to see beyond the surface of this poem makes us empathise rather too closely with the Trojans, who sleep drunkenly after an evening of celebration while Troy burns (*TH* 56).[19] From another angle, it is very important that the poem makes readers feel like true Trojans (Romans),

[16] As Slater (1988: 166) himself argues, 'The act of interpreting a pictorial work of art in the *Satyricon* is a miniature study of the multiple ironies of the whole work.'

[17] Walsh (1968) 209.

[18] E.g. Stübbe (1933: 40), Slater (1990: 118), Connors (1998: 87). The whole of the *Satyricon* is an eyewitness account, told by Encolpius.

[19] The *Troiae Halosis* fuses drunkenness and death (*inter sepultos Priamidos nocte et mero* / 'among Trojans buried in night and wine', v. 56; *hic graves alius mero / obtruncat et continuat in mortem ultimam / somnos /*

that the fall of Troy seems closer to home than ever before: as Connors points out, the *Troiae Halosis* hints that the Greek conquest of Troy is the original on which the later Greek cultural defeat of Rome is modeled: this parallel is brought to our attention in line 27 (*ibat iuventus capta, dum Troiam capit* / 'the prisoned youth went to make Troy their prisoner'), so reminiscent of Horace's formulation of Rome's subjugation to Greek influences in *Epist.* 2.1.156–7.[20]

As critics have discussed, there is a clear emphasis on repetition in the poem, on display in second-hand verbs given a new lease of life with a prefix: *re-plet* (19); *re-ducta* (20); *re-silit* (22); *re-plevit* (30); *re-sultat* (31); *re-fertur* (33); *re-spicimus* (35); *re-ferunt* (45); *re-tractant* (61).[21] Even Laocoön's axe, with which he strikes the horse a *second* time, is double-edged (*bipenni*, 24). Yet the joke that this is a stale, downright bad poem (told by Eumolpus, the poet who sings *so* well),[22] and that it is boring because we have seen it all before, is sharpened by the irony that *seeing* is precisely what we are now prevented from doing. The complex narrative of this short poem, which as it progresses includes such unimaginable things as movement (of the crowd to the gates, of Laocoön's spear, of the approaching ships), and sound (the gasping of the crowd, the rumbling of the horse's belly, the hissing of the snakes), makes our attempts to fathom exactly how this could be captured in a painting even more compulsive and frustrating.

Yet at the same time the salient ways in which this account differs from Virgil's in *Aeneid* II focus our attention on how imagined (that is, metaphorical) literary effects could possibly be painted. For example, whereas in the *Aeneid* the snakes which kill Laocoön and his sons foreshadow the stealthy movement of the Greek ships towards the Trojan shore, in Eumolpus' poem the snakes themselves are ships (or is it the

'one slaughters Trojans heavy with wine and makes sleep merge into final death,' vv. 62–4) just like in the *cena*, where over-indulgence in food and wine is staged in a dining room which is like an underworld, and also ends in death (Trimalchio's fake funeral, Ascyltos and Encolpius' close escape from drowning in *Sat.* 72).

[20] *Graecia capta ferum victorem cepit et artes / intulit agresti Latio* / 'Captured Greece took her savage victor captive and brought the arts into rustic Latium.'

[21] Sullivan's suggestion (1968a: 187) that repetitiveness in the poem is 'partly due to the poverty of the Latin vocabulary and certain metrical needs' and to the fact that Romans were 'more tolerant of verbal repetitiveness than we are' rather misses the point: the *Troaie Halosis* is *both* a bad, impoverished poem written by Eumolpus *and* a highly literary, Petronian exercise, in which repetition is thematised as an ironic and self-conscious strategy.

[22] I.e. εὐμολπεῖν = to sing well. His character possibly refers to the Eleusinian Eumolpus, so called because it was he who enunciated the sacred words of the Muses.

other way around, too?): *respicimus: angues orbibus geminis ferunt / ad saxa fluctus, tumida quorum pectora / rates ut altae lateribus spumas agunt* / 'We look back: twin coiling snakes push the waves to the rocks, their swollen chests like tall ships driving foam from their sides' (vv. 35–7). It is almost as if the poem predicts that the bored reader will impatiently leap ahead from the 'snake scene' to the 'ship scene' and so synthesises the two episodes in a single image. Even the island of Tenedos becomes one of the *alia monstra* ('other monsters'), raising its dorsal fin like a shark homing in on its shallow-water prey: *celsa qua Tenedos mare / dorso replevit* / 'The steep ridge of Tenedos blocked the sea' (vv. 29–30). The snakes which in Virgil are like ships now *become* ships, the threatening island becomes a predatory monster. How else can a picture portray a metaphor, in only two dimensions? Everything must be on the surface: in order to paint vv. 7–8 (*aperitur ingens antrum et obducti specus / qui castra caperent* / 'The huge cave was opened up, a hidden cavern which could hide a camp') one would have to leave nothing to the imagination. At every point we are reminded that this is a gallery for realist artworks.

Crucially it is repetition, the motivation and theme of this poem, which is the most difficult aspect to imagine in a picture. Perhaps the most salient departure from Virgil's account is the description of the actions of Laocoön in lines 18–26: instead of piercing the horse once with his spear as he does in the *Aeneid*, the spear bounces back and he is forced to go at it again with a double-axe which further emphasises the overt repetitiveness of the motion. This repetition would be almost impossible to portray in a picture, especially given the realist, or figurative emphasis, unless we are to imagine something approximating a narrative cartoon strip.[23] Again, we cannot imagine repetition because the point is that when we read this poem as a picture it is as if we have *not* seen it all before: we are bound to a limited, superficial viewpoint that can no longer transfix the surface, just like Laocoön's spear which bounces off the horse's ribs, or the blind Trojans who see events unfold with innocent eyes.[24]

The second significant departure from Virgil's narrative occurs at the end of the poem and at the dramatic fulcrum of the Greek victory: the

[23] Barnes (1972), cited by Slater (1988: 176) attempts to do something similar. In 71 ff., he suggests that Eumolpus is looking at a 'Trojan cycle' of four paintings.

[24] Slater sees, but does not see, the point (1988: 172): 'if the painting on the wall is indeed on a Trojan theme . . . we can never know what it looks like from Eumolpus' poem . . . It is mordantly ironic that what begins as a description at the hands of so ardently committed a realist as Eumolpus becomes rather a demonstration of the unknowability of the subject.'

opening up of the horse and the pouring out of soldiers into the heart of the city. Eumolpus recites (vv. 57–60):

> Danai relaxant claustra et effundunt viros.
> temptant in armis se duces, veluti solet
> nodo remissus Thessali quadrupes iugi
> cervicem et altas quatere ad excursum iubas.

> The Greeks unbarred the horse and poured out men.
> The leaders try their strength in arms, just like a steed
> loosed from the knot of a Thessalian chariot, will
> toss its neck and high mane as it leaps forward.

The men climbing out of the horse are themselves now compared to horses. This simile has been the cause of much critical perplexity. Connors deals with the problem extensively, suggesting that the scene could be read as funny, a mark of a barren aesthetic ability, or simply as an exaggerated but typical epic image similar to the description of Paris at the end of *Iliad* VI (506–11) or Turnus in *Aeneid* XI (492–7).[25] I would suggest that there is much more to say about this simile, which is even more intriguing and ridiculous when we visualise it (as we must).

First, the comparison of the soldiers who have been trapped in the horse with horses raises the all-important question which has been worrying readers from the beginning: can we tell what is inside from the image we see on the outside? What is the relationship between visible outsides and invisible insides? *Are* things or people what they look like?[26] Secondly, Eumolpus' picture-poem of the fall of Troy must make everything superficial, express everything on a surface level: thus (on paper) there can be no difference between what is outside and inside the horse. Men are horses because we are being reminded that this is a two-dimensional image with no capacity for distinguishing interior from exterior. Thus the flat image, as we have seen, mimics the viewpoint of the Trojans, who are not willing to believe that the horse is not what it seems. Yet thirdly, this is an image which double-crosses readers who

[25] Connors (1998) 92. Connors also notes here that the simile specifies that the horses were released and did not break free and so looks self-consciously contrived: 'epic models are evoked to be juxtaposed with a weakened re-enactment of their traditional glories'. See my discussion below.

[26] This dilemma was particularly acute in the *cena*, where Encolpius was faced with a series of layered dishes which never ceased to confuse and surprise him. Perhaps the most cunning of these recipes is the wooden hen in *Sat.* 33, which sits on fake eggs which in turn contain real baby birds (but not hen-chicks). The hollow *gallina lignea* is now recalled by the wooden horse, which also contains offspring which are not quite realistic (the men are only *like* young horses).

are being Trojans (again) as if for the first time: just as Encolpius at the *cena* thinks he is getting wise to Trimalchio's double-dealing but in his suspicions misinterprets the obvious,[27] the simile of the Greek horses rushing through the city tells us that the trick of the Trojan Horse was so obvious that we missed it. In reading this simile we are suddenly made aware not only of the strangeness of the image but also of the ridiculousness of the historical moment, the idea that the fall of Troy is a myth, a fiction that by definition is untrue, unbelievable: how could the Trojans not have suspected, what madness, and what naïvety it took to drag this equine time-bomb into the city and then party the night away, oblivious of danger!

We can see now that the description of the men pouring from the Trojan Horse as horses represents not only the dramatic culmination of the Greek ruse but also the crucial point of innovation in Eumolpus' poem, the striking departure from Virgil around which the difference of this poem's perspective spins. This slightly farcical but at the same time unsettling and guilt-provoking image stands out as Eumolpus' (or Petronius') original literary input into the standard versification of the fall of Troy. In particular our attention is drawn to the verb used to convey the 'pouring out' of soldiers from the belly of the horse: *effundunt* (the same verb is used at *Aen.* 2.329: *fundit equus*). True enough, as Connors observes, there is a neatly ironic correspondence between the pouring out of wine among the Trojans who end up 'buried in sleep and booze', and the pouring out of the Greek men.[28] Also, I would add, the use of this verb sets up another, this time very direct parallel between the complex layered recipes in the *cena* and the Trojan Horse: in *Sat.* 49.9–10 the pig's belly is cut open and the fake guts (sausages and black puddings) pour out: *effusa sunt*. Daedalus' hand as he cuts (*timida manu* / 'with a timid hand') is also recalled in Laocoön's attempted slicing open of the horse's belly in the *Troiae Halosis* (*confirmat invalidam manum* / 'he stayed his feeble hand') which replaces and reverses Virgilian Laocoön's strength as he throws the spear (*validis viribus* / 'with all his might', *Aen.* 2.50). Yet more importantly, we are to remember that the verb *fundere* ('to pour') and its cognates are used at significant points throughout the *Satyricon* to describe the flooding out of poetry from a body bloated to bursting point with literary foodstuffs.

27 The phrase at *Sat.* 41 is *sed res aperta*: if something is obvious it is 'open' (*aperta*), mirrored here in Eumolpus' explanation (opening up) of the painting/horse.

28 Connors (1998: 92). *fundere* is used twice in the *Satyricon* to refer to the pouring of wine: see Appendix I.

We have already seen evidence of this in the opening speeches by Encolpius and Agamemnon, which are vital in setting up images of (unsustainable) containment and (the rupture of) incorporation as metaphors for the learning and performance of literature: *his animum succinge bonis: sic flumine largo / plenus Pierio defundes pectore verba* / 'Gird up your souls for these great things: thus, full of this swelling torrent, you will pour out words from a heart the Muses love' (*Sat.* 5). In the *Troiae Halosis* however, it is as if this image of the sophisticate Neronian writer consuming and ejecting poetic knowledge finds its historical and mythic roots in the pregnant Trojan Horse pouring forth its Greek messengers of doom. Indeed, the phrase *plenus flumine* ('full of a river') here, alongside Eumolpus' later caricature of the contemporary poet as *plenus litteris* ('full of literature', not to mention the phrase *neque edere partum mens potest* / 'a mind cannot bring forth its fruit') in 118.3–6 also has connotations of pregnancy, as Fowler suggests.[29] The image for Roman literary knowledge and skill in poetic performance contains the ominous echoes of the great moment of Latin naïvety and superficiality of perception: the containment of the bloated horse within the walls of Troy. Meanwhile, if we pursue this line of thought, all the layered sophistication of contemporary Roman literature seems now to be parasitic on archetypal Greek trickery. The imaging of the Greek soldiers as horses, that is as the offspring of the pregnant wooden horse, has the further effect of introducing the image of reproduction as a metaphor for an inherited Roman outpouring of poetic material.[30] The body of the horse which continually repeats itself has become a potent symbol for literary succession, for a new generation of Neronian literary texts doomed always to resemble Greek parents.[31]

Roman writers are always trying to regain control of the Trojan horse, as Agamemnon's important image of the writer skilfully slackening the reins of his poem shows (*mox et Socratico plenus grege mittat habenas liber* / 'and soon, when he is full of the Socratic flock, let him loosen the reins',

[29] Fowler (forthcoming). He also goes on to suggest, as I do, that Eumolpus' second poem, the *Bellum Civile*, is written as a result of the poet's 'labour pains', and compares this to Catullus' image (95.1–2) of the work as a foetus gestating for nine years (the subject of Cinna's poem was Zmyrna's illicit sex with her father and subsequent pregnancy). All these images are fed by Platonic images of creation as giving birth. Note too that in the parallel marketplace scene, the 'worthless' cloak is *aureis plena* / 'full of gold' (13.3): finding the treasure (*thesaurum*, 13.2) is like reading (*litterae thesaurum est* / 'Literature is a treasure' 46.8).

[30] In *Aen.* 2.238, the horse is *feta armis* ('pregnant with arms'). *fundere* (*effundunt equos*) can be used of giving birth: e.g. Virg. *Aen.* 8.139 (*quam candida Maia . . . fudit*); Stat. *Theb.* 10.805–6 (*aut quae male pignora fudi / tam diversa mihi*).

[31] Aeschylus calls the Greeks 'the young of the horse' (*Ag.* 825).

Sat. 5 vv. 13–14).[32] I would suggest that the image of the horses being released rather than breaking free from the chariot has as much, if not more, to do with this image of self-conscious poetic control as with a simple weakening or comic parody of epic models, as Connors argues. Yet we have also seen that people in the *Satyricon* often behave like horses. In looking closely at the series of images of people horsing around in this novel, I emphasised first that the images of men being or riding horses always hark back to the poems at *Sat.* 5 and 23, which connect riding with literary and sexual manoeuvring, and secondly that the hierarchy of rider controlling horse is constantly undermined in a succession of contradictory images. The literary horse is never passive or tame even when harnessed, but is always a symbol for violence, danger, deception and foreign power.[33] It is this disturbing and tricky power which we see now embodied in the *Satyricon*'s poet figure, Eumolpus, and which begins to dawn on readers as soon as he stops reciting and Encolpius' narrative takes over.

We are now made aware that during the recitation of the *Troiae Halosis*, an audience was throwing stones at Eumolpus (*ex his, qui in porticibus spatiabantur lapides in Eumolpus recitantem miserunt* / 'Some of the people who were walking in the colonnade threw stones at Eumolpus as he recited', *Sat.* 90.1). Eumolpus, who interprets this reaction as a tribute to his genius (*plausum ingenii sui*), acts like every undercover trickster in the *Satyricon* and covers up his head (*operuit caput*): by now Petronius' readers are well tuned to the device of veiling as a trope for deception, and this metaphor is particularly acute in the context of this recitation, with its age-old theme of Greek trickery by concealment.[34] Eumolpus the poet no longer seems as straightforward as he did in *Sat.* 83, when Encolpius implied he could read him like a book (*ut facile appareret eum <ex> hac nota litteratorum esse*). Just like the Trojan Horse, with its misleading labelling

[32] Having 'control of the reins' is a trope for the power of gods (leaders, authors . . .), e.g. Aeolus in *Aen.* 1.62–3, cf. Pompey at Lucan, 7.124–6; Neptune at Virg. *G.* 1.12–14.

[33] The notion that the division between rider and horse can never be distinct, the relationship between the two never straightforwardly hierarchical, echoes perhaps Plato's famous description of the soul as a union of three parts: a charioteer (judgement or reason), and two horses, one noble and obedient, the other base and disobedient (*Phaedrus* 246a–b, 253c–54e); the charioteer (in you) must learn to manage the two different horses (in you). The danger of letting the horses run free is dramatised in the myth of Hippolytus (the 'horse-looser') who is killed when his horses bolt at the sight of a monster. Also see discussion of Hor. *Sat.* 2.1.17–20 and *Epist.* 1.10 in Ahl (1984b): man and horse may work together, but they are also always vying with each other: the rider may be cleverer, but the horse is stronger and faster.

[34] The caricature based on Sinon of the Greek character who seems to be *x* but is really *y* is common, e.g. in Tacitus: see Syme (1958) 548.

(*hoc titulus fero / incisus* / 'the inscription carved on the beast', *TH* 12–13), Eumolpus in *Sat.* 83 had something to hide.[35] And just like the Trojan Horse pouring out its stomach-contents, Eumolpus goes on to reveal all in his effusive recitation of a poem now characterised by Encolpius as a disease that until now has festered inside the poet's body: *quid tibi vis cum isto morbo?* / 'What's the deal with this disease of yours?' (*Sat.* 90.3). Eumolpus then promises to 'keep off this food for a whole day' to placate his audience, drawing another direct parallel between poetry and body-contents, and once more confusing the distinction between insides and outsides – is poetry a food eaten by the poet, or is it caught from somebody else, or bred inside you, like a disease, *morbus*?[36]

The containment of food and knowledge in the *Satyricon* is always plagued by an anxiety which envisages the consumed material as at the same time some kind of consuming force or disease eating away at its host from within. It is the poet, in Petronius' formulation, who must find a way to negotiate this anxiety, which in itself has come to stand for the difficulty of working within but at the same time incorporating and disguising a literary inheritance grounded, it seems, in the mythology of the fall of Troy and the nightmare vision of the swollen horse.[37]

Inevitably, our narrator Encolpius is at first deceived by Eumolpus' appearance, by his seductive stories and by his taste for realist art, which excels in portraying the superficial. It is only when Eumolpus starts reciting the *Troiae Halosis* (the equivalent of Sinon releasing the Greek soldiers from the horse) that Encolpius is suspicious: like a Laocoön figure determined to pierce the horse with his spear, he joins the audience in pelting Eumolpus with stones, intent on drawing blood (*ego quoque sinum meum saxis onerabo, ut quotiescunque coeperis a te exire, sanguinem tibi a capite mittam* / 'I too will load myself with stones, so that whenever you start to come out of yourself, I will make blood come out of your head', 90.4). Ostensibly, Encolpius wants to stop the recitation, yet at the same time the outpouring of verse is implicitly connected with the rupturing of the poet's body, especially as Eumolpus says *a te exire* ('to come out of yourself')

35 Eumolpus' success 'is measured by his ability to deceive' (Elsner 1993: 42–3).

36 As Williams discusses (1999: 180ff.), insatiable, effeminate men who sought to be penetrated were often said to be characterised by a *morbus* ('disease'), which was a catch-all term for all kinds of excessive or disgraceful behaviour. See e.g. Plaut. *Cas.* 810; Cic. *Tusc.* 4.25, *Verr.* 2.4.1; Sen. *Suas.* 2.17; Hor. *Sat.* 2.3.27; Mart. 1.89.5. Implicitly the poet is shameful because he happily contains that which should remain exterior to his body.

37 It's enough to turn any poet mad, just like in Horace, *Ars P.* 453–6, where the frenzied writer is plagued by a rash (*scabies*) and the disease of kings (*morbus regius*), which sends men of sound mind running.

to mean 'to perform poetry'. So how far is this a poetic challenge on Encolpius' part, an assertion of authorial power along the lines of Trimalchio's vision of the writer as comparable with a doctor, in the sense that both are privy to hidden disease (*Sat.* 56.1–3)? And how far is it another instance where we suspect that Encolpius has not understood the meaning or consequence of his actions? Similarly, how do we read the attack itself? Critics have invariably interpreted the stone-throwing as an exaggerated display of annoyance at this apparently bad poem.[38] Yet whatever its aesthetic value, this is a poem which is clearly powerful: it gets reactions, it rouses passions. To judge stone-throwing simply as evidence of the poem's failure, as Elsner does in particular, takes for granted the idea that Eumolpus' (and any author's) rationale is to entertain his audience. If that is not his reasoning, then perhaps he is justified after all in regarding the outburst as a tribute to his genius. His poem is an aggressive disease because it exemplifies, in the parallel image of the soldiers pouring out of the horse, the danger and threat of poetry itself. The audience throw stones at Eumolpus because the *Troiae Halosis*, like Eumolpus himself, has not lived up to their expectations: they misread him, just like the Trojans. The poet figure of the *Satyricon*, like the poetically innovative horse-men in his poem, has himself metamorphosed into a Trojan horse, standing firm despite the showers of stones that threaten to puncture his morale.[39] The Trojan Horse turns out to be a paradigm not only for the triumph of deception, as Elsner puts it, but more specifically, for the power of deceptive poetry, contained, as it is throughout the *Satyricon*, in the equally volatile and unpredictable human body.

The paralleling of violent outbursts of poetry, or poetic/narrative momentum in general, with the explosive release of dangerous, foreign, chaotic and chthonic forces, is implicit in most Greek and Roman epic, but spectacularly visualised in Petronius' take on *the* epic event, the fall of Troy. The *Satyricon* is especially parasitic here on the literary energy that fuels the *Aeneid*, the unlocked storm winds of Book I which are metaphorically re-released throughout the epic, and in particular in Book II, to propel the entire work. So the structures containing winds and Greek soldiers are both described as *molis*, a huge mass (*Aen.* 1.61, 2.32, 2.185);

[38] The only exception to this view that I have come across is Beck (1979: 246): 'we should, I think, avoid making the too easy judgment that because stones are thrown at Eumolpus, the poetry that elicits the volleys is *ipso facto* bad poetry . . . if there is an aesthetic moral to be pointed, it could as well be aimed at the philistinism of the audience as at the calibre of the poetry'.

[39] Just like the 'hybrid' author of prose fiction and satire: see Gowers (2001).

Aeolus hits the flank of the mountain with his spear (*cuspide, Aen.* 1.81), just as Laocoön hits the side of the horse with his (*hastam, Aen.* 2.50, *cuspide, Aen.* 2.230); Aeolus' control of the winds in their dark prison is visualized as a rider controlling the reins of a horse (*Aen.* 1.62–3), and the winds, rumbling as if in anticipation of release (*magno cum murmure, Aen.* 1.55), are recalled in the moaning that comes from the horse's womb after Laocoön has speared it (*insonuere cavae gemitumque dedere cavernae, Aen.* 2.53). The released winds at 1.81 ff. are like an *agmen* of soldiers rushing from a gate, or like a riot in a city stopped by an elder statesman (Neptune). Then again, in Book II, the city of Troy under attack rages like a torrent foaming from a mountainside (2.305–7), or a grassfire whipped up by southern winds, at least from Aeneas' perspective on a rooftop (*summi tecti, Aen.* 2.302), where he seems to have the perspective of a god, like Aeolus in Book I. The Trojans feel the Greek onslaught like a cyclone, when conflicting winds come together to trigger a sea storm (*Aen.* 2.416–19). And the breach of Priam's palace at *Aen.* 2.497–9 is the equivalent of a swollen river bursting its dykes (*moles* is again the word used, 497). In the cave-horse, Petronius has taken a foundational image imbued with all the potential of Greco-Roman epic and exploited its pregnancy by making explicit the latent notion that poetic recitation, the rupture of the suspect poetic belly, performs and re-enacts the unleashing of Virgil's storm winds and their human personifications. In the chapters that follow, we will see how Petronius' epic-scale text, like Virgil's, is littered with creative caverns whose provocative interiors are always threatening to blow.

CHAPTER 5

Bella intestina

Many critics have emphasised the connections between Eumolpus' two poems, the *Troiae Halosis* at *Sat.* 89 and the *Bellum Civile* at *Sat.* 119.[1] The similarities are clear: both poems have the same author, both are about war (indeed, about crucial conflicts in the ideological history of Rome) and both are preceded by moralising speeches lamenting failure in the arts (*Sat.* 88, *Sat.* 118). Moreover, as Zeitlin stresses, the two poems are clearly Virgilian:[2] whereas the *Troiae Halosis* follows the language and narrative of *Aeneid* II, the *Bellum Civile* and the narrative site of its composition continually evoke Virgilian and Trojan themes. For example, the poem is written on Lichas' ship during the poetically clichéd sea storm, which is Virgilian in detail and tone; 'civil war' on the ship is calmed when Tryphaena argues that this is not the kind of sea journey which starts a Trojan war (*non Troius heros / hac in classe vehit decepti pignus Atridae* / 'no Trojan hero carries the bride of Atreus' cuckold son on this fleet', 108.14 vv. 2–3); like the Trojan horse, the poem is a means of entering a city (Croton, the one-time first city of Italy which looks like a devastated Troy or Rome and is also implicitly compared to Carthage in *Sat.* 117.8,[3] as if it is being approached by a sea-worn Aeneas in *Aen.* 1); the images of disease and ruin in the poem itself draw much of their inspiration from Virgil's underworld in *Aen.* 6; the encounter between Dis and Fortuna in lines 79–121 recalls the meeting of Juno and Allecto in *Aen.* 7, while Fortuna's vision of the carnage of civil war looks much like the depiction of war on Aeneas' shield at *Aen.* 8; in line 83, the image of Rome struggling to 'hold up the mass' of its empire (*extollere molem*) revisits Trojan arrogance in accepting the wooden horse (*et molem mirantur equi* / 'and they marvelled at the mass of the horse', *Aen.* 2.32; *attollere molem* / 'They built an immense structure', 2.185); in lines 222ff., Romans leave their city

[1] See Walsh (1968), Zeitlin (1971b), Connors (1998). [2] Zeitlin (1971b).
[3] Eumolpus pretends he has so many slaves 'that he could have taken Carthage' (117.8).

just as Aeneas' people flee from a burning Troy;[4] in *BC* 293, Discordia instructs Pompey to take the walls of Epidamnus (*Epidamni moenia quaere*), echoing Hector's appeal to Aeneas in the dream at *Aen.* 2.294 (*hos cape fatorum comites, his moenia quaere* / 'Take these gods to share your fate, look for a new city to house them'). There are many more parallels.[5]

In privileging reminiscences of Virgil in order to twin the two poems, Zeitlin seems to skate around the question of Lucan's influence. Yet as critics such as Stübbe, Baldwin and George have shown, wherever we can find allusions to Lucan, we can equally find allusions to Virgil, overt and subtle, which often seem to have the closer fit.[6] It is crucial that what we see in Eumolpus' *Bellum Civile* is a dramatisation of the difficulty of writing about civil war, a difficulty which constrains and motivates Lucan, and decrees that you cannot write about the descent of Rome into civil war without writing about the fall of Troy, or more simply that you cannot write epic without incorporating Virgil, as well as Ennius, Lucretius, Ovid... As Eumolpus says in his introduction (*Sat.* 118), anyone who attempts civil war poetry is doomed to fail unless he is full of literature (*ecce belli civilis ingens opus quisquis attigerit, nisi plenus litteris, sub onere labetur* / 'For instance, anyone who tackles the enormous theme of civil war will sink under the burden unless he is full of literature'). The *Satyricon*'s *Bellum Civile* must be entwined with the *Troiae Halosis* because this is a poem that cannot escape its contents and must swallow what has already been written (or recited).

The *Bellum Civile* is necessarily incorporative, both within the context of the *Satyricon* and within a Neronian literary scene dominated and fuelled by the challenge to recycle repetitiveness as originality. Zeitlin's article takes the first step in arguing that Eumolpus' two poems are not designed to be seen as extractable entities, but are written for and enriched by each other and their contexts. Connors has recently elaborated this breakthrough at book-length, to consider extensively how the meaning of the poems is derived from their prose surroundings.[7] However, I want to take this contextualising strategy further to explore the *Bellum Civile* as a climactic moment in an all-pervasive strategy of incorporation,

[4] Here Petronius follows the narrative of *Aen.* II and contradicts Lucan's version (1.484–522) in which the fleeing Romans are said to behave precisely unlike the fleeing Trojans (they don't go back for aged relatives or household gods).

[5] Zeitlin gives the fullest analysis (1971b).

[6] Baldwin (1911), Stübbe (1933), George (1974). The question of how the *Bellum Civile* is related to Lucanian and Virgilian epic seems often to have been reduced to a competition between influencing authors, one of whom must always come out on top.

[7] Connors (1998).

imaged in an endlessly metaphorised and metamorphosing human body. It will not be the aim of my discussion to arbitrate on the aesthetic qualities of the poem, or to decide, as many critics have done, whether the poem is a (flattering or trenchant) parody of Lucan's *Pharsalia*; the critical history of this debate has shown that it is near impossible to read Petronius' intentions in this regard, and I would argue that parody is rather a weak, whitewashing term which fails to encompass the complexities of Petronius' relationship with his epic past and literary predecessors.[8] However the question of how the *Satyricon* articulates a relationship with previous texts is central to my concerns, and is inseparable from internal questions of the interplay between text and context, poetry and prose in the *Satyricon*. As I have emphasised throughout, it is precisely this dynamic – between text and context, inside and outside – which directs the *Satyricon*'s powerful imagistic structure.

As I argued in the previous chapter, it is in the poet's body that the *Troiae Halosis'* imagery of incorporation is finally focused, as it was in Encolpius and Agamemnon's programmatic speeches at *Sat.* 1–5: Eumolpus becomes a Trojan Horse who seduces Encolpius into a superficial, 'realistic' perspective before pouring out his diseased poetic insides in the shape of horse-soldiers, repeating the sack of Troy and the ridicule of the Trojans just as he captured the gullible boy at Pergamum in *Sat.* 5.85–7. There is something rather perverted in the association here, as we are blinded to share the Trojan perspective of being deceived by an image: like the boy at Pergamum who pretends to be asleep so that Eumolpus will 'trick' him again and again (or rather, so he can turn tricks for Eumolpus), we have to participate willingly in the fiction in order to fall for the horse-hoax. We are like the Trojans, but this time we are actors, feigning sleep while Troy burns. Petronius uses parallel images to spell out the masturbatory implications of reading (and enjoying) this repetitive poem: once again the *Satyricon*, so sophisticated it is scraping the gutter, links literary and sexual pleasures, positioning the reader's as well as the poet's body at the centre of its stage.

It should come as no surprise then, when we find that the poet's body is the focal point in the composition of the *Bellum Civile*: as Eumolpus scribbles his second poem on Tryphaena's ship, he appears to be a Trojan horse born-again. At *Sat.* 114.12, the ship is going down in a storm, and Encolpius is awaiting a watery tomb like a man dressed for his deathbed

8 For various perspectives on the 'parody' debate, see Baldwin (1911), Sullivan (1968a), Walsh (1968), George (1974) and Hutchinson (1982). On definitions of parody in Latin and Greek literature in general, see Silk (1993).

(*veluti lecto funebri aptatus*). As he clings onto Giton, both men hear a strange noise coming from the master cabin: *audimus murmur insolitum et sub diaeta magistri quasi cupientis exire beluae gemitum* / 'We heard a strange noise, and a groaning like a wild beast wanting to escape, coming from under the master's cabin', (115.2). It is Eumolpus, writing what we are to assume is the *Bellum Civile*: *invenimus Eumolpum sedentem membranaeque ingenti versus ingerentem* / 'We found Eumolpus sitting there, scribbling verse onto a huge parchment.'[9] At the first mention of Eumolpus' second masterpiece, we are taken back to his first, to the dramatic fulcrum of the *Troiae Halosis*: the groaning of the horse (and its contents) when Laocoön's axe almost cuts into the Greek ruse: *fremit / captiva pubes intus et, dum* ***murmurat***, *roborea moles spirat alieno metu* / 'The young soldiers shut inside gasped, and while the murmur lasted, the wooden mass breathed with a fear that was not its own' (*TH* 24–6). Now it is Eumolpus, trapped dangerously within the wooden cabin, whom they hear moaning (*audimus* ***murmur***). Meanwhile his groans (***gemitum***), like those of a caged beast, echo the same scene as staged in the *Aeneid*: *stetit illa tremens, uteroque recusso / insonuere cavae* ***gemitum****que dedere cavernae* / 'It stuck there vibrating, the creature's womb quivered, and the hollow caverns boomed and groaned' (*Aen.* 2.52–3).

As critics have noted, this scene recalls Horace's vision of the mad poet unable to control his inspiration as a wild animal caught in a hunter's pit or cage which will kill if it gets its paws on a reader (*Ars P.* 457–9, 472–6):[10] this image of entrapment is qualified by the resuscitated image of Eumolpus in *Sat.* 89–90 as a Trojan horse-poet containing his dangerous verse in a rumbling stomach, before unleashing it on an audience which reacts as if it has been attacked. Whereas in the *Troiae Halosis* Eumolpus was (in control of) the Trojan horse, now he appears to be inside it, to have, as it were, been consumed by it. This image suggests and forecasts that writing about civil war ruptures authorial control by confusing normative boundaries between insides and outsides (and between right and wrong, friend and foe) and by rejecting the perspective afforded by objectivity. The hierarchy of incorporation we envisaged in the recitation of the *Troiae Halosis* has been upturned: Eumolpus now writes from the dark cavern of the horse's belly, aggressively hurling his words (*ingerentem*)

[9] This implication is discussed by Stübbe (1933: 68–9); Rose (1966b: 298); Cameron (1970: 415).

[10] *quem vero arripuit, tenet occiditque legendo, / non missura cutem, nisi plena cruoris hirudo* / 'if he catches a man, he keeps hold of him and reads him to death, a leech that will not let go of the skin until gorged with blood' (475–6).

onto animal skin (*membranae*). As Fowler observes, *membrana*, the skin from which most notebooks widely used at Rome were made, can also mean a membrane like that of the womb,[11] while Eumolpus' groans 'are those of a woman in labour as well as of a madman'.[12] Is our poet still the Trojan horse, pregnant with literature, bellowing like an animal as he is dragged to safety (*in terram trahere poetam mugientem*)? Or has he lost control of the reins, the reverse of Agamemnon's 'free man' in *Sat.* 5, trapped within his own poetic material, inside the horse itself?

The *Satyricon*'s imagery and strategies of incorporation relate importantly to narrative structure, as Eumolpus' successive poems show on a grand scale: the *Bellum Civile* must contain the fall of Troy, yet its creator (from one perspective at least) is himself contained within a replica of the Trojan horse. We saw this relay of narrative incorporation imaged vividly in Trimalchio's layered dishes, whose hierarchies were deceptive and whose contents could well eat their consumer from within. Similarly, when we come to look closely at the *Bellum Civile*, we can see that as well as working within 'Trojan Horse' epic and within its immediate narrative context, it also seems to have gulped down chunks of the *Satyricon*'s storyline from a far wider arena.

For example, as Connors has argued, it is no accident that Eumolpus appears to write the *Bellum Civile* on a ship, or indeed that he scrambles to finish it as he is shipwrecked (Lucan's death and his unfinished *Pharsalia* are never far from the surface).[13] Long before we know that the poem is being composed, civil war, and more importantly *writing about* civil war, is already being staged. The seafaring episode of the *Satyricon* (100–15) exploits conventional figures of the 'ship of state' and 'the ship of

[11] *TLL* VIII 629, 55ff. See Fowler (forthcoming).

[12] Fowler (forthcoming): we may compare this passage of Petronius with Hor. *Ars P.* 386–90, also discussed by Fowler here, in which the work is pictured as a foetus stored in the womb (or notebooks, *membranae*) until publication (birth).

[13] Eumolpus tells us that his poem is unfinished (*nondum recepit ultimam manum* / 'It has not yet received the final hand', 118.6), which alludes to the abrupt ending of the *Pharsalia* and Lucan's premature death (Eumolpus has *almost* died in the shipwreck, and the wrecked ship itself ends up, like the poem, a *rudis atque infecta materies* / 'a raw and unfinished lump', 114.13), and also echoes the story that Virgil ordered the *Aeneid* to be burnt because it had not received his *summam manum*: 'ultimate hand' (see e.g. Servius, *Vita* 27–42). Eumolpus' poem also breaks off by alluding to the final lines of the *Pharsalia* (*Epidamni moenia quaere* / 'Let him take the walls of Epidamnus', *BC* 293; *respexit in agmine denso* / *Scaevam perpetuae meritum iam nomina famae* / *ad campos, Epidamne* . . . / 'He saw Scaeva in the close-packed ranks, the Scaeva who had already won immortal glory on the plains of Epidamnus', 10.543–5). See Connors (1998: 134–41) for further discussion on the unfinished ending of the *Bellum Civile*. See Masters (1992: 216–59) for discussion of whether Lucan's ending was the product of chance or design.

poetry', as well as Seneca's 'ship of philosophy' riding out the storms of fortune,[14] while also playing on Ovid's eroticisation of epic sea-voyaging in his *Ars Amatoria* and *Heroides*.[15] Fighting on board ship is described in terms of civil war: the travellers are divided into factions (*totiusque navigii turbam diducit in partes*, 108.7) and battle is called to a halt only when in *Sat.* 108.14, v. 1 Tryphaena echoes Lucan *Ph.* 1.8: *'quis furor' exclamat 'pacem convertit in arma?'* / ' "What madness", she cried, "is turning peace into war?" ' cf. *quis furor, o cives, quae tanta licentia ferri?* / 'What madness is this, my people, what orgy of slaughter?' The sinking of the ship of poetry at once calls a halt to Eumolpus' furiously written poem and also seems to provide further motivation for the poem's style and subject matter: after Lucan, it might seem that civil war poetry can only heap disintegration upon disintegration, for which shipwreck is a colourful metaphor.

As I have suggested, water imagery is endemic in the *Satyricon*, and is a central focus for incorporation.[16] Agamemnon's speech and poem in *Sat.* 3–5, which describe teachers as fishermen hooking pupils who swim in a dangerous sea of learning, and imagine the writer drinking in knowledge to bursting point before letting it all gush out in a river of free verse, set up a pattern for the rest of the fiction. We saw this imagery at work in Quartilla's brothel, where the gang had their private parts 'liquidised' by a *cinaedus* who is also a poet pouring out verse; and at the *cena*, where an arena enriched by interpretative challenges turned food and wine into literature to be swallowed and spewed out from soft, liquid bodies, and where the after-dinner bath suddenly transformed into a

[14] Seneca's philosophical writings picture sea storms as metaphors for the unpredictability of life, and depict philosophy as a helmsman (*gubernator*) who can guide men into safe harbours (see *Dial.* 6.6.3; 6.15.4; 7.19.1; 10.18.1; 11.9.6–7; *Ep.* 99.9). A bad teacher, on the other hand, is a sea-sick helmsman (*Ep.* 108.37). See discussion in Connors (1998: 78–83).

[15] Perhaps the most famous example of the 'ship of state' in Roman poetry is Horace, *Carm.* 1.14, as discussed by Quintilian, *Inst.* 8.6.44. In Ovid, the ship of poetry is also the ship of love: at the end of *Ars Am.* 1, the poet 'puts down the anchor' (*hic teneat nostras ancora iacta rates*, 772); by *Ars Am.* 2, he envisages his pupils sailing their own ships (or organs) of seduction, modeled on his ship of love poetry: *mediis tua pinus in undis / navigat* / 'your ship sails mid-ocean', 9–10; *sed non cui dederas a litore carbasa vento, / utendum, medio cum potiere freto* / 'but the wind to which you spread your sails when leaving the shore should not be used once you have reached the open sea', 337–8. When Encolpius embraces Giton on the boat of civil war (poetry) in *Sat.* 114 (*iuncta nos mors feret!* / 'a common death will bear us up'), we are reminded of Ovid's famous trope, *militiae species amor est* / 'love is a kind of war' (*Ars Am.* 2.233).

[16] See Wimmel (1960: 222–33) and Sochatoff (1970). Water is also a crucial theme in Ovid's *Metamorphoses*, a text which makes a huge impact on the *Satyricon*. From the story of the first flood (*Met.* 1.253–312), water is a source of continuous dissolution, the primal root of all metamorphosis. As Kilgour writes (1990: 32), water in the *Metamorphoses* is both 'a means of thematic continuity and a source of contagion'.

life-threatening fishpond. Even the entrance to Trimalchio's dining room, we now recall, was decorated to look like the prow of a ship (*Sat.* 30.1); and the *cena* (or perhaps the projected consequences of past troubles, it is not clear) was originally anticipated as an encroaching sea storm (*cum maesti deliberaremus quonam genere praesentem evitaremus procellam* / 'We were depressed, and making plans for how to avoid the oncoming squall', *Sat.* 26.8). In the *Troiae Halosis*, the innovative poetic content of the Trojan horse pours out (*effundunt*) from the beast's belly and from Eumolpus' sick stomach. And now the *Bellum Civile* is conjured up amid epic storms on a sinking ship, leaving poet and crew prey to fishermen (114.14); the poem is said to pour out of Eumolpus' mouth (*effudisset*) as if it is a lung-full of saltwater verse just recently inhaled (*Sat.* 124.2).

Moreover in *Sat.* 118, Eumolpus has already introduced civil war as a subject which demands that an author steep himself in a vast flood of literature (*neque concipere aut edere partum mens potest nisi ingenti flumine litterarum inundata* / 'The mind cannot conceive or bring forth its fruit unless it is drowned in a vast river of literature', 118.3); civil war is an *ingens opus* and the ship has always been set *ingenti cursu* / 'a huge course' (101.11). Contrary to popular belief, he says, writing poetry in general is not about relaxing in calm harbours (*sic forensibus ministeriis exercitati frequenter ad carminis tranquillitatem tamquam ad portum feliciorem* / 'And so people who are sick of forensic oratory often take refuge in the calm of poetry, as if in some happier haven', 118.2); anyone who attempts a civil war poem will sink unless he is laden with literature (*nisi plenus litteris, sub onere labetur*, 118.6). It seems that the Neronian poet faces the further challenge of both drinking *and* swimming in a literary sea, as if paradoxically he can only stay afloat if he has consumed enough liquid to weigh him down. Like civil war itself, as it throws society into a turmoil in which boundaries are reconceived and washed away all at once, the *Satyricon*'s poet figure seems trapped in a whirlpool where insides and outsides, liquids and solids, are perpetually rearranged and confused. Yet as I have suggested throughout, we can read the complexity of this imagery only if we envisage its scope throughout the *Satyricon*, rather than isolating the *Bellum Civile* in its immediate narrative context. As Encolpius remarks in *Sat.* 115.16, shipwreck is everywhere if you think about it: *si bene calculum ponas, ubique naufragium est.*[17]

[17] Tacitus says something similar when he tells the story of Nero's plot in 59 to kill Agrippina in the collapsible boat: *nihil tam capax fortuitorum quam mare* / 'nothing is so full of chance occurrences as the sea' (*Ann.* 14.3). The *Satyricon* is as full of *fortuna* as it is full of shipwreck (see Appendix II), yet

Let us look closely now at the location for the *Bellum Civile*, Croton. At one time the 'first town' of Italy, this city in the hills is not simply a nightmare inversion of a civilised Carthage in *Aeneid* I,[18] a satiric, modern take on fallen Troy or a caricature of Nero's immoral Rome. Crucially it is also the opening stage for the last book of Ovid's *Metamorphoses*, the site of a foundation narrative at the finale of this subversive epic. In *Met.* 15, Croton is the first Greek city in Italian territory, and it is where the intellectual King Numa goes to learn about the nature of the universe. For Croton is the home of Pythagoras, a learned Samian who preaches a vegetarian philosophy motivated by a golden-age idealism and by a theory of corporeal flux (metempsychosis) that seems to some extent to have driven the narratives of the *Metamorphoses* from the very beginning (or at least, on a metaliterary level, its patterns of narration and allusion): souls are perpetually reincarnated, moving randomly between humans and animals and taking on different shapes, just as in general our bodies are constantly changing as we move without stopping from birth to death. Because everything in the natural world, according to Pythagoras, is in a state of constant flux, it is sacrilegious to kill or consume an animal body, which may conceivably contain the soul of a long-lost relative. Carnivores are like Cyclopes, he says: *heu quantum scelus est in viscera viscera condi / … nil te nisi tristia mandere saevo / vulnera dente iuvat ritusque referre Cyclopum … /* 'How evil it is for flesh to be hidden inside flesh … you love chewing the tragic wounds with your savage teeth, repeating the Cyclopes' custom' (*Met.* 15.88, 92–3). Yet Pythagoras makes eating in general look risky, especially when we have read fourteen books of the *Metamorphoses*, in which human souls very often reside in such apparently harmless things as flowers and trees. Meat eating is simply an extreme example of the dangers *all* incorporation poses to the integrity of the human body and to the preservation of its inner self.

Metamorphosis, as we have seen, is an anxious undercurrent running throughout the *Satyricon*. Metamorphic ideas of corporeal flux seep into Petronius' interest in acting and performance, in the meaning of images and the deceptiveness of appearances, in the slippage between outsides and insides, and on a metaliterary level in an author's (and reader's) inability to control the welter of literary material which this novel changes

remembering Nero's manipulations (and Agrippina's retaliatory game, when she informs him of her good *fortuna* in escaping death: *Ann.* 14.6) reminds us that we should always be suspicious of this text's 'randomness': it may also be a sign of crafted ingenuity. According to Tacitus, Petronius even staged his own forced suicide as 'accidental': *mors fortuitae similis* (*Ann.* 16.19).

[18] In *Aeneid* I, Aeneas' view of Carthage under construction at first glance epitomises order, progress and peace. See *Aen.* 1.418–40.

in the process of incorporation but which always seems to have a life of its own. We saw all these concerns dramatised in Trimalchio's mind-boggling *cena* where, just as in Ovid's Croton, metamorphosis (in particular the constant exchange of human and animal roles) made eating especially risky. In fact there are points we have already looked at in the *Cena* where Trimalchio, we now realise, sounds just like a born-again Pythagorean regurgitating his master's speeches from *Met.* 15: compare *Sat.* 56.4–5 (***boves***, *quorum beneficio panem manducamus*; ***oves***, *quod lana illae nos gloriosus faciunt. et facinus indignum, aliquis ovillam est et tunicam habet* / 'cattle, because thanks to them we can eat bread; sheep, because their wool clothes us in splendour. So it's a terrible deed when someone eats lamb and wears a wool tunic') with *Met.* 15.116–21:[19]

> quid meruistis **oves**, placidum pecus inque tuendos
> natum homines, pleno quae fertis in ubere nectar,
> mollia quae nobis vestras velamina lanas
> praebetis vitaque magis quam morte iuvatis?
> quid meruere **boves**, animal sine fraude dolisque,
> innocuum, simplex, natum tolerare labores?

> What did you ever do, sheep, to deserve death,
> a peaceful flock born to serve mankind, bringing us
> nectar in plump udders, your wool for soft clothing,
> giving us more pleasure alive than dead?
> What have oxen ever done, those faithful, honest beasts,
> so innocent and simple, born to a life of toil?

Ovid's metamorphosis, the disruptive force which makes us all self-conscious and flaunts the collapse of epic decorum, takes place in bodies and indeed turns everything into a body, transforming Ovid's poetry into a living, breathing corpus with an ultra-modern energy and an ability to inject its genre with the power of change. As Henderson has suggested, Lucan reads Ovidian metamorphosis as disfigurement:[20] this is exactly what Petronius' commentary on civil war poetry wants to show, and it is exactly what we are seeing when we revisit with Encolpius the great city of Croton.

At *Sat.* 116 the gang is once again lost, and they are forced to ask a farm bailiff about the town they see on the nearby hill. They make

[19] We can always hear the nursery rhyme echo: *boves . . . oves. . . .*

[20] Henderson (1988) 143: 'Lucan shifts (Ovidian) metamorphosis away from slighting insouciance to defiling disfigurement. This epic defaces its city walls, unmakes its foundation and its history, implodes its tradition and ideologies along with the documents that bear them.'

inquiries like Homeric heroes who have travelled into the future: *cum deinde diligentius exploraremus qui homines inhabitarent nobile solum, quodve genus negotiationis praecipue probarent post attritas bellis frequentibus opes* / 'When we then inquired diligently what kind of men inhabited this noble soil and what kind of business pleased them best now that their wealth had been worn down by so many wars' (116.3). The man replies that they should steer clear of the town if they are businessmen, and should only approach if they are barefaced liars. For in this city there is no place for eloquence or learning (*in hac enim urbe non litterarum studia celebrantur, non eloquentia locum habet*, 116.6); men are divided into two classes, legacy-hunters and their prey (*nam aut captantur aut captant* / 'there are those who get captured, and those who do the capturing'). In both Petronius' and Ovid's Croton, the inhabitants are preoccupied with preserving bodily integrity. In the *Metamorphoses* this was explicitly to do with eating, and with Pythagoras' ideas about what one should and should not consume; here, it has to do with an ethos of extreme selfishness and with all kinds of social, marital and sexual relations: nobody in Petronius' Croton brings up children, because children are heirs who can drain a legacy-hunter's fortune – only the childless are admitted to dinner or the theatre (116.7);[21] similarly it is those who never marry and have no close relations who win the top jobs (*qui vero nec uxorem unquam duxerunt nec proximas necessitudines habent, ad summos honores perveniunt*). The bailiff predicts: *adibitis oppidum tamquam in pestilentia campos, in quibus nihil aliud est nisi cadavera quae lacerantur aut corvi qui lacerant* / 'You will enter a town that is like a plague-stricken plain, where there is nothing but corpses being torn to pieces and the crows that tear them' (116.9).

This is a city effectively in the midst of civil war.[22] The description of what is going on in Croton replays the civil war which wreaked havoc on Tryphaena's ship and (on a literary if not a literal level) ultimately caused it to sink, leaving its crew at the mercy of predatory fishermen (*Sat.* 114), while it looks forward to Eumolpus' poem, the *Bellum Civile*. The bailiff says that Croton's men are divided into factions (*partes*, 116.6), just as Tryphaena separates the crew in *Sat.* 108.7 (*totiusque navigii turbam diducit in partes*). On one level civil war both on board ship and within the

[21] On legacy-hunting and childlessness as a problem under Nero, see Tac. *Ann.* 13.52.3; 15.19.3. On childlessness as a social evil see Cicero, *Parad.* 5.239; Hor. *Sat.* 2.5; Hor. *Epist.* 1.1.79; Sen. *Ben.* 6.38; *Ad Marc.* 19.

[22] Indeed, the image of legacy-hunters as scavenging crows is reminiscent of the aftermath of Pharsalia at Lucan 7.825–46, where the birds which have long followed the *civilia castra* are joined by wild beasts and suck the marrow from the bones of the dead. Carrion birds also feed on the unburied body of Caesar's officer Curio at Lucan 4.809–10.

walls of Croton is a strife motivated by divisions and by the construction of aggressive hierarchies: there is no compromise in Croton, space only for the hunter or the hunted, the ruling class or the lowest of the low, the elevated or the despised. Similarly when fighting breaks out on the ship, there can only be two sides (*stante ergo utraque acie* / 'since both sides were drawn up in battle lines', *Sat.* 108.12), just like in a 'real war' (*referunt veluti ex proelio pedem* / 'they retired just like in an actual battle', *Sat.* 108.10); and even when ructions are calmed, it is clear that *different* hierarchies have merely been restored (between hunter and hunted). For in the image of idyllic fishing at 109.6, as I have argued, we are reminded again of Agamemnon's striking and programmatic image in *Sat.* 3.4 of the fisherman teacher hooking his pupils with choice bait. When the ship sinks, the idealistic *tranquillitas* of *Sat.* 109 is revealed to be deceptive as the *Satyricon*'s fishermen now hunt drowning men rather than fish. As in war, and as in Croton, the outcomes of this shipwreck are black and white: either you die or you survive, either you capture or you get caught (*aut captantur aut captant*).

Yet it is the paradox of incorporation and the power of metamorphosis that finally disrupt this version of what war is all about. The bailiff's final warning to the gang that they will find only *cadavera quae lacerantur aut corvi, qui lacerant* (116.9) seems at first reading to mirror his previous phrase (*nam aut captantur aut captant*) in describing this bleak, oppositional landscape. Yet the *cadavera* he talks about must surely be the corpses of the legacy-hunters, the egomaniacs who achieve so much in life but die childless and are left to rot with no relatives to bury them. In death, the aggressive hunters become the passive and vulnerable hunted, their never-penetrated (sexless, childless) bodies torn apart and consumed by crows.[23] Just as the crew who fish from Tryphaena's ship in *Sat.* 109 become the flailing prey in the water in *Sat.* 114, so Croton's legacy-hunters are eventually eaten because ultimately they cannot protect themselves from the bestial forces of penetration and consumption.

Literature about civil war may attempt guiltily to foster opposition, to maintain hierarchies and allow the objectivity of history to broadcast images in black and white. Yet finally, Petronius shows, it can (or should) never quite conceal civil war's anarchic core, written here in terms of Ovidian metamorphosis, which reminds us that in this kind of war

[23] Indeed legacy-hunters are described as birds of prey in Cat. 68.124 and Sen. *Ep.* 95.43. To be 'food for the crows' is an insult directed towards Giton at *Sat.* 58.2 (*quid faciat crucis offla, corvorum cibaria?* / 'What does he do, the gallows-meat, the crows' food?' cf. Hor. *Epist.* 1.17.48 (crucifixion is the standard punishment for slaves).

'enemies' may be brothers, murderers victims, hunters hunted. To enter into the kind of Croton imagined in *Sat.* 116 you have to be a *liar*. The Croton of *Met.* 15, where Pythagoras preaches his idealistic but potentially seditious vegetarianism, based on a philosophy of corporeal flux in which everything and everyone are related, forms the crucial subtext of Encolpius' approach or introduction into civil war. Petronius reads Ovidian metamorphosis as a kind of corporeal *Bellum Civile*, and the echoes of this association now reverberate disturbingly through the *Satyricon* as a whole. The more connections and similarities we see between Eumolpus' poem and its 'prose context', between its 'prose context' and earlier episodes (the ship, the *cena*, the brothel, the opening speeches), the more 'civil war' seems practically to infect this novel from beginning to end.[24]

Moreover the ultimate artificiality of Croton's social hierarchies is made emphatic in Eumolpus' strategy for entering the city in *Sat.* 117, in which they are to mime the same extreme opposition of roles. The poet is not at all perturbed by the bailiff's description of Croton, but rather enters into the spirit of the proposed deception: he suggests that the gang (now made up of Encolpius, Giton and Corax) appoint him as 'master', and take an oath to obey him at all costs like gladiators (*iuravimus: uri, vinciri, verberari ferroque necari, et quicquid aliud Eumolpus iussisset. tamquam legitimi gladiatores domino corpora animasque religiosissime addicimus* / 'We swore to be burned, tied up, beaten and put to death by the sword, and whatever else Eumolpus ordered. Like real gladiators we solemnly pledged our bodies and souls to our master', 117.5–6). Thus while Eumolpus recites a poem on civil war, the gang will also be acting as soldiers marching on a city, forced to surrender their bodies for the common good. They then rehearse a fake narrative in which their master Eumolpus has recently lost a son and has left his home country to escape the son's dependents and friends; he has also recently lost a fortune, two million sesterces, in a shipwreck, but is so rich this doesn't really bother him as *praeterea habere in Africa trecenties sestertium fundis nominibusque depositum* / 'He also had three million invested in Africa in farms and bonds' (117.8). Besides, he

[24] Indeed the *Satyricon* as a whole tells the story of bitter and often aggressive conflict between 'brothers', *fratres*, which is how Encolpius, Ascyltos and Giton refer to each other. All the central characters in this fiction are (sexually) related and divided. At *Sat.* 80, Encolpius and Ascyltos split into rival factions and plan also to split Giton's body in half (*partem meam necesse est vel hoc gladio contemptus abscindam* / 'I must cut off my share with this sword'), before the boy gets on his knees and begs them not to stage a Theban duel (80.3). As Barchiesi notes (1996: 200), this scene is explicitly also about the opposition of literary genres: '"Thebanum par" implica un tipico mito tragico, mentre taberna può essere collegato a tabernaria, definizione di un sottogenere del teatro comico (attestate per noi da Apul. *Apol.* 87.4).'

has so many slaves they could form an army to take Carthage (*ut possit vel Carthaginem capere*, 117.9). Just to tempt the legacy-hunters further, they are to pretend that Eumolpus is on the verge of death: he is to cough frequently, complain alternately of constipation and diarrhoea, and show signs of senility as he broods over his will and accounts. All of which, incidentally, is clearly reminiscent of the boasting of a certain stinking rich, prematurely aging Trimalchio, who complains about bowel problems (*Sat.* 47), rules his slaves and his dinner guests like a tyrant[25] and stages his own death (*Sat.* 78). In particular, the plan for Eumolpus to get confused over his slaves' names, hinting that he has far more slaves than he can ever remember, directly parallels the boast at 37.9 that Trimalchio has so many slaves, hardly one out of ten of them has ever even met his master (*non mehercules puto decumam partem esse quae dominum suum noverit* / 'I really don't believe that one in ten of them can recognise his master on sight').

Thus Eumolpus' *mimus* enacts both the sacrifices of civil war (the gang prostitute themselves like gladiators) and also the barbaric, war-like hierarchies that structure life in Croton (Eumolpus rules supreme as tyrannical master over his tortured, worthless slaves). Yet on one hand, this act is so obviously a farce that it makes the description of Croton we have just heard also sound like a fantasy: the kind of extremes on show here belong to the stage, to storytelling, not to real life civil war, which is far more complicated. Indeed Eumolpus' plan is so ridiculous that not even the gladiators can keep it up:[26] Giton cannot manage his load and Corax curses Eumolpus for his arrogance, saying, *quid vos iumentum me putatis esse aut lapidariam navem? hominis operas locavi, non caballi!* / 'What do you think I am, a beast of burden or a ship for transporting rocks? You hired the services of a man, not a horse!' (117.12). On the other hand, although it is explicitly theatrical, the *mimus* also seems to test out our ability to distinguish between what is 'real' and what is pure pantomime, not least because it seems to weave bits of 'real' narrative into its fiction (could it be *true*, for example that Eumolpus did lose money in the recent shipwreck – *proximum naufragium*)?

Petronius is always at pains to make it very difficult for his readers to split make-believe from reality. In *Sat.* 118, Eumolpus turns to the

[25] The most striking example of this is at *Sat.* 41.9: the guests are relieved of the pressure to eat when Trimalchio the tyrant leaves the room, and start talking.

[26] As Panayotakis notes (1995: 160), Encolpius and his friends are 'already typecast theatrical figures', as they are still wearing the blond wigs and false eyebrows given to them by Tryphaena at *Sat.* 110.

subject of poetry and writing about civil war, yet it is not clear where the mime stops and the discussion of poetry, or even the poem itself, begins. Is it the mime that gets them into Croton or the *Bellum Civile* itself? Eumolpus starts by saying that poetry (like mime) has deceived many people (*multos, o iuvenes, carmen decepit*, 118.1). Some are under the illusion, he says, that when they have written a poem they have climbed Mount Helicon (Eumolpus is far more modest: in reciting his poem he is merely climbing the hill up to Croton). To be a good poet one must avoid vulgarisms and use only unusual, elite language (*voces a plebe semotae* / 'words divorced from popular use', 118.4), just as Eumolpus will speak loudly in aristocratic tones to impress the legacy-hunters of Croton. Anyone who doesn't agree has missed the path that leads to poetry (*aut non viderunt viam, qua iretur ad carmen*, 118.6), or the road to Croton along which Eumolpus is heading: either that or they were afraid to walk on it (*aut visam timuerunt calcare*),[27] *calcare* being the regular Latin translation of πατέω, the verb used by Callimachus to describe the passage of wagons along the (epic) path an innovative poet should avoid.[28] This verb of (anti-) Callimachean poetic progress also draws us forward to a crucial event described in the *Bellum Civile* poem, Caesar's journey over the Alps in line 152 (*haec ubi* **calcavit** *Caesar iuga milite laeto* / 'when Caesar with his happy army trod these heights').[29] Finally, on the theme of civil war, Eumolpus declares that those who attempt such poetry will sink under the burden unless they are laden with literature, just as the patronised Giton and Corax are unable to bear their cargo (like a ship weighted down by stones: *lapidariam navem*, 117.12) as they trudge along a road which for them is very much a 'make-believe' narrative path constructed by the poet Eumolpus.

We must seriously question, then, what role Eumolpus is playing when he recites the *Bellum Civile*, and what function the poem really serves within the specific context and objective of getting into Croton. The age-old debate about what this poem is trying to do, and in what voice it is predominately written (Petronius', Eumolpus', Lucan's, Virgil's…) is

[27] *vi/s/am*, the imagined road, is cunningly captured here in a single word.

[28] *TLL* III.135 lines 20–5, 56, 81 and 136 line 45 cite examples where *calco* translates πατέω. See Callimachus *Aet.* 1, fr.1.22–8 Pf, where Callimachus says that Apollo told him not to tread the road that wagons go along (πατέουσιν), nor to follow anyone else's path, but to go his own way. For Latin examples of the path of poetry, used to describe the novelty or subtlety of a literary project, see Lucr. 4.1–2 (= 1.926–7); Prop. 3.1.18, 3.3.18, 26; Ov. *Pont.* 4.16.32.

[29] *calco* also appears in the last line of Lucan: *ubi solus apertis / obsedit muris calcantem moenia Magnum* / 'When the walls were breached he alone besieged Magnus, who had trodden the ramparts underfoot' (10.545–6).

a conundrum already explicitly staged in the prose narrative of *Sat.* 117 and 118. Again, as I have argued throughout, the point is always that episodes and poems in the *Satyricon* are not only never extractable, but are always related, like Pythagorean bodies, to their immediate and wider contexts: as a result it is very difficult to decide what is, for example, to be seen as *contained* within the *Bellum Civile* and what is intended to refer to something outside the poem in its 'prose context'. This dilemma mirrors the larger-scale challenge of reading this super-allusive novel, which seems to incorporate all the important Greek and Latin genres and authors we know: how to understand the relationship between what is inside the *Satyricon*, to be read and contained on the page, and the vast metamorphic 'outside-world' of literature to which this text continually refers?

Eumolpus' *Bellum Civile* is climactic in dramatising the artificiality of divisions between insides and outsides, reality and fiction, throughout the *Satyricon*. For full effect the imagery at work in this poem relies on Eumolpus' earlier poem, the *Troiae Halosis*, as well as many of the preliminary episodes of the *Satyricon*. When Eumolpus introduces the *Bellum Civile* he is pretending to have stomach pains caused by loose bowels (*solutioris stomachi*, *Sat.* 117.9) and to be struggling to keep the nasty contents of his body in. We are reminded that in *Sat.* 90 Eumolpus also has a disease (*morbus*) inside him which is implicitly compared to poetry: Encolpius begs him to stop reciting verse, that is, to keep his disease hidden. The entire *Troiae Halosis* is made to look like an outpouring of *morbus*, just as the Trojan Horse releases soldiers to destroy Troy from within. To return to *Sat.* 118, Eumolpus' philosophy of writing good poetry dictates that, 'thoughts must not stand out from the body of the speech, but must shine with a brilliancy woven into its fabric' (*curandum est ne sententiae emineant extra corpus orationis expressae, sed intexto vestibus colore niteant*, 118.5). Yet just as containment (of men inside the horse) resulted in rupture, war and destruction, so Eumolpus' struggle to keep everything in triggers the *Bellum Civile*, an effusive piece of poetry that pours from his body (*cum haec ingenti volubilitate verborum effudisset*, *Sat.* 124.2) like his Greek soldiers (*effundunt*, *TH* 57) to tell again of war and violence at the heart of Rome.

The *Bellum Civile* reads civil war as the rupture of incorporation. It is grandiose in that it swallows up everything that has already been narrated in the *Satyricon* before pouring it all out again in exaggerated form. In his guise as a filthy rich businessman bragging about his army of slaves, Eumolpus as poet of the *Bellum Civile* already looks like Trimalchio, while the image of Rome painted in *BC* 1–37 could easily capture Trimalchio's lifestyle in the *Cena*: he is the megalomaniac Roman who is never satisfied (*nec satiatus erat*, v. 3), a fan of Corinthian bronze (*aes Ephyre* †*cum*† *laudabat miles*, v. 9, cf. *solus sum qui vera Corinthea habeam* / 'I am the sole owner of genuine Corinthian plate', *Sat.* 50.2), of bright, exotic colours (*quaesitus tellure nitor* / 'vibrant hues dug from the earth', v. 10) and luxurious materials (*nova vellera* / 'pashminas', v. 11), and an aficionado of amphitheatre shows (vv. 12–18). The phrase *ecce aliae clades* / 'Look, another battle' at *BC* 12, describing the blood-thirsty displays of beasts in the arena, harks back to *ecce alia monstra* / 'Look, another monster' in *TH* v. 29, but also to *ecce alius ludus* / 'Look, another game' in *Sat.* 68.4, when Trimalchio calls a halt to a boy's impersonation of a nightingale (he will not allow birdsong in his dining room, just as the Phlegraean plain in *BC* vv. 72–3 is devoid of birds singing whatever the time of year: *non verno persona cantu* / *mollia discordi strepitu virgulta loquuntur* / 'the soft thickets never ring loud in springtime with the songs of rival birds').[30] Trimalchio's dining room is described as a labyrinthine hell on earth, just as in civil war, when the earth is cleft open and sucked into the underworld in a nightmare vision: *ad Stygios manes laceratus ducitur orbis* / 'the whole world is torn to shreds and pulled down to the Stygian shades' (*BC* v. 121).[31] Whereas Trimalchio's house is ruled by his wife Fortunata, the 'goddess' to whom he entrusts everything, even the time of day (*Sat.* 37.4–5), a Rome wrecked by civil war is controlled by the unpredictable goddess Fortuna, in whom generals and foolish Romans alike are forced to trust (*iudice Fortuna cadat alea* / 'Let Fortune decide how our fate falls', v. 174; *hic dat vela fugae Fortunaeque omnia credit*[32] / 'He sets sail and flees, and trusts all to chance', v. 237).[33] In the *Bellum Civile* a Rome split by civil war is shrouded in darkness (*caligine*, v. 128), but this is a

[30] As Connors points out (1998: 121–2), the Phlegraean plain is near Lake Avernus, and 'by asserting that there is no bird song in this place, Eumolpus alludes to the notion that the gases emanating from Lake Avernus would poison birds'. The juxtaposition of *non* and *verno* in this line 'momentarily re-etymologizes the name of Lake Avernus. *non verno*, with the Latin *non* replaced by the Greek alpha privative from *a-ornos*, is *A-verno*, Avernian birdsong, that is, no song at all.'

[31] Throughout the *cena* episode, Trimalchio's dining room appears as a microcosm: not only do the guests eat dishes that represent 'worlds', e.g., the zodiac dish (*Sat.* 35), eggs (*terra mater est in medio quasi ovum* / 'Mother Earth is at the centre of the universe like an egg', *Sat.* 39.15), but they look to the ceiling for surprises as if it were an overarching sky (*expectantes quid novi de caelo nuntiaretur* / 'We were wondering what the heavens were going to announce next', *Sat.* 60.2).

[32] This line is included in Müller (1961) but not in the 1995 edition.

[33] As Sullivan argues (1968a: 168), Petronius 'rejects Lucan's experiment of jettisoning divine machinery in favour of Stoic motifs of divination and omens, which indicate the involvement of the unseen and the divine in human affairs'. Yet by means of repeated imagery, such as this

darkness that has plagued Encolpius' journey ever since he began to wander the streets at *Sat.* 9 (*quasi per caliginem*). At the sight of war the deities of Olympus veil their heads and cover their faces (*Titan vultum caligine texit* / 'Titan veiled his face in darkness', v. 128; *extinxit Cynthia vultus* / 'Cynthia darkened her face', v. 130; *Pax… abscondit galea victum caput* / 'Peace hid her vanquished face under her helmet', vv. 249–50; *Furor… oraque mille / vulneribus confossa cruenta casside velat* / 'Madness veiled her face scarred by a thousand wounds with a bloody shield', vv. 258–60), reminding us that veiling has been a trope throughout the narrative of the *Satyricon* so far, a sign of deception and theatricality that was particularly prevalent in the marketplace episode at *Sat.* 12–15. In the scene where Peace veils her head in the *Bellum Civile*, we see Concord weeping with her cloak torn into pieces (*maerens lacera Concordia palla*, v. 253), which is again reminiscent of the little 'civil war' that erupts in the shady marketplace, where the gang fight over a torn cloak (*scissam tunicam*, *Sat.* 14.6). Similarly, when Eumolpus describes the traps of greed as a whirlpool in which ordinary Romans are drowning (*gemino deprensam* ***gurgite*** *plebem / faenoris ingluvies ususque exederat aeris* / 'Greed for usury and the lending of money had caught the public in a double whirlpool', vv. 51–2), he also echoes the dangerous pool into which Encolpius and Ascyltos fall in *Sat.* 72.7 after greedily stuffing themselves with Trimalchio's luxuries (*dum natanti opem fero, in eundem* ***gurgitem*** *tractus sum* / 'When I tried to help him as he swam, I was dragged into the same whirlpool'). And when at the end of the *Bellum Civile* Furor raises her bloody head like a horse (or a rider?) set free when the reins snap (*abruptis ceu liber habenis*, v. 258) we are reminded of the subversive poetic power invested in the horse throughout the *Satyricon*, from Agamemnon's image of risky poetic control in *Sat.* 5 (*mittat habenas / liber*) to the Trojan Horse in *Sat.* 89, which wreaks havoc despite and because of being 'tamed' within the walls of Troy.

The *Bellum Civile* overflows with references to the rest of the *Satyricon* which it cannot ultimately contain, despite Eumolpus' theory in *Sat.* 118 that thoughts should not stand out (*emineant*) from the 'body' of a recitation

parallel between Fortuna and Fortunata, Petronius makes gods look like human beings wearing theatrical masks, and vice versa, just as many of his characters are ordinary men with the names of heroes (Agamemnon, Menelaus . . .). Zeitlin notes (1971a: 657) that the concept or character of a cruel and random Fortune raises her head at several points in the *Satyricon*: see Appendix II. The entire text is shaped (literally) by the vacillating waves of fortune, and is an extended experiment in the 'fictions of chance' (see discussion in Connors 1998: 76–83, and my discussion in chapter eleven).

(*extra corpus orationis*). Like the *Troiae Halosis*, and like civil war itself, the *Bellum Civile* is born within the human body (Eumolpus' diseased or ailing belly), which it then inevitably ruptures, spurting out from all available orifices (*defudit pectore, BC* 102; *effudisset, Sat.* 124.2). Although the *Satyricon* until now has been obsessively concerned with *intestina*, it is in civil war (*intestinum bellum*) that this perverse focus on bodily investigation truly dominates the stage.[34] And this is where Petronius seems especially indebted to Lucanian imagery. Lucan's epic, to which Eumolpus' poem is clearly related, envisages civil war as a violence inflicted on and in the human body: Lucan's language, Bartsch explains,

> focuses sharply on the violation of soldierly bodies through the death-dealing wounds inflicted by their fellow Romans. In some ways his epic seems the prolonged expression of a crisis around the body, or rather the boundary that separates men from what is pointedly not-man, from the inanimate and the environment – a boundary which the weapons of civil war physically violate by spilling human blood and guts on the field of war and which the intrusive imperial government would violate too, if in another way.[35]

In this analysis, Lucan's tortured, wounded bodies are emotive metaphors for a social fabric which is also being ripped apart.[36]

In Eumolpus' poem, a long opening section (vv. 1–38) situates the origins of civil war in the bellies of ordinary Romans, citizens high on imperialism who will never be satisfied however much they consume (*nec satiatus erat*, v. 3), and who have a perverted obsession with bodies and sex (vv. 24–6):

> omnibus ergo
> scorta placent fractique enervi corpore gressus
> et laxi crines et tot nova nomina vestis,
> quaeque virum quaerunt.

> They get off on whores,
> those limping men with saggy frames,
> their flowing locks, their clothes with fancy names all new,
> everything that manhood isn't.

[34] E.g. *Sat.* 49.4: *porcus hic non est exinteratus?* / 'Has the pig not been gutted?', *Sat.* 56.1–2: *medicus, qui scit quid homunciones intra praecordia habeant . . .* / 'The doctor, who knows what poor men have in their insides', *Sat.* 63.8: *non cor habebat, non intestina, non quicquam* / 'He had no heart, no innards, no nothing', *Sat.* 66.5: *paene intestina sua vomuit* / 'She almost vomited her guts up'.

[35] Bartsch (1998) 12.

[36] See Scarry (1985: 81) for her exploration of the status of bodies in times of war: 'war is relentless for taking for its own interior content the interior content of the human body.'

Having drowned himself in wine like a Trojan about to be killed in burning Troy (*sepulta mero*, v. 31, cf. *sepultos mero, TH* 56),[37] this soldier of fortune physically *hungers* (*esurit*, v. 32) after his booty. It is gluttony (*gula*, v. 33), the physical urge for food and sex, which breeds corruption and eventually war: fish are shipped live from Sicily, oysters are torn from lake Lucrino, all to make a dinner saleable and to renew men's hunger for extravagance (*ut renovent per damna famem*, v. 36). The end result is madness, which spreads through the limbs like a disease sown in the dumb marrow (*sed veluti tabes tacitis concepta medullis / intra membra furens curis latrantibus errat*, vv. 54–5). Suddenly internal urges become external forces, contained madness bursts forth as an independent being (*feralis Enyo*, the goddess of war, v. 62), and all at once the earth's body cannot hold so many dead (*et quasi non posset tellus tot ferre sepulcra*, v. 65). The very surface of the earth, like the plebeian body unable to contain its disease, is split open to reveal Cocytus (vv. 67ff.), and now it gapes wide (*perfossa dehiscit / molibus insanis tellus*, vv. 90–1). In her speech at vv. 102–21, Fortuna directs Dis to open up his realm (*pande, age*) imaged as a 'thirsty' body (*sitentia regna*, v. 116), just as Eumolpus promised to 'open up' the picture of the fall of Troy at *Sat.* 89 in a gesture which mimics the 'opening up' of the Trojan horse (*itaque conabor opus versibus pandere*). The chthonic gods physically lust and thirst after civil war: Dis says, *iam pridem nullo perfundimus ora cruore* / 'It's been a long time since my lips dripped with gore' (vv. 96–7), and Fortuna cries, *et mihi cordi / quippe cremare viros et sanguine pascere luxum* / 'I will relish burning the men and feeding my lust on their blood' (vv. 109–10).

The rupture of greedily stuffed bodies, which I have explored as a unifying motif in the *Satyricon* so far, reaches a climax in civil war (as emphasized in Lucan's *Pharsalia*) and in Eumolpus' *Bellum Civile*. We have seen that the collapse of incorporation in times (and poems) of civil war explodes over a huge (narrative) area, blowing readers back to previous episodes which all seem, to various extents, to conceal the germs of civil war beneath the surface, just seething to emerge. The *Bellum Civile's* containment of the fall of Troy (as told in the *Troiae Halosis, Aeneid* II and a panoply of different versions),[38] which tells *the* story of the breach of

37 Echoing also *Aen.* 2.265 (*invadunt urbem somno vinoque sepultam* / 'They invaded a city buried in sleep and wine'). This repetition has the effect of implying that the people of Rome have not learnt from their mistakes because they are too concerned with present pleasures. This attitude is exemplified in Trimalchio and his freedmen guests, whose objective is to erase their slave-past and to enjoy each day as if it were their last.

38 See Erskine (1998) for an account of works themed around the Trojan war which have not survived.

incorporation, is just the most dramatic example of this poem's radical strategy of embodiment which exemplifies the heteroglossic strategy of the *Satyricon* as a whole.

Because of the detailed way in which Petronius has so far linked the hedonistic stuffing of the body with luxury food and the enthusiastic consumption of canonic literary texts, it seems almost that civil war in the *Satyricon* erupts as a direct result of the sophisticated learning processes now demanded of the young orator and scholar, as described in *Sat.* 1–5 by Encolpius and Agamemnon. Civil war seems to epitomise the kind of visceral, headline-grabbing poetry contemporary writers are *bound* to spurt out when they have filled themselves to bursting point with literary knowledge: as Agamemnon decrees in the poem at *Sat.* 5, the contemporary Roman writer reaches his peak when he sings of feasts and wars in bellicose tones (*truci canore*). It is not so much that one has to be 'full of literature' to compose poetry on civil war, as Eumolpus argues in *Sat.* 118.6, but rather that when a man is *plenus litteris*, *all* he can do is write about civil war, in one shape or form. *Epulae* and *bella* are not so much opposites as two sides of the same coin. When the contemporary poet comes to recite (that is to eject contained literary knowledge), he becomes a kind of *Furor*, raging free from the reins of classical discourse and revelling in the seditious energy embodied in civil war that is as creative as it is destructive.

What such lines of argument suggest is this: that when we approach Eumolpus' *Bellum Civile* as the oratorical exemplum it pretends to be in *Sat.* 118, a mediocre academic exercise in summarising 'civil war epic' which challenges studious readers to spot references to Lucan, Virgil, Ovid, Livy, with a view to deciding who comes out on top, we are partly, if not entirely, missing the point. As Eumolpus suggests in his introduction, poetry (like the *mimus*) intends to deceive; Eumolpus recites the *Bellum Civile*, we must remember, in the guise not only of Poet, but also of a bare-faced liar (the bailiff recommends deceit as the direct path to wealth at *Sat.* 116.5). This is not a set-piece which can continue to contain its material within its 'body', as Eumolpus advises in *Sat.* 118 (*ne sententiae emineant extra corpus orationis expressae*).[39] Rather, it is a poem which dramatises the complete collapse of such integration and self-containment as the core implication of civil war. Here as elsewhere, the *Satyricon* wants to prevent us from deciphering the relationship between what is inside and outside

[39] Cf. Zeitlin (1971a: 639), who argues that such 'formal exposition of cliches' at *Sat.* 5, 88 and here at 118 'are undercut in a complex way by those who make those formal expositions'.

the *Bellum Civile*, or from containing it (to use Petronius' metaphor) within our own bodies: as Connors rightly says, this is an 'indigestible lump of epic'.[40] This poem wants to defy contextualisation, to rubbish 'context' itself as a civilising term of division that has no place in the chaotic killing fields of civil war, where 'enemies' are compatriots and where everyone is always in the same boat.

I do not mean to imply that we can (or even are meant to) resist reading the *Bellum Civile* investigatively, noticing repeated images, references, quotations, allusions and trying to make sense of them in a deliberate, structured way. Therein lies the exhilarating pleasure of reading any complex piece of literature, and the *Satyricon* especially. I have avoided exploring the *Bellum Civile* on this level, partly because there are many excellent studies which already fulfil this role, but more importantly because my aim has been to examine how the poem's intense allusiveness contributes to a more general debate about the violent energy born of excessive consumption, which is imaged here and throughout the *Satyricon* in the human body. This poem tells us that it is impossible to write about civil war in a way that neatly *contains* and divides, just as civil war itself works to rupture incorporation, tearing bodies and ripping into the landscape. As writing about civil war, according to Eumolpus in *Sat.* 118, represents the difficulty of all writing in a Neronian era, so reading the *Bellum Civile* is a pivotal point in the *Satyricon*'s confrontation of its readers' interpretative abilities, their capacity to make sense of the confusing divisions and slippages between insides and outsides, poetry and prose, text and context.

[40] Connors (1998) 160.

CHAPTER 6

Regurgitating Polyphemus

After the chaotic flood of civil war poetry, which enacted the violent consequences of over-consumption (of luxury food and literature), the gang enter Croton – that infamous and problematic city of metamorphosis. From this point until the end of the text (as we have it), the focus is almost entirely on Encolpius, as he tells of his painful encounters with Circe, Chrysis, Proselenos and Oenothea in his role as *polyaenus* Odysseus. From chapter 124 onwards, the *Satyricon* is more difficult to read than ever. Not only is the text conspicuously fragmented, but so too is our perspective, as epic narratives are undone or reshuffled, and our narrator's credibility, as well as physical integrity, are undermined yet further. Recognisable names and epithets mean that these troublesome passages cannot fail to look 'Homeric', yet we are constantly challenged to decipher the relationship between the *Satyricon* and other works, and to question straightforward interactions between text and 'model'. In this chapter I will examine possible approaches to this dilemma, starting with the proposal, first formulated by Klebs,[1] that the *Satyricon* parodies the epic theme of a hero hounded by an avenging god: most famously, Poseidon's pursuit of Odysseus in the *Odyssey*. In the episodes at Croton, it is suggested, Encolpius comes face to face not with Poseidon but with Priapus, the god he first offends when he interrupts his rites at Quartilla's secret chapel at *Sat.* 16 (*vos sacrum ante cryptam turbastis*), and is then forced to worship (*etiam dormire vobis in mente est, cum sciatis Priapi genio pervigilium deberi?* / 'How can you even think about sleeping when you

[1] Klebs (1889). This argument is accepted by Sullivan (1968a, see 216), Walsh (1970: 76–7) and Conte (1996, e.g. 94), and developed by Connors (1998: 26–33). Cichorius (1922) argues for the possibility that Encolpius has committed some offence against Priapus at the beginning of the novel, for which he is being punished in the text we have. The theory of epic parody is problematised briefly by Slater (1990: 40, 182), who notes that Encolpius compares himself at 139.2 to a range of heroic figures and not simply to Odysseus, while Baldwin (1973b) attempts to refute the notion of any Priapus theme in the *Satyricon*.

know full well that it is your duty to devote a wakeful night to Priapus' genius?' 21.7).[2] I will argue that, far from presenting a comic, 'novelistic' alternative to the epic revenge plot as many critics suggest, the addition of Priapus undermines a rhetoric of definition and differentiation, epitomising the *Satyricon*'s voracious, sexualised incorporation of literature and its multiplication of perspectives on the literary past.

When he leaves Quartilla's brothel to dine at the house of Trimalchio, Encolpius encounters Priapus again, in a different guise. The guests are presented with a grand dish of cakes and fruits, crowned in the centre by a pastry Priapus depicted gathering up the delicacies in his wide apron.[3] However, when touched, the cakes ejaculate a nasty saffron liquid which stains the gobs[4] of the greedy (*omnes enim placentae omniaque poma etiam minima vexatione contacta coeperunt effundere crocum, et usque ad os molestus umor accidere* / 'For all the cakes and all the fruits, however lightly they were touched, began to spurt out saffron, and the horrid liquid even spurted into our mouths', 60.6). The guests assume the dish is sacred,[5] and promptly salute Augustus (*Augusto, patri patriae, feliciter* / 'God bless Augustus, father of his nation') before loading their napkins with fruit, thus mirroring the actions of Priapus himself. Throughout the *Satyricon*, as I have emphasised, we are made aware of the discomforting slippage between food and literature, and between eating, reading and sexual intercourse: for example, when the gang fall into Quartilla's clutches after offending Priapus, the sodomite offers an appetiser of lusty verse before getting to work on Encolpius (*consumptis versibus suis immundissimo me basio conspuit* / 'When we'd consumed his verses he smothered me with a filthy kiss',[6]

[2] As Connors discusses (1998: 28–9), Servius, commenting on *Aen.* 3.57, cites an episode from Petronius in which a plague at Massilia was expiated by feeding a poor man at public expense for a year and then driving him out of the city. This may indicate that the *Satyricon* began with a plague caused by the wrath of Priapus, although we can only speculate.

[3] We read about similar pastries in Martial, 14.69 and 9.2.3.

[4] I suggest that 'mouth' is a more appropriate translation of *os* than 'face' here: the joke, which perhaps exploits the ambiguity of *os* in Latin, is that eating the cakes is always preceded by and therefore interpreted as oral penetration, a violation that parallels Priapus' (Priapic poetry's) threat to rape and defile thieves who come near his orchards. These lines pick up on the use of *accidere* + *ad* to describe a voice or speech falling on ears/minds, e.g. Lucr. 2.1024; Livy 24.46.5; Quint. *Inst.* 12.10.75. *in os* is used at *Sat.* 67.2 to mean 'into her mouth' (*aquam in os suum non coniciet* / 'she won't let water come anywhere near her mouth').

[5] Perhaps because saffron was used in religious ritual, as well as in theatres, and as a perfume or air-freshener. Trimalchio has sawdust coloured with saffron and vermilion sprinkled on the dining room floor at *Sat.* 68.6.

[6] The filthy kiss probably refers to oral sex (Encolpius eats the *cinaedus*' verse, the *cinaedus* eats Encolpius), as it does throughout Martial, e.g. the Postumus poems in Book II (10, 12, 21, 23).

23.4),[7] while Quartilla refers to her sex slave Giton as her daily ration, not to be taken after such a rich meal (*hodie enim post asellum diaria non sumo*, 24.7).[8]

In *Sat.* 60, the priapic pastries spout unpleasant juices (*coeperunt effundere*) right into the mouths of the guests, mimicking oral rape and predicting that eating the cakes can never *not* be read as penetration: indeed Encolpius' follow-up remark that the guests gather up fruit into their napkins (*ipsi mappas implevimus*) just as he will make sure Giton's 'lap' gets well 'filled' (*ego praecipue, qui nullo satis amplo munere putabam me onerare Gitonis sinum* / 'me especially, as I reckoned I could never load Giton's lap with a large enough gift', 60.7) makes the joke even more blatant. Connors' wishful thinking that 'A pastry Priapus is a benign version of the sexual threat figured in the "real" Priapus'[9] underestimates the power of metaphor in the *Satyricon*, and assumes that the 'imagined' is more innocuous than the 'real' in a text which continually obfuscates such distinctions. Yet such comforting thoughts pinpoint precisely how cake-rape sets traps for its readers, as well as for its consumers. The use of the verb *effundere* to describe the spurting of sticky fluid sets the threats of Priapus (which are verbally as well as sexually aggressive)[10] alongside the performance of poetry throughout the *Satyricon*, imaged, as I have argued, as a liquid outpouring from the poet's body (*defundes pectore verba*, 5 v. 22; *eiusmodi carmina effudit*, 23.2; *haec mulier effudit*, 109.1; *cum haec… effudisset*, 124.2; *haec ut iratus effudi*, 132.11). As we swallow the implications of Trimalchio's, and Encolpius' bad jokes, we unfortunately cannot be as oblivious as the guests, who are being force-fed priapic verse and having words put straight into their mouths.[11]

We are perhaps reminded here of the goddess Fama in *Aen.* 4.195, who pours dangerous gossip and half-truths into the mouths of men (*haec passim dea foeda virum diffundit in ora* / 'Everywhere, the foul goddess poured

[7] The verses 'poured out' by the sodomite are written in Sotadeans, a metre especially associated with *cinaedi*, after the poetry of first-century Sotades. The implicit 'opening' up of his body in the gushing forth of poetry illustrates the *cinaedus*' role as passive, penetrated sexual partner, as reflected in the poem itself: bodies of the *spatalocinaedi* are soft (*molles*) and loose (*facili, agili*). For the remaining fragments of Sotades' work, see Powell (1925: 238–45). Compare *Sat.* 23.3 with *Iolaus* lines 14ff., Stephens and Winkler (1995: 369); Athenaeus, 14.620e; Strabo, 14.648; Martial, 2.86.2. See Connors (1998: 31–2) on the use of Sotadeans in the *Satyricon* as 'another form of novelty epic parody'.

[8] *asellus*, a kind of fish here, plays on the associations of hypersexual asses.

[9] Connors (1998) 30.

[10] Priapus is also poetry, *Priapea*.

[11] Compare Persius, 1.79–81: *hos pueris monitus patres* **infundere** *lippos / cum videas, quaerisne unde haec sartago loquendi / venerit in linguas?* / 'and when you see half-blind dads pouring lessons like this into their kids' ears, do you stop to wonder how their tongues came to be laced with that filthy ragu?'

these words into the mouths of men'). Fama here is mischievously allied with the (traditionally 'oral') epic poet: she and Virgil are both telling (singing) the same story, the same intoxicating, world-changing mix of truth and untruths (*et pariter facta atque infecta canebat* / 'She sang fiction and lies in equal portion', *Aen.* 4.190), passed on and retold by word of mouth. Inherent in Virgil's repulsive image of Fama is the equally disturbing idea of the manipulative power of poetry, the notion that readers can be quite literally *fed* ideology. At a crucial point in the text at which the tragedy of Dido demonstrates how difficult it really is to read the *Aeneid* as politically straightforward, the poet's voice whispers in our ears: 'What are you being made to feel? Do you really believe what you are reading?'

We hear little more of Priapus in the text as we have it until *Sat.* 133. Encolpius has been impotent since his unfortunate encounter with Circe, and attributes the curse to Priapus. He now arrives at Priapus' shrine, where he confesses in verse that he has sinned and asks to make amends (*quisquis peccat inops, minor est reus. hac prece quaeso, / exonera mentem culpaeque ignosce minori* / 'When a poor man sins, it's a lesser crime. This is my prayer: take a load off my mind and forgive my minor offence', 133.3 vv. 10–11). When the priestess of the shrine, Oenothea, offers to treat his condition, the resulting therapy, involving beatings (*Sat.* 134) and rape with a leather dildo (138), punishes Encolpius further, leaving him traumatised. Later, when he kills a goose which attacks him as he is making his escape, he soon learns that he has offended Priapus once again (*occidisti Priapi delicias, anserem omnibus matronis acceptissimum* / 'You have killed the darling of Priapus, the goose beloved of all married women', 137.2), and is forced to bribe Oenothea with gold pieces. In *Sat.* 139, Encolpius seals his self-image as Odysseus by claiming, in verse, that he has been a victim of Priapus' wrath all along, just as Laomedon had to face up to Apollo and Poseidon, Pelias felt Juno's anger, and Ulysses lived in fear of Neptune:[12]

> non solum me numen et implacabile fatum
> persequitur. prius Inachiae Tirynthius ora
> exagitatus onus caeli tulit, ante profanus
> Laomedon gemini satiavit numinis iram,
> Iunonem Pelias sensit, †tulit inscius arma†

[12] This poem mimics the beginning of Ov. *Tr.* 1.2, especially 9–12 (*saepe ferox cautum petiit Neptunus Ulixen* / 'Fierce Neptune often attacked the wily Ulysses' (9). Encolpius has already pictured himself as an exile in the wasteland of Croton (*dii deaeque, quam male est extra legem viventibus* / 'Gods and goddesses, how hard it is to live outside the law', 125.4).

Telephus et regnum Neptuni pavit Ulixes.
me quoque per terras, per cani Nereos aequor
Hellespontiaci sequitur gravis ira Priapi.

I am not the only one hounded by gods and cruel fate.
Before me Tiryns' son, driven from the Inachian shore,
bore heaven's weight. Profane Laomedon
sated the wrath of twin deities, Pelias felt
Juno's ire, Telephus bore arms unawares, and
Ulysses went pale at Neptune's realm.
Now Hellespontine Priapus is fired up and stalks his prey
through lands and over Nereus' white-haired waves.

Connors makes the neat point that the substitution of Poseidon for Priapus suits the novelistic genre: whereas Poseidon is grand, cosmic, epic, king of the ocean, Priapus is domestic, private, comic, his role merely to watch over gardens and threaten thieves with rape: thus 'Priapus is to Poseidon . . . as novel is to epic'.[13] Yet Priapus does not merely replace Poseidon in the *Satyricon*: the forces of Poseidon are present in the shipwreck at *Sat.* 114, for example, when the gang effectively 'escape' from the ship described by Eumolpus as the Cyclops' cave at 101, and Lichas and Tryphaena have complementary dreams at 104 in which they are given advice by Priapus and by a statue of Neptune:

videbatur mihi secundum quietem Priapus dicere: Encolpion quod quaeris, scito a me in navem tuam esse perductum. exhorruit Tryphaena et putes inquit una nos dormisse; nam et mihi simulacrum Neptuni, quod Bais <in> tetrastylo notaveram, videbatur dicere: in nave Lichae Gitona invenies. (104.1–3)

Priapus seemed to tell me in a dream, 'Know that the Encolpius you're looking for has been led by me on board your ship'. Tryphaena shuddered and said, 'You'd think we had slept together, because I dreamed that a statue of Neptune, which I noticed at a gallery in Baiae, said to me: "You will find Giton on Lichas' ship".'

In particular the figure of Poseidon's son Polyphemus is crucial from *Sat.* 97 onwards, when he becomes less a character than a role played alternately by many of the *Satyricon*'s 'actors'. By focusing my reading around the figure or role of the Cyclops, I hope to show that Priapus functions rather as a novelistic *supplement* to Poseidon, multiplying our perspectives on the literary past by summoning up and reinterpreting

[13] Connors (1998: 27). Her analysis follows Conte's (1996: 94): 'As Neptune is to Ulysses, so is Priapus to Encolpius'; there is a 'comic gap' opened up between the two figures of which Encolpius himself is 'unconscious'. Also see Richlin's discussion of the role of Priapus in the *Satyricon* (1992: 190–5).

Homeric narratives.[14] Specifically, the role of Priapus is not merely to retell epic tales in a bawdy, obscene way, but to interpret the suffering of heroes returning from Troy as a series of personal, private crises fought in and through their physical bodies. Priapus, I suggest, plays a key role in the *Satyricon*'s ongoing strategy of challenging the integrity of canonical texts via metaphors of destabilised, violated or metamorphosed male bodies. My argument takes issue with Connors' conclusion that Priapus emblematises the *Satyricon*'s delightful, rather than destructive, refashioning of its epic models.[15] Beneath the schoolboy humour, and the farcical spurtings of priapic pastries, we cannot forget that Priapus embodies (destructive) sexual aggression; he is the ithyphallic mascot for Roman satire's seething assaults on society, and on people (readers) in general, a *literary* rebel that is anything *but* sweet.[16] It is no coincidence that his role as motivating force in this, Encolpius' narrative, becomes more prominent when the gang reach Croton, where the aggressive hunting and 'eating' of one's fellow citizens is the norm, and where the poet Eumolpus finally seduces the sex-starved populace once and for all, by offering up his own body on a plate.

In what follows, my discussion of the Homeric characters and scenes encountered on the way to and in Croton will suggest that, within a framework of seeing Poseidon as, or alongside Priapus, we are continually encouraged to read sexual aggression and innuendo back into the *Odyssey*, to see it with completely new eyes. These episodes, I will argue, rehearse the question posed briefly but enigmatically back in *Sat.* 29, when we are told that Trimalchio has pictures of the *Iliad* and the *Odyssey* on his walls, which are then never described to us: how do we visualise Homer's stories? The challenge of perspective staged at the entrance

14 As I have argued throughout, the *Satyricon* continually incorporates, rather than substitutes, themes, characters, styles, rhythms and narratives, while its characters take on multiple identities. The text's dense, allusive texture ensures that our reading process is never linear, always veering off in different directions, so that it seems to be much 'bigger' than it is on the page. Critics, particularly of Senecan tragedy, have explored this effect of amplification as a key feature of Silver Latin literature. See Henderson (1983); Schiesaro (1994) argues that repetition, the incorporation of a mass of literary resources, is designed to make the crimes of Seneca's version of *Thyestes* yet 'more obsessive, more powerful, more guilty' (200), or as the Fury says at 56–7, *Thracium fiat nefas / maiore numero.* Conte (1996: 102 *et passim*) goes some way to discussing this theme or effect in Petronius, in his characterisation of Encolpius' multiple role-play as 'mythomania'.

15 Connors (1998) 30.

16 See especially Horace, *Sat.* 1.8, and discussion in Henderson (1999: 187–91): Horace (and all the male readers he makes stand up and listen) show that, just like the Priapus disguised in your posh dessert, the ironic, cultured Priapus of imperial gardens has lost next to nothing of his blunt brutality. Williams (1999: 18) calls Priapus 'the patron saint of Roman machismo', situating the god at the core of Roman articulations of masculinity.

to Trimalchio's dining room comes back to haunt us in the scenes at *Sat.* 89 and following, as we are drawn into a series of highly visual dramatisations of Homeric narratives.

A key figure in the *Satyricon*'s recollection of Poseidon as narrative motivator in the *Odyssey* is the Cyclops Polyphemus, Poseidon's son: it is the blinded Polyphemus who actually instigates the narrative of revenge when he calls on Poseidon to punish Odysseus by obstructing his return to Ithaca and ensuring that trouble awaits him when he eventually reaches home (*Od.* 9.528–35). In the *Satyricon*, the figure of the Cyclops and the scene of entrapment in Polyphemus' cave in *Odyssey* IX are recalled at three points: First, at *Sat.* 97–8, Encolpius hides Giton from Ascyltos and Eumolpus by tying him to the mattress under his bed, like Ulysses under the ram:

imperavi Gitoni ut raptim grabatum subiret annecteretque pedes et manus institis quibus sponda culcitam ferebat ac sic ut olim Ulixes †pro† ariete adhaesisset, extentus infra grabatum scrutantium eluderet manus. (97.4)

I ordered Giton to get under the bed at once and to hook his feet and hands under the straps which held the mattress to the frame so that, stretched out under the bed like Ulysses clinging to the ram, he might escape the detectives' grasp.

Giton enters into the spirit of the 'escape', and is said to surpass even Ulysses at trickery (*et Ulixem astu simillimo vicit*, 97.5). Ascyltos and Eumolpus fail to find their missing slave until Giton sneezes three times at *Sat.* 98: Eumolpus pulls off the bed-covers to reveal a Ulysses so puny 'even a hungry Cyclops would have passed on eating him' (*videt Ulixem, cui vel esuriens Cyclops potuisset parcere*, 98.5).

Shortly after this, the gang board ship, at *Sat.* 99. When night falls, Encolpius recognises a voice, and hears a woman complain loudly, *si quis deus manibus meis Gitona imponeret, quam bene exulem exciperem* / 'If only some god would deliver Giton into my hands, how well I'd accept the exile' (100.4). Eumolpus has to reveal that the owner of the boat is none other than Lichas of Tarentum, and the purpose of the voyage is to transport banished Tryphaena to Tarentum. Yet at first he does not realise the implications of this, asking *quae autem hic insidiae sunt? aut quis nobiscum Hannibal navigat?* / 'but what's the trap here, and who is the Hannibal on board this ship?' (101.4). After accounting for Lichas' good character, he mocks the others, saying sarcastically, *hic est Cyclops ille et archipirata, cui vecturam debemus* / '*This* is the Cyclops and pirate king to whom we owe our passage'. When Giton explains the story of their feud with Lichas, however, Eumolpus is horrified, repeating his joke about the Cyclops but this time in all seriousness: *fingite nos antrum Cyclopis intrasse. quaerendum est aliquod effugium* / 'Let's pretend we've entered the Cyclops' cave. We need to look for a way out' (101.7). They now begin to plot various escape routes from the monster's cave: in *Sat.* 102 Eumolpus suggests that he conceal the others in clothes and carry them out as luggage,[17] at which point Encolpius protests *ita vero, tamquam solidos alligaturus, quibus non soleat venter iniuriam facere? an tamquam eos qui sternutare non soleamus nec stertere?* / 'What, tie us up like hollow beings whose stomachs never give them any trouble? Or like people who never sneeze or snore?' (102.10), reminding us of Giton's failed imitation of Odysseus' escape from the Cyclops' cave at *Sat.* 98.4, betrayed by a sneeze caused by dusty bedclothes (*ter continuo ita sternutavit* / 'He sneezed three times in a row').

Eumolpus' first thought on how they are to escape is shipwreck: *nisi naufragium †ponimus† et omni nos periculo liberamur* / 'unless we suffer shipwreck and free ourselves from all danger' (101.7). In the *Odyssey*, Odysseus and his men live in constant fear of shipwreck after blinding Polyphemus, escaping from the cave and rousing the anger of Poseidon. Thus on the one hand the *Satyricon*'s reworking of the Odyssean narrative fuses the two threats (the Cyclops, shipwreck), adding the further twist that shipwreck may be their only way out from the cave. On the other, staging the escape from the cave scene on a ship renders literal some key metaphors operating in the *Odyssey*: in Homer's version, Odysseus and his men drive the stake into Polyphemus' eye as if they are drilling through the timber of a ship at 9.384–6. Polyphemus is also said to carry an olive-wood staff which is as big as the mast of a ship (321–3).[18] The same metaphor is used by Euripides in his satyr play, *Cyclops*: at lines 460–4, Odysseus plans to drill the stake into Polyphemus' eye 'just as a ship's joiner whirls his augur with a pair of thongs' (ναυπηγίαν δ'ὡσεί τις ἁρμόςων ἀνὴρ / διπλοῖν χαλινοῖν τρύπανον κωπηλατεῖ, 460–2), and at lines 503–6, the drunken Cyclops declares that his 'hull is full of wine right up to the top deck of my belly' (πλέως μὴν οἴνου / γάνυμαι <δὲ> δαιτὸς ἥβῃ, / σκάφος ὁλκὰς ὥς γεμισθεῖς / ποτὶ σέλμα γαστρὸς ἄκρας). When Eumolpus tells his audience to imagine they have boarded this ship only to have entered

[17] This plan recalls Cleopatra's idea to meet Julius Caesar secretly by wrapping herself inside a mattress, told by Plutarch (*Caes.* 49.1–2). In this analogy, both Giton and Encolpius would play Cleopatra, another instance of multiplying roles: see my discussion below.

[18] Ovid at *Met.* 13.782–3 changes the staff from olive wood to pine wood. Hopkinson (2000: 116–17) suggests that this might be designed to emphasise the ship simile from Homer, because *pinus* can (by metonymy) also mean a ship.

the Cyclops' cave (*fingite nos antrum Cyclopis intrasse*, 101.7), the image is made even more dramatic by the recollection of Homer's metaphor of Polyphemus as a great ship, steadied in the wind by a mast: Petronius' visceral rewritings situate the characters of the *Satyricon* not just in the Cyclops' cave, but in his stomach. They have already been eaten.

Yet they have also been here before. As well as imaging the dilemma of the gang on board ship, the *antrum Cyclopis* casts us back to the dramatic situations of the *Cena* and the *Troiae Halosis*, and forward to writing and recitation of the *Bellum Civile*. Indeed, throughout the *Satyricon*, Encolpius and his gang never get out of the dark, enclosed spaces in which they are perpetually trapped, but simply move from one metaphorical cave to another – from the rhetorical school and dark marketplace, to Quartilla's musty brothel, Trimalchio's house, the ship, and eventually Croton. As I have explored above, Trimalchio's dining room is described as a deadly underworld or labyrinth in which our heroes are trapped (e.g. *homines miserrimi et novi generis labyrintho inclusi* / 'us poor souls were locked into a new kind of labyrinth', 73.1); the menu itself is the work of a chef called Daedalus, and the monstrous Trimalchio looks even more like the Minotaur when he says that his rumbling stomach sounds like 'there's a bull in there' (*Sat.* 47.3). In chapter three, I argued that cannibalism is always a latent threat in the *cena*: the situation on board ship, in which the gang are trapped in the Cyclops' cave, is all too similar, particularly when we remember that Odysseus and his men were originally dinner guests of Polyphemus.[19] Trimalchio's dining room is also ship-like: its entrance is described as *quasi embolum navis aeneum* / 'just like the bronze prow of a ship'.[20] In *Sat.* 30.1, the fall-out from the adventures of the previous chapters, or perhaps even the *cena* itself, is anticipated as a sea-storm (*cum maesti deliberaremus quonam genere praesentem evitaremus procellam* / 'We were depressed and deliberated how best to avoid the looming squall', 26.7); just before they escape, Encolpius and Ascyltos nearly drown in a fishpond, and are pulled out trembling onto dry land (72.8), as if they are victims of a shipwreck; when Trimalchio is preparing for his funeral, he tells of his career as a shipbuilder, which was ruined when all his ships were wrecked in Neptune's storm (*uno die Neptunus tercenties sestertium devoravit* / 'Neptune swallowed three million, in one day!' 76.4) – and yet

[19] See Goldhill (1991: 31 ff.) for discussion of Polyphemus' violation of the expected norms of guest friendship.

[20] The adjective *aeneum* (evoking Aeneas) hints at an amalgamation of references, especially in retrospect after Trimalchio's epic story about Corinthian bronze at *Sat.* 50, melted down from *omnes statuas aeneas* following the fall of Troy.

he went on to build bigger, grander ships and a house, all vessels for his multiplying wealth (76.5ff.).

A further parallel for the *antrum Cyclopis* on board ship is Eumolpus' first poem, the *Troiae Halosis*. Like the ship-cave, the Trojan Horse is a hollow wooden structure described by Eumolpus as a cave (*ingens antrum et obducti specus*, v. 7), which like Polyphemus' den is the site and symbol for Greek guile and trickery in times of crisis.[21] Greek soldiers are contained within cave and horse, and escape by means of expert rhetorical deceit, by the confusion of identities: in Homer the men flee the cave as sheep, whereas in Petronius each heroic leader slips out of the horse like a 'four-legged animal' (*quadrupes, TH* v. 59). The Greeks kill Polyphemus (who has already become a cave-tomb for some of them) on the return from Troy by the same method used to defeat the Trojans: by lulling him into a false sense of security with the power of rhetoric, getting him drunk and waiting for him to fall asleep before making the fatal move.

Being trapped in and breaking out of caves provides the violent, symbolic energy for the writing and recitation of Eumolpus' second poem, the *Bellum Civile*, which I discussed at length in chapter five. As we have seen, the point in the *Bellum Civile* at which corrupt society is about to topple into civil war is envisaged as a landscape's inability to contain its volcanic, chthonic interior: the earth gapes wide, mountains are hollowed out, caves groan (*perfossa dehiscit / molibus insanis tellus, iam montibus haustis / antra gemunt*, vv. 90–3). Fortuna, like a man-eating beast let loose, salivates in expectation of human flesh (*iam pridem nullo perfundimus ora cruore* / 'It's been a long time since my lips dripped with blood', v. 96), a line which recalls Pythagoras of Croton's speech at *Met.* 15.96–8 (*nec polluit ora cruore* / 'nor did men defile their lips with blood', 98).[22] Cannibalism was the fuel for paranoia in Ovid's Croton and throughout the *Metamorphoses*, in which a world in perpetual flux could contain human souls in plants, liquids, even gases, as well as in animals we might ordinarily eat. In Petronius' Croton, the eventual port for Lichas' ship and the site for the recitation of the *Bellum Civile*, this threat of cannibalism is made horrifically real.

[21] In the *Aeneid*, the same word, *moles*, is used to describe both the Trojan Horse (*et molem mirantur equi* / 'They marvelled at the mass of the horse', 2.32) and Polyphemus (*videmus / ipsum inter pecudes vasta se mole moventem* / 'We saw his mighty mass shifting among the sheep', 3.655–6): both are gigantic structures, half-beast, and half-man, while both contain men, eaten or hidden, in their bellies.

[22] *ora cruor* is also a half-line at *Aen.* 10.728, describing the gory jaws of bestial, man-eating Mezentius. Also, *BC* 140 (*sanguineo . . . imbre*) echoes *Met.* 15.788 (*inter nimbos guttae cecidere cruentae*), as well as Lucan, 6.224 (*imbre cruento*).

As I have suggested, the eruption of monstrous, cannibalistic forces from caves is a metaphor not only for the raw, inhuman violence of civil war, but for the dark creative energy of the war poet, and indeed for poetry in general, imagined as gushing out of bodies crammed to bursting point with consumed material and digested ideas.[23] After conjuring up the image of the ship as a Cyclops' cave, Eumolpus the poet is eventually discovered groaning like a wild beast in his cabin (*quasi cupientis exire gemitum*) as the ship sinks, madly scribbling verses onto a vast parchment (*membranaeque ingenti versus ingerentem*, 115.2). Earlier, I suggested that as well as epitomising Horace's model of the mad poet as a bear trapped in a pit,[24] Eumolpus here seems almost to be writing the *Bellum Civile* from inside the belly of the Trojan Horse, hurling words onto animal hide; his moaning (*audimus murmur... et gemitum*) mimics the sound that echoes forth from the belly of the horse when it is struck by Laocoön's axe (*dum murmurat, roborea moles spirat alieno metu, TH* 25–6; *gemitum dedere cavernae, Aen.* 2.53). Instead of acting as a deceptive, aggressive Trojan horse himself, as he did in the recitation of the *Troiae Halosis*, the poet of the *Bellum Civile* seems to have lost control, to have been swallowed up by his own poetic trick – a powerful metaphor for the intellectually and emotionally suffocating (as well as politically risky) task of writing civil war epic.

Now, the image of the ship of civil war poetry as a Cyclops' cave adds a new dimension: in his bestial poetic frenzy, Eumolpus looks very much like a blinded Polyphemus, his animal cries reverberating round the walls of the cave which is also a grave for so many Greeks (*Od.* 9.395). As Encolpius pleads with him to leave the cabin before he drowns, Eumolpus resists furiously, saying, *sinite me sententiam explere; laborat carmen in fine* / 'Let me complete my thought; I'm struggling with the ending' (115.4): as he writes, he is deep in the jaws of civil war; madness is raising her gory head (*sanguineum late tollit caput, BC* v. 259), and Discord, her face caked in blood, gazes down onto the world's shores and predicts that the bays of Thessaly will be dyed with the blood of men (*BC* vv. 293–4): in writing

[23] The fearful, chthonic energy of caves and underworlds is the inspiration and source of poetry in Seneca's *Oedipus*, as Schiesaro argues (1997a, and forthcoming). In this play, poetry is a revelation of truths that had been carefully hidden away from an upper world dominated by reason. When poetry erupts from below, the Erinyes become the 'new Muses', and the poet a '*vates* who through his song can bring to life the frightening creatures buried in the underworld'. In his darkness, the blind seer Teiresias embodies 'a power deeply rooted in the chthonic realms of blood and passions' (96–7). Also see Segal (1983) on how Seneca's revelation of subterranean horrors is mirrored or magnified in images of enclosing or penetrating hidden bodily cavities.

[24] *Ars P.* 457–9, 472–3.

about the horror of war, Eumolpus has to (re)live it, and in some sense be responsible for *creating* it.[25] Trapped in his grave-cave, Eumolpus is not only 'swallowed up' by Virgilian epic, but as a man-eating beast, has to suffer for his ravenous consumption of literary resources.

The *Bellum Civile* provides the literary accompaniment to the gang's arrival at war-torn Croton, Petronius' city of cannibals which in Ovid was the spiritual home of Pythagoras where all meat-eaters (even, all *eaters*) were condemned as cannibalistic Cyclopes (*Met.* 15.92–3).[26] So too the poem's author, Eumolpus, is drawn onto the fictional stage set for civil war, becoming himself a cannibalistic figure whose literary output is seen to be the product of raw, uncivilised forces. As well as being reminded, as critics have often noted, of Horace's image of the mad poet in the *Ars Poetica*, we might also focus on his portrait in *Epist.* 2.2 of the creative genius, whose work looks effortless but conceals a tortuous creative process that mimics the animal lurchings of a satyr or a Cyclops: *ludentis speciem dabit et torquebitur, ut qui / nunc Satyrum, nunc agrestem Cyclopa movetur* / 'He will look like he's larking around when in fact he's being tortured, like a dancer who plays a satyr or a Cyclops' (124–5).[27] In Petronius, as in Horace, the Cyclops is made to represent the paradoxical power and vulnerability of Roman poetry and poet: although metaphorically gigantic in scale (the *Bellum Civile*, regardless of its length, is a huge work, an *ingens opus* written on an *ingens membrana*),[28] and fearsome in its consumption of lesser bits of literature, this poem is liable to reel out of control, dragging its writer with it. We might even see the Cyclops as a crucial visual symbol for the shape and structure of the *Satyricon*, which lurches wildly between scenes and styles within its vast, sophisticated frame.

Yet what do the figures of the Cyclops and his shipwrecking father Poseidon have to do with the superimposed narrative of Priapus' revenge? Let us return to the first 'escape from the cave' re-enactment at *Sat.* 97: at this point Giton, led by Encolpius, is not trying to hide from a monster who wants to eat him, but from a lover who wants to bed him. Priapus is exerting his ithyphallic influence even here, as the Cyclops' bestial desire to eat human flesh translates into an aggressive sexual urge, a hunger to penetrate. It is tempting, perhaps even irresistible, to

[25] As O'Higgins has argued (1988), the civil-war poet must be complicit with his material, and must create as well as rewrite the *nefas* of civil war: 'impiety and a taste for the *nefas* are virtual prerequisites for the singer of civil war'. The *vates* demonstrates 'loathing for his theme, and for himself' (217). These sentiments are echoed by Masters (1992) and Henderson (1988: 123): 'this poem . . . inflicts pain and suffering . . . this text screams a curse upon its readers and upon itself'.

[26] *iuvat ritusque referre Cyclopum* / 'You relish repeating the Cyclopes' custom.'

[27] Ahl (1984b: 55) discusses these lines briefly.

[28] *Sat.* 118, 115.

go back now to read the Odyssean narrative as a drama about male sexual power, in which Odysseus finally proves his virility by penetrating Polyphemus' eye, leaving him one big bloody hole. We are reminded of the filter through which Petronius reads Homer's Cyclops – the figure of Polyphemus in Ovid, *Met.* 13.744–897, whose cannibalism is transformed into sexual desire for Galatea. When he is told by Teiresias that Odysseus will take his one eye, he replies *altera iam rapuit* / 'Someone has taken it already', casting Galatea in the role of elegiac *puella*, after Corinna and Cynthia (*o facies oculos nata tenere meos* / 'That face was born to snare my eyes', Ov. *Am.* 2.17.12; *prima suis miserum me cepit ocellis* / 'She was the first to snare me, her victim, with her eyes', Prop. 1.1), and casting himself as *miles amator* ('soldier of love') on an epic scale. Polyphemus' blinding, foreseen by the blind prophet, becomes an unmissable erotic cliché, a predictable fantasy of submission which is made to look like brute macho pride before a fall: Odysseus' prophesied attack makes a castration scene out of the giant's clumsy Ovidian drag act.

Eating and sex are explicitly aligned in both Ovid and Petronius' Cyclops tales, just as they are in Quartilla's brothel, where submissive Giton is part of Quartilla's daily diet (*diaria*), in the *cena*, where the guests are force-fed the ejaculations of priapic cakes, and in Croton, where sexual pleasure is replaced by financial (and we are led to imagine, cannibalistic) consumption. As engineer of the plot to get Giton out of the cave, Encolpius is not merely punished by shipwreck (by Poseidon), but by impotence (by Priapus). The threat to his bodily integrity (as an impotent he can only be penetrated) is a constant reminder of the risk of being eaten in the Cyclops' cave, which after the farce of *Sat.* 97 becomes all too real a situation on board Lichas' ship.

Our perspective on the scenes of *Odyssey* IX has been skewed. A rewriting that centres on the figure of Odysseus as sexual object rather than as food for Polyphemus is both funnier, more light-hearted than the Homeric story we remember, and at the same time grossly disturbing: it is based on the idea, reflected in society at Croton, that all sexual activity is at some level cannibalistic, that sex involves the incorporation of (bits of) another person; and conversely that sexual contact, whether the participant is active or passive, directly threatens the boundaries of the individual and the integrity of the self. As the gang head towards Croton, we are reminded that this is just the kind of bodily and spiritual exchange that governs the narratives of Ovid's *Metamorphoses*, in which outward physical form becomes almost irrelevant in a literary microcosm in which beings (and texts) are perpetually in flux.

Sat. 97's redoubling of perspectives, and its implicit collapse of eater–eaten, penetrator–penetrated hierarchies, are also achieved through characterisation, or rather its confusion. The important thing to notice first of all is that the perspective of the narrator has changed *vis à vis* the *Odyssey*. It is Encolpius who is telling the story, as well as engineering the plot to hide under the bed, and it is Giton who is playing the role of Odysseus, despite the fact that Encolpius will later go on to live out Odysseus' role as *polyaenus* at Croton; Encolpius appears to be acting alongside Giton as a fellow Greek trapped in the cave, whereas Ascyltos and Eumolpus are both cast as Cyclops, out to eat (that is, to sexually overpower) Giton. Already there are two Polyphemuses (and we have also already seen this multiplication intertextually), yet Encolpius too is Giton's older lover, determined to keep him for his own dinner. When Giton is discovered, having failed, therefore, to 'escape from the cave', Encolpius observes, *videt Ulixem, cui vel esuriens Cyclops potuisset parcere* / 'He saw a Ulysses whom even a starving Cyclops would have spared' (98.5): we are reminded of Polyphemus' taunt at the end of *Odyssey* IX, just before he calls on his father Poseidon to curse Odysseus' fleet ('I always expected some hunk of a man to come along, and now a puny, good for nothing little runt gets me drunk and puts out my eye!' 513–16). To the giant Polyphemus, the Greeks must look like very small morsels indeed, and this is exactly the vantage point from which our grandiose narrator Encolpius is describing the scene, taking on the role (as if we didn't know it all along) of another Cyclops vying for Giton's flesh. With a hungry Cyclops creating as well as narrating the plot, it comes as no surprise that the Homeric tale as told by Odysseus runs off course, with traditional Greek trickery failing miserably and the hero falling rather pathetically into the jaws of Polyphemus. Is this what the monstrous Trimalchio has in mind when he performs a running translation of Homer into Latin at *Sat.* 59.3? *cum Homeristae Graecis versibus colloquerentur, ut insolenter solent, ille canora voce Latine legebat librum.* / 'While the reciters conversed in Greek verse, in their usual arrogant way, he read Latin out loud from a book, in a sing-song voice.' In Trimalchio's Roman version, well-known mythical characters are recast and act out alternative, original narratives: either he is simply confused, or, as I suggested in chapter two, the *Cena*'s eccentric director explicitly rewrites Homer, so that simultaneous translation from Greek into Latin becomes a trope for transformation, for the creative energies of a Roman literature working from Greek roots. This ambitious, and on paper rather wild ('confused') Latin translation of Homer is, I would suggest, precisely what we experience in Encolpius' restaging of

Odysseus' escape from the cave in *Sat.* 98–9. Importantly, our perspective is altered so that we get to see what it is like when the giant Polyphemus (or in true Neronian style, an actor in the role of Polyphemus), not Odysseus, narrates the scene, and when infamous Greek wit does not quite get its way. Moreover, we get to see how the epic narrator has privileged one cultural and political perspective over others. The question of how readers are influenced, often without realising it, by a narrator's viewpoint, is clearly a problematic one in the *Satyricon*: we are always suspicious of Encolpius as a narrator, both because he frequently shows himself up (whether ironically, self-consciously, or not...) as dense and forgetful, and because his character may or may not be, at any point, Petronius in disguise.

When the cast of Cyclopes and Odysseuses board the ship at *Sat.* 100, they ascend a different stage, and consequently change, or swap, roles. Encolpius indicates in 101.5 that Lichas is now the ogre, the ship is the cave, and Encolpius and friends are Greeks trapped and waiting to be eaten. As many critics have argued, the scenes that follow, in which the gang debate various means of escape, are mini theatrical productions, self-consciously acted and drawing heavily from Greek and Roman comedy, tragedy and satyr plays.[29] The result is often an amateurish drama that jumbles influences (and therefore acting roles) from many different sources. Thus, for example, *Sat.* 101–3 seems to be influenced in part by Euripides' *Cyclops*, so that, as Fedeli and Ferri argue, we might infer that Eumolpus is playing the role of Euripides' satyr, who functions as a mischievous intermediary between Polyphemus and Odysseus (like Silenus, Eumolpus has nothing to fear from Lichas).[30] Yet the point is always that literary sources (Homer/Euripides) overlap, so that in the rather adventurous, free-for-all spirit of Petronian theatre, characters are often playing more than one role, shifting between roles, or playing the same role (so three out of four of the actors in *Sat.* 97–8 want to play Polyphemus, it seems). As we approach Croton, city of metamorphosis, Petronius' world full of constantly performing, interchangeable actors becomes a powerful analogue for a universe governed by corporeal flux.

[29] See in particular Panayotakis (1995: 136–60).

[30] See Fedeli (1981) and Ferri (1988): Ferri argues that the Euripidean model is privileged here, because it is Euripides' addition of lengthy debate and consultation which forms the basis for the dramatic action.

CHAPTER 7

Scars of knowledge

Thus far, I have argued that in the course of the sea voyage, Lichas' ship becomes a metaphorical vessel in which Eumolpus rehearses poetic scenarios in the process of creating the *Bellum Civile* poem. I now want to look more closely at the scenes at *Sat.* 101–8, in which the gang of stowaways experiments with physical disguise as a means of escaping from the ship-cave. I will suggest that all the scenes on board ship are, as it were, preparatory jottings for the final flurry of writing as the ship sinks in *Sat.* 115. In stage-managing versions and revisions of the *Odyssey*'s 'escape from the cave' plot, Eumolpus is preoccupied with textual possibilities, with the (*Satyricon*'s) basic question of how to rework and transform epic narrative in new contexts: moreover, as befits the *Bellum Civile*'s obsession with metaphors of physicality (the diseased body of war, the ruptured body of a war-torn landscape) in a poem etched onto animal skin (*membrana*), Eumolpus' creative experiments for the poem are actually written on the bodies of his students.[1]

Encolpius is the first to suggest at 102 that, being a writer, Eumolpus must have some ink with which they can dye their skin and hair:

inspicite quod ego inveni. Eumolpus tamquam litterarum studiosus utique atramentum habet. hoc ergo remedio mutemus colores a capillis usque ad ungues. ita tanquam servi Aethiopes et praesto tibi erimus sine tormentorum iniuria hilares et permutato colore imponemus inimicis. (102.13)

Look what I've thought of. As a man of learning, Eumolpus is bound to have some ink. So let's use this medicine to dye our hair and everything apart from our nails; then we'll stand by you like Ethiopian slaves, torture-free, and trick our enemies with the change of colour.

The idea that they can get away with splashing writing ink indiscriminately all over their bodies is ridiculous, a comic display of Encolpius'

[1] As I mentioned above, *membrana* was used specifically to make notebooks on which works were first written before being copied out, or 'published' on papyrus. See Fowler (forthcoming).

lack of literary sophistication and an ironic slant on his own writing ability as 'author' of the *Satyricon*: given paper and a pen, the best our narrator can do is make a mess.[2] Even Giton is appalled, joking that even if the ink stayed on, they would merely look like dyed Caucasians, without the African characteristics of thick lips, frizzy hair, foreign-style beards and scarred foreheads: *color arte compositus inquinat corpus, non mutat* / 'artificial colour stains the body but doesn't change it' (102.15). Both Encolpius and Giton are using explicitly literary expressions: *color* can mean 'style' as well as skin tone, and *corpus* is commonly used to refer to the 'body' of a speech or text, for example at *Sat.* 118.5: *praeterea curandum est ne sententiae emineant extra* **corpus** *orationis expressae, sed intexto vestibus* **colore** *niteant* / 'You must also take care that thoughts do not stand out from the body of the speech, but shine like a colour woven into the material'; and in Encolpius' first speech (*Sat.* 2.2): *ut* **corpus** *orationis enervaretur et caderet* / 'so that the body of the speech is emasculated and dies'.[3] Giton's criticism that writing ink would be a cheap attempt at concealment mirrors Encolpius' claim in *Sat.* 1–2: it is no good peppering your bad prose with trendy jargon, or dressing it up with superficial frills, as any audience will see right through to the pale, limp flesh beneath.

The professional poet, however, has more elegant ideas. He will order his barber to shave the heads of each of the men, including their eyebrows (*supercilia*), creating a blank canvas on which Eumolpus can begin writing:

sequar ego frontes notans inscriptione sollerti, ut videamini stigmate esse puniti. ita eaedem litterae et suspicionem declinabunt quaerentium et vultus umbra supplicii tegent. (103.2)

Then I'll come and mark your foreheads with a neat inscription, so that it looks like you've been punished by branding. These same letters will divert nosy people's suspicions and also cover your faces with the shadow of punishment.

In sharp contrast to Encolpius' crude idea of splashing ink everywhere, Eumolpus' plan involves the skilful inscription of neat letters on their

[2] Fowler (forthcoming) argues that ink is generally referred to 'by periphrases and metaphors which often stress its links to other fluids, including bodily fluids like blood and tears'. For example, when Persius complains of the difficulties of writing in *Sat.* 3.12–14, 'he phrases his disgust at the recalcitrant ink in terms which associate it with pathological conditions of the body', i.e. the ink is the writer's black bile.

[3] See Seneca, *Contror.* 3. praef. 13–14, where a first-time orator in the forum, like a gladiator at his first show, is called a *cadet*: 'The school has always been regarded as a sort of gladiator's training camp and the forum as the arena.' For further discussion on Seneca's use of gladiatorial terms to describe the pugnacity of declaimers like Cestius Pius and Cassius Severus, see Sinclair (1995: 123–4).

foreheads in order to make them look like branded slaves, as well as to render them suppliants to his pen.[4] Again, the language he uses is metaphorical: as well as meaning 'forehead', *frons* is used by Tibullus and Ovid, among others, to refer to the outer end of a book roll,[5] whereas *caput*, as in English, is used metaphorically in many different contexts, including a literary one (*caput litterarum* is used by Cicero to mean 'the main argument' or the 'chief matter' in a speech).[6] Encolpius and Giton are to be read like books, and the brands on their foreheads are to stand as bold titles, the first thing a reader sees when he opens up the manuscript. These are tabloid-size, eye-catching advertisements for an exciting text that will impress for its sheer (metaphorical) scale, the *ingens opus* of the 296-line *Bellum Civile*, no less, previewed in the poet's *ingentes litterae* ('huge letters') sketched onto human skin.[7] The idea of preparing a manuscript by removing the hair (later referred to by Eumolpus at 105.2 as dirty: *horridi capilli*) is also a recognisable one. The cliché of Callimachean polish, a reference to the process of preparing the papyrus by pumicing it and smoothing down the fibres with oil,[8] is employed famously by Catullus (his *nugae* are well pumiced), and by Horace, whose image of his first book of *Epistles* as a freshly depilated slave ready for market resonates strikingly with Eumolpus' composition, designed to make Encolpius and Giton look like slaves:

> Vortumnum Ianumque, liber, spectare videris,
> scilicet ut prostes Sosiorum pumice mundus.
> odisti clavis et grata sigilla pudico;
> paucis ostendi gemis et communia laudas,
> non ita nutritus. fuge quo descendere gestis.
> non erit emisso reditus tibi. (*Epist.* 1.20.1–6)

4 This scene reminds us of the story in Herodotus (5.35) about the artistic ingenuity of the Ionian tyrant Histiaeus of Miletus: when Histiaeus was imprisoned by the Persian King Darius, he secretly shaved the head of his most trusted slave and tattooed a message on his scalp with pin and ink: the message read 'Histiaeus to Aristagoras, incite Ionia to revolt'. In a few weeks the slave's hair grew over the tattoo and he was dispatched to the son-in-law Aristagoras as a living letter. On reaching his destination, the slave shaved his head and on reading the message, Aristagoras launched an ill-conceived revolt that ended in the Persian invasion of Greece.

5 Tib. 3.13; Ov. *Tr.* 1.1.110. There are also examples of this usage in Martial, 1.66.10; 3.2.8 and Sen. *Dial.* 9.9.6.

6 *caput* can refer to a fundamental argument, the beginning of a speech, action, sentence or word, and can also mean 'heading' or 'summary': see e.g. Cic. *Verr.* 3.148; Quint. *Inst.* 3.8.10; Cic. *De Or.* 188; *Brut.* 164.

7 The imagining of the ship as a Cyclops' cave captained by a giant Polyphemus has already set a precedent for this creative manipulation of scale.

8 In the first passage of his *Aetia*, Callimachus asks the Graces to rub hair oil on his elegies 'so that they may last many a year'.

You seem, dear book, to be looking in the direction of
Vortumnus and Janus; you clearly want to go on sale,
shined up with Sosian pumice. You hate the keys and seals
so dear to modest volumes. You groan at meagre audiences,
but lap up the crowd – not that that was how I brought you up.
Away with you, go where you itch to go;
once you're let loose, there'll be no coming back.

Callimachean smoothness, the effect Eumolpus is apparently aiming for here, is frequently opposed to the virile hirsuteness of epic, or of other manly, aggressive genres like iambus and satire. Ovid's *Tristia*, in which the exiled author plays the battered Odyssean hero on a mission to get home, presents itself as 'hairy' (*nec fragili geminae poliantur pumice frontes / hirsutus sparsis ut videare comis* / 'Let no brittle pumice bring your double edges to a shine, I want you looking bristled, all roughed-up', 1.1.11–12), which is also how Propertius describes Ennius (4.1, 6.1), while Quintilian recommends that although this type of unshaven eloquence is now strictly passé, an excessively ornamental hair-style is also unacceptable (12.10.47), and that if the writing is good enough, all decoration in the form of either manicure or hairdressing can be dispensed with (8 *pr.*22).[9] Implicitly, then, this is not a good starting point for *real* epic (whether or not we read Eumolpus' barber trick as also a strategy for disguising the 'secret' composition of BIG poetry as *epigramma*). Those who read the *Bellum Civile* as an exercise in writing bad poetry should start laughing here.

The second stage in Eumolpus' experiment is to cover Encolpius' and Giton's faces with the 'usual marks of runaway slaves' (*notum fugitivorum epigramma*, 103–4). The scars of slavery, in Eumolpus' imagination, make a little poem (*epigramma*), scribbled down with the vivacious flair (*liberali manu*) of Agamemnon's educated Roman poet at *Sat.* 5, who has proved himself a free man (*liber*) through intellectual toil, and whose liberty manifests itself in fluent, grand verse, explicitly *written*, not performed, in a private rather than public space (*interdum subducta foro det pagina cursum* / 'Meanwhile let him withdraw from the courts and let his page run free', 5 v. 17). As Agamemnon's ideal Roman poet leaves oratory behind (*subducta foro*) for a private life of silent writing, so Eumolpus composes the first verses of the *Bellum Civile* in absolute secrecy, without an audience, and without even Encolpius and Giton realising what he is really up to.

9 On shaggy hair and hairdressing as metaphors for literary criticism, see Bramble (1974: 74).

Yet in another sense, for Encolpius and Giton the events of *Sat.* 103 are essential preparation for an oratorical performance in the arena of the ship-cave, which was the stage for Euripides' *Cyclops* and the platform for Odysseus' skill as an actor in *Odyssey* IX. They are being marked with false scars for a performance which reminds us again of Encolpius' act in *Sat.* 1.1, in which he pretends to be a young orator displaying his battle scars to seduce an audience (*haec vulnera pro libertate publica excepi* / 'These wounds I suffered for public freedom'; *hunc oculum pro vobis impendi* / 'This eye, I sacrificed for you'; *succisi poplites membra non sustinent* / 'My hamstrung knees can't support my body'). The most persuasive, emotive public speaker is the man who makes himself powerful by pretending to be physically and emotionally vulnerable, just like Encolpius and Giton here, dressed up as shamed, mutilated slaves in order to win the pity of, and eventually outwit, their captives. Odysseus himself was no stranger to this technique, and his triumph in the palace of Ithaca was made possible by his ability and strength to disguise himself as a worthless, streetworn beggar, just as he escaped from Polyphemus' cave by acting as *outis*, no one. Thus the orator's use of body language to construct an argument and to persuade an audience is literalised in the scene at *Sat.* 103, where physical performance is predicated on inscribing the actors' bodies with a written text. Encolpius and Giton plan not merely to use body language to back up their rhetoric: instead, their bodies *are* the rhetoric, and have incorporated the orator's written script.[10]

Similarly, there is a sense in which we cannot separate the writing (or the *writtenness*) of the *Bellum Civile* from its impact in performance: as I argued in chapter five, we must not forget that the *Bellum Civile* is itself part of the elaborate scheme to get into Croton, and its recitation is another layer in the *mimus* conceived by Eumolpus at *Sat.* 117. Eumolpus is a poet, but he also appears as a teacher of rhetoric: when his actors pledge their bodies to him like gladiators (*tamquam legitimi gladiatores domino corpora animasque religiosissime addicimus*, 117.5), they play the role of students signing up for their first term at a school of oratory, which was often likened to a gladiatorial training camp.[11] We might see the scenes on Lichas' ship, in which Eumolpus takes control of Encolpius and Giton's bodies, as well as body language, as preparatory work not only for the

[10] At 103.6, they are *silentio compositi*, which looks like an overt reference to their experience of the 'writing' process. Connors (1998: 144) makes a similar point about *Sat.* 117, when Eumolpus writes Giton and Encolpius into his mime as *auctorati* (gladiators).

[11] See e.g. Seneca, *Contr.* 3. praef. 13–14.

act on board ship, but also for the performance of the *Bellum Civile* and the cleverly orchestrated march on Croton.

The action on board ship now shifts to Lichas and Tryphaena, who have both been informed in dreams of Giton's presence (104). Lichas' suspicions are aroused further when he is told that men have been spotted cutting their hair, a terrible omen, because it looked like the final offering of a doomed crew (*quod imitaretur naufragorum ultimum votum*, 103.5). Eumolpus is forced to admit that he oversaw the hair-cutting incident, protesting however that it was all done innocently for reasons of hygiene (*quia [nocentes] horridos longosque habebant capillos, ne viderer de nave carcerem facere, iussi squalorem damnatis auferri* / 'It was because the guilty men had long dirty hair and I did not want to make the ship look like a prison, so I ordered the filth to be cleaned off the brutes', 105.2). Incidentally, he adds, their scruffy locks concealed the branding marks of slaves, which are there to be read (*simul ut notae quoque litterarum non obumbratae comarum praesidio totae ad oculos legentium acciderent* / 'Also, I wanted the branding marks to be fully exposed for everyone to read and not covered up by their hair'). Eumolpus wallows in the fiction of his superiority over a band of filthy, scarred slaves, and does nothing to prevent their punishment. Yet as Giton and Encolpius are whipped, their bodies marked by further scars, or 'letters', we as readers are propelled from Homeric scenes of disguise (in the Cyclops' cave) to Homeric scenes of recognition: Giton's cries identify him at once to Tryphaena and her maids, while Lichas runs up as if he has heard Encolpius' voice, only to greet his groin, announcing that no one need be surprised that Ulysses' nurse identified her master by a mere scar, when he himself has recognised a runaway in disguise by his one distinguishing feature:

Lichas, qui me optime noverat, tamquam et ipse vocem audisset, accurrit et nec manus nec faciem meam consideravit, sed continuo ad inguina mea luminibus deflexis movit officiosam manum et 'salve' inquit 'Encolpi'. miretur nunc aliquis Ulixis nutricem post vicesimum annum cicatricem invenisse originis indicem, cum homo prudentissimus confusis omnibus corporis indiciorumque lineamentis ad unicum fugitivi argumentum tam docte pervenerit. (105.9–10)

Lichas, who knew me well, ran up as though he had heard my voice and without even glancing at my hands or face immediately lowered his gaze to my groin, applied an obliging hand and said, 'Hi there Encolpius'. No one should be surprised that Ulysses' nurse found the scar which revealed his identity after twenty years, when some smart guy hits brilliantly on the one thing that identifies the fugitive, despite the fact that every feature of his face and body is blurred.

Ulysses' scar has become Encolpius' genitalia, and as soon as Lichas recognises Encolpius by looking at his groin, the scars written on his body by Eumolpus are also recognised, as fake: *tamquam vulnera ferro praeparata litteras biberint . . . nunc mimicis artibus petiti sumus et adumbrata inscriptione derisi* / 'as if these letters had really been made by the scars of the branding iron . . . now we've been done over by an actor's tricks, fooled by the mere outline of an inscription' (106.1). It is as if Eumolpus' action of *writing* scar-poems on Encolpius' face, so that an audience would literally read him like a book, is responsible for triggering the narrator's memory of the meaning of scars in literature.[12] At the same time the *mimicae artes* of the disguise result in a farce which has hilarious consequences for our reading of the *Odyssey*'s famous recognition scene in Book XIX. At best, Lichas' reaction makes it difficult for us to read the bathing scene with Eurycleia as innocently as we once did;[13] indeed, it reminds us that in the *Odyssey* itself, the virtuous, domestic picture of Eurycleia bathing Odysseus is intruded upon by the violent, sexual story of the scar's origin, Odysseus' rite of passage on a boar-hunt.[14] At worst, Lichas hints that perhaps it was not the scar she recognised, that a woman who has seen our hero naked since he was a baby would not have to rely on such signs to identify the body of her master. Petronius' gutter humour injects sexual tension into Eurycleia's poignant realisation, suggesting that she was as aroused by her delightful 'recognition' of Odysseus as Lichas is at the sight of his ex-lover Encolpius.[15] This is a crucial example of the way the *Satyricon* constantly wants to sexualise reading, invest it with a corporeality that not only makes this text become more 'alive' and

[12] Another famous scar is that of Orestes in Euripides' *Elektra*, which inevitably takes Odysseus' scar as its precedent. Goff's argument (1991: 260) for Orestes' confused identification with the hero of Homeric epic could equally apply to Encolpius here: Orestes' scar 'both compares Orestes to a heroic exemplar and simultaneously denies him the possibility of living up to the claims thus implied for him . . . His identity is thus put into a problematic relation with the identity of another.'

[13] As Goldhill reminds us (1991: 19), 'each use of the scar is different, as the sign is differently manipulated, tells a different story, and constructs a different relation between the partners in recognition'.

[14] And as Goff notes (1991: 263), 'it is well known that women and baths can be dangerous to returning heroes'. The bathing scene is thick with tension, risk and apprehension.

[15] As Murnaghan notes (1987: 112), in the *Odyssey* a bath is often the occasion for the removal of disguise, and sleeping in bed is often the result, most notably when Odysseus regains his marriage bed. It is precisely these traces of connections between recognition and sex, and between Eurycleia and Penelope, which the *Satyricon* picks up on and exaggerates out of all proportion. See also Henderson (1997b: 94): 'the sign "scar" . . . evokes . . . the relationship between the nurse and the boy, as against that of Penelope and Odysseus, for which an erotic "clue" is figuratively more fitting'.

theatrical (as if we are watching live bodies moving on a stage), but also blurs the divide between writing and flesh, or between the intellectual mind and the sensual body. As Eumolpus himself suggests at *Sat.* 92.11, brains and groins, the paronymic *ingenia* and *inguina*, are pretty much the same thing after all: *tanto magis expedit inguina quam ingenia fricare* / 'It's so much better to rub crotches than intellects.'

Eumolpus' faking of scar-tissue as *epigramma* in *Sat.*103 emphasises the idea that Odysseus' scar in the *Odyssey* functions as a literary marker, a scission in the text of *Od.* XIX which enables Homer to tell a story about an important event which played a role in making Odysseus the man he is today: as Eurycleia recognises Odysseus through his scar, so do we as readers. The scar is more than a focal point for recognition: it is itself a narrative, something Eumolpus' 'writing' of scars renders literal. However, as Cave argues in his famous critique of the bathing scene in *Od.* XIX, the narrative of Odysseus' scar predicts, or rather conceals, as much as it recalls and reveals: the story it recaptures is a sexually charged event in Odysseus' adolescence when he was gouged in the leg by a boar on his first hunt, but its revelation in the text also forecasts the final crisis of his homecoming, the equally sexually charged massacre of his wife's suitors and the hanging of the sluttish slave girls. Cave calls this finale, 'a second puberty rite . . . the crisis of the adolescent reenacted in the crisis of the middle aged man'.[16] The scar is now 'a mark of the treacherously concealed narrative waiting to break the surface and create a scandal'.[17] Petronius, however, is writing for a readership for whom the narratives of the *Odyssey*, read and reread, are no longer ever 'treacherously concealed'. It is perhaps not surprising that the *Satyricon*'s reworking of the recognition scene in *Od.* XIX drags all Homer's hidden innuendo and dramatic suspense to the surface, mapping out all the sexual implications of Odysseus' *cicatrix*, past, present and future, in Lichas' one, lingering look at Encolpius' crotch.

So Odysseus' scar is much more than a sign by which he is recognised: in Cave's words, 'it composes his identity by calling up retrospectively a fragment of narrative'.[18] In the *Satyricon*, the scar itself automatically recalls the Homeric narrative, yet it also functions as it does in *Od.* XIX, representing the history of a character within the text and acting as a point of interference between past and future events in the text. In the shadow of Odysseus' old wound, all scars in the *Satyricon* are framed as textual markers calling out to be recognised. For example, at *Sat.* 91,

[16] Cave (1988) 23. [17] Ibid. 24. [18] Ibid. 23.

when Encolpius and Giton are reunited as Encolpius emerges from the picture gallery, and Encolpius cries, *O facinus indignum, quod amo te quamvis relictus, et in hoc pectore, cum vulnus ingens fuerit, cicatrix non est* / 'It's amazing that I love you even though you ditched me, and that there's no scar left on my chest where the wound was so deep' (91.6), he imagines that events which have already taken place in the *Satyricon* should have left physical scars on his body.

All scars and wounds in the *Satyricon* are imaginary or metaphorical: at 54.2, Trimalchio pretends his arm is wounded (*bracchium tamquam laesum incubuisset* / 'He nursed his arm as if it was hurt'), rather than his pride; at 94.14, Giton prevents Encolpius from killing himself by stealing the limelight and drawing a blade across his own throat. It is all an act, like the orator's display of battle wounds before an audience: the blade is a blunt tool used to train barbers, and Giton is not even marked by the trace of a cut (*neque ulla erat suscipione vulneris laesus*). At *Sat.* 99.2, Encolpius declares that if Giton is to take him back, he will have to rid his mind of the scars caused by previous episodes (*tantum omnem scabitudinem animo tamquam bonarum artium magister delevet sine cicatrice*).[19] And in *Sat.* 113.7, every kiss Tryphaena plants on Giton's face is a wound (*omnia me oscula vulnerabant*). Giton refuses to talk to Encolpius because, Encolpius assumes, he is afraid of reviving old arguments, of opening a tender scar just as it has begun to heal (*credo, veritus ne inter initia coeuntis gratiae recentem cicatricem rescinderet*, 113.8). In the *Satyricon* as in the *Odyssey*, scarring is associated explicitly with the memory of events that have happened in literature. Petronius takes Homer's use of the scar as an opening in a linear narrative one step further, making it reveal not only the history of the *Satyricon*'s characters, but also the influence of other texts that have 'scarred' his own writing process.[20]

The idea that the body is a canvas on which scars or letters are inscribed is a unifying metaphor in the *Satyricon*. Yet in passages I have discussed above, it is the superficiality of scars, the idea that they are written merely on the skin and not in the body, that is perhaps most interesting, especially alongside the *Satyricon*'s investigation of the complex relationship between what is inside and outside bodies. For the most obvious implication of

[19] Cf. Henderson on the *Odyssey* (1997b: 87–8): 'we observe how the very same memory that fixes an identity round the marks left by life on the body takes shape in the insistence of signs and meaning as a "scarring" of the mind'.

[20] Cf. Goff on Orestes in Euripides' *Elektra* (1991: 261): 'The episode of the scar demonstrates that the whole drama is "scarred"; both made and marred by its inescapable relations to anterior texts.'

Eumolpus' metaphorical 'writing' of scars in *Sat.* 103 is that a text's signifiers are not only skilfully constructed and contrived, but may even be designed to deceive. Conversely, the meaningful 'scars' of Giton and Encolpius' love affair are invisible, felt only on the inside. Similarly, when we first meet Eumolpus in the picture gallery at *Sat.* 83, Encolpius thinks he can read him like a book: he is 'marked' (*hac nota*),[21] wearing his poet's identity on his sleeve, just like the other realist artworks in the gallery, portraits so clear and readable that as Encolpius remarks, *crederes etiam animorum esse picturam* / 'You'd think he had painted their souls'.[22] Yet the poet is not all he seems. He is an expert at seduction and deception, as his tale of the boy of Pergamum at *Sat.* 85–7 proves: Eumolpus lures the boy to stay with him by promising him a prize of a thoroughbred horse, a trick-gift which he has no real intention of bestowing. Thus when, in *Sat.* 89, Eumolpus tells the old story of the Greeks deceiving the Trojans with the 'gift' of the Trojan Horse, the parallels with the previous tale of the tricked boy from Pergamum (Troy) are plain to see. The audience respond like attacked Trojans, pelting Eumolpus with stones, while Encolpius interprets the *Troiae Halosis* as an offensive outpouring of inner disease (*quid tibi vis cum isto morbo?* / 'What's with this disease of yours?'). As I argued in chapter four, both Eumolpus and the Trojan Horse appear to a naïve or Trojan audience to be transparent artworks, readable by virtue of their labelling: Eumolpus is clearly a poet, because of his dress-code (*hac nota*), and the Trojan Horse is also marked by an inscription which is taken at face value (*hoc titulus fero / incisus*, *TH* vv. 12–13). Yet despite their readability, we soon realise that the one is as manipulative and deceptive as the other, and that exterior labels can conceal any number of sins. Giton makes a similar point at *Sat.* 102.15, when he says that they cannot alter their identity with Eumolpus' writing ink because their insides will still contradict external appearances (*color arte compositus inquinat corpus, non mutat*). The notion that the marks this poet makes on paper are to obscure 'inside' meaning has broad implications for the *Satyricon* as a whole. Not only is the body in the *Satyricon* a model for the literary text which is difficult to read; it also becomes a striking emblem of the *Satyricon*'s metaphoricity.

[21] As C. P. Jones notes (1987: 148), Plautus uses *litteratus* to mean both learned and tattooed (Pl. *Cas.* 401).

[22] Steiner (1994: 107ff.) has excellent discussion on the parallels between writing tablets (designed both to hide and reveal their contents) and the human body (which can conceal things within itself whilst presenting a different face to the world). Steiner notes that the same word used to describe the opening up of the leaves of a writing tablet to reveal its insides (*diaptússo*) is used of opening up the chest cavity of a human body to read mantric signs or indications of disease (e.g. Galen 2.520 Kühn).

CHAPTER 8

How to eat Virgil

The civil war that breaks out on board ship after Giton and Encolpius are recognised is short-lived. As order is restored and the decks ring out with songs, Eumolpus, in his new peacekeeping role as *periclitantium advocatus et praesentis concordiae auctor* / 'spokesman in peril and author of our present peace' (110.6) takes it upon himself to entertain the crowd with a story. All eyes and ears are fixed on him as he begins the tale of the widow of Ephesus, which is to exemplify female unpredictability (*multa in muliebrem levitatem coepit iactare* / 'He began to rant at the flightiness of women', 110.6).

The story of the widow of Ephesus seems to have been highly popular in antiquity,[1] and has been equally popular with literary critics. As Frow writes, 'narrative theorists have long had a predilection for this short tale: its peculiar effect of self-containment makes it possible and plausible to seek an equally self-contained point or a finite group of deep-structure categories'.[2] Bakhtin's reading of the story has proved particularly authoritative, to the extent that classicists have either shied away from challenging and unpacking his analysis, or have steered clear altogether. The tale is left undiscussed in most recent book-length readings of the *Satyricon*,[3] while McGlathery's recent attempt to fine-tune Bakhtin's thesis seems to take for granted the use of his work as a concrete foundation for further interpretation. This chapter therefore sets out to re-evaluate Bakhtin's and later narrative theorists' readings of the tale, and to discuss in what ways their approaches have been too readily accepted or in some cases underused in classicists' interpretations of the *Satyricon*. In particular, I aim to question Bakhtin's central idea that the tale is purely realistic, a thesis we have seen foregrounded and reflected in Auerbach's famous reading of Trimalchio's *Cena*, in Sullivan's key

[1] The story can also be found in Phaedrus, *Appendix Fabulae* 15. Walsh (1970: 11, n. 4) concludes that 'It must have been a favourite in the Greek world.'

[2] Frow (1986) 133. [3] Most conspicuously Slater (1990) and Connors (1998).

study and in Conte's more recent book, all of which continually differentiate between a low, real world apparently exemplified by the widow of Ephesus tale, dominated as it is by flesh, food and sex, and a higher intellectual and literary world.[4] As I have argued throughout, despite work on the tricky theatricality and literary complexity of the *Satyricon*, the ramifications of this realism thesis continue in subtle ways to prejudice our reading of Petronius, and they direct us to miss the point of this tale in particular. Further, I will suggest that the dominant perception or implication of the tale as extractable and self-contained, or in more sophisticated approaches, the perception of the tale's neglected context as consisting simply of the *Aeneid*, has severely limited our critical appreciation of the narrative and its significance in the *Satyricon* as a whole.

The story of the widow of Ephesus has often been extracted by critics as a prime example of the 'Milesian tale', and was famously singled out by Bakhtin in his *Dialogic Imagination* as the focal point for the modern, rejuvenating spirit of the novel: Bakhtin writes,

> Here we have without any omissions all the basic links in the classical series: the tomb – youth – food and drink – death – copulation – the conceiving of new life – laughter. At its simplest, the narrative is an uninterrupted series of victories of life over death . . . The elements of the ancient complex are presented in one unmediated and tightly packed matrix; pressed up against one another so that they almost cover each other up – they are not separated by any side-plots or detours in the narrative, nor by any lengthy discourses, nor by lyrical digressions, nor by any metaphorical sublimations that might destroy the dryly realistic surface of the story.
>
> . . . not only is there no trace of mysticism here, but even symbolic features are missing, not a single element is exploited as a metaphor. Everything occurs at the level of real life: it is completely credible that a widow should be aroused through food and drink to new life in the presence of the legionnaire's strong, young body; it is completely credible that new life should triumph over death in the act of conception; the sham resurrection of the dead man who climbed up on the cross comes about in a completely credible way and so forth. There are no sublimating processes of any kind in all this.[5]

Bakhtin's argument is strongly echoed by Conte:

> The story of the woman of Ephesus opens a window directly onto the function played by realism in the narrative . . . Here too is the tendency to exalt reality, a tendency to which Petronius constantly opposes the unconquerable energy of a 'low' world that knows only physical desires. We shall see that the body, food,

[4] Auerbach (1953), Sullivan (1968a), Conte (1996). [5] Bakhtin (1981) 222, 223.

sex and money are the forces that Petronius musters to demystify the pretenses of the false sublime in the *Satyricon*.[6]

There are several problems with these readings. As well as artificially isolating the tale from its literary context in the *Satyricon*, the idea that this is a strictly real-life narrative seems to ignore the fact that what motivates it is not the everyday chit-chat you might hear in any Roman province of the day, but lines (scenes, images, and textures...) from Virgil. It could equally be argued that the structure of the tale is reminiscent of a classic three-act drama, with the cave functioning as the stage (as in Euripides' *Cyclops*), and its own internal audience, the entertained *populus* marvelling at a *spectaculum* (111.1); or again, this might look rather like a dramatisation of another written text, a passage of Roman elegy, a scene from Ovid's *Ars Amatoria* perhaps, out to prove the sexual availability of *all* women.[7] What is clear is that when Encolpius reports that Eumolpus, 'was not thinking of old tragedies or names notorious in history but of an affair that happened in his own lifetime', this is itself an act, a superficial, conventional gesture, or rather an impossible claim.[8] The story he goes on to tell suggests that novelistic narrative, despite its everyday, contemporary themes, cannot be unconnected to a literary tradition, and nor can its author's *memory* be innocent of literary knowledge. Yet more than that, it shows that any kind of storytelling, in the context of a novel or in real life, can never be untouched by storytelling patterns consciously or unconsciously absorbed from many different sources, whether from famous epic and love poetry, religious hymns or folklore. This is precisely what this fiction enacts as a whole, in its pretence of being an eyewitness account of real-life events. What Eumolpus sells as a story picked up on his travels rather than an allusive piece of literature in its own right turns out to be a multi-layered narrative which plays on a series of references to literary works, from tragedy, epic, elegy, Greek novels, to other 'Milesian tales', as well as to the immediate and wider narrative of the *Satyricon*.

6 Conte (1996) 105. Conte's reading of Petronian realism does seem, nevertheless, to be more sophisticated than Bakhtin's here: he recognises the tale's high level of theatricality and its vacillating tone. I take issue rather with his key point that the 'high' literary or theatrical quality of the tale is set up in opposition to the role played by bodies and food, which represent the low, literal, non-metaphorical world.

7 E.g. *Ars Am.* 1.275; 343–4 (*ergo age, ne dubita cunctas sperare puellas / vix erat e multis, quae neget, una, tibi* / 'So come on, don't doubt that you can take your pick of girls; there'll hardly be one who'll turn you down'). We are reminded of Ovid's characterisation of the *ancilla* as an erotic intermediary, or even as an alternative object of the writer's (and readers') lust.

8 Slater (1990: 109) also notes this: the story 'is from the first presented in the language of theatre and role-playing'.

McGlathery has recently attempted to fine-tune or reorient Bakhtin's thesis by explaining in greater detail how the story reworks the tragedy of Dido in the *Aeneid*, using Bakhtin's own theories of carnivalesque to argue that the story brings privileged epic 'down to earth' by recasting its heroes as mundane, corrupt figures in a sordid fiction.[9] It is here, McGlathery argues, that we see the 'tomb' of epic transformed into the 'womb' for the novelistic genre. Both Bakhtin's and McGlathery's readings depend to a large extent on a polarisation of the lowly, realistic, happy-go-lucky novel and the lofty, serious, rigid genre of epic. McGlathery does attempt to deconstruct Bakhtin's parallel opposition of dialogic novel and monologic epic ('in this act of parody, the novel destroys the distance between the original, ostensibly monologic text and its dialogic double, this making it difficult to imagine a non-dialogic reading of the parodied text'),[10] yet in this instance neither critic, I will argue, fully explores the multiple perspectives suggested by the diagnosis of 'novel' as dialogic. The complexity of such a position is always cancelled out by the use of the misleadingly definitive term 'novel', so that the potentially disruptive dialogue between Petronius and his literary past is reduced to a simplistic contrariety: Virgil's tragic drama is replaced by Petronius' 'renewing power of laughter', as the widow of Ephesus chooses life and love over Dido's path of suicide.

My reading of the tale sets out to question this notion of neat reversal, which relies both on a rigid compartmentalising of genres and on a parallel conceptualisation of the *Satyricon* as a collection of insular fragments. I also aim to rethink Bakhtin's central premise that the apparently contemporary, everyday setting for the tale ensures that there can be no metaphorical structure at work here. I will suggest that the tale of the widow of Ephesus is, on the contrary, highly metaphorical, marking a difficult point in a text which continually stages so-called 'real life' as (literary) performance and which works to fuzz the conventional distinction between the literary and the everyday, or between intertextuality and physical/social exchange.

The reading offered by Frow, which is not recognised by McGlathery, is more intriguing.[11] Frow outlines the limitations of Bakhtin's structuralist interpretation of the tale,[12] suggesting instead, 'a more complicated model in which the movement of the text is not simply from death to

[9] McGlathery (1998). [10] McGlathery (1998) 316.

[11] Laird (1999: 245–6) also develops the case made by Frow.

[12] Bakhtin's account is compared to Schlegor (1970), cited by O'Toole (1975: 148), and also to Schlegor and Zholkovsky (1975).

life and vice versa, but from one form of life through death to a qualitively different form of life, and in this process a movement from the realm of social sanctions and decencies to the realm of profane values associated with bodily functions'.[13] Frow concludes: 'this is not a simple passage from one half of a dichotomy to another; far more important is the asymmetry that gives the story its paradoxical force'.[14] Although this shift in perspective is not developed with relation to the tale's narrative context, Frow makes a very important distinction.[15] The story resists being read as straightforwardly comic and optimistic in a number of ways. On a simple level, if we look at the reactions to Eumolpus' story within the text, we notice that not everyone on the ship reads it as a joyful and entertaining celebration of life after death. Only the sailors laugh: while Encolpius reports on the generally joyful scene, he feels depressed and starts to refuse food and drink, just like the widow of Ephesus herself (*ego maestus et impatiens foederis novi non cibum, non potionem capiebam*, 113.6); Tryphaena blushes with shame and Lichas is furious: *at non Lichas risit, sed iratum commovens caput 'si iustus' inquit 'imperator fuisset, debuit patris familiae corpus in monumentum referre, mulierem affigere cruci'* / 'But Lichas didn't smile. He shook his head angrily and said, "If the governor of the province had been just, he should have put the dead husband back in the tomb and hung the woman on the cross" ' (113.2).

Nevertheless, as Frow suggests, it might be argued that this scene exactly fits the speech-act structure described by Freud as characteristic of the dirty joke:

> In addition to the one who makes the joke, there must be a second who is taken as the object of the hostile or sexual aggressiveness, and a third in whom the joke's aim of producing pleasure is fulfilled. When the first person finds his libidinal impulse inhibited by the woman, he develops a hostile trend against that second person and calls on the originally interfering first person as his ally. Through the first person's smutty speech the woman is exposed before the third who, as listener, has now been bribed by the effortless satisfaction of his own libido.[16]

[13] Frow (1986) 134. [14] Frow (1986) 136.

[15] In his book *Marxism and Literary History*, Frow is attempting to theorise the concepts of system and history for a Marxist theory of literary discourse. His reading of the widow of Ephesus tale in chapter six seems to have been written to exemplify how his theories of system, which are influenced by the post-structuralism of critics like Foucault and Derrida, differ from those of more traditional Marxist formalist critics – in this case, Bakhtin and Schlegor. The tale is not discussed within a wider reading of the *Satyricon* as a whole, nor is Frow interested in the *Satyricon per se*, other than in terms of the part it plays in Bakhtin's work on the history of the novel.

[16] Freud (1966: 100), quoted by Frow (1986: 137).

Petronius' comic sketch is perhaps not as intricate as Freud's example, but this paradigm scenario usefully highlights the point that Lichas' misogynistic outburst is all part of the joke, that offending Lichas is part of the joke. Indeed this tension between the poet Eumolpus and the captain of this poetic ship has dominated the narrative of the sea voyage from the beginning. I have argued that the metaphorical ship has been a vehicle for the imagining and creation of fictions and for the recollection of literary narratives: Eumolpus' escape plots fuel the reinvention of alternative *Odysseys* and offer fleshy material for rough drafts of civil war poetry; the storm which wrecks the ship and kills its rival author and *gubernator* Lichas is itself a metaphor for civil war, yet the final sinking has been brewing all along, precipitated first by the hair-cutting incident devised by Eumolpus in the preparation of his human papyri, and then by the mini civil war called to a halt with a quote from Lucan. In writing the ultimate *ingens opus* of civil-war poetry, we have seen, you always have to risk drowning. The shipwreck is itself implicitly staged as the deciding round in a literary competition between Eumolpus and the ship's captain Lichas, a contest already begun in the image of Lichas as the Cyclops and Eumolpus as Odysseus. As in the *Odyssey*, this is about a battle of creative wits, about the poet and storyteller outmanoeuvring brute force. As soon as the audience settles down to listen to Eumolpus here, we are immediately made aware that he has taken on the stature and seductiveness of an epic bard: this is Aeneas (and all he represents), telling the tale of the fall of Troy which will have Dido swooning and dying in *Aeneid* IV, the very model, or anti-model, for the widow of Ephesus herself: *conversis igitur omnium in se vultibus auribusque* **sic orsus** *est* / 'So when all eyes and ears were on him, he began as follows' (*Sat.* 110.8); cf. *conticuere omnes intentique ora tenebant. inde toro pater Aeneas* **sic orsus** *ab alto* / 'Everyone was silent and fixed their eyes on him. And so father Aeneas began as follows from his high couch' (*Aen.* 2.1–2).[17]

As far as the widow of Ephesus tale goes, then, the joke is on Lichas in more ways than one. Eumolpus' skill at storytelling marks the lull before the storm. In the next chapter (114), the sky will darken, the seas will rise, and Lichas will be swept overboard to his death.[18] The ship of poetry is about to sink, and civil war is about to erupt, for real. The tale of the

[17] Collignon (1892: 123) also notes this parallel. He adds that the phrase *conticuere omnes* ('they were all silent') had become proverbial, and occurs twice in the graffiti found at Pompeii.

[18] As A. Barchiesi writes (1996: 199), prompted by Pecere (1975: 41), 'la novella di Efeso agisce da surrealistico anticipo della fine di Lica'.

widow of Ephesus exemplifies the dialogic nature of this text precisely because it is told at the climactic point at which Eumolpus is massing literary resources for the (conceptually) gigantic poem he is about to write, a poem which demands that its author be full of literary knowledge to the point of overflowing. It is a narrative, therefore, that can never *just* be extracted and set alongside *Aeneid* IV, or any other text to which it alludes, because its meaning must be partly determined by its context, the environment of the poetic ship. This story does not simply displace epic, but incorporates it, ensuring that Eumolpus' penultimate performance is not totally satisfying and cathartic but potentially disturbing and difficult to read.

In reading the tale of the widow of Ephesus, we are continually reminded of a network of metaphors that have so far coloured not only the episodes on board ship, but also key passages throughout the *Satyricon*. As I have suggested, the ship is another of the *Satyricon*'s dark enclosures in which Encolpius and his gang are trapped. The vision of the ship as a Cyclops' cave (*antrum Cyclopis*, 101.7), as a prison for branded slaves (*ne viderer de nave carcerem facere*, 105.2), or later on as a bear trap for the mad poet Eumolpus (*audimus... sub diaeta magistri quasi cupientis exire beluae gemitum*, 115.1) repeats the dramatic situations in which Petronius' characters have found themselves throughout the *Satyricon*.[19] We have seen that Trimalchio's dining room is at various points imaged as a deadly underworld, labyrinth, or cannibals' cave in which the guests are trapped;[20] the marketplace and Quartilla's brothel are similar dark enclosures from which the gang have to escape, and there are elements of all these episodes in the *Troiae Halosis*, in which the horse's belly containing the Greek soldiers is an *antrum* and a *specus* (v. 7), the *Bellum Civile* (where the world is turned inside out into the grottoes of hell), and in Croton, a hellish, apocalyptic landscape whose inhabitants have become uncivilised, man-eating beasts like the Cyclops in his unlit cave. The widow's cave, like Trimalchio's *cena*, is also an underworld, recalling the soldier Aeneas'

[19] M. Barchiesi (1981 : 124) dubs this 'la tendenza degli avventurieri del *Satyricon* a raggrupparsi in uno spazio chiuso, come in un rifugio (per quanto precario) contro il mondo che minaccia di irrompere'.

[20] Indeed there are parallels to be drawn between the widow of Ephesus tale, told during the dinner party on board ship, and Seleucus' interlude in the *Cena* at *Sat*. 42.7: Seleucus interrupts to tell a story about death and the failure of fasting which offers the same moral as Eumolpus gives at *Sat*. 110, the fickleness of women (*multa in muliebrem levitatem coepit iactare*; cf. *sed mulier quae mulier milvinum genus* / 'women are all kites'). In both stories the woman does not mourn sufficiently after the death of her husband.

journey to the underworld of *Aeneid* VI and his encounter with Dido, now faithful to the ghost of her husband Sychaeus:[21] when *this* soldier first goes to investigate and climbs down into the vault, he comes face to face with a ghost of hell: *descendit igitur in conditorium, visaque pulcherrima muliere primo quasi quodam monstro infernisque imaginibus turbatus substitit* / 'He climbed down into the vault, and on seeing a gorgeous woman, he stopped in his tracks, as stunned as if he had seen some monster or hellish spirit' (111.7). In the context of the ship-cave, this line has an ominous tone: on one hand we can read the soldier's hallucination as an effect of the woman's striking, otherworldly beauty, yet on the other, he sees precisely what the *Satyricon*'s repeated images of caves and underworlds have led us to expect: a monster. Once the widow of Ephesus descends into the vault of death, she begins to metamorphose into a hellish figure in an imaginary scenario that replicates the role-play of Trimalchio the Minotaur and Lichas the Cyclops. The woman's groans heard from outside her cavern (*cum gemitum lugentis audisset*, 111.6) echo the groans of blinded Polyphemus and predict the pained cries of the poet-turned-beast, as he composes the *Bellum Civile* from within the cave-hull of the ship: *audimus murmur insolitum et sub diaeta magistri quasi cupientis exire beluae gemitum* (115.1). At all these sites of entrapment, the bodily integrity of Encolpius and his companions is threatened: these are transgressive spaces which are enclosed so as to conceal aggressive, unlawful, shocking or uncivilised behaviour, from rape and kidnap to cannibalism. Trapped inside a series of monsters' caves, the gang continually fear that they will be eaten, literally or sexually.[22] Now, within the ship-cave, the tale of the widow of Ephesus is another extended metaphor for containment in which transgressive sex and eating, again aligned, are the inevitable

[21] Hence this tale contracts Dido and Aeneas' romance together with its aftermath in the *Aeneid*: here, contrary to Virgil's narrative, the affair seems to have a happy ending, but it is also set in Virgil's underworld in which Aeneas' encounter with Dido serves only to confirm the tragic consequences of the relationship. The widow of Ephesus revises Virgil twice over, it seems, yet the hellish backdrop is also a subversive subtext, disrupting the superficially straightforward narrative turn, especially since the environment of the underworld is a conventional metaphor for revisiting the past and for addressing the ghosts of literary predecessors.

[22] The cave itself can be identified with female genitalia, as Adams notes (1982: 85): 'the identification of the *cunnus* (or rectum) with a cave is an obvious enough image – it is exploited at length in the Priapic poem numbered 83: note lines 28–9: *inter atra cuius inguina / latet iacente pantice abditus specus* / "in her black groin there lay a hidden cave" and 35, *triplexque quadruplexque compleas specum.* / "you could fill her cave three or four times over." ' Also see Diom. *GLI* 512.28; Auson. *Cent. Nupt.* 113, p216P. The ship-cave perhaps reinforces this metaphor further, as *navis* is often used to mean womb or female genitals (e.g. Macrob. *Sat.* 2.5.9). Adams writes (89), 'A word denoting any hollow object or container (in this case the hollow hull of the ship) can readily be used metaphorically of the womb or vagina.'

threat and outcome. What begins as a lascivious tale told by Eumolpus simply to entertain, and unconnected to the wider narrative of the *Satyricon*, becomes a rather more ominous and complex story which repeats as well as predicts the dangers of entrapment.

Yet perhaps the most obvious way in which the tale mirrors and develops concerns of the *Satyricon* as a whole is in its metaphorical approximation of literature as food. When the widow does not respond to the soldier's platitudes on the inevitability of death (111.8), he persists in offering her food until the maid capitulates on her behalf, seduced, Eumolpus suspects, by the smell of wine (*vini odore corrupta*, 111.10).[23] As she regains her strength, the *ancilla* joins the soldier in persuading the woman to eat, taking on the role of Anna in *Aeneid* IV, as she talks Dido into forgetting Sychaeus and taking her chance on love and happiness with Aeneas. The line *id cinerem aut manes credis sentire sepultos?* / 'Do you think that ashes or the shades of the dead can feel anything?' (111.12) quotes the words of Anna at *Aen.* 4.34,[24] at the point at which she succeeds in changing Dido's mind about Aeneas and thus sets in motion the entire tragedy of *Aeneid* IV.

At the same time, the maid also adopts the role of Roman elegy's erotic intermediary, the *ancilla* who communicates between mistress and male lover (the *miles amator*), or even acts as a surrogate mistress in what is effectively a threesome.[25] At the sound of Virgil, the woman's resolution breaks down and she stuffs herself as greedily as the maid: *nec minus avide replevit se cibo quam ancilla quae prior victa est* (111.13). Eumolpus comments that people are always ready to listen when they are hungry (*nemo invitus audit, cum cogitur aut cibum aut vivere*, 111.13), and that everyone knows a full stomach triggers other desires (*ceterum scitis, quid plerumque soleat temptare humanam satietatem*, 112.1). As soon as she eats, the widow opens the floodgates to temptation. It follows that the soldier employs the same tactics to urge the widow to accept him as a lover, and the maid backs him again in quoting Anna at *Aen.* 4.38–9: *placitone etiam pugnabis amori? [nec venit in mentem, quorum consederis arvis?]* / 'Will you fight even a love that pleases you? Does it not occur to you, in whose lands you have

[23] The smell of wine is as dangerously pungent as that of a poet: Encolpius comments at 93.3, *nam si aliquis ex is, qui in eodem synoecio potant, nomen poetae olfecerit, totam concitabit viciniam et nos omnes sub eadem causa obruet* / 'If any one of those people who are drinking in the same tenement as us smells the name of Poet, he'll rouse the whole neighbourhood and ruin us all for the same crime.'

[24] The only difference is that *sentire* replaces *curare* here. See note 40, below.

[25] e.g. *Ars Am.* 1.351 ff.: *sed prius ancillam captandae nosse puellae / cura sit . . .* / 'But first, mind you get to know the maid of the girl you want to win.'

settled?'[26] The woman falls into his arms, and like Dido and Aeneas consummating their fake marriage in a cave in the woods (*Aen.* 4.160–72), the soldier and widow sleep together in secret inside the closed tomb. By letting her sacred body be penetrated by food, the woman implicitly makes herself sexually available to the soldier, as satisfaction from eating precedes sexual arousal. Food and sex are both acts of incorporation which rupture the integrity of her abstemious body, so that we are encouraged to see her 'swallowing' of Virgilian lines of seduction and her physical acceptance of food and sex as sitting metaphorically side by side.

The incorporation of food or the 'consumption' of a sexual partner has been the *Satyricon*'s core model for the absorption of literary knowledge: literature has been imaged as food since the programmatic speeches at *Sat.* 1–5, where Encolpius delivers 'honey-balls of phrases' (*mellitos verborum globulos*, 1.3) and speaks of the 'diet' of poetry (*quasi eodem cibo pasta* / 'all fed on the same food', 2.8), while Agamemnon imagines the teacher of oratory 'feeding' his fish-pupils with tasty bait (3.4); the scholar must 'drink' Homer (*Maeoniumque bibat…fontem*, 5, v. 12), and when he has had his fill, he should change his taste (*mutet saporem*) and pour out his knowledge in poetry about food (*epulae*) and bloodshed (*bella*, 5, v. 19). This metaphor is extended spectacularly in the *Cena*, as we have seen, where dishes are layered literary texts or dramas split into acts which have to be interpreted before they are eaten. Meanwhile Agamemnon's notion that the good Roman scholar must stuff himself to bursting point

[26] This interesting line is found in the oldest MSS of the O-class, but is missing from the *Florilegia* and from one of the L-class MSS, the Lambeth codex r, where it is deleted by the copyist; it was omitted from the *codex Memmianus*, which has not survived. Müller, following Bücheler, deletes the verse in all his editions: as Rose notes (1968: 257), Müller 'presumes that Daniel Rogers, the scribe of r, deleted the line because it was absent from one of his sources, the *Memmianus*, and he also explains the presence of the verse in the L-MSS by contamination with the O-class'. It does remain possible, as Rose adds, that the line was in L, and that only the *Memmianus* omitted it, whether intentionally or not. Reasons for the line being an interpolation, if given at all, are generally that a scribe must have let his memory run away with him, or was showing off his literary knowledge, and that the line makes little or no sense in the context of the tale. Arguments for keeping the line fall into two overlapping groups: Cesareo and Terzaghi (1950), Marmorale (1950: 80–1), Campanile (1957), Ciaffi (1967), and Walsh (1970: 12, n. 3) suggest that *arva* here refer to the dangerous corpse-strewn margins of the city of Ephesus, in parallel with Virgil's menacing African plains. The argument put to both Dido and the widow, therefore, is that a woman needs a noble young soldier to protect her. Other critics (e.g. Rose (1968: 257–8), Díaz y Díaz (1968–9: 95)) have argued that the line includes an obscene joke: *arva* are a metaphor for *pudenda*, while *consedere* is used in an erotic sense, as *sedere* is at *Sat.* 126.10 and 140.7: for general examples of an erotic use of *sedere*, see Herescu (1959). This argument is strengthened by a similar obscene use of a passage of *Aeneid* VI involving Dido at *Sat.* 132.11, and by the notion that the line was omitted precisely because of its inappropriate connotations (although it is equally possible to argue that the line was *added* by an interpolator who had such a joke in mind). For further discussion of this reading, see appendix III.

with literary knowledge, until he 'pours out' verse from a swollen belly, is developed in Eumolpus' speech at 118 in which he warns anyone brave enough to take on the *impetus* of civil-war poetry to be full (*plenus*) of literature if he is not to sink under the burden. We have seen that the poem, or civil war itself, is the violent result of a frenzied poetic process in which the poet struggles and inevitably fails to contain a bellyful of literary knowledge. *intestinum bellum* always translates as *intestinal* war.

The maid in the tale of the widow of Ephesus employs precisely the same tactic as Encolpius' orator in *Sat.* 1, persuading the hungry widow to eat (and to have sex) by feeding her delicious titbits of literature. Yet in his recent article, McGlathery argues that the maid looks like an 'unsophisticated reader of Virgil' because she does not realise that the words of Anna in *Aeneid* IV turn out to be bad advice.[27] This sounds logical, yet it is not necessarily true, or even likely: on a simple level we might argue that, despite the comic opportunity for us to pretend otherwise in this context, a reader who can quote *Aeneid* IV verbatim will surely know what happens at the end. Indeed the effectiveness of the quotation is predicated precisely on a mutual familiarity with the original text. Perhaps we should ask instead what it would mean if the maid quoted Anna's lines to persuade her mistress despite knowing full well their final implications in the *Aeneid*. What *is* the function of a quotation, and how does it relate to its context in the original narrative?

One answer might be that the lines of Virgil have taken on a sensual power here that far exceeds the rationale of their impact within the narrative of Dido's love affair with Aeneas. In the erotically charged atmosphere of the cave-tomb, where she is as seduced by the soldier (and the situation)[28] as her mistress, the maid compulsively repeats Virgil as she is drawn into the intensity of the moment (here and in *Aeneid* IV), so that the sexual frisson of the scene replicates her pleasure in remembering (reading) Virgil's words.[29] The Ovidian *ancilla* has been taking notes

27 McGlathery (1998) 329.

28 Arguably all romantic encounters are conceptualised in terms of (and therefore to some extent directed by) the behaviour of lovers in books and films, which often offer unique opportunities to witness intimate exchanges between people not involving oneself. Sharrock (1994: 291) puts this another way: 'we make sense of relationships against the background of other relationships, both our own and those we encounter at second hand; likewise, we make sense of reading, as of any other act of communication, by means of reference to other readings'. In Barthes' frequently quoted analysis (1990: 147), lovers are always bound to enact formulas, to quote or reiterate the words of others: ' "I love you" has no meaning whatever; it merely repeats in an enigmatic mode – so blank it does not appear – the old message.'

29 Remembering is the pleasurable bit: *forsan et haec olim meminisse iuvabit* / 'perhaps one day it will be a pleasure to remember this' (*Aen.* 1.203). The introduction to the *Oxford Book of Quotations* (1979)

from Ovid's *Ars Amatoria*, in which, as Sharrock has shown, repetition is a means of seduction, the root of and key to all erotic success.[30] The pleasure she offers her mistress is the pleasure of rereading (even to the point of 'reliving') the romance and tragedy of Dido,[31] as distinct from naïvely encouraging her to fall into the trap of making a tragic hash of her own circumstances.[32] Like many other quotations, Anna's words are a unit or formula strangely disconnected from a narrative context which is nevertheless the source of its complex, emotive force. The quotation of these lines may be reckless, but it is also compulsive, representing both the seductive power of epic and the reader's inability to control what his literary memory will throw up at any time. In the responses of the maid and the widow, we see a theatrical demonstration of what it is to be affected physically by literature.[33] The use of Virgil here does not so much 'debase' epic, as McGlathery argues, but highlights how epic inevitably infects fiction, plaguing the memory (and *bodies*) of both writer and readers.

To put it slightly differently, it shows that in the transmission and rereading of texts, a narrative never goes the same way twice: we can never recapture the instant of reading, any more than the instant of writing. In the dense context of the *Satyricon*, we cannot presume that a remake of Dido and Aeneas' illicit love will have the same consequences, transmuted as it is by countless later texts and readings. This is Anna read through Ovid's erotic poetry, no longer a naïve advisor or disinterested third party but a sexual object and predator completing a heavily

begins with the sentence: 'Quotation brings to many people one of the intensest joys of living.' The editor remembers a famous speech by Churchill in which he quoted the nineteenth-century poet Arthur Hugh Clough, and writes: 'When the Prime Minister said that there were some lines that he deemed appropriate, we sat up rigid, waiting in mingled pleasure and apprehension. How agreeable it would be if we were acquainted with them and approved the choice! How flat and disappointing should they be unknown to us! A moment later we heard, "for a while the tired waves, vainly breaking" and sat back in a pleasant agony of relief. We whispered the lines affectionately to ourselves, following the speaker, or even kept a word or two ahead of him to show our familiarity with the text.'

30 Sharrock (1994) 1–20 *et passim*.

31 Long (1990) discusses the reality of feeling and seeking pleasure in (re)reading, and describes rereading a cherished book: 'the passage isn't where we thought it was (toward the back, top of a right hand page), and it's, well, pretty different. In fact, we remember not so much the words as the resonance they created in us – we remember an instant in our reading lives. Rereading, we try to reclaim that instant, the frisson that set it off' (65).

32 This tale tempts us, like the widow, to read the quoted line *id cinerem aut manes credis sentire sepultos?* as hinting at the non-existence of connections between 'dead' and 'living' texts: this claim is perhaps what makes the *Satyricon* as a whole so seductive in its appeal. See my discussion in chapter eleven.

33 On the idea that literature affects the body, producing sensual, physical reactions, see the collection of essays in Halpern (1990).

charged love triangle. In *Fasti* 3.633–8, Anna specifically becomes a surrogate for Dido, winning Aeneas' sympathy and attention and making his new wife Lavinia jealous and desperate for revenge. Laird's conclusion that Petronius' tale serves to 'excavate' or to bring to greater prominence the comical resonances 'buried' in Virgil's epic therefore seems to miss the point:[34] it is not that comic elements have necessarily lain undiscovered in Virgil all along, but rather that any reworking of the *Aeneid* is interpretative and transformative, as is any rereading, even by the same person, of any text. The *Satyricon* as a whole is concerned precisely with the harnessing of this creative instability and unpredictability.[35] Moreover, this idea is powerfully expressed and reflected in an exploration of the metaphor of text as food, of bodies as temporary, unstable containers for literary knowledge: what goes in is never the same as what comes out.

I have suggested that the widow of Ephesus tale dramatises the impact and implications of gorging on literature within the confined environment of the cave, the cave that is both the tomb of the dead husband and the prison of Lichas' ship, *as well as* the cave of Dido and Aeneas' unlawful union, the underworld of *Aeneid* VI, and the *specus* of the Trojan Horse. As the *Satyricon* reminds us, caves in the *Aeneid* and the *Odyssey* are sites for unlawful eating and sex, erotic, fantastic places in which sexual urges and hunger spiral out of control: man-eating Cyclopes live in caves, and uncivilised Eastern women consummate fake marriages in them. In this cave-tomb, the widow's gorging on food and wine and her shameful union with the soldier are paralleled by her compulsive 'eating' of seductive lines of Virgil. In the ship-cave of poetry, meanwhile, Eumolpus is writing a poem which demands that he stuff his body full of literature, to be spewed out as the waves of civil war. For if we know anything about caves in epic literature and in the *Satyricon*, we should realise that what is trapped in the freakish space of the cave must eventually burst out, just as literature, accumulated in the body, finally erupts in a swelling torrent (*sic flumine largo / plenus Pierio defundes pectore verba*, 5, vv. 21–2). As I have argued, this image is a defining one in the poem itself, which

[34] Cf. Frow (1986: 138): 'the woman of Ephesus can be read as a direct reversal of the heroic ideology of the epic poem' . . . it even 'actively undermines it'.

[35] This is a story which fosters suspicion and uncertainty, centred around the figure of a woman, in a text full of dangerous, deceptive women (Fortunata, Quartilla, Tryphaena, Circe, Oenothea) who control and trick men. Conte (1996: 106) concludes that the 'ultimate meaning' of the tale is that 'all appearances are deceptive', and makes the link with other deceptive women in the *Satyricon* by comparing the widow's change of mind with Oenothea's change of attitude to the murdered goose (*Sat.* 107–9).

describes the outbreak of civil war in terms of an explosive breach of caves and of all dark, chthonic spaces, culminating in the laying bare of hell itself:

perfossa dehiscit
molibus insanis tellus, iam montibus haustis
antra gemunt, et dum vanos lapis invenit usus,
inferni manes caelum sperare fatentur.
(*BC* 90–3)

The earth gashed deep for her madmen's foundations
gapes wide, and now the caves groan in the hollowed hills,
and while men find empty uses for nature's stone,
the ghosts of hell confess their hopes of winning heaven.

Implicit then, in every tale of entrapment, and/or culinary, sexual or literary overindulgence in caves, is the idea that something has to give, that the escapist, fantastic bubble will eventually burst: Greeks break free from the cave of the 'peaceful' Trojan Horse to raze Troy; once Aeneas leaves his idealistic marriage-cave, he must leave Dido to her tragic death; when Odysseus escapes from the Cyclops' cave he must also flee a fairy-tale world of nymphs and monsters to face grim reality in Ithaca; when the very land of Italy is swollen with the gluttony of empire, civil war (poetry) breaks out.[36] The widow of Ephesus tale ends happily, apparently, with soldier and new bride still cosy in their cave. Yet if we see the tale within the *Satyricon*'s repeated imagery of the rupture of containment, it is very difficult not to read this ending as rather more ominous and foreboding. The soldier's first warning to the widow is that

[36] The idea reminds us of Bakhtin's image of the grotesque carnival body which is always bursting its confines with a utopian generosity (1968: ch. 5). The notion that things trapped in bodies or caves will eventually get out is the subject of one of the poems attributed by Scaliger to Petronius (fragment XXXV, Müller 1995), found in the codex Vossianus L.Q.86, a manuscript of the ninth century (the poems here follow a number of epigrams attributed to Seneca): it goes:

sic et membra solent auras includere ventris,
quae penitus mersae cum rursus abire laborant,
verberibus rimantur iter; nec desinit ante
frigidus, adstrictis qui regnat in ossibus, horror
quam tepidus laxo manavit corpore sudor.

And so the limbs lock in the belly's wind
when it fights to exit its dungeon deep and prises
its way with blows; there is no end to the sick chill
which racks your shaking bones, till that tepid sweat
soaks your slackened body.

Compare Trimalchio's speech at *Sat.* 47: 'nobody is born solid. I can imagine no greater torture than holding oneself in . . . the doctors forbid retention'.

she risks 'pouring out' her spirit if she does not drink or eat (*'quid proderit' inquit 'hoc tibi, si soluta inedia fueris, si te vivam sepelieris, si antequam fata poscant, indemnatum spiritum* ***effuderis****?* / ' "What will you gain from this", he said, "if you waste away from hunger, if you bury yourself alive, if you pour out your undoomed soul before the fates demand it?" ', 111.11), yet Eumolpus has already expressed drinking wine as being 'buried alive' when he sung of the Trojans trapped in a prison of their own making and facing certain death at the hands of the Greeks (*cum inter sepultos Priamidas nocte et mero / Danai relaxant claustra et* ***effundunt*** *viros, TH* 55–6):[37] it is wine which the soldier implicitly first exhorts the 'dry' widow to drink (the maid has already been 'corrupted' by it): *itaque mulier aliquot dierum abstinentia sicca passa est frangi pertinaciam suam* / 'and so the woman, dried out after several days of abstinence, allowed her resolution to be broken down' (111.13).[38] If we have learnt the lessons of Troy's fall,[39] we cannot help but read the soldier's quoted exhortation rather differently: he does not say, as Anna does, 'Do you believe that the ashes or the spirits of the buried dead [i.e. your husband] can feel your pain?' but 'Do you believe that *you* will be able to feel anything when you're dead and "buried"?'[40] Wine will numb the widow's pain, dissolving her guard and allowing the soldier to seduce her and to murder her reputation as a *singularis exempli femina* / 'woman of unique character' (111.3).[41] Alongside the *Troiae Halosis*, the (Greek) soldier pours out wine together with the widow's soul.[42]

37 As I suggested in chapter four, the movement of the Greeks 'relaxing' the bars and 'pouring out' of the horse echoes the pouring of wine and general relaxing of spirits among the Trojans.

38 *siccus* has overtly sexual connotations: with the help of alcohol, this dried-up matron won't feel a thing . . .

39 Perhaps this text is only funny if we (realise we) haven't.

40 Hence the replacement of *curare* with *sentire* may not be so accidental: our attention is focused on the widow's *physical* reaction to the soldier. Note that a metaphorical usage of 'drunkenness' as well as 'sobriety' is common in Latin and Greek literary discourse: adjectives such as *sobrius, ebrius, vinolentus* and *siccus* were stylistic terms. Bramble (1974: 48–9) gives examples: Cratinus dismissed the sober 'water-drinkers' as inferior poets (fr. 199.2), Isocrates drew a distinction between drunkenness and temperance in literature (8.13, Van Hook 1905: 32), Callimachus calls Archilochus a drunkard (fr. 544), Cicero compares the passionate, immoderate orator to a drunkard (*De Or.* 99) and Quintilian parallels chanting delivery and inebriated speech (11.3.57). It is tempting to see the widow's acceptance of wine as directly connected to the change of direction in the narrative/style/feel of *Aeneid* IV, and as a metaphor in general for Petronius' manipulation (or corruption) of literary sources.

41 As Eumolpus puts it, the soldier plans an 'assault' on the woman's virtue: *isdem etiam pudicitiam eius aggressus est* (112.2), and emerges *victor* (112.2).

42 From outside the closed tomb, it looks as if the widow has died with her husband (*ut quisquis ex notis ignotisque ad monumentum venisset, putaret expirasse super corpus viri pudicissimam uxorem*, 112.3). Not such an illusion, as the 'virtuous wife' has indeed perished. This post-Virgilian audience is reminded that surface appearance does not always correspond with interior reality, and the joke here is that the townsfolk remind us of the Trojans misinterpreting the disastrous Trojan Horse

The tale of the widow of Ephesus can only end 'happily' if it remains self-contained, unrelated to the narrative which surrounds and precedes it. As soon as we stop reading the tale as an extractable narrative, our impression of its comfortable closure tends to disintegrate, replaced by tension, expectation, suspense. The widow's final gesture, the fixing of her husband's body on the cross in place of the stolen corpse, is particularly problematic. I am puzzled by Bakhtin's conclusion that the act of lifting the husband's body onto the cross signifies a 'resurrection' in parallel with what is defined as the rejuvenating spirit of this novelistic narrative in general.[43] Even if we may (impossibly) presume the influence of Christian cult symbolism here, what we are reading is surely not resurrection but precisely the opposite: Christ is taken down from the cross to his cave-tomb from where he ascends into heaven, not back onto the cross.[44] The shame of being crucified as a criminal (a man who, in Christian thought, will descend to hell not ascend to heaven) is something the husband cannot escape: this is his final resting place. His crucifixion may have saved the soldier's life, but it is a sign not of hope and rebirth but of a lowering and degrading of human life:[45] it advertises the widow's guilt, and suggests that the sanctity of the cave-tomb cannot be breached without the ominous release of its chthonic, creative power.

I have tried to show that although, on one level, we are directed to see the tale as rather flimsy entertainment detracting from, rather than reflecting, the wider narrative situation, on another, this is a complex narrative that develops imagery and marks a significant point in the writing process of the *Bellum Civile*. Readings of the tale as comic have implied a curiously limited view of comedy which moves to cancel out tension and complexity in favour of a laddish, bawdy humour. I have argued instead that comedy in this tale is always double-edged; the ending constitutes not so much a resolution as a cliffhanger, for the visceral, uncontrollable

as a happy ending to an idealised narrative. But the joke is also that we too react gullibly if we think this story ends where it ends, if we think this counts as a happy ending.

43 Bakhtin (1981: 222–3).

44 Could it be that this narrative is as much about regression to tragedy as about transcendence to novelistic comedy? Like this tale itself, a romance set in hell, the husband's crucifixion is always a paradoxical or ambivalent gesture, as the conflicting reactions of the audience demonstrate: for the townsfolk, the husband's fate is a hilarious punchline, while Lichas is anything but amused.

45 The crucified criminal is also a sex symbol, pigeonholed by Chrysis in *Sat.* 126 along with actors, slaves, gladiators, and men with scars: *ego adhuc servo numquam succubui, nec hoc dii sinant, ut amplexus meos in crucem mittam. viderint matronae, quae flagellorum vestigia osculantur* / 'I never yielded to a slave yet, and god forbid that I should fall into the arms of a gallows-bird. The married women can see to that, the ones who kiss scars after a flogging' (126.9–10). By hooking up with a soldier and crucifying her husband, the widow of Ephesus fulfills all her (stereotypical, matronly) erotic fantasies at once.

energy trapped in the cave-tomb is about to blow. To presume otherwise, or to brush over the anxious conflicts in audience response to the tale, is to repeat (again) the infamous misreading of the Trojans, caricatured here as a townsfolk oblivious to the machinations concealed inside the closed tomb that resonates so powerfully alongside *all* the *Satyricon*'s spectral spaces, from labyrinth and horse-belly, to the visualised guts of Trimalchio's guests, and ultimately of Eumolpus himself. When all eyes and ears focus on Eumolpus at 110.8, our memories stir in expectation of the gloriously seductive Fall of Troy, the story which, in Petronius, comes to stand for Virgil's (for literature's) power to affect readers physically. This is a tale about the seductiveness of poetry, its power to move and corrupt even the most impenetrable and virtuous of minds, just like, we can always say, the *Satyricon* itself, the disjointed and disjointing *satyrion*, or the delicious, poisonous dishes from Trimalchio's kitchen which will have you enthralled as well as make you sick. The more we enjoy this tale, the more we are sucked into the *Satyricon*'s core problematisation of what literature does to its readers, its concern with the pernicious dangers of eating, and of reading itself. If you've read this far, there's no leaving the literary table: as Eumolpus' take on Virgil suggests, not even *good* taste insures against heartburn.

CHAPTER 9

Ghost stories

I have argued that the writing and performance of the *Bellum Civile* reverberates throughout the ship voyage and march to Croton, as well as in Croton itself, the city which seems to mimic the conditions of civil war. Parallels and overlaps between apparently distinct episodes make it difficult to determine when the poem ends and where 'real-life' narrative begins, or vice versa, thus problematising distinctions between and definitions of fiction and reality, poetry and prose. When Eumolpus and his gang enter Croton, therefore, just as the *Bellum Civile* ends at *Sat.* 124, they seem to be entering into the landscape represented in the poem itself. The 'invasion' of Croton by the leader Eumolpus and his 'army' of 'gladiator' slaves, followed by their greedy exploitation of foreign luxuries (*quotidie magis magisque superfluentibus bonis saginatum corpus impleveram* / 'every day I filled my stuffed body with an ever-growing supply of goodies', *Sat.* 125.2),[1] and Encolpius' fear of vengeful Fortuna (*putabamque a custodia mei removisse vultum Fortunam* / 'I thought that Fortune had turned away her face from keeping a watch on me') restage the scenes at the beginning of the *Bellum Civile*, where war is precipitated by insatiable imperialistic greed and directed by Fortuna. As critics have suggested, Eumolpus' descent into Croton is imaged as a repetition of Caesar's (and Hannibal's, and Hercules'...) crossing of the Alps in the *Bellum Civile*, a poem which, as Connors puts it, has already figured history as 'a series of re-enactments'.[2] As we saw in chapter six, progress along the Callimachean path of poetry, which is also the road to Croton (*viam, qua iretur ad carmen... timuerunt* ***calcare***, 118.5) is explicitly aligned with Caesar's historic advance (*haec ubi* ***calcavit*** *Caesar iuga milite laeto*, *BC* 152).

[1] Note that *sagina* has a specific association with the fattening of gladiators or soldiers before battle: see Tac. *Hist.* 2.8 and Prop. 4.8.25.

[2] Connors (1998) 130. See also Beck (1979: 248) and Connors (1998: 125–134).

Yet it is equally important that the acting roles required for the recitation of the *Bellum Civile* are not cast aside when the poem is finished but are continued, adding to the impression that the characters to some extent now remain suspended in poetic performance. For the entire Croton episode (*Sat.* 124–40), the gang are in disguise, working continually on the plot to seduce the legacy-hunters which was conceived back in *Sat.* 117. Eumolpus is playing a rich African businessman with one foot in the grave, and the others are to act as his devoted slaves, who have pledged their bodies to him like gladiators. The approximation of the recitation of the *Bellum Civile* and the performance of the characters inside Croton is indicated specifically at *Sat.* 124: whereas Eumolpus 'pours out' the poem with immense fluency (*cum haec Eumolpus ingenti volubilitate verborum effudisset*), at the first meeting with the fortune-hunters the actors spurt out the agreed fictional account in unison, in the same manner (*ex praescripto ergo consilii communis exaggerata verborum volubilitate* / 'Then, as we'd arranged between us, we blurted out our prepared speech in a torrent of words', 124.3).[3] In this chapter, I will explore more extensively the spectrum of ways in which the dramas in Croton are not only performances but reperformances. As well as living out the poetic environment of Eumolpus' poem on civil war, itself influenced, implicitly, by imagining what life will really be like in this city of death and greed, the characters are also all acting out roles devised and imposed by the poet Eumolpus just before the recitation of the *Bellum Civile*.

The scenes at Croton, I suggest, develop an association between acting and poetic performance. For the self-consciousness of 'putting on an act' coincides with Encolpius' sudden creative impulse, as he now responds to and even usurps Eumolpus' role as poet of the *Satyricon*.[4] As he transforms his body to play a character invented by Eumolpus, Encolpius is also forging an identity as poet which entails his 'embodiment' as or in his work. Maintaining a series of acting personas involves an increased awareness of physical appearance and body language, and

[3] This point is made by Beck (1979: 248).

[4] This sense of empowerment as a performer culminates at *Sat.* 140 when Encolpius makes an aggressive sexual move on Eumolpus, who has until now been the sexual predator (*sustuli tunicam Eumolpoque me totum approbavi. at ille primo exhorruit, deinde ut plurimum crederet, utraque manu deorum beneficia tractat* / 'I lifted my tunic and offered my whole body for Eumolpus to feast his eyes on. At first he was terrified, and then, so that it could really sink in, he fondled the gifts of the gods with both hands', 140.13). The roles of orator and actor are so anxiously intertwined, both here and in the rhetorical treatises, that as soon as Encolpius announces he is acting, we are conscious that he is also a literary performer.

from the outset Encolpius is paranoid that his fragile, superficial identity will collapse:

'quid' aiebam 'si callidus captator exploratorem in Africam miserit mendaciumque deprehenderit nostrum? quid, si etiam mercennarius praesenti felicitate lassus indicium ad amicos detulerit totamque fallaciam invidiosa proditione detexerit?' (125.3)

I kept saying to myself, 'What if some clever-dick legacy-hunter sends a spy over to Africa and finds out we're lying? Or what if the servant tires of his present luck and drops a hint to his friends, or just betrays us out of spite and exposes the whole scam?'

Here and throughout the *Satyricon*, bodily self-consciousness, implying psychological as well as physical vulnerability, seems almost to be a condition for writing, which is always envisaged as a product of digested learning. Like acting, writing poetry in the *Satyricon* can be dangerously self-revelatory:[5] its internal source constantly threatens to penetrate Encolpius' disguise, to reveal his real, *inside* body in all its potential inadequacy.

For example, in his guise as a scarred slave, complete with wig, fake eyebrows and make-up provided by Tryphaena to cover up Eumolpus' writing experiments on board ship, Encolpius the actor is received by Chrysis in terms suggestive of literary criticism;[6] Here Chrysis, apparently convinced by his guise as gladiator/slave, surveys Encolpius' appearance as if she is commenting on elegant Callimachean verse:

quo enim spectant flexae pectine comae, quo facies medicamine attrita et oculorum quoque mollis petulantia, quo incessus arte compositus et ne vestigia[7] quidem pedum extra mensuram aberrantia, nisi quod formam prostituis, ut vendas? (126.2)

What is the point of that nicely combed hair of yours, that face plastered in make-up, that soft fondness in your eyes, the walk artfully measured so that not even a footstep is out of place? The only answer is that your beauty is up for sale.

[5] Does Encolpius become impotent with Circe precisely because he is acting? These scenes play on the anxiety surrounding the approximation of theatrical performance and public speaking, derived from the notion that acting is lowly and unmanly because it transcends or subverts the male citizen's self-controlled, self-contained, body. The encounter with Circe shows that in becoming an actor (and in attracting women with his fake actor's appearance), Encolpius risks becoming unvirile and like a woman.

[6] As I have argued, the poet Eumolpus has already set precedents for the writer's 'embodiment' of or in his work: e.g. as a Trojan horse ejecting dangerous poetic material in *Sat.* 89–90.

[7] Petronius uses *vestigia* to mean marks on the body as well as 'steps': e.g. *flagellorum vestigia* / 'marks of the whip' (126.10). The 'scars' resulting from the slave-act on board ship are still a feature of his disguise.

The rhetorical-sounding phrase *arte compositus* immediately recalls Encolpius' poetic status on board ship, where his body, I have argued, served as the poet's note-pad for his experimental jottings in preparation for the *Bellum Civile*. At *Sat.* 102.15, as the gang discuss various 'writing' plans, Giton rejects Encolpius' crude idea to cover their bodies in writing ink, saying: *color arte compositus inquinat corpus, non mutat* / 'artificial colour stains but does not change the body'. This verbal parallel hints that Encolpius could easily look like a neatly-turned poem here, artfully composed, with not a foot out of place. In this context, Chrysis' description could be construed as making ample use of a critical rhetoric rooted in metaphors of physical appearance, health and performance: in particular, *facies* can be used to mean style or form,[8] *attritus* to indicate 'worn down' or 'attenuated' oratorical style,[9] *pecten* is a quill for striking lyre strings, as well as a comb for the hair,[10] the adjective *flexus* can signify artful 'turning' of the voice in public speaking,[11] while *pes* and *mensura* are clearly terms used in the discussion of poetic metre. Similarly, later on at *Sat.* 131.4, Oenothea receives Encolpius by wrapping threads around his neck and marking his forehead with a seal, as if he is a rolled-up manuscript about to be dispatched (*illa de sinu licium protulit varii coloris filis intortum cervicemque vinxit meam. mox turbatum sputo pulverem medio sustulit digito frontemque repugnantis signavit*).[12]

Chrysis' potentially metaphorical[13] speech would again seem to raise the issue of literature's potential to affect a reader physically, to stir hunger or sexual arousal. Moreover, Encolpius' embodiment of an emotive, arousing piece of poetry or oratory renders all too real an established rhetorical discourse which describes speeches in physiognomic terms, or figures literature as a food to be consumed in the process of reading and learning. Yet in the *Satyricon*, the result of 'eating' literature, it seems, is that the student *becomes* what he reads, a literary body marked legibly with

[8] E.g. Quint. *Inst.* 12.10.69: *plures etiam eloquentiae facies* / 'eloquence has many faces'.

[9] E.g. Tac. *Dial.* 18.5: *ex quibus facile est deprendere Calvus quidem Ciceroni visum exsanguem et attritum* / 'from which one quickly gathers that Cicero thought Calvus bloodless and rather worn'.

[10] E.g. Juv. *Sat.* 6.382 (*crispo numerantur pectine chordae* / 'She runs through the cords with quivering quill'); Virg. *Aen.* 6.647 (*eadem ... pectine pulsat eburno* / 'He plucked the notes with an ivory plectrum').

[11] Quint. *Inst.* 1.8.1 cf. Sen. *Dial.* 10.12.4.

[12] *signo* can mean to mark with writing, imprint, inscribe, or to fix a seal on a letter or contract (e.g. Cic. *Att.* 11.1.1; Hor. *Epist.* 1.13.2; Ov. *Tr.* 5.4.5). It can also be used to indicate tattooing (Pliny, *HN* 6.11) and branding (Nov. *Com.* 42): i.e. this scene is reminiscent of the 'branding' or 'tattooing' escapades on board ship. *frons*, as I discussed above, means both 'brow' and the flat ends of a papyrus roll (e.g. Ov. *Tr.* 1.1.110; *Pont.* 4.13.7; Sen. *Dial.* 9.9.6).

[13] For discussion of the possible criteria for distinguishing metaphorical usage in ancient literate discourse, see Silk (1974: 27–56).

the scars of his own knowledge. The parallel between the 'written' bodies of *Sat.* 102–3 and the 'legible' desirability of Encolpius here is hinted at also in Chrysis' discussion of the sexual appeal of the slave or gladiator further on in *Sat.* 126: her mistress, Circe, is the kind of woman who can only be attracted to rough, low-class men, and who is particularly turned on by a gladiator's scars (*viderint matronae, quae flagellorum vestigia osculantur* / 'let the married women see to that, the ones who kiss the scars caused by flogging', 126.10). It is as if Encolpius is still playing the role of branded or 'written' slave which he was instructed to adopt on board ship.[14] However, Chrysis' naïve belief that she can see a man's character in his face, his thoughts by the way he walks (*ex vultibus tamen hominum mores colligo, et cum spatiantem vidi, quid cogitet scio*, 126.3) threatens even now to puncture Encolpius' superficial act, to repeat the recognition and punishment scenes on Lichas' boat.[15] In Croton, of course, the threats of cannibalism imagined in the ship-cave are even more immediate.[16]

The eroticisation of scars, which recalls the comparison of Lichas' 'recognition' of Encolpius to Eurycleia's recognition of Odysseus by means of his scar at *Sat.* 105, is the first in a series of identifications of the Odyssean past triggered by Encolpius' encounter with a woman named Circe. Like Encolpius in his role as Odysseus, Circe is acting: both characters are intensely aware of the power of their Homeric names and the narratives that accompany them, so that their interaction is envisaged as a meeting of (embodied) literary signifiers: Encolpius is perceived by Circe as an extract from Homeric verse, while she also appears to him as an artistic creation (*mulierem omnibus simulacris emendatiorem*, 126.13); both are consummate poseurs, and Circe keeps stopping to check contrived 'looks' in a mirror.[17] Although she is not the *real* Circe, she claims her

[14] Indeed the two 'roles', actor and slave, are already associated in Chrysis' speech about female desires: *quaedam enim feminae sordibus calent, nec libidinem concitant, nisi aut servos viderint aut statores altius cinctos. harena aliquas accendit aut perfusus pulvere mulio aut histrio scaenae ostentatione traductus* / 'Some women, you know, get the hots for vile men, and can't get turned on at all unless they set eyes on a slave-boy, or some servant in a hitched-up tunic. Some go for the arena talent, either a muleteer covered in dust or an actor disgraced after exposing himself on stage' (126.5–6).

[15] Chrysis' confidence in metoposcopy recalls Petronius' restaging of the Trojan belief in determining insides from outsides, in the *Troiae Halosis* and also in Trimalchio's *cena*. Yet it is also as if she can 'read' Encolpius, or at least see the traces of previous 'scars' under his wig.

[16] Especially when Circe reveals she is fainting with hunger (*spiritus ieiunio marcens*, 128.1). Hunger is implicitly (frustrated) sexual desire, 'eating' the satisfaction of that desire.

[17] 128.4–5: *rapuit deinde tacenti speculum, et postquam omnes vultus temptavit, quos solet inter amantes risus fingere* . . . / 'Then she snatched a mirror from the dumbstruck girl, and after trying out a look which brings a smile to most lovers' lips . . .' Petronius' Circe is a mere reflection of her Homeric self. Yet the mirror hints also at her dangerous feminine powers: a woman with a mirror can

name encapsulates Circean magic when combined with *polyaenus*, the epithet granted to Odysseus by the Sirens in *Od.* 12.184 when he survives their deadly song with the help of Circe's advice:

'ita' inquit 'non dixit tibi ancilla mea me Circen vocari? non sum quidem Solis progenies, nec mea mater, dum placet, labentis mundi cursum detinuit. habebo tamen quod caelo imputem, si nos fata coniunxerint. immo iam nescio quid tacitis cogitationibus deus agit. nec sine causa Polyaenon Circe amat: semper inter haec nomina magna fax surgit.' (127.6–7)

'So', she said, 'didn't my maid tell you my name is Circe? I'm not the Sun-child, mind you, and neither has my mother ever stopped the world in its course when she felt like it. But I will have a debt to pay to heaven if fate brings the two of us together. I'm sure some god is scheming silently as we speak. Circe does not love Polyaenus without good reason: when these names meet, there's always fireworks.'

As Connors suggests, Encolpius also attempts to 'playfully authenticate' his Odyssean identity by observing that Circe's voice sounds like that of the Sirens (*ut putares inter auras canere Sirenum concordiam*, 127.5), implying that, as Odysseus, he has heard the song of the Sirens and lived to tell the tale, thanks to Circe.[18] In wooing Circe, Encolpius parades his knowledge of Homer further in the poem at 127.9, in which he compares their embraces to the 'wedding' of Zeus and Hera on Mount Ida in *Iliad* XIV:

Idaeo qualis fudit de vertice flores
terra parens, cum se concesso iunxit amori
Iuppiter et toto concepit pectore flammas:
emicuere rosae violaeque et molle cyperon,
albaque de viridi riserunt lilia prato:
talis humus Venerem molles clamavit in herbas,
candidiorque dies secreto favit amori.

Such flowers spread by mother earth on Ida's peak
when Jupiter swept her up in lawful love
and all his heart caught fire.
Roses shone there, violets and soft galingale;
white lilies laughed in the green meadow.
Such a turf called Venus to its tender plants, and
the day grew bright to bless their secret love.

make-up, act and deceive, even paralyse and kill (Medusa's gaze is represented, as well as deflected, by Perseus' mirror-shield).

18 Connors (1998) 40. Odysseus learns how to master the Sirens' song from Circe (*Od.* 12.39–54).

Encolpius' poem is clearly recognisable as a loose paraphrase of its Homeric model, in which Hera uses Aphrodite's spells to seduce Zeus in order to divert his attention from what is happening at Troy. Yet instead of the lotus, crocus and hyacinth that bloom around Hera and Zeus, here the flowers are the rose, violet, galingale and lily;[19] and instead of being shrouded in a bright cloud like Homer's modest couple,[20] Encolpius and Circe embrace openly in broad daylight (*candidiorque dies*). Encolpius' Latin translation sets the scene for the superficiality of this coupling, hinting that there is no room for subtlety and concealment in repetition: drained of the impact of originality, the poem already looks 'soft' (*molle cyperon . . . molles in herbas*), offering little inspiration for Encolpius' virility; clearly, the Homeric precedent already tells us that this seduction is about a woman using erotic magic to control her male partner. Yet we also know that such a contrived alignment of signifiers (Circe and *polyaenus*) cannot be as predictable as the combination of chemical elements foreseen by Circe: reperforming, or translating Homer, however knowledgeable the 'actors', will inevitably introduce different experiences of reading, new perspectives and agendas, so as to produce new, potentially more complex narratives. The interaction of reading bodies at *Sat.* 127.10, lying down (*compositi*) like 'composed' poems,[21] is about to send the story of *Odyssey* X reeling off on an altogether different course.

In *Sat.* 128, Encolpius' metrical neatness disintegrates as soon as he attempts to consummate his relationship with Circe. He is impotent, and his body seems to have lost its shape, or its wholeness (*etiam si quid habueram virium perdidi, totoque corpore velut laxato*, 128.2). He has failed where Odysseus triumphed, perhaps because he has not received a drug from Hermes to protect himself against Circe's magic (*Od.* 10.301, 341). Encolpius embodies his own description of bad oratory, or bad literature in general, as unvirile in *Sat.* 2.2:[22] like the amateur speech sustained

[19] Courtney suggests (1991: 31) that the galingale, *cyperon*, is a reference to Aphrodite's meeting with Anchises amid oaks and galingale on Mount Ida in Theocritus, *Id.* 1.106. Connors (1998: 42) proposes that the roses are introduced here because their absence in Homer was remarked upon by readers (the scholia record that Homer left out the rose because of its thorniness Schol b T ad *Il.*14.347). Now, 'the roses (thorns and all) bring hints of love's discontents into the very heart of a poetic landscape perfect for love'.

[20] τῷ ἔνι λεξάσθην ἐπὶ δε νεφέλην ἕσσαντο / καλὴν χρυσεῖην / 'Here they lay, veiled by a beautiful golden cloud' (*Iliad* 14.350–1).

[21] *In hoc gramine pariter compositi mille osculis lusimus, quaerentes voluptatem robustam* / 'We lay together on the grass and exchanged a thousand kisses as we went in search of rougher pleasures' (127.10).

[22] Cf. Tac. *Dial.* 18.5: *Ciceronem et Calvo . . . male audisse tamquam solutum et enervem* / 'Cicero was in turn criticised by Calvus for being spiritless and weak.'

by surface flourishes and lacking in real substance, his literary prowess is based on a mere name, the superficiality of which is revealed as soon as he has to involve his body in the performance. Beneath the surface, his *corpus* betrays his ignorance, and his floppy physique takes on the shape of a clumsily written speech or poem. Encolpius is paralysed by Circe because even after she has emphasised that her name is a narrative trigger (127), he does not fully grasp the implications, the learned notion that 'a woman called Circe is poisonous'.

We can take the parallel between Encolpius' erotic failure here and his caricature of the impotent young orator/speech further: not only does his literary ignorance reveal itself in an unmanly 'body' of speech, hidden beneath a veneer of appeal; he has attracted Circe by posing as a scarred soldier, capitalising on the seductiveness of the gladiator just like the orator in *Sat.* 1 who displays and exaggerates his wounds in order to win over his audience (*haec vulnera pro libertate publica excepi*, 1.1); impotence, as Circe says, can prevent the afflicted from walking (*negant enim medici sine nervis homines ambulare posse* / 'For doctors say that people who have lost their sinews cannot walk', 129.5),[23] just as the caricatured orator claims that he is hamstrung and cannot walk (*qui me ducat ad liberos meos, nam succisi poplites membra non sustinent?* 1.1). Like the students rendered starry-eyed by the unreal environment of the rhetorical school (*putent se in alium orbem terrarum delatos* / 'they think they have been transported into another world', 1.2), Encolpius has entered naïvely into a world of fiction, unprepared for the consequences. At *Sat.* 128, his response to his affliction is to muse dizzily about dreams and shadows (128.6 v. 1): he compares losing Circe to finding treasure in a dream and waking up to find it does not exist, recalling Ascyltos' condemnation of Agamemnon's speeches as nothing more than *somniorum interpretamenta* ('dream interpretations', 10.1). Croton itself, the city where people are more concerned with financial gain and self-promotion than literature (*non litterarum studia celebrantur, non eloquentia locum habet* / 'The pursuit of learning is not valued, nor does eloquence have a place here', 116.6), could look like an exaggerated satire of the rhetorical school in the vein of *Sat.* 1–5, in which teachers are greedy, illiterate parasites who can only think about seducing and trapping an audience (*nihil prius meditantur quam id quod putant gratissimum auditoribus fore*, 3.3). The images of the master of oratory baiting his victims like a fisherman (to the point where we imagine him consuming his audience),

[23] Impotence is this Circe's version of Homeric metamorphosis: the enervated man is bestialised, since he can no longer walk (on two legs).

and the voracious legacy-hunter seducing his prey in order to 'eat' his fortune/flesh, are perhaps too close for comfort.

The entire episode at Croton, as told by our disreputable narrator Encolpius, might be read as a confused recollection or regurgitation of *Odyssey* X. In Encolpius' mixed-up version, Circe succeeds in poisoning Odysseus but does not mean to; she invites Odysseus to bed *before* she poisons him, and Mercury eventually reverses the effects of the magic, rather than giving Odysseus a prophylactic potion in the first place (*Mercurius enim, qui animas ducere et reducere solet, suis beneficiis reddidit mihi, quod manus irata praeciderat* / 'for Mercury, who directs and redirects our souls, has used his powers to restore to me that which his angry hand had stolen away', 140.12). From one angle it is ironic that Encolpius' role as Odysseus here is defined by the epithet *polyaenus* given to Odysseus by the Sirens as a mark of his heroic ability to withstand their enchanting song: Encolpius seems so oblivious it is as if he has not really listened to the story of the *Odyssey* at all. Yet another way of reading this 'confusion' is as an imaginative rehash or multiplication of literary influences (including earlier parts of the *Satyricon* itself), which render a straightforward reperformance of the Homeric narrative impossible. Fittingly, *polyaenus* means 'a man of many stories'. Petronius' literary bodies are what they eat, and Encolpius has clearly consumed much more than just Homeric epic.

His courtship of Circe at *Sat.* 129–30, for example, is also conducted as if it were an erotic exchange from Roman elegy: the couple exchange fraught letters via an intermediary slave-girl, Chrysis, and Encolpius plays the role of an amateur elegiac 'soldier of love', who has mistakenly surrendered one weapon too many (*paratus miles arma non habui* / 'I was a ready soldier but had no arms', 130.4).[24] There are parallels here with the tale of the widow of Ephesus, the narrator of which simply cannot make us think about the epic love affair between Dido and Aeneas without at the same time referring to, or conjuring up, images and scenarios from elegiac love poetry. Encolpius' allusion to the *miles amator* of Ovidian elegy within the fantasy of his Homeric affair with a woman called Circe is implicitly one of the reasons for his impotence: elegy's playful rejection of traditionally masculine epic roles makes it very difficult for an educated reader to play a convincing Odysseus, especially

[24] Cf. Ov. *Am.* 3.7.71 (*per te deprensus inermis* / 'because of you I've been caught unarmed'). Richlin (1983: 118) suggests that *inermis* is reminiscent of Priapic poems, as Priapus regularly describes his genitalia as his weapons (Pr. 9.20, 11.3, 25.7, 31.3, 43.1, 55.4).

when it comes to acting out love scenes.[25] In particular, Ovid's manly poem on his bed-time failure with Corinna (*Am.* 3.7) (which encapsulates the ongoing irony that in his solitary role as poet the one thing he is *not* doing is performing between the sheets),[26] has clearly poisoned (or is that inspired?) Encolpius' mind. In Ovid, Corinna acts with an outrage that mirrors Circe's: *'quid me ludis?' ait* (' "What are you playing at?" she said', *Am.* 3.7.77) cf. *'quid est?' inquit* (' "What is it?", she said', *Sat.* 128.1). Corinna assumes her lover is a victim of Circe's spells (*aut te traiectis Aeaea venefica lanis / devovet*, 79–80); either that or, as Circe accuses Encolpius, he is exhausted from another partner (*aut alio lassus amore venis* / 'or you come to me tired from another love', *Am.* 3.7.80 cf. *recipies, inquam, nervos tuos, si triduo sine fratre dormieris* / 'I think you will recover your sinews if you sleep without your brother for three days', *Sat.* 129.8). Later on, Encolpius, like Ovid, talks to his inactive member as if to a rebellious homuncule (*'quid dicis' inquam 'omnium hominum deorumque pudor?'* / ' "What have you got to say for yourself", I asked him, "you shame of all gods and men?" ', 132.9; cf. *quin istic pudibunda iaces, pars pessima nostri?* / 'Are you going to just lie there in shame, you despicable bit of me?', *Am.* 3.7.69).[27]

Meanwhile the 'disease' with which Encolpius is afflicted (*numquam ego aegrum tam magno periculo vidi* / 'I've never seen a sick man in such great danger', 129.6) reminds us of his own reaction to (what he apparently perceives as) Eumolpus' poor poetic performance at *Sat.* 90.3: *'rogo' inquam 'quid tibi vis cum isto morbo? minus quam duabus horis mecum moraris, et saepius poetice quam humane locutus es.'* / ' "Do me a favour", I said, "can't you get rid of that disease? You've been hanging round me for less than two hours and already you've talked more often as a poet than as a man." ' Poetry is imaged as the dangerous revelation of disease otherwise concealed within the body, in this case in parallel with the expulsion of Greek soldiers from the belly of the Trojan Horse. At Croton, Encolpius' malaise

[25] Ovid titillates with erotic suspense and deferral, and even with his own inability to perform (*Am.* 3.7): in fact, anything *but* graphic scenes of consummation. For then what more would there be to write about?

[26] See Sharrock (1995), who reminds us that for a Callimachean poet, 'whose every word must be painstakingly weighed, one might almost consider the experience of difficulty in performing obligatory . . . the sexual and poetic impotence which the poem celebrates are a reflection on the nature of elegy, doomed as it is to perpetual "failure" through which it achieves success' (157). This is poetry which 'thrives on rejection and is structured around exclusion' (162).

[27] Horace, *Sat.* 1.2.68–71 imagines this in reverse, when disastrous Villius' cock pipes up to ask him what on earth he thinks he's doing; cf. Martial, who says his penis protests when he refuses to buy a *puer* at a high price (1.58.3), and asks it its opinion on women (9.37.10). As Richlin argues (1983: 116), the god Priapus is often imagined as a walking, talking phallus: some poems compare a man's penis to the god (Juv. *Sat.* 6.375–6; Mart. 11.51, 11.72).

is also implicitly a comment on his status as a poet and his poetic ability. When he first meets Circe's maid Chrysis and she howls with laughter at his inept turn of phrase (*multum risit ancilla post tam frigidum schema*, 126.8), the adjective *frigidum* predicts the frigidity of his sexual response: *namque illa metu frigidior rigente bruma / confugerat in viscera mille operta rugis* / 'for that thing, colder with fear than the stiffest mid-winter, had retracted into my flesh covered in a thousand wrinkles' (132.8 vv. 5–6).[28] Encolpius' verbal and intellectual impotence forecasts, and is manifested in, his inability to perform sexually, and in *Sat.* 132 it follows that even the sword with which he 'castrates' himself will be merely verbal:

ita non potui supplicio caput aperire,
sed furciferae mortifero timore lusus
ad *verba*, magis quae poterant nocere, fugi.
(132.8 vv. 7–9)

I couldn't uncover its head to give it some,
so as mere plaything of the fucker's deadly fear
I took refuge in words, which could hurt all the more.

Yet in a city in the midst of civil war, Encolpius' affliction is also a reminder of the plague that penetrates the flesh and bones of greedy Romans in the *Bellum Civile*, an outbreak of disease sown in the marrow (*sed veluti tabes tacitis concepta medullis, BC* 54) that will in turn cause war (and poetry) to erupt. The outbreak of disease and the debilitation of the human body is connected to the energy and production of poetry at crucial points throughout the *Satyricon*.

It is crucial, then, that Encolpius becomes 'impotent', and at the same time poetically effusive, at the very point at which he encounters Circean spells, the *Aeaea carmina*[29] which rely precisely on the power of words to control and alter nature. Latin elegy in particular associates Circean

[28] *frigidus* can be used of lame, unappealing speech or speakers (e.g. Cic. *Fam.* 10.16.1; Ov. *Pont.* 4.2.45; Quint. *Inst.* 4.1.77), as well as of sexual frigidity (Ov. *Am.* 2.1.5: *me legat in sponsi facie non frigida virgo* / 'I want a reader who isn't frigid at the sight of her lover-to-be's face'). Encolpius reacted the same way to the abuse of his body in Quartilla's brothel (*ego autem frigidior hieme Gallica factus* / 'I turned colder than a Swiss winter', 19.3; *sollicitavit inguina mea mille iam mortibus frigida* / 'She stirred my groin, which had been blasted with the chill of a thousand deaths', 20.2). Ovid in *Am.* 3.7 also describes his lazy genitalia as frozen: *gelida mea membra* (13).

[29] Songs of Aeaea, Circe's birthplace. Connors suggests (1998: 43) that Petronius 'takes to a logical extreme the literary representations which tend to count "Circean" erotic magic, *Aeaea carmina*, as the expertise of an old dipsomaniacal procuress (*lena*)'. Oenothea, she argues, 'is clearly meant to recall the universal magical powers of a *lena*, such as Ovid's Dipsas, who knows the *Aeaea carmina* (*Am.* 1.8.5); the name Dipsas ("thirsty") carries the same connotations of drunkenness as are obvious in the name Oenothea ("wine goddess").'

magic with femaleness and with the enchanting, seductive power of all poetry (cunningly appropriated by 'feminine' elegy itself).[30] Ovid's versified sweet nothings outside Corinna's bolted door at *Am.* 2.1.23–8 are conjured up again in *Sat.* 129 and 134: compare *carmina sanguineae deducunt cornua lunae / et revocant niveos solis euntis equos* / 'Song lures down the horns of the blood-red moon and calls back the snow-white steeds of the departing sun' (*Am.* 2.1.23–4) with *in hac civitate, in qua mulieres etiam lunam deducunt* / 'In this town, the women can even draw down the moon from the sky' (the warning of Chrysis at 129.10) and *lunae descendit imago / carminibus deducta meis, trepidusque furentes / flectere Phoebus equos revoluto cogitur orbe* / 'The shape of the moon is drawn down by my spells, and trembling Pheobus must turn his horses as he is forced to reverse his path' (the Circean Oenothea at 134.12 vv. 8–10). Love poetry is constructed as embodying the spellbinding (Circean) potency of love itself. In Petronius, Circe's (woman's/poetry's) ability to control Phoebus' horses rings with echoes of Agamemnon's programmatic image of the Roman writer intuitively controlling the wild, unsaddled horse of contemporary literature (*mox et Socratico plenus grege mittat habenas / liber*, *Sat.* 5 vv. 13–14)

In the epithet *polyaenus*, Encolpius' status as Odysseus has already been explicitly connected with the hero's survival of the Sirens' typically esoteric, female song, a success which, as Blanchot argues, comes at a price: because Odysseus lives, he lives to tell his tales, and thus metamorphoses into the Homeric poet, the singer of songs we know. 'Every narration' writes Blanchot of the *Odyssey*, 'resists the encounter with the Sirens'.[31] Hence Encolpius' failure to be Odysseus and thus to withstand Circe's power over bodies and language results in an erotic and narrative aporia, so that his fundamental position as narrator of the *Satyricon* is both accented and undermined. Ironically, Circe's verbal power in the *Satyricon* is *just* the power of the word, the name, Circe. Unhindered by the hapless Encolpius, the name Circe not only disempowers her victim (the equivalent, here, of metamorphosis),[32] but also changes (metamorphoses) the Homeric story, allowing space for innovation. Nobody is actually turned into a pig, wolf or lion in Petronius' version, as

[30] See Sharrock (1994: 50–78): 'while purporting to reject the use of magic in love, Ovid in fact highlights the very indissolubility of the charms of magic and of love poetry . . . the *Ars Amatoria* is, of its nature, an *Ars Magica*. Ovid . . . is the *magus* of love as well as the *magister*' (65).

[31] Blanchot (1982: 61).

[32] It is also a literal reading of Hermes' warning to Odysseus that Circe will try to 'rob him of his manhood' (*Od.* 10.300–1).

metamorphosis is dealt with on a metaphorical, rather than a literal plane, and takes place at the level of language and narrative.[33]

Croton, we must remember, is the locus for the climax of Ovid's *Metamorphoses*, and the home of Pythagoreanism, the philosophy of eating founded on a belief in corporeal flux, on the idea that we cannot eat flesh of any kind because human souls are repeatedly and unpredictably reincarnated in animal bodies. Despite the fact that Circe claims she does not know Circean magic (*non sum quidem Solis progenies*, 127.6), Chrysis reveals that the women in Croton can 'draw the moon down from the sky' (129.10). Indeed at various points all the other female characters at Croton seem to be playing the role of, or metamorphosing into, Circe. At first Encolpius wants the maid Chrysis to be Circe (his lover) (*numquid illa, quae me amat, tu es?* / 'It is not you, I suppose, who love me?', 126.8), and at *Sat.* 139, his fantasy comes true (*Chrysis intervenit amplexuque effusissimo me invasit et 'teneo te' inquit 'qualem speraveram: tu desiderium meum, tu voluptas mea, numquam finies hunc ignem, nisi sanguine extinxeris'* / 'Chrysis came in, ran up, embraced me warmly and said, "Now I have you as I hoped; you are my desire, my pleasure, you will never put out this flame unless you quench it with my blood" ', 139.4). Meanwhile the two women introduced to Encolpius by Chrysis in the hope that they will cure him are both sorceresses in the Circean mould: Proselenos chants magic spells (131.5); Oenothea is a *sacerdos* (134.3) who can make earth and water obey her spell. In a reversal of Circe's initial use of her magic to turn men into animals, Oenothea wills tigers and snakes to stand up like humans (*Hyrcanaeque tigres et iussi stare dracones*, 134.12 v. 7).[34] In Croton *everyone* is a Circe.

It is striking, as critics have noted, that the people of Petronius' Croton seem to preach a philosophy antithetical to the Pythagoreanism of Ovid's Croton in *Met.* 15: far from feeling revulsion at the thought of eating animal flesh, to the point where they are nervous of eating anything at all, the inhabitants of Croton hunger not only for meat, but also for roast human. Yet in a sense, one might argue, the two philosophies are simply different perspectives or responses to the same idea that people are also animals, or potential meat. After reading Ovid's account, cannibalism at Croton is an utterly horrifying concept, implying a complete liberation

33 At cannibalistic Croton, one could argue, the divide between human and animal life (between eaters and eaten) has already collapsed.

34 Cf. Circe at Ovid, *Met.* 14.299–305, who changes the animals back into men in exchange for winning Odysseus as her 'husband'.

of the anarchic forces of metamorphosis. As in the *Cena*, where, I argued, the transformative process of acting is a trope for metamorphosis, so in Petronius' Croton the Circean power of metamorphosis seems to go hand in hand with role-play, or rather with the confusion of acting parts. Everyone at Petronius' Croton is a flesh-eater, and each inhabitant therefore incorporates a variety of different characters (or consumed personalities). Fittingly, the role or name of Circe has become a paradigm and metaphor for the effect of corporeal flux on individual identity in this epic city of metamorphosis.

It is no coincidence then that Croton, like other spectral spaces throughout the *Satyricon*, is imagined as an underworld. For this is a city in which dead spirits survive and multiply inside the living, as represented by the agglomeration of roles and appellations (as if everyone has been eating the same Circean meal). The notion that old souls continue to be present and to exert their all too vital energies is a hard-hitting metaphor for the influence of 'past' texts, and of past experience in general, on present writing and reading activities. Croton is a self-consciously fictional space inhabited by walking poems and narratives which enact just how embodied ghosts of texts (or our own literary memories) drive and complicate social and sexual interactions.

The vision of Croton as an underworld or hell is itself another instance of *polyaenus* Encolpius' embroiled recollection (or ambitious revision) of the narrative of the *Odyssey*. In Virgil, Circe is connected to the underworld in that she lives near Cumae, and in Homer, she instructs Odysseus to visit Hades in *Od*. X; in the *Satyricon*, however, she lives in ghostly Croton, and is responsible for luring Encolpius into his own private hell. For example, when in *Sat*. 132.10 he addresses his own impotent organ, he asks, *hoc de te merui, ut me in caelo positum ad inferos traheres?* / 'Did I deserve being dragged down to hell by you when I was in heaven?' Encolpius' experiences in Croton are dream-like, and he often thinks he has seen a ghost: when he realises he is impotent, he is horror-stricken (*ego contra damnatus et quasi quodam visu in horrorem perductus interrogare animum meum coepi, an vera voluptate fraudatus essem* / 'But I was horrified as if I had seen a ghost, and began to ask myself whether I had been cheated of real pleasure', 128.5), and in the poem that follows, he talks of snatching at treasure in a dream, only to wake with nothing but images: *nocte soporifera veluti cum somnia ludunt / . . . veraque forma redit, animus quod perdidit optat / atque in praeterita se totus imagine versat* (vv. 1, 8–9). At *Sat*. 139.1, he writhes on the bed and searches for a 'ghost' of his love (*torum frequenti tractatione vexavi, amoris mei quasi quandam imaginem*), while elsewhere he describes himself as partly dead (*funerata est illa pars corporis, qua quondam Achilles eram* / 'That part of my body which was once Achilles is now dead and buried', 129.1; *medius [fidius] iam peristi* / 'I declare that you are as good as dead', 129.6). Later, when Proselenos enters Oenothea's chamber at *Sat.* 134.7, where Encolpius is receiving 'treatment', it is as if she is visiting a freshly made grave (*tamquam ante recens bustum*). And when Encolpius is finally cured at *Sat.* 140.12, it is by Mercury, the god who guides souls in the underworld. The restoration of Encolpius' virility is equivalent to being allowed to revisit the earth after being confined to hell, which was the favour granted by Mercury to Protesilaus, the leader of the Thessalians who was also the first man to be slain in the war between Troy and Thessaly.[35]

The scenes at Croton continually play on the idea that the underworld is a poetic landscape in which characters (and readers) revisit people and narratives from the past. At 132.8, Encolpius' castration poem, in which he seizes the axe three times and three times flinches from the blade, sounds like a remake of Aeneas' attempts to embrace the ghost of Creusa in *Aeneid* II and of Anchises in the underworld of *Aeneid* VI:

> **Te**r corripui **ter**ribilem manu bipennem,
> **ter** languidior coliculi repen**te thyr**so
> ferrum timui, quod trepido male dabat usum.
> nec iam poteram, quod modo conficere libebat;
> namque illa metu frigidior rigente bruma
> confugerat in viscera mille operta rugis.

> Three times I seized the dreaded axe,
> three times, fainter than a cabbage stalk,
> I feared the steel, no use to me I shook so much.
> So now I couldn't do what I wanted to do a moment before;
> That thing, stiffer with fear than a frozen winter, had
> sunk back in my flesh, hooded by a thousand wrinkles.

[35] Bowersock (1994: 111–13) argues that Protesilaus epitomises both the resurrected hero and the 'theme of resurrection' in ancient fiction in general. He notes in particular: Chariton's *Callirhoë*, in which Chaereas assumes Callirhoë has been carried off by a god when her body disappears from its tomb; Xenophon's *Ephesiaca*, in which Anthia is presumed dead and is laid in a tomb, but regains consciousness and is abducted by pirates; Achilles Tatius' *Leucippe and Clitophon*, where the heroine seems to die and is resurrected three times; and Apuleius' *Met.*, in which 'communication with the dead, necromancy and visits to the Underworld are all conspicuous'. On Protesilaus, Bowersock (130) discusses Philostratus' *Heroikos* 11.17–32 (Kayser), where the various rectifications of Homer are introduced by Protesilaus, and *Callirhoë*, 5.10.1 ('What Protesilaus is this, who has come back to life to plague me?').

Compare *Aen.* 2. 792–3 (repeated at 6.700–1):[36]

> ter conatus ibi collo dare bracchia circum;
> ter frustra comprensa manus effugit imago

> Three times I tried to put my arms around her neck,
> Three times, in vain, the phantom slipped my grasp.

Encolpius triples and retriples Virgil's *ter . . . ter* patterning, using the force of amplification as a fearsome (*trepidus*) weapon of words which advertise and impugn his intellectual, as well as sexual impotence, his inability to do anything other than passively copy, repeat and echo. Even his blade is doubled (*bipennem*), and the choice of word here (as well as the fear of making the cut) duplicates Eumolpus' innovative repetition of Laocoön's assault on the Trojan Horse in the *Troiae Halosis*, which itself reverberates, I have argued, with Daedalus' nervy slicing of the stuffed pig at *Sat.* 49: in the *Troiae Halosis*, Laocoön hits the horse twice, not once, the first time with a spear, as in the *Aeneid*, but the second time with a double-edged axe:

> mox reducta cuspide
> uterum notavit, fata sed tardant manus,
> ictusque resilit et dolis addit fidem.
> iterum tamen confirmat invalidam manum
> altaque bipenni latera pertemptat.
> (*TH* vv. 20–4)

> Then he drew back the spear and hit the
> horse's womb, yet fate slowed his hand,
> the blow rebounded, built up our faith in tricks.
> Again he steadied feeble hand and
> struck deep flanks with the double axe.

The poem at *Sat.* 132 is written in Sotadeans, a 'passive' metre associated specifically with *cinaedi*, as I noted in chapter six. As Connors explains, the process of 'converting' hexameters into Sotadeans (from *Aen.* 2.792–3/6.700–1 to *Sat.* 132) is described as reading 'backwards' (*retro* or *retrorsus*).[37] Hence Encolpius' impotence, manifested in the physical retraction of his penis (*illa . . . confugerat in viscera*), is written in a poem whose metre bends (epic, manly hexameter) over backwards, and which dramatises its regressive, reiterative strategies by recalling epic passages

[36] Zeitlin (1971b: 71) and Connors (1998: 31) comment on this comparison.

[37] Connors (1998) 31. Dion. Hal. *Comp.* 24 (Usener), Quint. *Inst.* 9.4.90, Mart. 2.86.2, and cf. Plin. *Ep.* 5.3.2.

which also concern revisitations of the past, either in the underworld, or in Eumolpus' reworking of the Fall of Troy.

Encolpius now addresses his recalcitrant member in a brief speech (*oratio*), and it promptly responds to his appeals like Dido to Aeneas in the underworld of *Aeneid* VI:

> illa solo fixos oculos aversa tenebat,
> nec magis incepto vultum sermone movetur
> quam lentae salices lassove papavera collo.
> (132.11)

> It turned away, eyes fixed to floor, its face
> moved no more by my unfinished speech
> than bendy willows or poppies hung on tired necks.

Reference to the ghost of Dido in *Aeneid* VI, alongside Eumolpus' manipulation of her 'living' character from *Aeneid* IV in *Sat.* 111–12 could itself be read as a conscious attempt by Encolpius to extend narratives begun by the pedagogic poet, particularly as there are clearly parallels between the strongly elegiac (or elegised) widow of Ephesus tale and Encolpius' 'soldier of love' antics here. But again Encolpius seems to have identified to such an extent with Eumolpus' creative output that he has immersed himself directly in the narrative, becoming like the widow herself part-Dido, a womanly body whose sexual organs are infused with Virgilian anxieties and desires, throbbing away in hexameters.

While the first two lines of this poem quote *Aen.* 6.469–70 (the description of Dido's scornful refusal to speak to Aeneas in Hades) and play on Encolpius' previous portrayal of his organ as a body with a head (*caput*, 132.8 v. 7) covered and bowed like a woman in mourning, the third line (again the number is a cue for revision and multiplication) is also a clatter of repetitions: *quam lentae salices* replaces Virgil's *quam si dura silex aut stet Marpesia cautes* / 'just like a block of hard flint or rock quarried from Mount Marpessus' (*Aen.* 6.471), which would be wildly contradictory in this case (and is still funny, of course, for its conspicuous absence). The pliant willow now supplements the abscised line about adamantine flint, which is also a castration tool.[38] The adjective *lentus* attached to *salix* reminds us of the conversation between poets Mopsus and Menalcas in Virgil's fifth *Eclogue*: Menalcas assures Mopsus that poet Amyntas will agree to a singing contest 'as surely as supple

[38] E.g. Catullus 63 (the castration of Attis): *devolsit ili acuto sibi pondera silice* / 'He cut off the weights of his groin with a sharp flint' (5).

willow yields to the pale olive, or humble red valerian to the crimson rose' (*lenta salix quantum pallenti cedit olivae, / puniceis humilis quantum saliunca rosetis, / iudicio nostro tantum tibi cedit Amyntas*, 16–18).[39]

This poem is itself fast becoming a live contest between poetic influences and images, while Encolpius' over-flexible, malleable body is again framed as a blatant index of his poor literary performance. The second half of the third line, *lassoque papavera collo*, repeats the death of Euryalus at *Aen.* 9.436, and also alludes to Catullus 11.21–4, where the ditched poet sends a bilious message to Lesbia in which he accuses her of crushing him like a wildflower at the edge of a field. Both Virgil and Catullus play on the epic image of the young hero in the 'flower' of his youth which can be traced back to Homer.[40] Now the entire sluggish line, with its perceptible split in the centre (*quam lentae salices* ✂ *lassove papavera collo*) *looks like* the droopy body of its subject, and vice versa: poem and poet collapse into one as Encolpius' impotence continues to manifest itself as a physical symptom of inadequate or fragmented literary knowledge.[41]

Yet, like the 'impotent' Ovid or the callously 'victimised' Catullus displaying all the while their poetic power (the self-evidence of which is highlighted by a willingness to versify their own *erotic* failure), Encolpius is never *just* a bad poet, a defective caricature. Throughout much of the *Satyricon*, as we have seen, Encolpius is a highly metaphorical figure, enacting not only the tricky, shifting identity of the poet (and of the author of the *Satyricon*), but also embodying the text itself, as it is written, scarred, coloured, cut and pasted. His attempted castration (and actual chopping up of lines of poetry) equally evoke a conceptual vocabulary for analysing rhetorical style. As I mentioned earlier, Horace famously talks of *disiecti membra poetae*, and the adjective *abscisus* frequently refers to admirably neat, clipped composition in Valerius Maximus, Quintilian and Pliny.[42] The question of how to read Encolpius' body-text is always as slippery as metaphor itself: does he enact the self-evident impotence of his authorial voice, both in his desire to castrate himself (and thus to produce the

[39] The resulting poetic performance is staged in a cave (*successimus antro*, 19), in parallel to the (re-)creative environment of Virgil's underworld.

[40] See *Iliad* 8.306–7.

[41] It may also be worth noting that, in Aeneas' speech in *Aen.* VI, to which Dido responds by averting her eyes (6.469, the line quoted here by Encolpius), his key statement *invitus, regina, tuo de litore cessi* / 'I left your shores unwillingly, Queen' (6.460) gains its force partly by alluding to actual physical severance (*invita, o regina, tuo de vertice cessi* / 'I was parted from your head unwillingly, Queen'), the cutting of a lock of hair from Berenice's head in Catullus 66.39.

[42] Hor. *Sat.* 1.4.62. Val. Max. 2.7.14; 3.7; 3.8.3; 6.3.10. Quint. *Inst.* 8.3.85; 9.4.118. Plin. *Ep.* 1.20.19. For discussion of rhetorical 'dismemberment' see Most (1992).

unmanly body of speech he condemned in *Sat.* 1–2), and in his failure so to do (that is, his inability to achieve a pointed, 'cut off' rhetoric)? Or is his sexual failure (and the way he repeatedly ensures that canonical narratives are snarled and frustrated) evidence for precisely the opposite, a maverick creative formula which ensures narrative twists and turns and a tragi-comic plot infinitely more entertaining than the Homeric hero's romance? Once more, bound up in these questions is always the *Satyricon*'s core riddle of authorial identity, the impossibility of separating narrator from author which entails that Encolpius' 'ignorance' and 'impotence' are always as opaque as they are suspicious.

To conclude: we have seen how the confused self-image and anxious introspection which now seem to stain our narrator's first poetic ventures and newfound sense of his own responsibility seem to coincide with a more self-conscious revisitation of past events in the text and of literary narratives in general. Yet in the *Satyricon*, poetic projects are never without their fretful physical implications and consequences: a Pythagorean philosophy of corporeal flux, concomitant with this fiction's overarching metaphor of text as body, ensures that tracing (your readings of) past narratives is always about self-examination. These scenes, more overtly than any in the *Satyricon*, dramatise intertextuality as social/sexual interaction and exchange, and vitalise texts as brews of memories, experiences and feelings, in readers' heads. The fiction of embodied texts entails Encolpius' corporal vulnerability as well as his/the freedom to make it up, yet for the *Satyricon*'s readers dissecting authorial personas while able to spy no further than their own noses, such liberties are inevitably poisoned, perhaps even paralysed, by constraint.

CHAPTER 10

Decomposing rhythms

We have now seen extensively how the city of Croton is mapped as an overtly poetic environment. In Petronius' dark restaging of an Ovidian landscape, the suppressed energy of Pythagoreanism erupts in a chaos of corporeal and literary flux. The impotent Encolpius comes to incarnate not just the metaphor of civil war (poetry), but also his own bloated and slippery corpus of literary knowledge: his is a fragile condition reflected back on an audience impotent to discover whether sexual failure is canny or farcical, seductive or repellent. We can only be sure that 'soft', 'fluid' flesh in the *Satyricon* is a prerequisite to creative output, the breeding ground for passionate poetry: as a choleric freedman yells in Trimalchio's *Cena, in molli carne vermes nascuntur* / 'worms breed in soft flesh' (57.3). Yet in another twist, it seems that the women of Croton's sexual frustration with the afflicted Encolpius is also an act, that their interest in his pulpy, disintegrating self threatens to reveal itself as a sexualised cannibalism, playing on the metaphor of eating as sexual intercourse which we can see traced throughout the *Satyricon* as a whole. In the Pythagorean cityscape of civil war, the way to a woman's heart is almost certainly through her stomach. In this chapter, I will explore in greater detail how the final scenes of the *Satyricon* as we have it sexualise the consumption of human/literary bodies, culminating in a rotten recycling of Philomela's myth which frames the ultimate exhibition of Eumolpus' poetic flesh.

By *Sat.* 134, impotent Encolpius is at a loss. His self-castigation and verbal castration have been to no avail, and his latest prayers to Priapus and Bacchus, including promises to sacrifice a horned goat and the young of a squealing sow, have remained unanswered. As he kneels at the altar, he is seized by a vile old woman clad all in black, who drags him out through the porch claiming he has riled the gods against her: *nec contentus ipse peccare, mihi deos iratos excitasti* / 'and not content with sinning yourself, you have roused the angry gods against me' (134.2). His punishment, now so familiar that he does not even resist (*nihil recusantem*, 134.3), is a thorough caning which nearly smashes his head and arm (*forsitan etiam bracchia mea caputque fregisset*, 134.4). As both Encolpius and Proselenos sit on the bed in tears, the priestess Oenothea enters and learns of the patient's predicament. She boasts: *istum morbum sola sum quae emendare scio. et ne putetis perplexe agere, rogo ut adulescentulus mecum nocte dormiat... nisi illud tam rigidum reddidero quam cornu* / 'I am the only woman alive who knows how to cure this disease. And in case you think I'm having you on, I ask that the young man sleep one night with me... if I don't make that thing stiffer than horn' (134.10–11). However, this promise of a remedy marks the onset of more overt cannibalistic plotting which exposes the real, grizzly concerns of Croton's female population: the consumption, as well as the control, of Encolpius' poetic corpus in his incarnation as *polyaenus* Odysseus. It is tempting, therefore, to see the disjointed narrative of Encolpius' erotic crises in Croton as always mirroring and foregrounding the showdown in which the poet Eumolpus is forced to bargain with his own body.[1]

Chrysis' warning in *Sat.* 129.10 that the women of Croton can draw down the moon from the sky is confirmed at 134, where Oenothea claims to have Circean powers displayed in 'magic' verse (*quicquid in orbe vides, paret mihi* / 'Whatever you see in the world, obeys me', 134.12 v. 1).[2] Yet once she begins to prepare her paraphernalia for 'curing' Encolpius, her resemblance to Circe veers in a more ominous direction. She has already boasted, in her poem, of being able to make tigers and lions 'stand upright' as humans, reminding us of Circe's farmyard of human-animals; now she leads the already victimized Encolpius right into her den – a kitchen equipped with a hearth, a huge (man-sized?) cooking pot (*cucuma ingens*, 135.4) and a great deal of rotting meat, including a mouldy pig's head tenderised by a thousand blows (*sincipitis vetustissima particula mille plagis dolata*, 135.4). Gruesome implications are all there if we want to read them: is this unfortunate pig's head the remains of the last of Odysseus' men, who fell into Circe's trap all the way back in Homer's day, in *Odyssey* X – an archaic (*vetustissima*) meat forming the core ingredient

[1] Although the perception of *Sat.* 139–41 as climactic could look artificial, given the uncertain length and shape of the original text, the scene would arguably be extremely striking whatever its precise context in the *Satyricon*.

[2] In vv. 11–13, which are deleted by Müller in all three editions, she compares herself directly to Circe (*taurorum flamma quiescit / virgineis extincta sacris, Phoebeia Circe / carminibus magicis socios mutavit Ulixes*).

for Petronius' satirical melting pot? Has Encolpius been beaten to a pulp by Proselenos (who tries to smash his stupid, porcine head) to ensure that his flesh is extra juicy (for it is already soft)? Oenothea's first words to Encolpius ('What screech owls have eaten your groin?' 134.1) look even more threatening in retrospect.

The notion that we always have to look back to understand this aged, decaying literary recipe is emphasized by Encolpius' poem at *Sat.* 135.8, which follows the preparation of the dubious casserole: in this verse, which like its author survives fragmented, Encolpius compares Oenothea to Hecale, alluding both to Callimachus' *Hecale* and also to Ovid's comparable tale of the simple, rustic hospitality of Baucis and Philemon in *Met.* 8.[3] As Connors shows, lines 15–16 of the poem represent a free translation of the first line of *Hecale*, and also allude to its probable conclusion, Theseus' establishment of rites in Hecale's honour after her death: *qualis in Actaea quondam fuit hospita terra / digna sacris Hecale* / 'Such a hostess there once was on Athenian soil, Hecale, worthy of worship', cf. Ἀκταίη τις ἔναιεν Ἐρεχθέος ἔν ποτε γουνῷ / 'Once upon a time there lived an Attic woman in the hill country of Erechtheus' (fr. 1).[4] When Encolpius says that Oenothea's *cella* could not be further removed from a marble palace (*non Indum fulgebat ebur, quod inhaeserat auro / nec iam calcato radiabat marmore terra / muneribus delusa suis* / 'No Indian ivory set in gold shone here, nor did the earth gleam with marble trodden on or mocked for the gifts she gave', vv. 1–2), he reminds us that Baucis and Philemon's reward for entertaining the disguised Jupiter and Mercury was to have their humble home transformed into a magnificent temple complete with gold roof, carved doors and marble columns (*vertitur in templum: furcas subiere columnae / stramina flavescunt, adopertaque marmore tellus / caelataeque fores aurataque tecta videntur* / 'It was changed into a temple: marble columns replaced the forked wooden supports; the straw grew yellow and became a golden roof', *Met.* 8.700–3). Just like Oenothea, the rustic couple had also welcomed their guests by preparing a pot on the fire, cleaning vegetables, and taking down some smoked ham from

[3] The two stories are explicitly connected in *Met.* 8: Theseus, the guest of Hecale, is in the audience and is very moved by the tale (*desierat, cunctosque et res et moverat auctor, / Thesea praecipue* 725–6). On the relationship between the Oenothea episode, Callimachus' Hecale story and Ovid's Baucis and Philemon story, see Garrido (1930: 10–11), Sullivan (1985: 86–7) and Connors (1998: 43–7). Persius, 4.21 mentions Baucis as an example of a poor old woman, and Pliny talks of Hecale's humble larder (*HN* 22.88; 26.82).

[4] Also line 17 of the poem (*Bachineas veteres*) probably alludes to Callimachus (the poet of Cyrene, founded by Battus, or 'the son of Battus'): see Müller (1995) in his apparatus criticus.

the rafters (*Met.* 8.647–50). Yet their meat was 'long-cherished' (*servatoque diu*, 650): by the time Petronius gets his dirty hands on it, it is well and truly past its sell-by date.[5]

Encolpius' idealistic poetic offerings are obviously anachronistic and frayed around the edges, a suitable response to the out-of-date pig's head, born on Oenothea's birthday (*coaequale natalium suorum sinciput*, 136.1). Even Oenothea's stool turns out to be decomposing and collapses under her weight, throwing the old woman into the hearth and sending the broth flying, thus extinguishing the fire: *fracta est putris sella, quae staturae altitudinem adiecerat, anumque pondere suo deiectam super foculum mittit* (136.1). The old domestic literary scene of a couple preparing the humble hearth disintegrates beneath the weight of cliché and repetition, reminding us of Eumolpus' earlier lesson on tackling the burden of literary influence (you have to be 'full' of literature before tackling a theme like civil war, 118.6). Oenothea's face is covered in the ashes she has scattered everywhere (*faciemque totam excitato cinere perfundit*, 136.2), again stirring up images of death and bodily remains:[6] are these the ashes of metamorphosed men? Whereas Baucis and Philemon's old table was a little unsteady and needed propping up with a tile (*mensae set erat pes tertius inpar: / testa parem fecit*, *Met.* 8.661–2), Oenothea's furniture falls apart explosively, with a violence that is repeated in the ensuing scene, in which Encolpius tears off a table leg to beat to death the ferocious goose, darling of Priapus: *oblitus itaque nugarum pedem mensulae extorsi coepique pugnacissimum animal armata elidere manu. nec satiatus defunctorio ictu, morte me anseris vindicavi* / 'and so, forgetting all trivialities, I wrenched a leg off the little table and began to hammer the aggressive creature with the weapon I had in my hand. I was not satisfied with just one blow, and got my revenge with the goose's death' (136.5).[7]

[5] As in the *Odyssey* (and Encolpius, we may assume, is still playing the heroic, Homeric narrator here), the prospect of return or going back in time always evokes the potential to descend into barbarism (see Horkheimer and Adorno 1982: 43–80): Encolpius' poetic return involves not just encounters with cannibalistic monsters and metamorphosing witches, but with their rotten remains and leftovers. As Pythagoras of Croton says, time (*tempus edax*) is the greatest cannibal of all (*Met.* 15.234–6): *Chronos* (time) and son-eating Kronos (Saturn) could be easily confused. Note that talking about cannibalism, in Eumolpus' final analysis (141.9–11) always involves looking back into the past for *exempla*.

[6] Connors suggests (1998: 46) that Oenothea's fall 'self-reflexively acknowledges the way Petronius has lowered and dirtied the Callimachean and Ovidian models'.

[7] This reminds us that Baucis and Philemon tried to catch a goose for dinner to impress their guests (*Met.* 8.684: *unicus anser erat, minimae custodia villae, / quem dis hospitibus domini mactare parabant* / 'They had one goose, the guardian of their tiny estate, which the hosts were preparing to kill for their divine guests'): killing the goose, in this analogy, is bound to anger the gods.

An amused Encolpius helps Oenothea up from the dirty floor, yet as soon as she is on her feet, she runs off to her neighbours to fetch more fuel for the fire, so as not to delay the *sacrifice* (*ne res aliqua sacrificium moraretur*, 136.3). It looks as though her victim may not be laughing for long. Indeed at *Sat.* 137, cooking is again under way, and it is Encolpius who is being primed for the pot. First his fingers are marinated in wine, leeks and celery: *infra manus meas camellam vini posuit, et cum digitos extensos porris apioque lustrasset, avellanas nuces cum precatione mersit in vinum* (137.10). Then he is ceremoniously stuffed with a leather prick dipped in oil, pepper and the bruised seed of nettles: *profert Oenothea scorteum fascinum, quod ut oleo et minuto pipere atque urticae trito circumdedit semine, paulatim coepit inserere ano meo* (138.1). Finally, his thighs are anointed with the same sauce, his loins seasoned with the juices of cress and southernwood, and a *bouquet garni* of nettles is used to gently strike the area below his navel (*hoc crudelissima anus spargit subinde umore femina mea*... *nasturcii sucum cum habrotono miscet perfusisque inguinibus meis viridis urticae fascem comprehendit omniaque infra umbilicum coepit lenta manu caedere*, 138.2). Increasingly, as the fragmented narrative builds up to Eumolpus' demand (or trap) that the legacy-hunters cut up his body and consume it in public, there are hints that Encolpius' treatment for his 'disease' (*morbus*) at the hands of Croton's Circean females has less to do with restoring his virility than with perfecting his flesh for the final sacrifice. As Eumolpus observes in his last moments, some countries still observe the law whereby sick people are blamed for spoiling their own meat: *apud quasdam gentes scimus adhuc legem servari, ut a propinquis suis consumantur defuncti, adeo quidem, ut obiurgentur aegri frequenter, quod carnem suam faciant peiorem* (141.3).[8] Indeed, there have already been hints that Encolpius should be highly suspicious of women in Croton who appear to pursue him sexually: before they entered the city, the gang was informed of the sexlessness of the inhabitants, who never bring up children (presumably it is also dangerous to have children in the first place) and rarely marry, if they know what's good for them:

in hac urbe nemo liberos tollit, quia quisquis suos heredes habet, non ad cenas, non ad spectacula admittitur, sed omnibus prohibetur commodis, inter ignominiosos latitat. qui vero nec uxores umquam duxerunt nec proximas necessitudines habent, ad summos honores perveniunt, id est soli militares soli fortissimi atque etiam innocentes habentur. (116.7–8)

[8] This recalls Herodotus' tale (3.99) of the cannibalistic Indian tribe called Padaei, who immediately kill those among them who become ill, reasoning that a man who wastes away with sickness is depriving the healthy of his flesh.

In this city no one brings up children, because anyone who has heirs is not admitted to the theatre, but instead is deprived of all advantages and lies at the bottom of the social pile. Those on the other hand who have never taken a wife and have no close relations reach the highest positions; they alone can serve in the military, and they're the only men considered really tough, or even the only men considered *good*.

For the people of Croton, it is clear that to some extent they have to choose between enjoying dinner parties and enjoying close sexual and family relationships. Yet we have seen that sex and eating, both acts of incorporation, have been intertwined and assimilated throughout the *Satyricon*, most clearly in Quartilla's brothel and in the Cyclops seduction scenes at *Sat.* 97–8, and now in the stuffing and basting of Encolpius.[9] First faced with Encolpius' disappointing performance, Circe expresses her frustration in terms of hunger (*numquid te osculum meum offendit? numquid spiritus ieiunio marcens?* / 'Does my kiss offend you in some way? Is it my breath that faints with hunger?' 128.1), and Encolpius uses the same metaphor himself when he wonders, *forsitan dum omnia concupisco, voluptatem tempore consumpsi* / 'Perhaps, while I desired so much, I ate up all my pleasure in the meantime' (130.5), while Oenothea, as we have seen, connects castration with eating (*quae striges comederunt nervos tuos?* / 'What screech-owls have eaten your sinews?' 134.1). Encolpius' first instinct is to treat his affliction by consuming strong foods, like onions and snails (*mox cibis validioribus pastus, id est bulbis cochlearumque sine iure cervicibus, hausi parcius merum*, 130.7–8). As well as being prepared and fattened for the pot, Encolpius' body has already undergone the dissection and dismemberment required by Eumolpus in *Sat.* 141.2. Our narrator's impotence has been represented as a self-conscious disconnection of body parts and a collapse of physical wholeness. Ironically, the more he attempts to arouse women's hunger in Croton, the more he risks being treated as a passive sexual object to be cut up and eaten, rather than proving his maleness. His brief interlude of virility, in which he comes to Circe *totus* ('whole') and boasts, *totoque corpore in amplexum eius immissus* / 'I threw my entire body into her arms' (131.11), is in sharp contrast to his general state of bodily disintegration: *toto corpore velut laxato* / 'It was as though my whole body had got slack' (128.2); *funerata est illa pars corporis, qua quondam Achilles*

[9] Like eating, sex makes two bodies one: See discussion in Rawson (1977, 1978) and Kilgour (1990: 7ff.) on the relationship between eating and sexual intercourse in modern and ancient myth and idiom. An anthropological interpretation of this relationship is suggested by Lévi-Strauss (1972: 106), who emphasises the French pun (*consommer* = to eat, to consummate). For discussions that combine psychoanalytical and anthropological approaches to the subject, see Pontalis (1972).

eram / 'That bit of me that was once Achilles is dead and buried' (129.1); *sed inops et rebus egenis / attritus facinus non toto corpore feci* / 'When I was poor and worn with deprivation I sinned, but not with my whole body' (133.3 vv. 8–9); *forsitan rediret hoc corpus ad vires et resipiscerent partes veneficio, credo, sopitae* / 'Maybe then my body would regain its strength and the parts of me that were soaked in poison would be themselves again' (138.7). At *Sat.* 132, as we have seen, Encolpius suffers from more than a split personality when he addresses his groin as a separate entity, comparing his behaviour to that of Homer, the tragedians, or sick people (like the 'gout-striken' Eumolpus)[10] who feel disconnected from their own bodies:

aut quid est quod in corpore humano ventri male dicere solemus aut gulae capitique etiam, cum saepius dolet? quid? non et Ulixes cum corde litigat suo, et quidam tragici oculos suos tamquam audientes castigant? podagrici pedibus suis male dicunt, chiragrici manibus, lippi oculis, et qui offenderunt saepe digitos, quicquid doloris habent in pedes deferunt. (132.13)

And then there is the fact that in the human body we often damn our guts, our throats, even our heads, when they ache. Why? Did Ulysses not argue with his own heart, do some tragedians not curse their eyes as if they could hear? People with gout attack their feet, people with arthritis moan at their hands, people with sties curse their eyes, and men with painful toes blame every grief they suffer in life on their feet.

Encolpius has already attempted to cut himself up (into *partes*: bite sized morsels), the threatened slicing multiplied in verse by an ever-echoing *ter*...*ter* (132.8); as I have argued, the response of his 'disconnected' organ, which seems now to have a voice and character of its own, is then described in a poem which is itself conspicuously chopped up, a jagged assortment of quotations: *quam lentae salices* ✂ *lassove papavera collo.*[11] Like Croton itself, Encolpius ends up *in duas partes divisos*, as the farm-bailiff predicts in *Sat.* 116: he embodies the civil war epitomised by Croton's war-torn and corrupt society and perpetuated by the final dissection of Eumolpus (into rival factions): *si corpus meum in partes conciderint* / 'if they cut up my body into bits' (141.2). Interestingly, the fake civil war on board ship at *Sat.* 108, in which the crew is divided into factions (*Tryphaena*...

[10] Eumolpus has told everyone he suffers from gout, i.e., he is on his last legs (*sed et podagricum se esse lumborumque solutorum omnibus dixerat, et si non servasset integram simulationem, periclitabatur totam paene tragoediam evertere*, 140.6).

[11] Being reduced to a series of separate body parts is the price to pay for being an edible sex symbol: in *Sat.* 79–80 the older men even think of dividing their shared plaything, Giton, in two, or slicing off a part of him (*'age' inquit 'nunc et puerum dividamus'* / ' "Come", he said, "now let's divide the boy" ', 79.12).

totiusque navigii turbam diducit in partes) and takes up battle lines (*stant ergo utraque acie*), is also dominated by (feigned) self-mutilation, when both Giton and Encolpius threaten to cut themselves:

tunc fortissimus Giton ad virilia sua admovit novaculam infestam, minatus se abscissurum tot miseriarum causam, inhibuitque Tryphaena tam grande facinus non dissimulata missione. saepius ego cultrum tonsorium super iugulum meum posui, non magis me occisurus, quam Giton quod minabatur facturus. audacius tamen ille tragoediam implebat, quia sciebat se illam habere novaculam, qua iam sibi cervicem praeciderat. (108.10–11)

Then brave Giton held a deadly razor to his genitals and threatened to solve our troubles by self-mutilation, but Tryphaena put a stop to the terrible deed with a genuine offer of freedom. Several times I put a barber's knife to my own throat, no more meaning to kill myself than Giton meant to carry out his own threats. Nevertheless, he was more reckless in playing the tragic part, because he knew that he was holding the same razor he'd already used to cut his neck.[12]

This violent performance is halted by Tryphaena's civil war poem, which itself alludes to the mutilation of a body: *nec Medea furens fraterno sanguine pugnat* / 'nor does crazy Medea fight with her brother's blood' (v. 4) is a reference to Medea's murder of her brother Absyrtus and the subsequent cutting up of his corpse, which was then thrown overboard to delay Jason's pursuers. Cutting up the body (and/as poem) into *partes* by turning weapons of war against the self rather than against the enemy has become a blatant analogue of civil war, as well as a metaphor for Petronius' anatomisation of canonic bodies of literature.

Let us look now at the final scenes of the *Satyricon*, which take self-harm to its furthest extreme. Here we discover that cannibalisation (the eating of your own flesh) is not only the ultimate tragedy and disgrace of war, as Eumolpus shows in his historical *exempla* at *Sat.* 141, but is also a means of exploring and advertising the *Satyricon*'s incorporative strategies, which risk killing the poet even as they draw in the crowds.

The marinating of Encolpius' tender loins with spicy juices is precisely what Eumolpus recommends for his own body at *Sat.* 141: no meat is pleasant in itself, he explains, but has to be artificially disguised to be reconciled to the unwilling digestion: *accedit huc quod aliqua inveniemus blandimenta, quibus saporem mutemus. neque enim ulla caro per se placet, sed arte quadam corrumpitur et stomacho conciliatur averso* (141.8). Yet we have heard the inspirational phrase *saporem mutare* ('to change taste') before, back in

[12] Note that this is probably another of Encolpius' howlers: he has forgotten that the razor Giton used previously at *Sat.* 94 was blunt and did not cut.

Agamemnon's programmatic poem in *Sat.* 5, when he advocates that the student immerse himself in the waters of Greek literature before 'changing taste' and moving onto solids – the richer, more complicated dishes of Latin writers, which are always about food and wars (or food wars):

> hinc Romana manus circumfluat et modo Graio
> †exonerata† sono *mutet* suffusa *saporem*.
>
> (*Sat.* 5. vv. 15–22)

> Then let the band of Roman writers pour around him,
> let him leave Greece behind, steep his soul and change his taste.

The *Satyricon* is (or wants to taste like) shockingly *nouvelle cuisine*,[13] especially because it is always tempted to tell you that its peppered gravy is designed to (almost) disguise the nauseating flesh (Eumolpus' *noxissimum corpus*) that constitutes its real body:[14] you will never be able to transform your taste enough to stomach this vile literary concoction – although the taste of it might well change *you*. The *Satyricon*'s performances, like Trimalchio's over-elaborate and eventually sickening food in the *Cena*, are emetic: *ibat res ad summam nauseam* / 'things were getting really nauseating' remarks Encolpius at *Sat.* 78.5, referring both to Trimalchio's funeral show and to the food that now sits heavy in his bloated stomach.[15]

[13] Flower and Rosenbaum (1958: 19ff.) remark on the Roman passion for disguising food, both in appearance and taste. See e.g. Apicius 4.12.4: *nemo agnoscet quid manducet* / 'No one will recognise what they're eating.' This practice is perhaps also described, or hinted at, in Hor. *Sat.* 2.8.27–8, where a fish dish is *longe dissimilem noto celantia sucum* / 'hiding a flavour very different from any we know'. See Gowers (1993: 161–79).

[14] Quintilian (9.3.4) employs the same metaphor when he writes that the more unattractive the subject matter, the greater the need for seasoning (*condimentum*). See Bramble (1974: 52–4) on metaphors of sauce and vinegar in Quintilian, Aristophanes and Martial, e.g. Mart. 7.25.5: *nec cibus ipse iuvat morsu fraudatus aceti* / 'There is no pleasure in food deprived of vinegar's bite'. Bramble concludes (54), 'it emerges quite clearly that literature was frequently conceived as some kind of foodstuff, to be seasoned before consumption'.

[15] By *Sat.* 69, Encolpius says that he would prefer to die than to eat any more (*ut vel fame perire mallemus*, 69.7). Eating is associated with the death of eater as well as eaten throughout the *Satyricon*. The *cena*, a feast which ends in a fake funeral, directly parallels this last supper, in which Eumolpus' death is also a *mimus* (gone wrong?). As Slater discusses (1990: 133), commenting on Conte (1987), we cannot be sure whether or not Eumolpus' gruesome demands are a bluff to quiet the greed of his would-be heirs, which backfires when they are prepared to meet the conditions. Neither can we be certain whether or not he is already dead, whether he is reading out his will or whether it is being read out over his corpse, and whether, if he is already dead, this will turn out to be a *Scheintod*. Conte, on the other hand (1987: 530) argues that this scene is all Eumolpus' 'last joke' on the *heredipetae*. I am not convinced, however, of Conte's supporting point that, alive or dead, Eumolpus is obliged to keep up the pretence to protect his accomplices, simply because there is no evidence that concern for his friends has *ever* been a priority. Feasts are of course associated with death throughout Greek and Latin literature, from the *Odyssey* to the tragedies of Agamemnon and Thyestes.

Yet, like Tereus or Thyestes, we may not realise the implications of eating until, too late, they rumble away in our insides. *No* flesh tastes nice without a sauce, warns Eumolpus, suggesting that not just human, but *all* meat is inherently repulsive and inedible, recalling again Crotonian Pythagoras' message that non-vegetarians are always in danger of tearing apart and consuming a human soul: 'We should not load our bellies with a Thyestean banquet', he preaches (*Met.* 15.461–2).[16] Petronius has already hinted at the Daedalean writer's ability[17] to dress up his meat in whatever guise he chooses in *Sat.* 70.2: Trimalchio boasts that his chef can make a fish out of a sow's womb, a woodpigeon out of bacon, a turtledove out of ham, or a chicken out of a knuckle of pork (*volueris, de vulva faciet piscem, de lardo palumbum, de perna turturem, de colepio gallinam*).[18]

Throughout the *Satyricon*, we are reminded that outsides do not necessarily correspond to insides, and that exteriors are often contrived to deceive and mislead. Eumolpus' surrender of his body instead of or as his inheritable fortune (*operi modo oculos et finge te non humana viscera sed centies sestertium comesse* / 'Just shut your eyes and imagine you're eating a million in cash rather than human flesh', 141.7) recalls Trimalchio's wise words at *Sat.* 56, when he compares the writer to the money-lender and the doctor (and hence silver plated coins to the similarly deceptive human form), all of whom are privileged to see the cheap, diseased insides of bodies, real or metaphorical (56.1–4). Who knows (apart from the writer) what we are really eating when we chew over the *Satyricon*'s narratives? Stuck in this entrapping text, are we as blind, in effect, as the legacy hunters, who can think only of Eumolpus' wealth (*excaecabat pecuniae ingens fama oculos animosque miserorum* / 'His great reputation for wealth blinded the eyes and minds of these pathetic creatures', 141.5)? Are we truly devouring a luxurious, rich text, or a tacky, sickeningly bad substitute? Do we find ourselves set up, as well as fed up, dumb creatures snared by food, as Eumolpus puts it (*sicut muta animalia cibo inescantur, sic homines non caperentur, nisi spei aliquid morderent* / 'Just as dumb animals are hooked by food, so human beings would not be caught unless they had some hope to nibble on', 140.15)?

As we have seen, being baited by literary titbits has been a model for learning about and being seduced by literature from the beginning of

[16] *neve Thyesteis cumulemus viscera mensis.*

[17] See Sharrock (1994: 133–46) on the image of the poet as Daedalus and Daedalean flight as a metaphor for poetry in Ovid.

[18] Trimalchio continues to say that he bought Daedalus some knives from Rome as a present, and allows guests to try the blades on their cheeks (*etiam nobis potestatem fecit, ut mucronem ad buccam probaremus*, 70.3). Which one of them is to be chopped up (and disguised) next, we wonder?

the *Satyricon*: in *Sat.* 3, Agamemnon painted a caricature of the master of oratory as a fisherman (*tanquam piscator*) dangling delicacies before his students and waiting for a catch, just like the parasites of comedy wangling free dinners from rich hosts (3.3–4).[19]

Reading is like being hounded down by a trickster who (thinks he) knows exactly what you'll fall for, and as *we* know, in Croton you're either the hunter or the hunted (*nam aut captantur aut captant*, 116.6).[20] Eumolpus plays the paradigmatic rhetorician and poet when he reels in the audience of legacy-hunters with promises of his own barbed flesh:[21] *unde plani autem, unde levatores viverent, nisi aut locellos aut sonantes aere sacellos pro hamis in turbam mitterent?* / 'But how would cheats and pickpockets live, if they didn't send out little boxes or purses jingling with money, like hooks, into the crowd?' (140.15).[22] In comparing a crowd snared by cheats jingling their purses to animals lured by food and men given some hope to 'chew on' (140.15), Eumolpus hints that it is his flesh that seduces, as well as (or just like) the cash reward. Yet in these final scenes, it seems, Petronius also has his readers hooked, teasing us with the certainty that, like the myopic inhabitants of Croton, we are still seduced by delicious tales of cannibalism (in the tradition of the myths of Saturn, Polyphemus, Tereus, Thyestes), but can no longer perceive them as examples of what we are not, since we have been gulping down a *charcuterie* of unlabelled meats from the beginning. Even readers with impeccable taste could be fooled, up to the point at which they start to digest the contents of their dinner. As soon as the exotic flavour-enhancers wear off, this scene is bound to turn tragic, which is exactly why Eumolpus is compelled to sustain his act to the very end (*et si non servasset integram simulationem, periclitabatur totam paene tragoediam evertere* / 'If he couldn't keep up all his pretence, he ran the risk of upsetting the whole tragedy', 140.6).

For Petronius' audience, there seems to be no way out of this labyrinth: in the world of the *Satyricon*, eating or tasting is the primary model for knowing; to read is to consume, yet to eat at all is to enter into a maze of uncertainty and risk in which positions and hierarchies of power cannot

[19] Walsh (1970: 108–9) suggests, 'Petronius doubtless has some contemporary rhetoricians in mind when he gives the name Gorgias to one of the most shameful of Eumolpus' pursuers' (*Gorgias paratus erat exsequi*, *Sat.* 141.5).

[20] In Horace, *Sat.* 2.5, Teiresias advises the impoverished Odysseus to return home to Ithaca as a legacy-hunter, and to 'fish cunningly' for old men's wills. As you get better at sycophancy, he assures, 'more and more fish will come swimming up and your ponds will grow'.

[21] For images of *captatores* as fishermen ensnaring prey with baited gifts, see, e.g. Martial 4.56; 6.63.5, Hor. *Sat.* 2.5.44; *Epist.* 1.1.71–9. This image is discussed by Tracy (1980).

[22] His defence of cannibalism in the final lines of the *Satyricon* also sounds like a predictable school oratory project.

be preserved. To eat is always in a sense to be eaten: the poet who baits an audience is dependent on being fed himself, while the reader and pupil are desperate to eat, knowing full well that this makes them the writer's or teacher's latest catch. This double-bind is embodied finally by Eumolpus, who on one hand appears to be completely in control and pulling off the ultimate authorial trick, and on the other seems to have fallen into his own net, as he is about to be cut up and eaten for real. This dilemma and contradiction is further perpetuated, of course, by the prospect that the legacy-hunters will gag on and be poisoned by the poet's sick flesh, which will not be 'rich' in the way they bargained for, thus reversing and regurgitating the hierarchy of control.[23]

As we have seen throughout, bodily continuity is also a metaphor in the *Satyricon* for the changeability and inheritance of literature, which is perpetually consumed and poured forth from bodies. Vomiting is always imaginable as recitation, an often violent ejection of contained knowledge, which in the bellies of Thyestes and other 'meat-eaters' may be too much to bear. Literature, says the *Satyricon*, is always changing, moving from reader body to reader body like the Pythagorean soul, and affected by age as visibly as people. Encolpius sees contemporary literature, alongside today's precocious scholars, as too unhealthy to reach old age: *ac ne carmen quidem sani coloris enituit, sed omnia quasi eodem cibo pasta non potuerunt usque ad senectutem canescere* / 'nor does poetry have a healthy glow, but is all fed on the same diet and can't reach the grey hairs of old age' (2.8).[24] Now, in Petronius' Croton, a putrefying dystopia alongside Pythagoras' vision of civilisation in Ovid's *Metamorphoses*, our adolescent narrator has been teetering constantly on the verge of death (*medius [fidius] iam peristi* / 'You are as good as dead', 129.6), and has fallen in with old women: it is uncertain whether Proselenos is referring to herself or to Encolpius when she curses elderly sluggishness: *aetatisque longae moram tremulis vocibus coepit accusare* / 'She began to curse the delays of old age in a shaky voice' (134.6). Eumolpus has also been faking old age and senility (117) and is now about to die before his time, while the props of Callimachean poetry (in the house of Hecale) are rotting, along with the remains of Homeric Circe's dinner. This text, implicitly, is constituted by the mutating leftovers of classical literature: fascinating to read, but tough to chew.

[23] Aelian writes (*VH* 13.22) that the painter Galaton depicted Homer being sick, with other poets drawing on his vomit.

[24] See Gowers (1994) on how Neronian writers image themselves, paradoxically, as premature latecomers, a reflection of boy-king Nero's concentrated reign and a reaction to the balanced, well-timed construction of Augustan Rome as *aeterna urbs*. I discuss this in the Conclusion.

Now, in *Sat.* 140, we meet a figure who dramatises more vividly the *Satyricon*'s metaphor of the 'aging' of literature. The well-known mythical character Philomela becomes, in Petronius' hands, one of the geriatric legacy-hunters who approach Eumolpus in *Sat.* 140. Like Circe, Philomela's inauthenticity in the *Satyricon* is emphasised by the qualification *nomine*, which reminds us not only that all characters in the *Satyricon* are masked actors, but also that 'Philomela' is a powerful signifier, lugging a baggage of narratives from other texts.[25] In the *Satyricon*, Philomela is no longer a vulnerable, damaged young girl but a venerable matron: *matrona inter primas honesta, Philomela nomine, quae multas saepe hereditates officio aetatis extorserat, tum anus et floris extincti* / 'A most honorable woman by the name of Philomela, who had often extorted legacies thanks to the well-managed virtues of her youth, was now an old lady and well past her blooming years' (140.1). When she was younger she often extorted legacies, presumably by seduction (like Circe, Chrysis, Proselenos and Oenothea), but these days she uses her attractive son and daughter as bait (*per hanc successionem artem suam perseverabat extendere* / 'through this succession, she hoped to continue the use of her art', 140.1). Philomela now offers her children to Eumolpus, in the hope, it is assumed, that he will write them into his will before his looming death.

Repeating a now familiar pattern, this seedy plot is disguised as literary education. Eumolpus will not use their bodies, he will 'teach' them, just as he 'taught' the sexy boy of Pergamum: the pupil and reader are always 'fucked over', yet equally, the *Satyricon* shows, the sexually aggressive writer has made himself vulnerable precisely by entering into such a dialogue.[26] For this is Philomela, we must remember, the dangerous victim-woman who was raped and mutilated by her brother-in-law but who fought back in silent, written poetry to tell of the tragedy that ruined her. Tereus' punishment was to have his crime of violation turned back

[25] Circe talks about her relationship with Encolpius as an interaction of names (*semper inter haec nomina magna fax surgit* / 'There's always fireworks when these two names get together', 127.7). Both passages recall the male writer's appropriation of Sappho's authorial and signifying power in Ov. *Her.* 15 (*at nomen, quod terras implet omnes / est mihi mensuram nominis ipsa fero* / 'but my name fills every land. I am only the measure of my name', 33–4): a woman's name encapsulates her reputation and her past – she is often *just* a name and nothing else. See Rimell (1999).

[26] In *Totem and Taboo* (1983) and *Moses and Monotheism* (1939), Freud imagines a foundational myth in which the primal sons eat the original father to incorporate his power and thus essentially become him, but then discover that they have merely internalised the father's power against them. As Kilgour explains, 'the dualism of eater/eaten is not transcended or sublimated through internalisation, but perpetrated. In such instances, to eat the father is the same as being eaten by him' (1990: 13). This happens in reverse in the Tereus and Thyestes myths: the all-powerful father is 'eaten up', i.e. destroyed, by the act of eating his sons.

upon himself, when Procne and Philomela kill Itys and serve him to his father on a plate, diced and roasted.

In the *Satyricon*, Philomela's abuse of her own son and daughter dramatically repeats both her own violation and the sacrifice of Itys, casting the poet Eumolpus as the guilty rapist blind to what he is actually eating for his last meal:[27] the 'art' Philomela wants to perpetuate (*per hanc successionem artem suam perseverabat extendere*) clearly refers not only to the crafty career of legacy-hunting, but also to the artistry she displayed in communicating Tereus' unspeakable crime in a tapestry, and in tricking him into swallowing his own son. As one of the legacy-hunters lining up to consume Eumolpus' flesh, Philomela's new power is implicitly cannibalistic, reminding us of her complicity in the monstrous killing and cooking of beloved Itys. We are drawn back again to her original crime in Eumolpus' last words, as he recalls the story of the mothers in besieged Numantia, found clutching the half-eaten bodies of their children to their chests, in a gross inversion of breastfeeding:[28] *cum esset Numantia a Scipione capta, inventae sunt matres quae liberorum suorum tenerent semesa in sinu corpora* (141.11).[29] Regressive repetition, the engine of Senecan tragedy[30] and a powerful metaphor for a text's ideological negotiation of the past, locks Petronius' Philomela in an endless victim/perpetrator cycle.[31] Through her children she is raped again and again, yet she is doomed not only to avenge the crime, but more tragically still to play the role of Tereus – the cunning mind behind the sexual abuse, and the cannibal no longer spared by initial ignorance of what she consumes.[32] In hunting

27 Acting in the *Satyricon* is always liable to get out of control: Eumolpus, performing here as a gout-stricken millionaire, now slips into the role of Tereus (and perhaps by association, Thyestes), and later on (when it seems he is about to be eaten) of Itys. Moreover, the reminder in 140.6 that he is forced to engage in this tragic farce with Philomela and her daughter because he is suffering from gout, the disease which causes acute pain in the joints of the foot, marks him physically with the tragic prop of Oedipus' mutilated foot, dredging up similar stories of incest and blindness.

28 The mother's natural role as feeder and nurturer is warped into the role of cannibalistic eater. See Kristeva (1982: 105) for discussion of the symbolism of breastfeeding, and for biblical examples where distortion of the breastfeeding bond is a metaphor for incest.

29 In Croton, Philomela's children are themselves a crime: in *Sat.* 116 the gang are told that those who bring up children in the city are deprived of all advantages and 'lie in obscurity among the low-born'.

30 On this topic see Schiesaro (1997b, and forthcoming).

31 Like the boy of Pergamum in the parallel story of Eumolpus' didactic exploits at *Sat.* 85–7, the tragedy is also that Philomela can never be satisfied by repetition (*sed non fuit contentus iteratione*, 87.7). Sexual desire in the *Satyricon*, like the coital movement of Eumolpus, Corax and Philomela's daughter, and like Pythagorean time, is suspended *veluti oscillatione* / 'like a see-saw' (140.9): it is never satisfied, but moves backwards and forwards from anticipation to disappointment or frustration.

32 Ovid, *Met.* 6.652: *tantaque nox animi est: 'Ityn huc accersite' dixit* / 'and in his complete and utter blindness, he said, "Call Itys here to me."'

Eumolpus, she waits to eat and overpower her aggressor,[33] yet in this very 'victory' she suffers Tereus' punishment, so creatively designed by her own hand. Again the *Satyricon* forces a radical disintegration of the hierarchy of eater/eaten: the eater invades, yet is always also invaded, while what is eaten and thereby concealed is all the more pernicious for its invisibility.

Philomela is compelled to use her children in the same way she was used herself: indeed she is helpless to teach, or give them, anything else (*quae sola posset hereditas iuvenibus dari* / 'this was the only inheritance her children could be given', 140.3). Her beautiful daughter seems similarly constrained: in the following scene, which is made even grimmer by its farcical frame and by Eumolpus' dirty laughter (*hoc semel iterumque ingenti risu, etiam suo, Eumolpus fecerat* / 'Eumolpus didn't just do this once, he did it again, amid raucous laughter including his own', 140.10), her responses are described as *automata*: compulsive, machine-like.[34] In parallel with Eumolpus' tirelessness (*semel iterumque*)[35] as well as with the see-saw thrusts of the pantomime threesome (*sic inter mercennarium amicamque positus senex veluti oscillatione ludebat* / 'in this way the old man, sandwiched between the servant and the girlfriend, sported a kind of swinging to and fro between one and the other', 140.9), the girl is made to re-enact the forced movements of her violated mother, as if the repetition of the crime is an uncontrollable reflex.[36] The Philomela myth predicts that children are condemned to embody the guilt (and punishment) of their parents, for which a legal inheritance of property is now a powerful metaphor. In Ovid's version of the tragedy, for example, Itys is murdered precisely because he is the duplicate image of his father (*quid possit, ab illo / admonita*

[33] The association Tereus–Eumolpus is strengthened by the pretence that Eumolpus is suffering from gout, a disease often thought to be precipitated by gross overeating or overindulgence in sex. Lucian considered gout one of the curses of the rich who had no self-discipline (*Somn.* 23). Celsus recommended the disease be treated by blood-letting, diuretics, emetics, hot fermentations, refrigerants and repressants or, in periods of remission, with gentle exercise and a spare diet. He observes (*Med.* 4.31) 'some have obtained lifelong security by refraining from wine, mead and venery for a whole year'. On this topic, and specifically on gout as an after-effect of lust, see Bramble (1974: 87–9). Elsewhere in the *Satyricon*, the freedman Plocamus from the *Cena* claims to be suffering from gout (*'iam' inquit ille 'quadrigae meae decurrerunt, ex quo podagricus factus sum'* / ' "Now", he said, "my galloping days are over, ever since I was taken with the gout" ', 64.3), and later on in 64, an unhealthy-looking boy is force-feeding an obese puppy, which threatens to be sick. At *Sat.* 96.4, Bargates has to be carried into the brawl involving Eumolpus and some drunken lodgers because he has gouty feet (*nam erat etiam pedibus aeger*).

[34] *dum frater sororis suae automata per clostellum miratur* / 'while the brother was marvelling at his sister's routine through the keyhole' (140.11).

[35] Repetition is overtly thematised here, as it is in Senecan tragedy.

[36] We might see the fact that there are two men involved in this 'rape' as symbolic of this doubling or repetition, as if Tereus' ghost is still present.

est oculisque tuens immitibus, 'a! quam / es similis patri!' / 'His coming suggested what she could do, and looking at him with pitiless eyes she said, "Ah, how like his father he is" ', *Met.* 6.621–3). Procne's relationship with her son is irrevocably damaged by Tereus' desecration of familial relations, leading her to ask, 'Why does he [Itys] call me mother, when she [Philomela] cannot call me sister?'[37]

This scene is contrived as well as compulsive: the girl's genitals are presented to Eumolpus as an *artificium*, the legacy-hunter's trap which also recalls and represents Philomela's artistic trick, the telling of her violation in a tapestry.[38] The choice of word here recalls Trimalchio's speech at 56.1 (*quod...putamus secundum litteras difficillimum esse* ***artificium****?* / 'So, what do you think is the hardest profession after writing?') and a similar usage at 58.14 (*ego, quod me sic vides, propter* ***artificium*** *meum diis gratias ago* / 'I thank the gods for my education, which made me the man you see before you now');[39] *artificium* is education, knowledge, art, a graduate's profession, and it runs in the family. For this girl's mother, Philomela, is the paradigmatic storyteller, and the myth of her rape and the revenge on Tereus has often been read as a myth of the origin of poetry: as Kilgour argues, the Philomela myth shows how 'poetry is produced by the disorder of relations and the confusion of identity represented as incest, cannibalism or civil war'.[40] Even in old age Philomela is propelled (and condemned) to keep on telling, and vicariously to re-enact her narrative, as if she could heal her muteness and memory through the reiteration of her power to write. As she admits, the only inheritance she can pass down to her son and daughter is the desire and opportunity to learn literature (*ad summam, relinquere se pueros in domo Eumolpi, ut illum loquentem audirent... quae sola posset hereditas iuvenibus dari*, 140.3), and thus to read and reread her pained communication to the world. Her children, it might be said, are living proof of her creative ability, even as they are also evidence of her sexual experience, and therefore of her original (or repeated) violation, the catalyst for all future reproduction. Children, who resemble their parents and share the same blood but are necessarily different from their 'originals', make neat metaphors for successive narratives, or successive readings of texts. Through children, parents (and poets) live

[37] *Met.* 6.633: *quam vocat hic matrem, cur non vocat illa sororem?*

[38] *artificium* can signify anything from talent and craft or profession to a trick, device or work of art (*Oxford Latin Dictionary* 1: 177).

[39] Also see *Sat.* 46.7–8: *quod si resilierit, destinavi illum* ***artificium*** *docere* / 'if he is restless, I want him to learn a trade'; *litterae thesaurum est, et artificium nunquam moritur* / 'Literature is a treasure, and culture never dies', *Sat.* 53.12; *mirabatur haec solus Trimalchio dicebatque ingratum* ***artificium*** *esse* / 'Only Trimalchio was excited by this, and kept on saying it was a thankless profession.'

[40] Kilgour (1990: 33).

on, and indeed Philomela recognises that her son and daughter are her mightiest weapons with which to defeat her rival poet Eumolpus, who conspicuously (in this mime) no longer has children of his own (*elatumque ab Eumolpo filium pariter condiscimus, iuvenem ingentis eloquentiae et spei* / 'We learnt all together that Eumolpus had lost a son, a young man of great eloquence and promise', 117.6).

In the context of seduction routines, erotic artifice (and Eumolpus' role as 'teacher' here) must also recall another perpetuated *ars*, Ovid's *Ars Amatoria.* Post-Ovidian erotics can never *not* be directed by the teacher–pupil, lover–rival semiotics of the *Ars Amatoria*: this is a compulsive pattern which parallels Philomela's inevitable reproduction of inflicted roles. To unlearn Ovid's models and precepts of seduction is as impossible for readers as it is for Philomela to regain her virginity, to un-write her myth.

Petronius' vision of the cannibalistic inheritance of texts, which like Pythagorean flux emphasises circular over linear change, is captured in these final images and echoes of children being fed back into the bodies of their parents. Alongside this, civil war, which wreaks its metaphorical havoc in Croton, is seen to reverse the foundation myth of mother earth, who now gapes open to devour her own offspring. These last scenes are the culmination of the *Satyricon*'s subversion of the authority and perspective of age and time: a cannibal's murderous distortion of linear familial relations is refracted throughout this cleverly disjointed, vacillating, anti-narrative text. Petronius imagines a literary system in which there is never any position of superiority or certainty from which to write or read, for we never write or read after or above our predecessors, but in a system of perpetual flux in which we can never be sure exactly what has landed on our plate, or even what is coming out of our mouths. Thus this chapter has attempted to expose the dangerous limitations of reading *Sat.* 140 as 'the narrative equivalent of theatrical farce'. Panayotakis' conclusion that 'the clearly theatrical conception of the scene, as well as other scenes in the novel, its specific comic elements and its farcical tone suggest its purpose and forbid us to accept it as anything else than amusement'[41] is itself comically repressive. I hope to have shown that comedy, in the limited sense in which it has been used by critics of the *Satyricon*, is only one element of this deceptive mime, which sucks in its stuffed and sickly audience as farcical participators, and which is always embroidered with a mass of competing narratives.

[41] Panayotakis (1994a) 466–7.

Conclusion
Licence and labyrinths

This study has attempted to map out the intricate ways in which the act of reading Petronius' hyperactive fiction is always implicated in and tricked by its paradoxical, corporeal visions. We began, in chapter one, with the opening speeches outside rhetorical school, where the environments of learning and the relationship between teacher and pupil, poet and patron/audience, were imagined in terms of eating and cannibalisation, and more specifically in terms of the ultimate instability of hierarchies positioning eater over eaten: everyone is part of a food-chain, unable ultimately to escape their corporeality. Moreover, the intensity of such environments of learning, together with the overpowering tang of contemporary literature, dampen the physical senses and render them useless, so that nobody, it seems, really knows what they are eating: students are trapped as if in a *culina* ('kitchen'), where they not only smell bad, but implicitly lose their ability to smell at all (2.1). From the very beginning of the *Satyricon*, these environments of learning are set up as caricatures of worlds of fiction (students 'think they have been transported into another world', 1.2) and, by implication of this text, a *satura* which aims to overload its readers with flavours until they cannot distinguish one from another,[1] and are rendered blind to the 'outside' world (not least our looming, 'exterior' author).

As I have hinted, like Encolpius in Quartilla's brothel, we get fed *satyri_on* (or a *S-a-t-y-r-i-c-o-n* whose narratives were always disjointed, fragmented), an aphrodisiac drug designed to 'loosen you up' and make you have a good time, but which in fact renders you physically and mentally vulnerable: when Encolpius inadvertently downs an entire cup

[1] Seneca (*Ep.* 95.26–7) compares the confused state of Roman morals to an elaborate dish of mixed seafood designed for people who do not have time to savour each ingredient, but want to wolf it down in one mouthful: it is as if the dinner has already been chewed. The *Satyricon* inflicts social and moral inadequacies on its readers, makes immersion and implication in Encolpius' 'lowly' world a condition of reading.

of Petronius' medicine in *Sat.* 20.7 (*adulescens, solus tantum medicamentum ebibisti?* / 'Boy, did you drink all that medicine by yourself?' 20.7), he reacts as if he is being tortured (*volebamus miseri exclamare, sed nec in auxilio erat quisquam* / 'We wanted to cry out in our misery, but there was no one to come to our rescue', 21.1), while Ascyltos is 'threatened' (*puella Ascylton opprimebat*) by a sponge soaked in the same poison (21.1). Just before he is made aware of the contents of his drink, Encolpius reports that the thread of conversation was suddenly broken (*iam deficiente fabularum contextu*, 20.5): was this the point at which *satyri_on* went to his head? Similarly, is the incoherent form of the *Satyricon*, which stumbles from scene to scene like a drunk unable to walk in a straight line, all a matter of perspective, a perspective which is necessarily distorted by the very act of reading (that is, imbibing) such fictions? As I stressed in the Introduction, this is in part the unique dilemma of the *Satyricon*'s modern-day readers, unable to perceive how the fragmented state of the text conditions interpretation, but that is not to say that such difficulties are not (ironically, for us) negotiated in the text itself, which shows every sign of being mischievously anti-Aristotelian.

As Agamemnon explains in *Sat.* 5, reading contemporary Latin literature always involves 'changing your taste'. Yet as we saw in chapter ten, this ambitious, liberating metaphor repeats on us in Encolpius' torture at the hands of Croton's witches and in the grim last scenes, where Eumolpus tries to convince the legacy-hunters to eat his body by reassuring them that they can add a sauce to 'change the taste', for no flesh is pleasant by itself. The opening speeches by Encolpius and Agamemnon, in which literature (and especially Latin poetry, which is all about food, *epulae*) is consumed and then ejected in performance, haunt the entire work: their programmatic visions are reflected climactically in Eumolpus' imagined death, where the consumption and transmission of poetic knowledge (embodied in the wise old poet) is enough to make us want to vomit.

I have suggested that the subversive act of cannibalisation, which radically upsets the fixed status and separation of eater from eaten, is a threat that lurks throughout the *Satyricon*, continually dramatising the anxieties and risks germane to a range of literary and interpretative arenas. We have seen how Agamemnon's image of the power-hungry but ever exposed fisherman-teacher finds parallels in the caricature figure of Trimalchio, whose guests fall hook, line and sinker for his tasty tricks. As I explored in chapter three, the guests at the *cena* eat, or report eating, man-eating bear steaks and human personalities from the zodiac platter, while they themselves are implicitly food for the beasts (this is a *libera cena*, the last supper before slaves are thrown to the lions) and also for the Minotaur in this, Daedalus' labyrinth. Cannibalism is also the barbaric, anarchic force at the heart of civil war, as we saw in chapter five: Eumolpus' *Bellum Civile* depicts Dis and Tisiphone lusting after the taste of human flesh,[2] and the very cracking open of the earth to pour forth chthonic forces cannot help but regurgitate the image of the greedy scholar who swallows so much knowledge that he vomits it forth. Human greed, the specific catalyst for civil war here, leads to a rupture and opening up of bodily cavities, a physical vulnerability already inscribed in the continued threat of cannibalism. Petronius' civil war is *intestinal*, just as Horace sees the larger intestinal conflicts of his poetic collection seething in his insides in *Epode* 3.[3] The disease or garlic-poison of poetry, like civil war, comes from within.[4] Again we are reminded that Latin poetry is about 'feasts and wars', in that order.

The *Satyricon* shows that the contemporary poet can in a sense *only* write about civil war (or 'civil war'), because the volume of literature he has to consume to be up to the task amounts to an uncontrollable, uncontainable mass that is bound to erupt violently, in poetry about violence.[5] Well before we are even thinking about civil war (poetry), the *Cena* demonstrates all too dramatically both what you have to go through to be a poet, or a good reader, and the horrific implications of that process: at (very) close hand, we watch the guests tuck into those implicit poetic creations and interpretative riddles which are Daedalus' layered dishes, until they are not just stuffed, but painfully nauseous. This uncontrolled, forced, obsessive and excessive eating, culminating in the rupture of incorporation (that is, *war*), finds its guilty roots in the fall of Troy.

As I argued in chapter four, the *Satyricon* sets Trojan Horse and aggressive poet in parallel, both pouring out violent forces that until this point have been well concealed inside their bodies. The Trojans' fatal error was to throw themselves into partying and to get 'buried' in darkness and wine (*inter sepultos Priamidas nocte et mero, TH* 55). This is just what

[2] And as I have argued, Dis' plea to Fortuna at *BC* 96 (*iam pridem nullo perfundimus ora cruore* / 'It has been a long time since my lips dripped with gore') echoes *Met.* 15.98 (*nec polluit ora cruore*), where Pythagoras refers to an age where people did not yet eat meat, that is, before the age of cannibalism.

[3] See Fitzgerald (1988) on the intestine as a civil metaphor, Gowers on *Epod.* 3 (1993: 280–310) and Henderson (1999: 93–108) for more general investigation of Horace's 'bio-scripts'.

[4] 'The stomach is the real muse of poetry', says Persius (*Prol.* 10–11).

[5] The etymology of *Satyricon* always reminds us of this potentiality: *satur* means 'full'.

Trimalchio and his guests do in the *Cena* (*plane matus sum. vinus mihi in cerebrum abiit* / 'I am completely soaked. The wine has gone right to my head', 41.12; *Trimalchio ebrietate turpissima gravis* / 'Trimalchio was deep in the most vile drunkenness', 78.5; *accedebat huc ebrietas* / 'We were pissed by this point', 79.2), especially when things get really nauseating (*ibat res ad summam nauseam*), at the point just before the gang make their escape from the labyrinth. Trapped on Lichas' menacing ship, just before the storm breaks, Eumolpus tells the story of the widow of Ephesus in her tomb, who gets drunk ('buried') slurping wine and Virgil: the poet has himself been described as *vino solutus* ('loosened by wine') at 109.8. By the time we get to war-torn Croton, the old women pursuing Encolpius for dinner are all *solutae mero* (again, 'loosened by wine', 138.3). Loosening up the body is a necessary precursor for poetry and war, which are inevitably felt in the gut.

Moreover, Agamemnon has already pictured the contemporary poet as 'loosening the reins' on the wild horse of literature in his poem at *Sat.* 5, in preparation for the free, creative outpouring (*defundes pectore*) of literary inheritance, an image which is redoubled in the *Troiae Halosis* when the horse-soldiers are untied from their horse-prison as self-consciously as the poem itself (*TH* vv. 58–60), and subsequently in the *Bellum Civile* when the poetics of Furor are unleashed on the world (*quas inter Furor, abruptis ceu liber habenis / sanguineum late tollit caput* / 'Among them Madness, like a horse let loose when the reins snap, throws up her bloody head', 258–9). All post-Troy, post-Virgilian literature has to cope with (and, the *Satyricon* says, *incorporate*) the image and implications of the pregnant, bloated wooden horse, doomed always to repeat this pattern of stuffing/enclosure followed by violent rupture of the creative belly/womb. If we learn one thing about Petronius' vatic visions, it is that this is where all knowledge, all poetry comes from. Yet one of the things the *Cena* dramatises is the suspicion that perhaps we never learn, that restaging the fable of Troy's fall always tragically repeats Trojan blindness and failure: the layered dishes that take centre stage in Trimalchio's feast are always opaque to the guests, who can never tell what is inside however many times they are shown the patterns of Daedalean (Greek, poetic . . .) trickery.[6]

In chapters six, seven, eight and nine, I argued that the journey by ship to Croton, the city of cannibalism which realises the full horror of Pythagoras' fears in Ovid's Croton (*Met.* 15), stages self-conscious

[6] As Seneca writes, *aliud autem est meminisse, aliud scire* / 'It's one thing to remember, another to know' (*Ep.* 33.8).

exercises in poetic composition, culminating in the bestial outpouring of the *Bellum Civile*. The ship itself, imagined as a Cyclops' cave in which the gang face the constant threat of a giant, man-eating monster, reiterates the pattern of dark, entrapping spaces enclosing chthonic forces encountered throughout the text. I have suggested that these sites of entrapment are always creative environments, analogous to the dark confines of the scholar's belly, the source of poetry itself. Thus Eumolpus' poetic experiments are focused on the bodies of his subjects: scarring their foreheads like book-rolls in an attempt to deceive is just what (his) poetry is all about (*multos, o iuvenes, carmen decepit* / 'Poetry, my boys, has tricked many people', 118.1). The scenes on board ship are all rehearsals for civil war: violence results in the crew splitting into factions, and the chaos is called to a halt with a quote from Lucan's *Pharsalia*; the gang imagine in fate-dealing Lichas the cannibalistic forces that forecast Tisiphone's blood-lust, while Eumolpus enacts the intestinal content, source and impact of civil war poetry by writing it first on human skin (as tattoos), then on animal hide (*membrana*, 115.2) when he scribbles the final version, after flaunting the implications of greedy literary consumption in the tale of the widow of Ephesus.

When the ship reaches Croton, a city which looks ravaged by civil war, there seems to be little distinction between the recitation of the *Bellum Civile* and the scenes in Croton itself. Encolpius is still a literary body, branded with Eumolpus' violent verse. We saw in chapter nine that as such he is incapable of repeating Homeric or other narratives without corrupting them and hacking them to bits, which is exactly what he imagines doing to his own body: the factions (*partes*) of civil war are enacted in the cutting-up of poems and of Encolpius' poetic *corpus*. Encolpius' failed attempts to become a poet, and to use and display his literary knowledge, exhibit the extent to which contemporary creativity, and the contemporary body/self in general, are infected by the dissolving, destructive, transformative spirit of civil war (poetry). The writer, like the trainee scholar/poet/reader at the mercy of the fisherman's hook in Agamemnon's first speech, is always rendered physically vulnerable by the threat of civil war's engulfing, cannibalistic power. The city of Croton, where everyone 'is either caught or gets caught' (or where, indeed, everyone gets caught in the end, preyed on by legacy hunters/vultures), exactly mirrors the frustrating, perilous literary environments imagined by Agamemnon at the beginning of the *Satyricon*, where it is clear that each hierarchy is always swallowed up by a bigger one, that in the end there is no telling who is the fisherman, who the fish. This dynamic was spotlit more obviously, as I have hinted, in the *cena*'s zodiac dish, where the sign of the fish (*Pisces*) is at one at the same time a *rhetor* and *obsonator* (rhetorician and caterer), the bait as well the hunter, the dinner as well as the chef.[7] The more Encolpius tries to become a poet, therefore, to take on the role of (storyteller) Odysseus and to get involved in a self-consciously 'literary' relationship with Circe (with texts of the past), the more he renders himself vulnerable to Croton's legacy-hunters, who are all the while preparing his body to be eaten.

TAKING LIBERTIES

I have argued that the *Satyricon* is about reinvisaging literary systems, about taking Ovid's images of bodily-as-textual exchange/transformation from the arena of mythology to the fiction of reality, to explore their threatening implications not only for the self, but for the containment and status of literary knowledge, and therefore for the status and power of the reader as well as writer. The idea, developed so strikingly in the *Satyricon*'s narratives, that literature is/gets inside you, is an invasive force subject to corporeal flux and ephemerality, forces us to contemplate issues of freedom of speech and originality, as well as the concept of whether literary knowledge, which we must amass in order to read the ultra-allusive texts of Neronian Rome, makes us physically vulnerable or even intellectually incapacitated. In this concluding chapter, however, I aim to explore just how double-edged or paradoxical the *Satyricon*'s rebellious, chaotic upheavals really are: to what extent do they constitute a posture of originality, a plea to rubbish the past and live for the (Petronian) moment, and to what extent is this plea always at the same time self-destructive, deconstructed in the *Satyricon*'s narratives? In asking these questions we are always regressing to a basic dilemma, or prejudice: how weird/different/incomparable is the *Satyricon*, how disorganised/schizophrenic is it, how novel is the 'novel'?

Let us begin by turning the spotlight on the concept of freedom or liberality, which lies at the heart of the problematic implications invested in Petronian corporeality. As we have seen, many critics have found freedom inscribed in the 'looseness' of the *Satyricon*, its collapse of generic boundaries, its chaotic form, and its riddle-like quality which (according to Slater) can only evoke or result in an interpretative free-for-all. Yet,

[7] *in piscibus obsonatores et rhetores* (39.13). *obsonator* is well-chosen, because *obsonium* often refers specifically to fish (e.g. Varro. *Rust.* 3.17.7; Apul. *Apol.* 27).

as I have argued throughout, this is a self-exculpatory and dead-ended reading, superficially reliant on the *Satyricon*'s disconcerting appearance, one which fails to look at the work as a whole to investigate how the concept of liberality is explored and contested within the text itself. Such an investigation is central to understanding the impact of the *Satyricon* as a complex, interrogative text which repeatedly challenges its own literary status as well as the interpretative powers of its readers. For *libertas*, as it is enacted and discussed in the *Satyricon*, is plagued by paradox, set up on one hand as an ideal, a condition of ambitious contemporary writing empowered to break free from biology and the constraints of the past, and on the other as an uncontrolled and uncontrollable excess, which ultimately serves to demonstrate the tortuous pull of the past on the present and our continued enslavement to corporeality.

In Agamemnon's poem at *Sat.* 5, Latin literature is associated with letting go, running free, allowing the reins of poetry to slacken. The freedom begins with the weapons of Demosthenes (*liber* / 'like a free man', v. 14), but then the student leaves the Greeks behind to gush poetry about heady, passionate topics like feasts and wars. Emotive, modern verse is about loosening oneself from the shackles of 'tradition', represented by Homer, Socrates, and all the Greek writers one studies at the preliminary stages of education, and going on to develop an original, ambitious voice, one true to the present. This construction is explicit elsewhere, for example in Eumolpus' introduction to the *Bellum Civile*, where he talks of the writer's 'free spirit' plunging headlong into allusive, mythological poetry just like an inspired *vaticinatio*, looking into the future and leaving the past to historians:

non enim res gestae versibus comprehendendae sunt, quod longe melius historici faciunt, sed per ambages deorumque ministeria et fabulosum †sententiarum tormentum† praecipitandus est *liber spiritus*, ut potius furentis animi vaticinatio appareat quam religiosae orationis sub testibus fides: tamquam, si placet, hic impetus, etiam si nondum recepit ultimam manum. (118.6)

It is not a matter of recording real events in verse, something historians do far better. No, the *free spirit* of genius must plunge right into ambiguities and divine interpositions, and the contorted style of mythological narrative, so that the end result looks more like the visions of an inspired seer than an exacting statement made on oath before witnesses: the following effusion will show you what I mean, if you'd like it, bearing in mind it hasn't received the final touches.

We might also note that in the earlier 'writing' scene on board the ship of poetry, Eumolpus inscribes the epic-sized letters on Encolpius' forehead *liberali manu* ('freehand', 103.5). Throughout Trimalchio's *cena*, meanwhile, the well-lubricated freedmen in a sense embody the excited, liberated spirit of the contemporary Roman writer. In them the true meaning and implications of free citizenship are exaggerated and spill out over every aspect of their lifestyle and philosophies: Trimalchio encourages loose bowels and bladders, and visits the toilet regularly throughout the evening as if setting a good example of 'liberal' behaviour. For the free body never holds anything in, and constipation is the worst possible torture (*ego nullo puto tam magnum tormentum esse quam continere. hoc solum vetare ne Iovis potest* / 'I can think of no greater torture than holding oneself in. Release is the one thing that Jupiter cannot forbid', 47.4); the perfect host encourages his guests to relax, let it all hang out (*itaque si quis vestrum voluerit sua re causa facere, non est quod illum pudeatur* / 'so if anyone of you needs to do his business, there's no need to be shy', 47.4). Trimalchio goes on to describe manumission as 'tasting the water of freedom' (*aquam liberam gustabunt*, 71.1), a physical metaphor which parallels Agamemnon's visions of the free man's learning progress in *Sat.* 5 (he is to drink of Homer's 'font' and pour it out again in a regurgitated 'river'). Needless to say, this free(d)man's father is Liber himself (*'non negabitis me' inquit 'habere Liberum patrem'* / 'I'm sure you won't deny that the god of liberation is my dad', 41.8)[8] while the *cena* is one long celebration of Bacchic excess, dominated by overeating and drinking. If we missed the pun, we can rely on Trimalchio to state the obvious: *Liber esto* ('Be free', 41.7), he declares, on freeing a young slave whose name also happens to be Bacchus. Of course, Liber stands for wine as well as for 'loosening up', and, to quote Trimalchio, *vinum vita est* ('wine is life'). Life for the free(d)men flows as freely and creatively as Latin verse.

Just as the writer's 'freedom' is to some extent envisaged as a liberation from the literature of the past (if only in the sense that the scholar is now educated enough so as not to be constrained by the pressures of learning his Homer), so the *cena* is also freed from the normal constraints of time, taking place through an endless evening which continues even after the cock has crowed (74.1), and long after the guests have had their fill. The dinner party is set up to digest the creative spirit of the *Satyricon* as a whole: its liberality echoes and motivates both this text's anti-narrative form, and the impatience and lackadaisical attitude of the narrator, who is so ironically unbothered by past events, and who

[8] Trimalchio also has a slave called Bacchus (41.6), who displays the inherent slipperiness or flexibility of the god by impersonating him: *modo Bromium, interdum Lyaeum Euhiumque confessus.* / 'He impersonated Bacchus first as the Noisy One, and then sometimes as the Loosener or GoodJoy.'

boasts an atrocious memory (*tardum est differre quod placet* / 'It's difficult to put off pleasures', 10.7; *longum erat singula excipere* / 'It would take too long to recount the details', 28.1; *non licebat †multaciam† considerare* / 'I couldn't take in the whole multiplicity at once', 30.1; *sexcenta huiusmodi fuerunt, quae iam exciderunt memoriae meae* / 'There were any number of these jokes, which have now slipped my mind', 56.10). Forgetfulness seems to plague Encolpius even more in the *Cena* than in the rest of the text,[9] perhaps implicitly because the food and drink have upset his stomach and blurred his vision so as to make it impossible to concentrate. (Habinnas, who arrives late and inebriated from another dinner party, with greasy ointment running down his forehead into his eyes, has such a poor memory that he often forgets his own name: *nam tam bonae memoriae sum, ut frequenter nomen meum obliviscar*, 66.1.) Likewise, even outside this debauched atmosphere, the gang of characters on the move through this fiction are always on the run from law and order: *quid faciunt leges?* / 'What's the point of laws?' chants Ascyltos in *Sat.* 14.2; *effugi iudicium* / 'I'm on the run from justice', boasts Encolpius at 81.3. Our narrator later bemoans his outlaw life (*quam male est extra legem viventibus* / 'How hard it is living outside the law', 125.4) and accuses Ascyltos of taking liberties with Giton in defiance of all human justice (*oblitus iuris humani*, 79.9).[10]

Liberty seems to be directly associated with rebellion against chronology, and against the constraints (or for the freedmen, literally the slavery) of the past in general. Yet throughout the *cena* Trimalchio also demonstrates his obsession with time, suggesting that he feels as haunted by the past as he is liberated from its clutches. The *Satyricon* caricatures the freedman as a paranoid, paradoxical figure whose enthusiasm for making up for lost time and for packing a lifetime's worth of privilege and fun into his few remaining years always betrays a guilt and self-consciousness about his previous identity. In *Sat.* 72.4 for example, Habinnas remarks: *de una die duas facere, nihil malo* / 'I like nothing better than making two days out of one'. Time must happen in concentrate because there is

[9] We may suspect that this is because the *cena* is the longest surviving chunk of the *Satyricon*, and so seems to be more coherent in terms of the construction of Encolpius' narrating persona.

[10] See A. Barchiesi (1996) on the relationship between narration and illegality in the *Satyricon*. Barchiesi takes as his starting point Gide's perspective on the nineteenth-century novel as used by Brooks (1993: 155): 'André Gide referred to the novel as a "lawless" form, using this word in English to suggest the novel's freedom from rules. Yet he might with equal pertinence have used the French term, "hors-la-loi", since it is what lies outside the law, the state of infraction and deviance in its interaction with the controlling pressures of the law, that increasingly in the nineteenth century preoccupies narrative . . . in the banal nineteenth century where . . . everything is becoming standardized and boring, the world of social depth – of the professionally deviant, so to speak – comes to appear the last place of stories ready to hand, the last refuge of the narratable.'

implicitly so little of it left. Dinner-couch talk often turns to mortality and the shortness of life (*'dies' inquit 'nihil est. dum versas te, nox fit. itaque nihil est melius quam de cubiculo recta in triclinium ire.'* / ' "Day," he said, "is nothing. Night is on you before you can turn around. So there's nothing better than going straight from bed to dinner" ', 41.10; *utres inflati ambulamus. minoris quam muscae sumus, <muscae> tamen aliquam virtutem habent, nos non pluris sumus quam bullae* / 'We strut about like bladders of wind; we're worth less than flies, but flies have their virtues, whereas we're worth no more than bubbles', 42.4).

Indeed Trimalchio is so petrified of death that he wants to be able to exert full control over it: he has a clock and trumpeter to inform him how much of life is gone (26.9), calendars on each doorpost marked with lucky and unlucky days (30.4); he relishes quoting dates (*Falernum Opimianum annorum centum* / 'One-hundred-year-old Falernian of Opimius' vintage', 34.6),[11] and has a clerk recite statistics of happenings on his estate as if he is reading a daily newspaper (53); when he gives orders for the design of his own tomb, he specifies that a clock take pride of place (*horologium in medio*, 71.11), and goes on to stage his own funeral, complete with death bed and shroud (78). All this despite the fact that he actually has 'thirty years, four months and two days' left to live (*quod vobis non dixerim, etiam nunc mi restare vitae annos triginta et menses quattuor et dies duos*, 77.2). As a teenager, he reports, he wanted to grow up too quickly and used to oil his chin to simulate beard growth (75.10), reminding us of other instances of prematurity in the *Satyricon*: Pannychis and Quartilla losing their virginity as children at *Sat.* 25,[12] or Agamemnon's attack on teachers who fulfil Trimalchian ambition by forcing the 'unripe' schoolboy into the lawcourts (*deinde cum ad vota properant, cruda adhuc studia in forum [im]pellunt et eloquentiam, qua nihil esse maius confitentur, pueris induunt adhuc nascentibus* / 'Then when they're in a hurry to satisfy their ambitions, they drive the unripe schoolboys into the lawcourts and thrust eloquence – the noblest of callings, they confess themselves – upon children who are still growing up', 4.2).[13]

[11] Although since Trimalchio is presumably supposed to be a character of Nero's reign, this is likely a laughable error, as Opimius was consul in 121 BC. Or is it not so funny, for some people? If the joke works, this luxurious tipple is probably poisonously bad, adding a venomous aftertaste to Trimalchio's quip, *eheu. ergo diutius vivit vinum quam homuncio* / 'Alas, wine lives longer than poor man' (34.7).

[12] Quartilla was so young when she lost her virginity that she jokes she does not remember ever having been a virgin (*Iunonem meam iratam habeam, si unquam me meminerim virginem fuisse*, 25.4).

[13] M. Barchiesi (1981) sees the pathological impatience of the *Satyricon*'s characters mirrored in the pace of the narrative itself. He quotes Nietzsche in *Beyond Good and Evil* (1990) where he labels Petronius 'der Meister des Presto', with 'die Füsse eines Windes'.

The dinner becomes a funeral feast, a deadly labyrinth (plus hungry Minotaur), an underworld guarded by a Cerberus and exited via the gate of dreams,[14] a *libera cena* which twists liberty into a licence to manipulate and kill. Our narrator is a nervous, squeamish guest, constantly on his guard for unseen attacks: the one time he refers to his own *libertas* is when Trimalchio has left the room, at which point the guests permit themselves to relax (*nos libertatem sine tyranno nacti coepimus invitare... [convivarum sermones]* / 'with the tyrant away we had our freedom, and began to chat with our neighbours', 41.9). Wine, the symbol of liberty and a synonym for Liber, Trimalchio's father and presiding deity at this dinner, becomes an accessory to death when Trimalchio gives instruction that it be poured over his bones: *profer et unguentum et ex illa amphora gustum, ex qua iubeo lavari ossa mea* (77.7).[15] It is tempting to see this scene, in which the funeral director orders wine to be poured into a large bowl, in parallel with an earlier scene at 64 (*nam vinum quidem in vinarium iussit infundi* / 'for he ordered wine to be poured into a bowl', 78.4 cf. *Trimalchio camellam grandem iussit misceri <et> potiones dividi omnibus servis* / 'Trimalchio ordered a great bowl of wine to be mixed, and drinks to be served round all the slaves', 64.13). Slaves who refuse to drink will have the wine poured over their heads (*'si quis' inquit 'noluerit accipere, caput illi perfunde'*), a punishment which becomes all the more threatening when framed as a final dedication to the dead.[16]

As Gowers argues, Neronian writers (into whom we cannot help but read Nero's own obsessions and life-story)[17] are preoccupied with the

[14] Petronius' Cerberus is painted on the dining room wall, but it is just as scary as the real thing: and like the real thing, it is encountered both on entering and leaving this hell (see *Sat.* 29.1 and *Sat.* 72.8–9, where Giton, like Aeneas, throws the dog food as a distraction): does Encolpius hallucinate *again* at 72? Also like Aeneas in *Aen.* 6, Encolpius and Giton are forbidden to leave the house by the door through which they entered: *alia intrant, alia exeunt* / 'Enter by one door, leave by another' (72.10).

[15] This practice is also referred to by Habinnas as he recounts the *funeral* feast he has just attended: *sed tamen suaviter fuit, etiam si coacti sumus dimidias potiones supra ossucula eius effundere* / 'It was a pleasant event, even if we had to pour half our drinks over his bones' (65.11).

[16] Similarly at 34.8, Trimalchio produces a silver skeleton which symbolises the free, loose, flexible body aimed for in the *cena*: it has been specially made so that its joints and sockets can be manipulated in any direction. Yet clearly this is not possible in a living body: this symbol of liberality was apparently often present at Roman dinners, reminding the guests that though one eats now, one will die later. The word used of skeleton here, *larva*, usually means ghost. On this custom see Dunbabin (1986).

[17] As Gowers discusses (1994), Nero's reign was itself concentrated and precocious, lasting precisely one third of Augustus' (comparisons of this kind were common in antiquity); he is said to have hit puberty early, later outgrowing adolescence but not immaturity. Tacitus' image of Nero (*Ann.* 13.15) as the Saturnalian boy king (his birthday was 15 December: Suet. *Ner.* 6) seems to define the reign as a whole. The historians also emphasise his pathological impatience: we are told that

construction of themselves and their work as late, hurried, immature, concentrated[18] and paranoid, in contrast to the grown-up Augustans, who apparently had written everything in advance, 'timed the golden age of literature in one glorious *kairos*, or perfect hour'.[19] Persius and Horace are particularly biting examples, giving us a sharp taste of their place in history as 'thwarted latecomers, burnt-out prodigies and predestined bankrupts'.[20] The later historians, Suetonius, Tacitus and Dio, participate in, reflect and inflate this inspiring formula, latch onto it as the defining energy of an era. Neronian constructions of time are about the explosive pressures and anxieties of (re)creation, and their stimulating, fertile potential can be traced throughout the *Satyricon*.[21]

Trimalchio's paranoid and exhibitionist plea to his guests to imagine they are at a funeral (*'putate vos' ait 'ad parentalia mea invitatos esse'* / 'Make believe you've been invited to my funeral', 78.4; *'fingite me mortuum esse'* / 'Imagine I am dead', 78.5) makes emphatic his role as Neronian creative director, a composer of fiction alongside Encolpius/Petronius (and alongside the *Satyricon*'s poet figure Eumolpus, who later advocates similarly horrific imaginings: *fingite nos antrum Cyclopis intrasse* / 'Imagine we have entered the Cyclops' cave', 101.7). As I have argued, this parallel is particularly overt when Trimalchio instructs one of the freedmen to capture the dining room scene down to the last tiny detail in the representation on his tomb (there's even a carving of a boy weeping over a urn which, in 'real' time, has just been broken, 71.11), forecasting in true

he could not wait for the five-yearly festivals in Greece to come round again, so he conflated them all into one year (*cogi in unum annum*, Suet. *Ner.* 23) and speeded up their anniversaries. His own festival, the Neronia, was also revived before time (*ante praestitutam diem*, Suet. *Ner.* 21). And according to Tac. *Ann.* 13.10; 16.12, after first resisting the attempts of the Senate to bring the new year in early in his honour, he jumped the gun by re-naming April, May and June Neroneus, Claudius and Germanicus after himself, leaping in ahead of Julius and Augustus. As Gowers also reminds us, Nero's impatience all too often extended to other people's lives.

[18] Gowers (1994) frames her article around the use of the verb *decoquere*, to boil down, both in Neronian texts and in histories about them. She notes (133) how the word conveys a sense of cooking too fast, or unnaturally, or of overcooking at too intense a heat. It can also be used metaphorically, of stewing or shrivelling one's body in a bath, of reducing the excesses of early rhetorical exuberance, of squandering one's worldly substance, or of being insolvent. Trimalchio's *cena*, punctuated by oven-like baths, is one (long) exercise in overcooking, in which each dish consists of a gamut of ingredients and animals concentrated in a 'single body'.

[19] Gowers (1994) 133.

[20] Gowers (1994) 131. In Persius 3.62, the young student is accused of living just for the moment and not caring where his feet take him (*securus quo pes ferat, atque ex tempore vivis?*), reminding us both of Trimalchio's debauched existence and of Encolpius' haphazard wandering/narrating.

[21] As Rose remarks (1966b: 289), 'it is a well-known cliché among classicists to refer to the *Satyricon* as timeless'. Yet once the above point is made, it becomes extremely difficult to mythologise the *Satyricon* as incomparable with the other first-century texts and therefore 'beyond' politics: this fiction seems in many ways acutely conscious of its place in time and culture.

vatic style Encolpius' 'later' reconstruction of the *cena* as we are reading it. The funeral scene also amplifies the potential for social exchange and storytelling which have already been a focal point (*the* point?) of the dinner party: this is authorial, authoritative Trimalchio's excuse to tell autobiographical narratives (75–7), which in a sense now become paradigms for narrative in general, reminding us of the normative role of chronology and teleology in storytelling and serving in turn to accent the *Satyricon*'s 'unnatural' anti-narrative construction. Trimalchio's mock funeral, like the *cena* itself, is a vehicle for creative manipulation in which control (and hyper-awareness) of time exemplify artistic power.[22]

Indeed much of the poetic composition dramatised in the *Satyricon* is achieved under the inspiring threat of extinction.[23] When Eumolpus writes his *epigramma* on Encolpius' and Giton's heads at *Sat.* 103 (an act which involves shaving off the hair, thus prematurely eliminating a powerful symbol of youth, and which itself precipitates a poem on hair at *Sat.* 109.8),[24] it is to escape certain punishment and possible death at the hands of Lichas; hair-cutting on board ship is itself interpreted as the last offering of a crew threatened by shipwreck (103.5). Later on in this fraught voyage, the *Bellum Civile* is scrawled in a rabid frenzy just as the ship (of poetry) sinks,[25] and Eumolpus barely escapes alive. Then,

[22] The idea that poetic power is a Circean ability to distort time and reverse the laws of nature occurs frequently in Latin poetry, especially in Ovid (e.g. *Tr.* 1.8, 1–10). See Beard (1987) and Newlands (1995) on imperial manipulations of time as the ultimate display of political power.

[23] See Connors (1994) on the relationship between authorship/writing and death in the *Satyricon* and in Neronian literary culture: at Tac. *Ann.* 15.70, Lucan uses his own poetry as a script for his death; in *Ep.* 77.20 Seneca explicitly figures suicide as the construction of a text or performance by an author, while Nero apparently dies claiming *qualis artifex pereo* / 'What an artist the world is losing' (Suet. *Ner.* 49.1) and even Tacitus' Petronius makes literary conversation and listens to poetry as his blood drains from his slit wrists (*Ann.* 16.20).

[24] Eumolpus' little elegy on hair, 'the corporeal icon par excellence' (Hall, Laqueur and Posner 1992: 16), plays on the idea that hair is a symbol of youth and a reflection of a person's age, punning like Ovid (*Met.* 1.3–4; *Fast.* 4.11–12, 15–16) on *tempora* as times/forehead: shaving off the hair reveals a man's forehead, but it also makes him look old, exposes the time he has left to live. The paralleling of hair-loss with falling leaves (both are *coma*) during the last season of the year, winter, stretches the rusty Ovidian joke further (vv. 1–4). The last two lines of this poem only rub salt into vain Giton's wounds (*ut mortem citius venire credas, / scito iam capitis perisse partem* / 'So you may know how quickly death shall come, know that a part of my head has died already', vv. 12–13): his hair is dead not only because it has been cut off, but also because hair is always dead, a brittle and insentient accessory to the living body. The idea that everybody is always half-dead is truly in the Neronian spirit as discussed above: the free man is perhaps not so superior to the slave or freedman, whose heads are normally shaven (witness Trimalchio's *adrasum caput* at 32.2, which he naturally tries to cover with a cloak).

[25] This has often been used to support assessments of the aesthetic value of the poem. E.g. Rose (1966b: 298) writes: 'either the poem was written in a hurry and Petronius contented himself with making it sufficiently Lucanic, or else it deliberately sets out to seem like hurried, bombastic poetry'.

on the march to the menacing, death-filled city of Croton, the same poem is recited by Eumolpus as he gets in role as a sick old man on the verge of death. In Croton itself, the adolescent Encolpius' metaphorical and premature 'death' (*malo astro natus est* / 'He was born under a bad star', 134.8) inspires a string of poems. The entire drama at Croton seems on one level to be about a poet consciously putting himself in a threatening and deathly environment, that of civil war (although it is impossible to know whether Eumolpus really does mean to get himself executed in our dramatic finale, or whether this is another poetic trick).[26]

It is no accident that the beginning of the *Bellum Civile*, where modern greed and arrogance are the catalyst for civil war (and for civil war poetry), reminds us precisely of the rich freedman lifestyle dramatised in the *Cena*: like Trimalchio, hubristic Romans want their empire to extend even to the heavens (Trimalchio's dining room ceiling is his sky[27]), and to control the course of the sun and moon (*orbem iam totum victor Romanus habebat, / qua mare, qua terrae, qua sidus currit utrumque* / 'The conquering Roman now held the world, the sea, the land, the course of the sun and moon', vv. 1–2); like our neophile symposiarch, they love Corinthian bronze, take pleasure in their own bodies, and 'gain no happiness from familiar joys' (*BC* 7–8 cf. 39.4: *nam mihi nihil novi potest afferri* / 'nobody can bring me anything new'). As we have seen, in Croton, the city of civil war itself, all the women can apparently control nature and time, just like spellbinding Circe, the goddess of creative empowerment whose poetic talents are matched only by great storytellers like Odysseus, and certainly not by would-be Odysseuses like Encolpius.

Yet as the pure theatrics of the *cena* and the subsequent failed act of *polyaenus* Encolpius can but demonstrate, Trimalchio's demonic control (like that of the gluttonous Romans in *BC* 1–52) is doomed to self-destruct: the more he displays the gilded accessories of imperialism, evidence of his mastery over nature and time, the more paranoid and comic he looks. The more he preaches liberality in every sphere, from excess spending, eating and drinking to loosening the bladder and bowels, the more he spells out a human inability to transcend his own corporeality, his ultimate lack of control. Ultimately, he too is one of the freedmen, the larger than life caricatures symbolising the general Roman public as

[26] Cf. Empedocles coolly leaping into burning Aetna in the hope of becoming immortal (Hor. *Ars P.* 465–6).

[27] See *Sat.* 60, where the ceiling rumbles with 'thunder' (*nam repente lacunaria sonare coeperunt totumque triclinium intremuit*, 60.1) and the guests wonder what new portent will be announced 'from the heavens' (*de caelo*, 60.2).

described at the start of the *Bellum Civile*, who embody a cheap parody of liberty. Freedmen in a sense are hyper-free, for they alone perhaps know the real meaning of freedom; yet they are also emphatically not truly free, not born free. They serve to demonstrate how even the man who indulges in the most liberal excesses, who really takes freedom to an extreme, will always be bound and controlled by the limits of his own body, and also by fate.[28] As I have argued, the *cena* plays on name-etymology, painting Fortunata as Fortuna, the goddess who rules Trimalchio's life:[29]

nunc, nec quid nec quare, in caelum abiit et Trimalchionis topanta est. ad summam, mero meridie si dixerit illi tenebras esse, credet. ipse nescit quid habeat, adeo saplutus est; sed haec lupatria providet omnia, est ubi non putes. (37.4–6)

No questions asked, she lives in the heavens and is Trimalchio's be all and end all. In fact, if she tells him it's dark at midday, he'll believe it. He's so rich, he doesn't even know himself what he owns; but that bitch foresees everything, even where you wouldn't think it.

nihil autem tam inaequale erat: nam modo Fortunatam <verebatur> modo ad naturam suam revertebatur. (52.11)

But never was anything so unpredictable: one minute he'd be frightened of Fortunata, the next he'd be back to his old self.

Fortuna is the goddess who presides over war in the *Bellum Civile*: she is the essence of civil war's disruptive, anarchic force, the goddess roused by the hubris of Roman liberality who, just like the free(d)man, epitomises *both* the extremes of *libertas and* the destruction or meaninglessness of human liberty.[30] Moreover, as we have but glimpsed so far, *fortuna* is a concept or impetus woven throughout this fiction, one whose doubleness reflects the real trickiness of the *Satyricon* as well as the inevitable double-bind in which its readers find themselves. The next section of this chapter will take its chances with fortune.

[28] As Fitzgerald writes (2000: 5), 'freemen lived with slaves as one "lives with" death, since slaves provided a constant reminder of something terrible that might befall any of them'.

[29] The name Trimalchio could also mean 'thrice lucky', implying that his present fortune is just a trick of fate.

[30] The chaos she provokes, reflecting Masters' interpretation of Lucan's civil war as creating 'as many boundaries as it demolishes' (1992: 64), is never formless, but instead vacillates between loosening and paralysing the forces of nature: see especially *BC* 185–98 (*et paulo ante lues iam concidenda iacebat* / 'and the water that flowed free a moment before now stopped, hard enough to cut', 192).

FICTIONS OF CHANCE

As we have seen throughout, the critical consensus on the *Satyricon* (with one or two notable exceptions) is to deal with the work as a series of dislocated, potentially extractable episodes. This kind of positioning, I have suggested, is in many ways rather seductive, letting the overworked critic off the hook of narratological intricacy and cleaving plenty of space for Slater's entertaining comedy of confusion. It is, moreover, a straightforward response not only to the *Satyricon*'s fragmented appearance (and to the historical reality of its corruption), but also to Trimalchian constructions of time and events in the *Cena*, which seem to brainwash the narratives that follow. Yet, as I have suggested throughout, a stubbornly 'episodic' packaging of the *Satyricon* falls, like the naïve dinner guests, straight into the Freedman's labyrinthine trap. For Trimalchio, as 'author' and director of the *cena*-drama, an obsession with Fortuna (and with the divine control-freak Fortunata) is on one hand all part of his hyper-freedom, his rebellious lack of responsibility or self-determination (everything's completely out of my control, all down to chance, so I'm just going to go with the flow...). Yet on the other it is an authorial construction designed to maximise the novelty of his culinary and dramatic tricks. For if everything is down to chance and accident, then one can never predict or control what is going to happen next: every writer wants suspense and plot-twists up both sleeves.[31]

The inevitability that *complete* chaos/anti-narrative/episodic patterning is always fake or constructed is never more in evidence than in *Sat.* 54–5: this is the point in the dinner party when a slave falls ('accidentally'?) against Trimalchio's arm, who pretends to be hurt: doctors are called, the slave is begging for his life, while the guests are worried something terrible is going to happen, especially when another slave is beaten for dressing the bruise on his master's arm with white wool instead of purple. A distraught Encolpius writes:

pessime mihi erat, ne his precibus per <rid>iculum aliquid catastropha quaereretur. nec enim adhuc exciderat cocus ille qui oblitus fuerat porcum exinterare.

[31] Connors suggests (1998: 82–3): 'Petronius is *Fortuna* in devising these fictions of chance for his literary creations'. M. Barchiesi (1981: 129) pinpoints the dynamic of the dinner party when he writes 'nella cena nulla è casuale'. The prevalence of fortuna in the *cena* is inspired by Hor. *Sat.* 2.8, where Nasidienus' dinner is fraught with anxiety over things which may be beyond the host's control (the bread could be overbaked, the sauce underseasoned, a dish might get smashed). But when a ceiling canopy falls down, ruining the culinary *pièce de résistance*, this is the perfect excuse for the host to shine by overcoming 'unforeseen' disaster with inspired improvisation.

itaque totum circumspicere triclinium coepi, ne per parietem automatum aliquod exiret. (*Sat.* 54.3)

I was really scared that his begging act was leading up to some comic twist, because the cook who had forgotten to gut the pig had not faded from my recollection. So I started to scan the whole dining room, in case some clockwork contraption was about to jump out of the wall.

He is referring to the earlier incident at *Sat.* 49, yet as I hinted in chapter two, our narrator is so caught up in the episodic thrill of Trimalchio's theatre that he seems to have forgotten that the cook did *not* forget to gut the pig, that remembering and forgetting in the *Cena* are liberating postures whose relationship to 'reality' is always indecipherable.[32] When finally Trimalchio frees the slave instead of punishing him, so that he never has to admit to being wounded by a mere servant (54.5), this sparks off small talk about the uncertainty of men's affairs, which Trimalchio gets to mark with an *inscriptio* bowing to the powers of Fortuna:

> quod non expectes, ex traverso fit <ubique,
> nostra> et supra nos Fortuna negotia curat.
> quare da nobis vina Falerna, puer. (*Sat.* 55.3)

> Things always happen when you're least expecting,
> And high above us Fortune rules our lives.
> So, slave, pass us the Falernian wine.

Of course, this is all 'off the top of his head'. The entire scene is described as a *casus*: an accident, precipitated literally by a 'fall', not planned or contrived in the least. But this little farce is clearly not about freedom, freeing, Fortuna, but about the opposite: control and manipulation of an audience. The performance stars Trimalchio as Fortuna, lauding it over the small, fated lives of his dinner guests. Meanwhile the notion

[32] For example, when Habinnas arrives drunk from another funeral feast, he doubts whether he can tell the guests about his evening because his memory is so bad (*'dicam' inquit 'si potuero; nam tam bonae memoriae sum, ut frequenter nomen meum obliviscar'* / 'I'll tell you if I can, but my memory is in such fine shape, I often forget my own name', 66.1). Yet he proceeds to recount the minutiae of every course, even remembering that some guests took three fistfuls of olives after the dessert. His drunkenness, we suspect, was just part of the act in his grand entrance, which impresses the guests (*Habinnamque intrantem cum admiratione ingenti spectabam* / 'I watched Habinnas enter with great admiration', 65.6) and even entertains Trimalchio (*delectatus hac Trimalchio hilaritate* / 'Trimalchio was delighted by his sense of humour', 65.8). This is one of the points at which the *Satyricon* seems to strike an acutely modern note: part of the fun of a drunken pub-crawl is to reconstruct (often in much greater detail than one would after a sober evening) hazy movements and events, while everyone today recognises the character who boasts complete inebriation only to give the funniest account of the night's happenings, or conversely the character who always claims drunken memory loss to cover up socially unacceptable behaviour.

that Encolpius may have forgotten (or, remember, 'forgotten') exactly what happened in a previous scene (as well as admitting to memory loss elsewhere) nudges us to think about how we are reading the *Satyricon* in general: did *we* not remember the previous scene, convinced as we are that this text is irredeemably 'episodic'? Have we been similarly seduced by authorial guile, by the (liberating) idea that this is all just superficial, raucous entertainment devoid of any clever patterning, ring-composition and the like (which is why it makes such a refreshing change from other classical Latin texts, and the painstaking critical approaches they demand)? Are all texts about Fortuna (on a literal and metaliterary level) always really also about *constructed* chaos (and the construction of poet as fate-controlling *vates*),[33] about the self-conscious orchestration of free, anarchic, metamorphic forces as symbolic fodder for creativity/poetry itself? For that is precisely what happens on a miniature scale in the above scene, where *casus* inspires Trimalchio to compose verses on paper, which then prompt a discussion on poets (*ab hoc epigrammate coepit poetarum esse mentio* / 'a debate about poets arose from this epigram', 55.4) followed by Trimalchio's grandiose poem on the futility of materialism,[34] and finally by the conversational gambit, *quod autem putamus secundum litteras difficillimum esse artificium?* / 'Now what do we reckon's the hardest profession after writing?' In this short sequence alone, we see the powers of *artificium* and narrative at work, rounded off by the poet's advertising blurb outlining the difficulty of the exercise. The striking image which we have come back to again and again of the writer as (like) a doctor who knows what poor men have in their insides, implicitly sets the 'poet' Trimalchio in the same league as his own astrologer, who 'knew the secrets of the gods' as well as his own 'insides', and stopped just short of telling him what he had eaten for dinner the previous evening (*intestinas meas noverat; tantum quod mihi non dixerat quid pridie cenaveram*, 76.11). Trimalchio's comment that

[33] The poet who dominates the literary discussion at 55.4ff. is Mopsus, which is also the name of several soothsayers (indeed we know of no poet called Mopsus).

[34] Between opulent courses, this awful poem, quoted apparently from Publilius Syrus the mimographer, with its aggressive address (*tuo, tibi*), looks particularly sick: you can almost hear the jaws of luxury (*luxuriae rictu* ***M****artis* ***m****arcent* ***m****oenia*, v. 1) masticating on the stuffed guests in this grating first line, not to mention pulverising their palates in vv. 2–3 (*tuo palato clausus pavo pascitur / plumato*) before force-feeding them the indigestible, tongue-twisting stork in v. 6 (*pietaticultrix gracilipes crotalistria*). Within this drama of constructed liberality, it is an opportune moment for Trimalchio to remind his guests that they are eating exotic game only as a result of (it? them?) being imprisoned (v. 2). Courtney (1991: 21) suggests that the poem mocks the frequent use of quotations from Publilius by Seneca (nine in the letters, two in the dialogues) to illustrate his moral teaching, and that the piece is itself a parody of such moral tirades. I am dubious about the latter point: as Smith argues (1975: 148), the style and content of the poem do not remotely resemble the extant aphorisms of Publilius.

he resents doctors because they are always prescribing him antidotes to poison (*quod mihi iubent saepe anatinam*[35] *parari*, 56.3) implicitly illustrates his superiority over the (less talented, and less fortunate) guests: just as he is privileged to predict the insides of layered dishes, is he the only diner equipped with an antidote to the food he *knows* the other guests have eaten?[36] Wherever you find honey, watch out for the sting (*ubicumque dulce est, ibi et acidum invenies*, 56.6).

A similar incident surrounding the manipulation of *casus* occurs on Lichas' ship at *Sat.* 107. In 104, by a strange 'trick of fate', Lichas and Tryphaena have similar dreams in which Priapus and Neptune inform them of Encolpius' and Giton's presence on board.[37] Lichas agrees to search the ship, if only to show that he has some respect for *divinae mentis opera* / 'the workings of a divine agent' (104.4), and is immediately told that men have been spotted shaving their hair by moonlight. The villains are to be punished to avoid the risk of shipwreck, and Eumolpus intervenes in their defence, claiming their ignorance of seafaring laws and rationalising that their long hair needed cutting to stop the ship looking like a prison (105.2). Despite his pleas, Giton and Encolpius are beaten, yet without their clothes they are soon recognised by ex-lovers Tryphaena and Lichas, who is infuriated: *nunc mimicis artibus petiti sumus et adumbrata inscriptione derisi* / 'Now we've been done over by an actor's tricks, fooled by the mere outline of a inscription' (106.1). Quick-witted Eumolpus is on the defensive once more, arguing that they *intended* to board the ship in order to be reunited with old friends, and so had no need to disguise themselves (the slave-marks on their faces were a self-imposed punishment, he says): you are mistaken if, by chance (*forte*) you believe they have fallen (*incidisse*) into your snare by chance (*casu*) (107.2). Yet Lichas interrupts, warning him not to confuse the issue: a man who disguises himself wants to play a trick, not to make amends: *ex quo appareat*

35 *anatinam* means 'a dose of duck'. This makes sense: Pliny, *HN* 15.6 says that Mithridates VI, King of Pontus, who allegedly drank remedies daily in order to make himself immune from poisoning, mixed with antidotes the blood of Pontic ducks which, says Pliny, live on poison. Also, Smith (1975: 150) notes that the Younger Cato is said to have included duck in his little book of prescriptions for the family (Plut. *Cat. Min.* 23.3) and that the animal also figures in bizarre remedies of folklore: Columella (6.7.1) says that pain in the stomach and intestines of oxen is eased if the patient catches sight of swimming creatures, especially ducks, and that the sight of a duck is even more successful in curing mules and horses. Pliny notes further that if someone suffering from colic has a duck placed beside his stomach the ailment disappears and the duck perishes (*HN* 30.61).

36 The implication that the food contains a dangerous poison is in a sense confirmed by Trimalchio's vegetarian, Pythagorean speech that now follows.

37 Even this 'coincidence' gets a nudge and a wink: on her way into exile for crimes of passion, Tryphaena remarks *putes una nos dormisse* / 'you'd think we had slept together' (104.2).

casu incidisse noxios in plagas et te artem quaesisse, qua nostrae animadversionis impetum eluderes / 'All of which makes it quite clear that the vagabonds fell into the net by accident, and that you then hunted for some trick to avoid the force of our displeasure' (107.9). Hitting back at this *declamatio* in what is fast becoming (or was set up to become) a law-court debate, Eumolpus encourages his audience to distinguish between appearances and reality: *hoc argumento incidisse in navem videntur, non venisse* / 'This looks like proof that they boarded the ship by chance and not on purpose' (107.12). Lichas loses his temper, the branding marks are unveiled as water-soluble handwriting, and the mini-civil war breaks out, complete with phony battle-lines and mutilation. Unlike Trimalchio in the *Cena*, then, this arrogant poet weaves fictions of *intent*, not of chance, arguing that the gang deceived no one because they *meant* to board the ship and be recognised by their 'friends'. Lichas' counter-argument is that these events were accidental: i.e., they *were* tricksters, but getting caught was the point at which the trick failed. Yet we may suspect that Eumolpus has the last laugh. In naming the discovery a *casus*, and in grounding his cross-examination in the language of chance, Lichas reminds us of the prominent parallel scene at *Sat.* 54–5, where, as we have seen, Trimalchio is on a roll as trickster dramatist/poet, particularly as the key element of Eumolpus' design to be revealed as fake, the *inscriptio*, described as *epigramma* at 103.4, mirrors the poetic climax to Trimalchio's stageshow: *non oportet hunc casum sine inscriptione transire* / 'We should not let this chance slip without an inscription' (55.2)... *ab hoc epigrammate*... / 'from this epigram...' (55.4). This recollection (or Lichas' unawareness of it) is fatal, because it dredges up unforgettable resonances of *casus* not as chance or accident but as fakery *disguised* as chance or accident. Lichas is still a firm believer in *casus* and thinks fate is on his side, whereas the *Satyricon*'s readers are drawn back to a point in the text where the gullibility and exploitability of such beliefs are cleverly exposed. In the ship scene, the boundary between what is accident and what is 'accident' is confused. Does Eumolpus mean for his illusion to be found out, for his make-up job to run, just as the punchline to Trimalchio's magic consists in the revelation of fakery (what seemed like intestines are in fact sausages), rather than the perpetuation of suspense and deception? Lichas looks double-crossed, as his protestations of coincidence (it was fate that revealed the truth) can also be read ironically as advertisements for Eumolpus' creative machinations, concealed, like Trimalchio's, beneath the distracting veil of chance. Eumolpus' trick succeeds in failing, while the punishment and threats inspired by the recognition are just the initiatives he requires to conjure up scenes of civil war and to rouse Fortuna from the waves. Lichas accuses Eumolpus of searching frantically for a way to avoid the impetus of his displeasure (*ex quo appareat... et te artem quaesisse, qua nostrae animadversionis* ***impetum*** *eluderes*, 107.9), yet this reaction is precisely the inspiration he has been looking for, as he finally proves at 118.6: *tamquam, si placet, hic* ***impetus*** / 'this effusion will show you what I mean'.

These complementary scenes, then, mark crucial points in the *Satyricon* at which our privileged awareness of 'authorial' contrivance raises our suspicions as to the reading patterns we may be led to follow for the text as a whole: do we want to look as stupid as Encolpius (contrives to look), or stand as deluded as Lichas, who literally falls victim, finally, to the seas of fortune? If not we had better look sharp and stay sober, we had better recall what has already happened in this tricky anti-narrative, even if we cannot really ever predict what is going to happen next. As the freedmen prove (or betray in their paranoia), we should never, and can never, erase or deny the past and live just for the moment: as Lowenthal argues, 'the past is essential to our sense of identity: the sureness of "I was" is a necessary component of "I am". The ability to recall and identify with our own past gives existence meaning, purpose and value'; amnesiacs are bereft of personality.[38] Memory is an essential cognitive tool when it comes to reading the *Satyricon*, as well as any other complex text, and especially the dense, self-consciously secondary literature of Neronian Rome. In order to understand Petronian riddles, you have to be educated in Homeric, Virgilian and post-Virgilian epic, in mime, Greek and Roman comedy, satire, love poetry, *ad infinitum*... It is difficult to think of a genre that critics have not 'found' in this text. As I have argued throughout, the *Satyricon* is never simply 'unique', never unrecognisably 'different' from any other ancient text we have, never concerned with a straightforward displacement and substitution of known narratives and motifs. Its innovation is always grounded in incorporation, whereby it enacts its dependency on the past *alongside* its will to break free from its literary inheritance. This is just the model of learning we get in Agamemnon's poem at *Sat.* 5, replicated in the

[38] Lowenthal (1985) 41. One of the rare points at which it is possible to argue for signs of narrative development in the *Satyricon* is at *Sat.* 125ff., where Encolpius seems more hesitant and self-reflective, and his poetry seems to be in part a self-deprecating commentary on his earlier naïvety: it is clear at this point that our narrator can no longer maintain his Trimalchian, 'novelistic' disregard for the past, which, I have argued, returns to haunt him in the form of literary knowledge, texts of the past which he now ignores, forgets or misremembers at his peril.

freedman's inner battle between ambitions for a free present and future, and a guilty relationship with his constrictive past. It is also the pattern compulsively perpetuated in the story of the fall of Troy, the foundational myth grounded paradoxically in the destruction of a civilisation.

CLAIMS TO FAME

The *Satyricon* constantly problematises its own idea of modern literature's impatiently futuristic, liberal visions and radical breach with the constraints of the past. Yet we have also seen how its complex imagistic structure, its discussions of literature and its anti-narrative form in general, are geared precisely towards undermining or confusing memory, and models of learning grounded in remembering. Throughout, it is only the scholar full of literature, drowned in it (*sic flumine largo plenus* / 'full of a wide river', 5 vv. 21–2; *ingenti flumine litterarum inundata* / 'flooded in a huge river of literature', 118.3; *plenus litteris* / 'full of literature', 118.6) who can cope with writing and understanding literature in the spirit of the age. If he is not sufficiently learned, he is sure to sink under the weight of ignorance (*sub onere labetur*, 118.6). Yet there is a fine line between drowning in knowledge and sinking in ignorance, as the scene of the composition of the *Bellum Civile* shows, for despite his efforts Eumolpus barely escapes death in the shipwreck. As Quintilian discusses, knowledge (or rather memory, the retention of knowledge) becomes a dangerous and debilitating burden when you are required to consume such an overwhelming mass of information.[39] Eumolpus' speech at *Sat.* 118 resonates with the *Satyricon*'s ongoing symbolism of literature as an internalised food which can trigger nausea, constipation and indigestion if consumed in excess (or in the tyrant's poisonous dining room, if consumed at all). Literature is the beast within, glimpsed in the scene of Eumolpus' creative frustration at *Sat.* 115.1 as he scribbled his masterwork like a caged beast groaning with frustration, which can make you 'mad with learning' (*prae litteras fatúum esse*, 46.1).

Moreover the *Satyricon*'s imaging of poetic creation/recitation as the effusion of contained knowledge is totally at odds with Quintilian's similarly metaphorical model of learning whereby knowledge is sipped slowly in small quantities so that the body may retain it permanently (*Inst.*

[39] Quint. *Inst.* 11.2.27: *proderit per partes ediscere; laborat enim maxime onere* / 'It's a good idea to learn in bits: there's nothing so bad for the memory as being overburdened.'

1.2.26–8).[40] This text suggests that in a literary and socio-political arena satisfied with nothing less than epic gesture and civil war-scale literature, traditional models of learning based on memory have reached breaking point.[41] Knowledge can no longer be contained within the human body, which is so stuffed full that it has to burst, just as the pupils in the rhetorical school (alongside the readers of this dark fiction) are so overloaded with flavours that, ironically, they have lost their tastebuds. Furthermore, the *Satyricon* suggests that all knowledge and indeed all literature is subject to corporeal flux: like memory, literature consists in what the reader, in all his human and bodily fallibility, can recall – it survives as fragments, subjectively cut and reordered.[42] Throughout, the notion that texts, like bodies, change and age (and in Neronian spirit, age prematurely: *non potuerunt usque ad senectutem canescere* / 'they couldn't reach the grey hairs of old age', 2.8) directly challenges the concept of memory as preserving, rather than continually recreating, the past.

Nevertheless, in locating anxieties of knowing and remembering within a framework of corporeal fallibility, the *Satyricon* could be construed as formulating standard epic claims to classic status: elaborating metaphors of text as body, or text as a physically internalised food, is a sideways take on an Ennian bid to 'live on the lips of men', and is borrowed directly from Ovid's (albeit deconstructed and deconstructable) image of the *Metamorphoses* as an oral artefact, a *perpetuum carmen* surviving 'in the mouths' of his audience.[43] Both Ovid's and Petronius' poetics of corporeal exchange constitute, to a point, a legitimating strategy echoing a long tradition of vatic immortality claims. The *Satyricon* seems on

40 'Vessels with narrow mouths will not take liquids if too much is poured into them at once, but are easily filled if the liquid is admitted in a gentle stream or even drop by drop; similarly, you must consider how much a child's mind is capable of receiving. The more difficult lessons will not enter minds that have not been opened up sufficiently to take them in' (Quint. *Inst.* 1.2.28). We may compare Hor. *Ars P.* 335–7: 'Whenever you instruct, be brief, so that what is said quickly the mind can readily grasp and faithfully hold; every word in excess flows away from the full mind' (*omne supervacuum pleno de pectore manat*).

41 Quintilian states that all education depends on memory (*nam et omnis disciplina memoria constat*, *Inst.* 11.2.1).

42 Cf. Quint. *Inst.* 11.2.4 (memory depends on our physical condition); 11.2.6 (memory is inconsistent: we remember childhood, but not yesterday); 11.2.7 (memory can come and go, it's not reliable).

43 E.g. *ore legar populi* / 'I shall be read on men's lips' (*Met.* 15.878); *nunc incorrectum populi pervenit in ora / in populi quicquam si tamen ore meum est* / 'But now it has come to men's lips unrevised, if anything of mine is on their lips' (*Tr.* 3.14.23). See Farrell (1999) for an excellent discussion of Ovid's 'thematically charged opposition between the materiality of the text and the immateriality of the poetic voice'. Farrell concludes (136) that the opposition between oral artifact and bookish body is 'maintained and intensified throughout the poem, surfacing at key moments and tending finally to validate the claims of the voice over that of the book'.

one hand to envisage the transmission of literature as an oral, or cerebral, system that finally transcends materiality, living only in the mind (and rumbling in the belly), before being regurgitated and transformed, like the Pythagorean soul. Yet fundamentally, we have seen, the *Satyricon* further entangles Ovid's complication of a clichéd opposition between the fragile, material book and the immutable, transcendental poetic voice: here, there is *no such thing* as disembodiment, as all speech, writing, ideas and ideologies are ultimately subject to corporeality. Just as papyrus can be burnt, so minds can hallucinate or forget, memory trick, voices be misheard and misinterpreted. Thus while on one hand the *Satyricon* plugs into its predecessors' cultivation of 'classic' status, on the other it violently debunks the very notion of a 'classic' text, with all its connotations of permanence, unchangeability and metaphysicality.

Yet Petronian materiality forges another version of epic arrogance, one which situates the mortal 'classic' solely in the present, the here and now: like all great works of fiction expanding to cocoon readers in its world, the *Satyricon* pulls out all the stops to ensure its audience partakes in its Trimalchian philosophy of living (and reading) for the moment. It says: this is the best, forget the rest (they're past it, old, decayed, defunct...). Does Petronius see Bloom's anxiety of influence dead and buried, is *this* freedom for the Neronian writer?[44] There may even be a sense in which we are meant to grasp an implicit connection between the material book (*liber*),[45] and the *free* (*liber*) Roman writer who has withdrawn from the forum (*subducta foro*) to write, rather than declaim, in private not in public (5 vv. 13–14, 17–18), which is only possible when one is educated enough to be liberated from the reins of tradition; there is certainly evidence of such punning in Latin texts.[46]

This idea is traceable throughout the *Cena*: Latin literature is removed from (Greek) oral performance, a matter for silent, private contemplation rather than for social entertainment. For example, at *Sat.* 59, Trimalchio shows off his 'refined' Romanness and independence of thought by *reading* a Latin version from a book while the slaves act out the Greek; when he wants to compose a poem, he asks for some paper (55.2). Encolpius later remarks that something he did not understand and found offensive

[44] Bloom (1973).

[45] *Satyricon* (a Greek genitive plural) is likely to have had *liber* supplied in its original title (cf. *Georgicon liber*).

[46] Maltby (1991: 337) documents *liber* puns of this kind in antiquity: e.g. Cassiod. *Inst.* 2. praef. 4 *liber . . . dictus est a libro, id est arboris cortice dempto atque liberato.* / 'liber, from liber (book), that is, the bark of the tree removed and "liberated" '.

turned out to be Greek (64.5). Trimalchio boasts of his libraries, one Greek and one Latin (*II bybliothecas habeo, unam Graecam, alteram Latinam*, 48.4), and says, '*nam et comoedos... emeram, sed malui illos Atell <ani> am facere et choraulen meum iussi Latine cantare.*' / 'For I once bought a Greek comedy company... but I preferred them to play Atellane plays, and I ordered my pipe-player to play Latin songs' (53.13). Even a comic drama is enclosed in the pages of a book (*mox ubi ridendas inclusit pagina partes*, 80.9), while we are frequently reminded that the *Bellum Civile* has been *written* (*nondum recepit ultimam manum* / 'It hasn't received the final touches yet', 118.6). The physicality of Latin literature, together with the 'freedom' of the writer who has progressed from school-style recitation to the contemplative, material pursuit of writing, are continually emphasised, culminating perhaps in the secret tattooing scene on Lichas's ship, where writing is so fragile it can be obliterated with a wet sponge (108.2). The *liber spiritus* of contemporary writing (of which the *Satyricon* wants to be read as a prime example), buzzing with present-day vibes and determined brazenly to discredit the past, always sets itself up to showcase its own limitations.[47] Empowering the reader by ensuring that interpretation matters (because texts are, and can be *changed* in the process of transmission), inevitably backfires, at least for the author. Because the day after reading this masterpiece, you can just as easily wash it off.

I have attempted to explore how the *Satyricon* situates its readers in a series of double-binds: in order to understand this text you have to have mastered an apparatus of literary memory, not only to grasp the links/repetitions between 'episodes',[48] but to tune into its hyper-allusivity. Yet the more sensitised we are to the intricacies of this fiction and to what it constantly suggests about reading and learning processes, the more we are made conscious both of its construction of the past (and

[47] Indeed, as Fitzgerald (2000: 80) reminds us, in Hor. *Epist.* 1.20 the finished opus is addressed as if it were a young and recently manumitted slave, eager to display himself to a broader public and see something of the world. The published book (*liber*) is not associated with a free citizen, but with a freed (*liber*) slave. This pun is echoed in Ov. *Tr.* 1.1. (1–2, 15–16, 57–8), where ironically it is the book that is free to go to Rome while the master is not. Even the most creative (liberated) Roman writer is also in some way enslaved by the very materiality or uncontrollability of his creation.

[48] The repetition of images which, I have argued, runs throughout the *Satyricon*, forges links and triggers memory, reminding us too of Quintilian's discussion of mnemonics at *Inst.* 11.2.17–22 (we remember in symbols: *imagines voces sunt, quibus ea quae ediscenda sunt notamus ut quomodo Cicero dicit, locis pro cera, simulacris pro litteris utamur* / 'Images are the voices by which we distinguish the things we have to learn by heart. In fact, as Cicero says, we use places like wax tablets and symbols in place of letters', 21).

of literary knowledge) as *just* memory (literature is all in the mind/body, and so subject to corporeal vicissitudes), and of the necessary limitations of memory as learning or reading tool. Fundamentally, the fiction of the *Satyricon* itself depends on its having been written down from Encolpius' memory, and the central joke or dilemma of reading it is that our narrator's memory is conspicuously fallible, subjective and inadequate. We can never feel intellectually 'liberated' by the *Satyricon's* disjointed, schizophrenic appearance because we are made all too aware that its liberality is rooted in limitation, not *freedom*, of thought.[49] This text makes it difficult, to various degrees, to decide what is controlled, and what is beyond a character's control, or what is merely constructed as control/freedom. As we have seen throughout, it is as tough for readers as for Encolpius (whose narrow perspective on life we share) to tell whether something is an act or not. Ultimately this discussion reflects and embraces another central dilemma of reading the *Satyricon*: the impossibility of deciphering the relationship between 'interior' narrator and 'exterior' author, of deciding when/if ever Encolpius is just posing as a forgetful, passive, impotent *scholasticus*, manipulating an audience doomed never to be any the wiser.

The *Satyricon* suggests that any such conclusion must be aware of being skewed by perspective. Our view of the whole of the *Satyricon*, like the picture painted of the *cena*, is always labyrinthine, and as Penelope Reed Doob has argued, labyrinths are 'characteristically double'.[50] Not only does their circuitous design prescribe a constant doubling back, but they also presume a double viewpoint: what you see depends on where you stand. From above or as a diagram in a work of art, the viewer is dazzled by its complex and symmetrical artistry. Yet Petronius' readers, who view the world according to Encolpius, are never permitted to forget that inside Daedalus' creation, vision behind and ahead is extremely constricted and fragmented.[51] Labyrinths, like the *Satyricon*, 'simultaneously incorporate order and disorder, unity and multiplicity, artistry and chaos'. They 'encode the very principle of doubleness, contrariety,

[49] This point has much in common with Hershkowitz's (1998: 195–6) on Ovid's *Met.*: 'While it is a good idea to reconsider the meaning of the metamorphosis of Ovid's poem in the light of postmodernism, we should be wary of obscuring the negative, terrifying aspects of the loss of self, or of transferring the madness into an excessively cheerful picture of fluidity and freedom. One of the lessons of the *Metamorphoses* is that such fluidity and freedom of mind and world can only be bought at the price of loss and madness.'

[50] Reed Doob (1990) 1–2 *et passim*.

[51] Strabo recommends viewing a labyrinth from the top of a building, so that one can appreciate its design (17.1.37).

paradox'. Stuck in this maze, a work of art decipherable, we remember, only by means of super-human memory, we are aware of the paradox that our constricted vision is the price to pay for a fleeting vindication of (what looks like)[52] a freedom to mean.

[52] As Fowler reminds us in his discussion of Zeitlin's 'paradox' (2000: 300–1), at the end there are always buts, in which readers are implicated: as far as the *Satyricon* is concerned, 'thematisation (i.e. whether of closure, openness, or a pomo dialectic between the two) can always be refused' (301). I would like to see this constant potential for reversal or refusal playing a frustrating/energising role at the core of Petronian paradox.

APPENDIX I

The use of fundere *and cognates in the* Satyricon

1. TO POUR OUT, IN OR OVER, TO EMPTY (*FUNDERE, EFFUNDERE*)

plus vini sub mensa effundebatur (38.15)
coeperunt effundere crocum (60.6)
etiam si coacti sumus dimidias potiones supra ossucula eius effundere (65.11)
et nummos in publico de sacculo effundentem (71.9)
vinum sub mensa iussit effundi (74.1)
nam spiritus, extra / qui furit effusus (*BC vv.* 69–70)
crines ingenio suo flexi per totos se umeros effuderant (126.15)
nullis precibus effusis (132.4)
florida tellus... fundit opes (134.12)
partem leguminis super mensam effudit (135.5)
passimque per totum effusam pavimentum collegerant fabam (136.7)
amplexuque effusissimo me invasit (139.4)

2. TO POUR OUT WORDS/POETRY/EMOTIONS (*EFFUNDERE, DEFUNDERE*)

defundes pectore verba (5 v. 22)
haec aliaque cum effusissimis prosequeremur laudationibus (48.7)
haec ut turbato clamore mulier effudit (109.1)
tunc Fortuna levi defudit pectore voces (*BC* v. 102)
cum haec Eumolpus ingenti volubilitate verborum effudisset (124.2)
haec ut iratus effudi (132.11)

3. TO EMIT FROM THE BODY: BLOOD, TEARS, SWEAT, LAUGHTER, LIFE (*FUNDERE, EFFUNDERE*)

risum effusa est (18.7)
Giton... risum iam diu compressum etiam indecenter effudit (58.1)
effundunt viros (*TH* v. 57)

haec cum inter gemitus lacrimasque fudissem (91.8)
funde sanguinem (97.9)
deinde ut effusus sudor utriusque spiritum revocavit (101.2)
Tryphaena lacrimas effudit (105.11)
si antequam fata poscant, indemnatum spiritum effuderis? (111.11)

4. TO DRENCH OR COVER, TO ANOINT (*PERFUNDERE*)

et nos legitimo perfusus oleo refecerunt (21.4)
unguento perfusus (28.2)
rati ergo sacrum esse fer[i]culum tam religioso apparatu perfusum (60.7)
'si quis' inquit 'noluerit accipere, caput illi perfunde' (64.13)
perfusum os lacrimis (91.4)
illos proxima nocte extraxi mero unguentisque perfusos (105.3)
Iulius ingratam perfudit sanguine Romam (*BC* v. 64)
Cocyti perfusus aqua (*BC* v. 69)
iam pridem nullo perfundimus ora cruore (*BC* v. 96)
totasque per Alpes / fervere Germano perfusas sanguine turmas (*BC* vv. 213–14)
perfusus pulvere mulio (126.6)
perfusus ego rubore (128.2)
coepi secretoque rubore perfundi (132.12)
non sanguine tristi / perfusus venio (133.3 vv. 6–7)
faciemque totam excitato cinere perfundit (136.2)
perfusisque inguinibus meis (138.2)

5. TO POUR ON OR IN (*INFUNDERE*)

lucernis occidentibus oleum infuderat (22.6)
scr[i]bl[i]ta frigida et supra mel caldum infusum excellente Hispanum (66.3)
vinum quidem in vinarium iussit infundi (78.4)

6. TO MINGLE, JUMBLE, CONFUSE, UPSET (*CONFUNDERE*)

qua voce confusus Trimalchio (74.1)
video Gitona... parieti applicitum tristem confusumque (91.1)
confusus hac denuntiatione (94.7)
confusus ille (101.7)
poteris hanc simulationem et vultus confusione et lacrimis obumbrare (101.8)
cum homo prudentissimus confusis omnibus corporis indiciorumque lineamentis (105.10)

Lichas et 'noli' inquit 'causam confundere' (107.7)
atramentum omnia scilicet lineamenta fulginea nube confudit (108.2)
totaque familia . . . quaeritque quis dominae hilaritatem confuderit (132.5)
nec minus illa fletu confusa (134.6)
confusaque regia caeli (136.6 v. 5)
confusus itaque (136.14)

7. TO POUR FROM ONE VESSEL INTO ANOTHER, TO EXCHANGE (*TRANSFUNDERE*)

haesimus calentes / et transfudimus hinc et hinc labellis / errantes animas (79.8 vv. 2–4)

8. TO POUR OVER, TO STAIN (*SUFFUNDERE*)

sono mutet suffusa saporem (5 v. 16)

9. TO POUR IN DIFFERENT DIRECTIONS, TO SPREAD OR DIFFUSE (*DIFFUNDERE*)

nobilis aestivas platanus diffuderat umbras (131.8 v. 1)

APPENDIX II

The occurrence of fortuna *or Fortuna in the* Satyricon

et fortuna sonet celeri distincta meatu (5 v. 18)
o lusum fortunae mirabilem (13.1)
sed etiam quod fortuna me a turpissima suspicione dimiserat (13.4)
praesto erat Fortuna <cum> cornu abundanti [copiosa] (29.6)
plane fortunae filius (43.7)
et supra nos Fortuna negotia curat (55.3)
et paulo ante carissimum sibi commilitonem fortunaeque etiam similitudine parem in loco peregrino destituit abiectum (80.8)
cum fortuna manet (80.9)
suam habet fortuna rationem (82.6)
nos casus in eandem fortunam rettulisset (87.1)
sed non crudelis fortuna concedit (114.8)
tres tulerat Fortuna duces (*BC* v. 61)
ac tali volucrem Fortunam voce lacessit (*BC* v. 78)
tunc Fortuna levi defudit pectore voces (*BC* v. 102)
iudice Fortuna cadat alea (*BC* v. 174)
ut Fortuna levis Magni quoque terga videret (*BC* v. 244)
amplioris fortunae domum quaerentes (124.2)
et Eumolpus felicitate plenus prioris fortunae esset oblitus (125.1)
putabamque a custodia mei removisse vultum Fortunam (125.2)
quisquis habet nummos, secura navigat aura / fortunam suo temperat arbitrio (137.9)
Chrysis, quae priorem fortunam tuam oderat (138.5)

FORTUNATA

'uxor' inquit 'Trimalchionis, Fortunata appellatur' (37.2)
rides, Fortunata, quae soles me nocte desomnem facere? (47.5)
'nemo' inquit 'vestrum rogat Fortunatam meam ut saltet?' (52.8)
et inter primos Fortunata crinibus passis cum scypho (54.2)

nisi signo dato Fortunata quater amplius a tota familia esset vocata (67.3)
iam coeperat Fortunata velle saltare (70.10)
ad dexteram meam ponas statuam Fortunatae meae columbam tenentem (71.11)
in aliud triclinium deducti sumus, ubi Fortunata disposuerat lautitias (73.5)
itaque Fortunata, ut ex aequo ius firmum approbaret, male dicere Trimalchioni coepit (74.9)
sed Fortunata vetat (75.6)
hoc loco Fortunata rem piam fecit (76.7)

APPENDIX III

Aen. 4.39 *at Sat.* 112: *nec venit in mentem, quorum consederis arvis?*

I would argue that this line cannot, as Rose suggests,[1] be used in a simple erotic sense. Rose's argument relies on understanding *arva* as a very general, non gender-specific term for genitalia (with the implication that here it is being used of a man, presumably the soldier), yet there is no evidence of *arvum* being used in any erotic context other than female: the fertility of field/furrow/land/earth is conventionally associated with women, just as ploughing or digging up land is often used metaphorically to refer to penetration by a male.[2] The example Rose gives of a similar use of garden/field to mean male pudenda is Priapea 5.3–4:

> Quod meus hortus habet, sumas impune licebit
> si dederis nobis quod tuus hortus habet
>
> (Bücheler)

However, this poem, set in Priapus' domain, clearly puns on *hortus* to express Priapus' sexual proposition: 'I'll show you my garden, if you promise to let me have yours.' *hortus* here therefore refers not to his penis, but to the victim's rear end, about to be penetrated by the mischievous ithyphallic god. As Adams notes in his discussion of fields, etc. referring metaphorically to female genitalia, 'Nominal metaphors of the type in question were readily transferable to the male anus'.[3] Admittedly, it *is* tempting to see *arva* refer to men in the context of the *Satyricon*, given the use of *sedere* at 126.10 and 140.7: if this were the case, Pecere's note on the possible discrepancy in the line's reference to past happenings (*consederis*) rather than the future erotic opportunities we are dealing with here, might be redundant if we were to view the line as referring to the widow's past sexual experiences which, the maid now argues, are of a very low rank compared to this 'pleasing love'.[4] For this is the joke of the

[1] Rose (1968). [2] See Adams (1982) 24, 82–4.
[3] Adams (1982) 83. [4] Pecere (1975) 117.

tale, that no woman, even (or especially) a chaste one, is what she seems, that given a lithe young soldier and a little abstinence, even a paradigm of virtue can become a hungry Tryphaena.

Yet this cannot be what the line means here, as we have no evidence of *arvum* being used of male genitalia. Nevertheless, this does not necessarily rule out all erotic connotations, not does it offer up a watertight argument for deleting the line. The argument which suggests that the *ancilla* here is convincing the widow of the dangers posed by the *arva* she finds herself in is very persuasive, especially if we approach this on a metaphorical as well as a literal level. By reference to real environments, this line reminds Eumolpus' and Petronius' audiences of the *literary* space in which the tale of the widow of Ephesus and the widow herself are situated. It recalls not only the 'menacing fields' of *Aeneid* IV, and their inevitable tragic forewarning of the dangers that await Dido *if* she falls for Aeneas, not if she rejects him; it also reaffirms the notion that, as I have argued, the fictional environment of the cave parallels other sexually threatening spaces throughout the *Satyricon*. It is possible, I would suggest, that the strong erotic connotations of *arva* reinforce this sexual threat, the idea that the cave-tomb is a sexualised literary location, a dark enclosure invisible to outsiders which nevertheless contains uncontrolled desires, just like the hungry belly/womb of the widow herself. We have seen that throughout the *Satyricon*, sites of entrapment are overtly female arenas (the uterus of the Trojan horse in the *Troiae Halosis*, Quartilla's brothel, Trimalchio's dining room, ruled by Fortunata's capricious wiles, the chthonic female monsters who wage civil war in the *Bellum Civile*, and the grotto-like hell of Croton, inhabited by Circean witches). It should come as no surprise that, at a crucial point in a narrative fundamentally concerned with what is or gets inside Ephesus' most famous widow, in both sexual and moral terms, the maid should be advising her mistress to contemplate the highly sexual literary environment in which she finds herself, an enclosed dark space invisible to the audience outside it which is a metaphorical dramatisation of her own mysterious insides, about to be revealed not only to the lucky soldier but also to Eumolpus' seduced audience.

Bibliography

Abbot, F. F. (1907) 'The theatre as a factor in Roman politics under the Republic', *TAPhA* 38: 49–56.

Adamietz, J. (1987) 'Zum literarischen Charakter von Petronius *Satyrica*', *RhM* 130: 329–46.

(1995) 'Circe in den Satyrica Petrons und des Wesen dieses Werken', *Hermes* 123: 320–34.

Adams, J. N. (1982) *The Latin Sexual Vocabulary*. London.

Adler, T. P. (1974) 'Pinter's night. A stroll down memory lane', *Modern Drama* 17: 461–5.

Ahl, F. (1976) *Lucan: An Introduction*. Ithaca, N.Y., and London.

(1984a) 'The art of safe criticism in Greece and Rome', *AJP* 105: 174–208.

(1984b) 'The rider and the horse: politics and power in Roman poetry from Horace to Statius', *ANRW* 2.32.1: 40–110.

(1985) *Metaformations: Soundplay and Wordplay in Ovid and other Classical Poets*, Ithaca, N.Y., and London.

Anderson, G. (1982) *Eros Sophistes: Ancient Novelists at Play*, Chicago.

(1984) *The Novel in the Ancient World*, Sydney.

Armstrong, N. and Tennenhouse, L. (eds.) (1989) *The Violence of Representation: Literature and the History of Violence*, London and New York.

Arrowsmith, W. (1959) *Petronius Arbiter: The Satyricon*, Ann Arbor, Mich.

(1966) 'Luxury and death in the *Satyricon*', *Arion* 5: 304–31.

Auerbach, E. (1953) *Mimesis: The Representation of Reality in Western Literature*, trans. W. R. Trask, Princeton, N.J.

Bacon, H. H. (1958) 'The sibyl in the bottle', *Virginia Quarterly Review* 34: 262–76.

Bakhtin, M. (1968) *Rabelais and his World*, trans. H. Iswolsky, Cambridge, Mass.

(1981) *The Dialogic Imagination: Four Essays*, ed. M. Holquist, trans. M. Holquist and C. Emerson, Austin, Tex.

(1986) *Speech Genres and Other Late Essays*, ed. M. Holquist and C. Emerson, trans. V. McGee, Austin, Tex.

Baldwin, B. (1971) 'Trimalchio's poetry', *CJ* 66: 254–5.

(1973a) 'Trimalchio's Corinthian plate', *CP* 68: 46–7.

(1973b) 'Ira Priapi', *CP* 68: 294–6.

(1976) 'Petronius' Tryphaena', *Eranos* 74: 53–7.

(1979) 'Petronius 34.10', *Maia* 31: 145.
(1984) 'Trimalchio and Maecenas', *Latomus* 43: 402–3.
Baldwin, F. T. (1911) *The Bellum Civile of Petronius*, New York.
Barasch, F. K. (1971) *The Grotesque. A Study in Meanings*, The Hague.
Barchiesi, A. (1984) 'Il nome di Lica e la poetica dei nomi in Petronio', *MD* 12: 169–75.
(1996) '*Extra legem*: consumo di letteratura in Petronio, Arbitro', in Pecere and Stramaglia (1996), 191–208.
(1999) 'Traces of Greek narrative and the Roman novel' in Harrison (1999), 124–41.
Barchiesi, M. (1981) 'L'Orologio di Trimalchione (Struttura e Tempo Narrativo in Petronio)', in Della Corte (1981), 109–46.
Bardon, H. and Verdière, R. (1971) *Vergiliana: Recherches sur Virgile*, Leiden.
Barkan, L. (1975) *Nature's Work of Art: The Human Body as an Image of the World*, New Haven, Conn., and London.
(1986) *The Gods Made Flesh: Metamorphosis and the Pursuit of Paganism*. New Haven, Conn., and London.
Barker, F. (1984) *The Tremulous Private Body: Essays in Subjection*, London and New York.
Barnes, E. J. (1972) 'The poems of Petronius', dissertation, University of Toronto.
(1987) 'Hannibal at Troy: some sources of Trimalchio's confusion', *PSN* 17: 6.
Barthes, R. (1990) *Pleasure of the Text*, trans. R. Miller, Oxford.
Bartoňková, D. (1976) 'Prosimetrum, the mixed style in ancient literature', *Eirene* 14: 65–92.
Bartsch, S. (1994) *Actors in the Audience: Theatricality and Double Speak from Nero to Hadrian*, Cambridge, Mass.
(1998) *Ideology in Cold Blood. A Reading of Lucan's Civil War*, Cambridge, Mass.
Baxandall, M. (1985) *Patterns of Intention: On the Historical Explanation of Pictures*, New Haven, Conn.
Beard, M. (1987) 'A complex of times: no more sheep on Romulus' birthday', *PCPhS* 33: 1–15.
Beck, R. (1973) 'Some observations on the narrative technique of Petronius', *Phoenix* 27: 42–61.
(1975) 'Encolpius at the *Cena*', *Phoenix* 29: 271–83.
(1979) 'Eumolpus *poeta*, Eumolpus *fabulator*: A study in characterisation in the *Satyricon*', *Phoenix* 33: 239–53.
(1982) 'The *Satyricon*: satire, narrator and antecedents', *MH* 39: 206–14.
Bérard, C. (1984) *La Cité des images: religion et société en Grèce antique*, Paris.
Bevan, D. (ed.) (1988) *Literary Gastronomy*, Amsterdam.
(1993) *Literature and Sickness*, Amsterdam.
Blanchot, M. (1982) *The Sirens' Song. Selected Essays*, ed. G. Josipovici, trans. S. Rabinowitz, Brighton.

Bloom, H. (1973) *The Anxiety of Influence: A Theory of Poetry*, Oxford.
Boa, E. (1996) *Kafka: Gender, Class and Race in the Letters and Fictions*, Oxford.
Bodel, J. (1994) 'Trimalchio's underworld', in Tatum (1994), 237–59.
Bourdieu, P. (1984) *Distinction: A Social Critique of the Judgement of Taste*, trans. R. Nice, Cambridge, Mass.
Bowersock, G. W. (1994) *Fiction as History: Nero to Julian*, Berkeley, Calif.
Boyle, A. J. (ed.) (1983) *Seneca Tragicus. Ramus Essays on Senecan Drama*, Victoria, Australia.
(1988) *The Imperial Muse. Ramus Essays on Roman Literature of the Empire*, vol. I, *To Juvenal through Ovid*, Victoria, Australia.
(1990) *The Imperial Muse. Ramus Essays on Roman Literature of the Empire*, vol. II, *Flavian Epicist to Claudian*, Victoria, Australia.
(1993) *Roman Epic*, London and New York.
Bradbury, M. (1978) *Eating People is Wrong*, London.
Bramble, J. (1974) *Persius and the Programmatic Satire: A Study in Form and Imagery*, Cambridge.
Braund, S. (1986) 'Juvenal on how to (tr)eat people', *Omnibus* 11: 15–17.
(1996) *Juvenal. Satires Book 1*, Cambridge.
Braund, S. M. and Gill, C. (eds.) (1997) *The Passions in Roman Thought and Literature*, Cambridge.
Braund, S. M. and Gold, B. K. (eds.) (1998) *Vile Bodies: Roman Satire and Corporeal Discourse. Arethusa* 31.
Brillat-Savarin, J. A. (1975) *Physiologie du goût*, Paris.
Brilliant, R. (1974) *Visual Narratives: Storytelling in Roman and Etruscan Art*, Ithaca, N.Y.
Brink, C. O. (1971) *Horace on Poetry: The Ars Poetica*, Cambridge.
Brooks, P. (1984) *Reading for the Plot: Design and Intention in Narrative*, New York.
(1993) *Body Work: Objects of Desire in Modern Narrative*, Cambridge, Mass.
Brown, P. (1989) *The Body and Society: Explorations in Social Theory*, London.
Browning, R. (1962) Review of K. Müller, *Petronii Arbitri Satyricon* (Munich 1961), *CR* 12: 218–21.
Brunette, P. and Wills, D. (1994) *Deconstruction and the Visual Arts: Art, Media, Architecture*, Cambridge.
Bryson, N. (1981) *Word and Image: French Painting of the Ancien Régime*, Cambridge.
(1983) *Vision and Painting: The Logic of the Gaze*, London.
(1990) *Looking at the Overlooked: Four Essays on Still-Life Painting*, Cambridge, Mass.
Bücheler, F. (ed.) (1862) *Petronii Arbitri Satirarum Reliquae adiectus est Liber Priapeorum*, Berlin.
Butler, J. (1993) *Bodies that Matter: On the Discursive Limits of 'Sex'*, New York and London.
Cameron, A. M. (1969) 'Petronius and Plato', *CQ* 19: 367–70.
(1970) 'Myth and meaning in Petronius: some modern comparisons', *Latomus* 29: 397–425.
(1995) *Callimachus and his Critics*, Princeton, N.J.

Campanile, E. (1957) 'Osservazioni sulla lingua di Petronio', *ASNP* 26: 54–69.
Canali, L. (1986) *L'Erotico e il Grottesco nel Satyricon*. Rome and Bari.
Casali, S. (2000) 'The Making of the Shield: Inspiration and Repression in the *Aeneid*', unpublished paper presented at the Classical Association conference, 2000.
Cave, T. (1988) *Recognitions: A Study in Poetics*, Oxford.
Caws, M. (1985) *Reading Frames in Modern Fiction*, Princeton, N.J.
Cèbe, J. P. (ed.) (1974) *Varron: Satires Ménippées II*, Collection Ecole française de Rome IX.
Cesareo, G. A. and Terzaghi, N. (1950) *Petronio Arbitro: Il Romanzo Satirico*, Florence.
Chambers, R. (1984) *Story and Situation: Narrative Seduction and the Power of Fiction*, Manchester.
Ciaffi, V. (1967) *Petronio: Il Satyricon* (second edition), Turin.
Cichorius, C. (1922) 'Petronius and Massilia', *Römische Studien*, 438–42, Leipzig.
Coccia, M. (1973) *Le Interpolazioni in Petronio*, Rome.
Coleman, K. M. (1990) 'Fatal charades: Roman executions staged as mythological enactments', *JRS* 80: 44–73.
(1993) 'Launching into history: aquatic displays in the early empire', *JRS* 83: 48–74.
Collignon, A. (1892) *Etude sur Pétrone*, Paris.
Connors, C. (1994) 'Famous Last Words: authorship and death in the *Satyricon* and Neronian Rome' in Elsner and Masters (1994), 225–36.
(1995) 'Beholding Troy in Petronius' *Satyricon* and John Barclay's *Euphormionis' Lusinini Satyricon*' in *Groningen Colloquia on the Novel*, vol. VI, 51–74.
(1998) *Petronius the Poet: Verse and Literary Tradition in the Satyricon*, Cambridge.
Conte, G. B. (1987) 'Petronius, *Satyricon* 141.4', *CQ* 37: 529–32.
(1996) *The Hidden Author: An Interpretation of Petronius' Satyricon*. Berkeley, Calif.
Corbeill, A. (1996) *Controlling Laughter. Political Humor in the Late Roman Republic*, Princeton, N.J.
Corbett, P. B. (1967) 'Petroniana', *CP* 62: 260–1.
(1970) *Petronius*, New York.
Courtney, E. (1970) 'Some passages of Petronius', *BICS* 17: 65–9.
(1980) *A Commentary on the Satires of Juvenal*, London.
(1987) 'Petronius and the underworld', *AJP* 108: 408–10.
(1991) *The Poems of Petronius*, Atlanta, Ga.
Crowther, N. B. (1979) 'Water and wine as symbols of inspiration', *Mnemosyne* 32: 1–11.
Crum, R. H. (1952) 'Petronius and the Emperors', *CW* 45: 161–7, 197–201.
Culler, J. (ed.) (1988) *On Puns: The Foundation of Letters*, Oxford.
Dalby, A. (1996) *Siren Feasts. A History of Food and Gastronomy in Greece*, London.
Davidson, J. (1997) *Courtesans and Fishcakes*, London.
Della Corte, F. (1981) *I Moderni alla Ricerca di Enea*, Rome.
Derrida, J. (1974) *Of Grammatology*, trans. G. Spivak, Baltimore, Md.
(1982) *Margins of Philosophy*, trans. A. Bass, Chicago.

(1987) *The Truth in Painting*, trans. G. Bennington and I. McLeod, Chicago.
(1998) 'The retrait of metaphor', in Wolfreys (1998), 102–29.
Dewar, M. (1994) 'Laying it on with a trowel: the proem to Lucan and related texts', *CQ* 44: 199–211.
DeWitt, N. J. (1941) 'Rome and the "road of Hercules" ', *TAPhA* 72: 59–69.
De Yong, I. J. F. (1985) 'Eurykleia and Odysseus' scar: Odyssey XIX 393–466', *CQ* 35: 517.
Díaz y Díaz, M. C. (1968–9) *Petronio Árbitro: Satiricón*, Barcelona.
Dominik, W. J. (ed.) (1997) *Roman Eloquence: Rhetoric in Society and Literature*, London.
Dronke, P. (1994) *Verse with Prose from Petronius to Dante: The Art and Scope of the Mixed Form*, Cambridge, Mass.
Dubin, S. C. (1992) *Arresting Images: Impolitic Art and Uncivil Action*, New York and London.
Dunbabin, K. (1986) '*sic erimus cuncti*: The skeleton in Greco-Roman art', *JDAI* 101: 185–255.
Dupont, F. (1997) 'Recitatio and the reorganisation of public discourse', in Habinek and Schiesaro (1997), 44–60.
Edwards, C. (1993) *The Politics of Immorality in Ancient Rome*, Cambridge.
Elsner, J. (1993) 'Seductions of art: Encolpius and Eumolpus in a Neronian picture gallery', *PCPhS* 39: 30–47.
Elsner, J. and Masters, J. (eds.) (1994) *Reflections of Nero: Culture, History and Representation*, London.
Emanuele, D. (1989) '*Aes Corinthium*: fact, fiction and fake', *Phoenix* 43: 347–58.
Erskine, A. (1998) 'Trojan horse-play in Rome', *Dialogos* 5: 131–8.
Farrell, J. (1999) 'The Ovidian corpus: poetic body and poetic text', in Hardie, Barchiesi and Hinds (1999), 127–41.
Favazza, A. R. (1987) *Bodies under Siege: Self-Mutilation in Culture and Psychiatry*, Baltimore, Md.
Fedeli, P. (1981) 'Petronio: il viaggio, il labirinto', *MD* 6: 91–117.
Feder Kittay, E. (1987) *Metaphor: Its Cognitive Force and Linguistic Structure*, Oxford.
Feeney, D. (1998) *Literature and Religion at Rome: Cultures, Contexts, Beliefs*, Cambridge.
Feher, M., Naddaff, R. and Tazi, N. (eds.) (1989) *Fragments for a History of the Human Body*, New York.
Ferber, M. (1999) *A Dictionary of Literary Symbols*, Cambridge.
Ferguson, M. W., Quilligan, M. and Vickers, N. J. (eds.) (1986) *Rewriting the Renaissance: The Discourses of Sexual Difference in Early Modern Europe*, Chicago.
Ferri, R. (1988) 'Il ciclope di Eumolpus e il ciclope di Petronio. *Sat*.100ss', *MD* 21: 311–15.
Fitzgerald, W. (1988) 'Power and impotence in Horace's *Epodes*', *Ramus* 17.2: 176–91.
(2000) *Slavery and the Roman Literary Imagination*, Cambridge.

Flower, B. and Rosenbaum, E. (1958) *Apicius: The Roman Cookery Book*, London.

Foucault, M. (1978) *The History of Sexuality: An Introduction*, trans. R. Hurley, London.

(1985) *The History of Sexuality: The Use of Pleasure*, trans. R. Hurley, London.

(1986) *The History of Sexuality: Care of the Self*, trans. R. Hurley, London.

Fowler, D. (1991) 'Narrate and describe: the problem of ekphrasis', *JRS* 81: 25–35.

(2000) *Roman Constructions: Readings in Postmodern Latin*, Oxford.

(forthcoming) *Unrolling the Text: Books and Readers in Latin Poetry.*

Fowler, R. (ed.) (1975) *Style and Structure in Literature*, Oxford.

Freud, S. (1939) *Moses and Monotheism*, London.

(1966) *Jokes and their Relation to the Unconscious*, trans. J. Strachey, London.

(1983) *Totem and Taboo*, London.

Freudenburg, K. (2001) *Satires of Rome: Threatening Poses from Lucilius to Juvenal*, Cambridge.

Freudenburg, K. (ed.) (forthcoming) *The Cambridge Companion to Roman Satire*, Cambridge.

Frow, J. (1986) *Marxism and Literary History*, London.

Frye, N. (1957) *Anatomy of Criticism: Four Essays*, Princeton, N.J.

(1976) *Spiritus Mundi: Essays on Literature, Myth and Society*, Bloomington, Ind., and London.

Furbank, P. N. (1970) *Reflections on the Word 'Image'*, London.

Fyfe, G. and Law, J. (eds.) (1988) *Picturing Power: Visual Depiction and Social Relations*, London.

Gagliardi, D. (1981) 'Eumolpo o dell'ambiguità', *Orpheus* 2: 360–5.

(1993) *Petronio e il Romanzo Moderno*, Florence.

Galinsky, K. (1972) *The Herakles Theme: Adaptations of the Hero in Literature*, Oxford.

(1989) 'Was Ovid a silver Latin poet?', *ICS* 14: 69–88.

Gallop, J. (1988) *Thinking Through the Body*, New York.

Garrido, I. M. (1930) 'Note on Petronius' *Satyricon* 135', *CR* 44: 10–11.

George, P. A. (1966) 'Style and character in the *Satyricon*', *Arion* 5: 336–58.

(1974) 'Petronius and Lucan *de belli Civili*', *CQ* 24: 119–33.

Giardina, I. C. and Melloni, R. C. (1995) *Petronii Arbitri Satyricon*, Turin.

Giddens, A. (1991) *Modernity and Self-identity: Self and Society in the Late Modern Age*, Cambridge.

Gill, C. (1973) 'Sexual episodes in the *Satyricon*', *CP* 68: 172–85.

Gill, C. and Wiseman J. P. (eds.) (1993) *Lies and Fiction in the Ancient World*, Exeter.

Gleason, M. W. (1995) *Making Men: Sophists and Self-Representation in Ancient Rome*, Princeton, N.J.

Glenn, J. (1971) 'The Polyphemus folktale and Homer's kyklôpeia', *TAPhA* 102: 133–81.

Goff, B. (1991) 'The sign of the fall: the scars of Orestes and Odysseus', *CA* 10: 259–67.

Goffman, E. (1974) *Frame Analysis: An Essay on the Organisation of Experience*, New York.
Goldhill, S. D. (1988) 'Reading differences. *The Odyssey* and recognition', *Ramus* 17: 1–31.
(1991) *The Poet's Voice*, Cambridge.
(1995) *Foucault's Virginity: Ancient Erotic Fiction and the History of Sexuality*, Cambridge.
Goldhill, S. D. and Osborne, R. (eds.) (1994) *Art and Text in Ancient Greek Culture*, Cambridge.
Gordon, R. (ed.) (1981) *Myth, Religion and Society: Structuralist Essays*, Cambridge.
Gowers, E. (1993) *The Loaded Table. Representations of Food in Roman Literature*, Oxford.
(1994) 'Persius and the decoction of Nero', in Elsner and Masters (1994), 131–50.
(2001) 'Apuleius and Persius', in Kahane and Laird (2001), 77–87.
Greenblatt, S. (1980) *Renaissance Self-Fashioning: From More to Shakespeare*, Chicago.
Greimas, A. J. (ed.) (1970) *Sign–Language–Culture*, The Hague.
Grimal, P. (1977) *La Guerre civile de Pétrone dans ses rapports avec la Pharsale*, Paris.
Guido, G. (1976) *Dal 'Satyricon' il 'Bellum Civile'*, Bologna.
Gunderson, E. (1998) 'Discovering the body in Roman oratory', in Wyke (1998), 169–89.
Habinek, T. and Schiesaro, A. (eds.) (1997) *The Roman Cultural Revolution*, Cambridge.
Hägg, T. (1983) *The Novel in Antiquity*, Berkeley.
Hall, D. (1990) 'The way to say pleasure', in Halpern (1990), 101–9.
Hall, D., Laqueur, T. and Posner, H. (eds.) (1992) *Corporal Politics: Essays*, Boston.
Hall, E. (1989) *Inventing the Barbarian: Greek Self-Definition through Tragedy*, Oxford.
Hallett, J. and Skinner, M. B. (eds.) (1997) *Roman Sexualities*, Princeton, N.J.
Halperin, D., Winkler, J. and Zeitlin, F. (eds.) (1990) *Before Sexuality: The Construction of Erotic Experience in the Ancient Greek World*, Princeton, N.J.
Halpern, D. (ed.) (1990) *Antaeus: Literature as Pleasure*, London.
Hardie, P. R. (1986) *Virgil's* Aeneid. *Cosmos and Imperium*, Oxford.
(1992) 'Augustan poets and the mutability of Rome', in Powell (1992), 59–82.
(1993) *The Epic Successors of Virgil: A Study in the Dynamics of a Tradition*, Cambridge.
(1995) 'The speech of Pythagoras in Ovid, *Met.* 15: Empedoclean epos', *CQ* 45: 204–14.
Hardie, P., Barchiesi, A., and Hinds, S. (eds.) (1999) *Ovidian Transformations: Essays on Ovid's* Metamorphoses *and its Reception*, *PCPhS* suppl. 23.
Harpham, G. G. (1982) *On the Grotesque: Strategies of Contradiction in Art and Literature*, Princeton, N.J.
Harrison, S. J. (ed.) (1999) *Oxford Readings in the Roman Novel*, Oxford.
Haskell, F. (1993) *History and its Images: Art and the Interpretation of the Past*, New Haven, Conn., and London.

Hassan, I. (1982) *The Dismemberment of Orpheus. Towards a Postmodern Literature* (second edition), Madison, Wis., and London.
Hawthorn, J. (1983) *Multiple Personality and the Disintegration of Literary Character from Oliver Goldsmith to Sylvia Plath*, London.
Heffernan, J. A. W. (1993) *Museum of Words: The Poetics of Ekphrasis from Homer to Ashbery*, Chicago.
Henderson, J. G. W. (1983) 'Poetic technique and amplification; Seneca *Medea* 579–669' in Boyle (1983), 94–113.
(1988) 'Lucan: the word at war', in Boyle (1988), 122–64.
(1993) 'The pupil as teacher: Persius' didactic satire', *Ramus* 20: 123–48.
(1997a) *Figuring out Roman Nobility: Juvenal's Eighth Satire*, Exeter.
(1997b) 'The name of the tree: recounting Odyssey XXIV 340–2', *JHS* 112: 87–116.
(1998a) *Fighting for Rome: Poets and Caesars, History and Civil War*, Cambridge.
(1998b) 'Dead eyes and blank faces': review of Vasily Rudich's *Political Dissidence under Nero: The Price of Rhetoricisation, London Review of Books*, 2 April.
(1999) *Writing Down Rome: Satire, Comedy and other Offences in Latin Poetry*, Oxford.
Henisch, B. A. (1976) *Fast and Feast*, University Park, Penn.
(1984) *Cakes and Characters*, London.
Hepworth, P. and Turner, B. S. (eds.) (1991) *The Body: Social Process and Cultural Theory*, London.
Herescu, N. J. (1959) 'Sur le sens "érotique" de *sedere*', *Glotta* 38: 125–34.
Hershkowitz, D. (1998) *The Madness of Epic. Reading Insanity from Homer to Statius*, Oxford.
Herzog, R. (1989) 'Fest, Terror und Tod in Petrons *Satyrica*', in Warning (1989), 120–50.
Heseltine, M. and Rouse, W. H. D. (1987) *Petronius Satyricon and Seneca Apocolocyntosis*, rev. E. H. Warmington, Loeb edition, Cambridge, Mass., and London.
Hexter, R. and Selden, D. (eds.) (1992) *Innovations of Antiquity*, London.
Highet, G. (1941) 'Petronius the moralist', *TAPhA* 72: 176–94.
Hillis Miller, J. (1982) *Fiction and Repetition: Seven English Novels*, Oxford.
Hinds, S. (1998) *Allusion and Intertext: Dynamics of Appropriation in Roman Poetry*, Cambridge.
Hofman, J. B. and Szantyr, A. (1965) *Lateinische Syntax und Stilistik*, Munich.
Hofmann, H. (ed.) (1998) *Latin Fiction: The Latin Novel in Context*, London and New York.
Holzberg, N. (1995) *The Ancient Novel: An Introduction*, trans. C. Jackson-Holzberg, London and New York.
Hopkinson, N. (2000) *Ovid Metamorphoses* Book XIII, Cambridge.
Horkheimer, M. and Adorno, T. W. (1982) *Dialectic of Enlightenment*, trans. J. Cumming, New York.
Horsfall, N. (1989) ' "The uses of literacy" and the *Cena Trimalchionis*', *G&R* 36: 74–89, 194–209.

Hubbard, T. K. (1986) 'The narrative architecture of Petronius' *Satyricon*', *A Class* 55: 190–212.
Huet, M. H. (1997) *Monstrous Imagination*, Cambridge Mass., and London.
Hutcheon, L. (1985) *A Theory of Parody: The Teachings of Twentieth-Century Art Forms*, New York and London.
Hutchinson, A. C. (1982) 'Petronius and Lucan', *LCM* 7: 46–7.
Huxley, H. H. (1970) ' "Marked literary inferiority" in the poems of the *Satyricon*', *CJ* 66: 69–70.
Imbert, C. (1980) 'Stoic logic and Alexandrine poetics', in Schofield, Burnyeat and Barnes (1980), 182–216.
Ingvarsson, K. (1950) 'Ingens dans la poésie et chez Tacite', *Eranos* 48: 66–70.
Johnson, W. R. (1987) *Momentary Monsters: Lucan and his Heroes*, Ithaca, N.Y., and London.
Jones, C. P. (1987) 'Stigma: tattooing and branding in Graeco-Roman antiquity', *JRS* 77: 139–55.
(1991) 'Dinner theatre', in Slater (1991), 185–98.
Jones, F. (1987) 'The narrator and narrative in the *Satyricon*', *Latomus* 46: 810–19.
Josipovici, G. (1982) *Writing and the Body*, Brighton.
Kahane, A. and Laird, A. (eds.) (2001), *A Companion to the Prologue to Apuleius'* Metamorphoses, Oxford.
Kayser, C. L. (1870–1) *Flavii Philostratus Opera*, Leipzig.
Keller, C. (1986) *From a Broken Web: Separation, Sexism and Self*, Boston, Mass.
Kennedy, D. F. (1993) *The Arts of Love: Five Studies in the Discourse of Roman Elegy*, Cambridge.
Kennedy, G. A. (1978) 'Encolpius and Agamemnon in Petronius', *AJP* 99: 171–8.
(1994) *A New History of Classical Rhetoric*, Princeton, N.J.
Kilgour, M. (1990) *From Communion to Cannibalism: An Anatomy of Metaphors of Incorporation*, Princeton, N.J.
Klebs, E. (1889) 'Zur Composition von Petronius *Satirae*', *Philologus* 47: 623–35.
Knight, C. (1989) 'Listening to Encolpius: modes of confusion in the *Satyricon*', *University of Toronto Quarterly* 58: 335–54.
Knox, B. (1985) 'Wine, water and Callimachean polemics', *HSCP* 89: 107–19.
Konstan, D. (1993) *Sexual Symmetry: Love in the Ancient Novel and Related Genres*, Princeton, N.J.
Kragelund, P. (1989) 'Epicurus, Priapus and dreams in the *Satyricon*', *CQ* 39: 436–50.
Kristeva, J. (1982) *Powers of Horror: an Essay in Subjection*, New York.
Kühn, C. G. (1964) *Claudii Galeni Opera Omnia*, Leipzig.
Laing, R. D. (1965) *The Divided Self: An Existential Study in Sanity and Madness*, London.
Laird, A. (1999) *Powers of Expression, Expressions of Power: Speech Presentation in Latin Literature*, Oxford.
Lakoff, G. and Johnson, M. (1980) *Metaphors We Live By*, Chicago and London.
Lapidge, M. (1979) 'Lucan's imagery of cosmic dissolution', *Hermes* 107: 344–70.

Laqueur, T. (1990) *Making Sex: The Body and Gender from the Greeks to Freud*, Cambridge, Mass. and London.
Lawall, G. (1995) *Selections from the Satyricon* (third edition), Chicago.
Lecercle, J. J. (1990) *The Violence of Language*, London.
Lee Too, Y. and Livingstone, N. (eds.) (1998) *Pedagogy and Power: Rhetorics of Classical Learning*, Cambridge.
Lefevere, A. (1992) *Translation, Rewriting and the Manipulation of Literary Fame*, London.
Leigh, M. (1995) 'Wounding and popular rhetoric at Rome', *BICS* 40: 195–212.
(1997) *Lucan: Spectacle and Engagement*, Oxford.
LeLièvre, F. J. (1954) 'The basis of ancient parody', *G&R* 1: 66–81.
Lessing, G. E. (1984) *Laocoön: An Essay on the Limits of Painting and Poetry*, trans. E. A. McCormick, Baltimore, Md.
Lévi-Strauss, C. (1970) *The Raw and the Cooked*, London.
(1972) *The Savage Mind*, Chicago.
Litvak, J. (1997) *Strange Gourmets: Sophistication, Theory and the Novel*, Durham, N.C., and London.
Long, D. (1990) 'On re-reading' in Halpern (1990), 62–8.
Lowe, J. C. B. (1985a) 'Cooks in Plautus', *CA* 4: 72–102.
(1985b) 'The cook scene of Plautus' *Pseudolus*', *CQ* 35: 411–16.
Lowenthal, D. (1985) *The Past is a Foreign Country*, Cambridge.
Lowrie, M. (1997) *Horace's Narrative Odes*, Oxford.
Luck, G. (1972) 'On Petronius' *Bellum Civile*', *AJPh* 93: 133–41.
McCulloch, G. (1989) *The Game of the Name: Introducing Logic, Language and the Mind*, Oxford.
McDermott, M. H. (1983) 'The *Satyricon* as a parody of the *Odyssey* and Greek romance', *LCM* 8: 82–5.
McGlathery, D. B. (1998) 'Petronius' tale of the woman of Ephesus and Bakhtin's material bodily lower stratum', *Arethusa* 31: 313–36.
Maclean, M. (1988) *Narrative as Performance: The Baudelairian Experiment*, London and New York.
McMahon, J. (1998) *Paralysin Cave: Impotence, Perception and Text in the Satyrica of Petronius*, Leiden.
Maltby, R. (1991) *A Lexicon of Latin Etymologies*, Leeds.
Manning, C. E. (1975) 'Acting and Nero's conception of the principate', *G&R* 22: 164–75.
Marmorale, E. V. (1950) *Naevius Poeta*, Florence.
(1961) *Petronii Arbitri Cena Trimalchionis. Testo Critico e Commento* (second edition), Florence.
Martin, L. (1989) *Food for Thought*, Baltimore, Md.
Martindale, C. (1993) *Redeeming the Text: Latin Poetry and the Hermeneutics of Reception*, Cambridge.
Masters, J. (1992) *Poetry and Civil War in Lucan's* Bellum Civile, Cambridge.
Mayer, R. (1982) 'Neronian classicism', *AJPh* 103: 305–18.

Michie, H. (1987) *The Flesh Made Word: Female Figures and Women's Bodies*, New York and Oxford.
Miller, S. (1967) *The Picaresque Novel*, Cleveland, Ohio.
Mitchell, W. J. T. (1986) *Iconology: Image, Text, Symbol*, Chicago and London.
Mitchell, W. J. T. (ed.) (1981) *On Narrative*, Chicago.
Mondi, R. (1983) 'The Homeric Cyclops: folktale, tradition and theme', *TAPhA* 113: 17–38.
Montserrat, D. (ed.) (1998) *Changing Bodies, Changing Meanings*, London.
Most, G. (1992) '*Disiecti membra poetae*: the rhetoric of dismemberment in Neronian poetry' in Hexter and Selden (1992), 391–419.
Müller, K. (1961) *Petronii Arbitri Satyricon*, Munich.
(1995) *Petronius Satyricon Reliquiae*, Teubner and Leipzig.
Müller, K. and Ehlers, W. (1965) *Petronius Satyrica. Schelmengesichten*, Munich.
Murnaghan, S. (1987) *Disguise and Recognition in the* Odyssey, Princeton, N.J.
(1988) *Porneia: On Desire and the Body in Antiquity*, Oxford.
Natanson, M. (1970) *The Journeying Self: A Study in Philosophy and Social Role*, Reading.
Nelson, H. L. W. (1971) 'Bemerkungen su einem neuem Petrontext', *Mnemosyne* 24: 60–87.
Newbold, R. F. (1979) 'Bodies and boundaries in late Antiquity', *Arethusa* 12: 93–114.
Newlands, C. (1995) *Playing with Time: Ovid and the Fasti*, New York.
Newton, R. M. (1982) 'Trimalchio's hellish bath', *CJ* 77: 315–19.
Nietzsche, F. (1990) *Beyond Good and Evil: Prelude to the Philosophy of the Future* (second edition), trans. R. J. Hollingdale, London.
Nimis, S. (1999) 'The sense of open-endedness in the ancient novel', *Arethusa* 32: 215–38.
Nisbet, R. G. M. (1962) Review of K. Müller, *Petronii Arbitri Satyricon* (Munich 1961), *JRS* 52: 227–32.
O'Hara, J. J. (1996) *True Names: Vergil and the Epistemological Tradition of Etymological Word Play*, Ann Arbor, Mich.
O'Higgins, D. (1988) 'Lucan as *vates*', *CA* 7: 208–26.
O'Toole, L. M. (1975) 'Analytic and synthetic approaches to narrative structure', in Fowler (1975), 143–76.
Otto, A. (1962) *Die Sprichwörter und Sprichwörtlichen Redensarten der Römer*, Hildesheim.
Panayotakis, C. (1994a) 'A sacred ceremony in honour of the buttocks: Petronius, *Satyrica* 140. 1–11', *CQ* 44: 458–67.
(1994b) 'Quartilla's histrionics in Petronius, *Satyrica* 16.1–26.6', *Mnemosyne* 47: 319–36.
(1995) *Theatrum Arbitri: Theatrical Elements in the Satyrica of Petronius*, *Mnemosyne* Suppl. 146, Leiden, New York, Cologne.
Pecere, O. (1975) *Petronio. La novella della matrona di Efeso*, Padua.
Pecere, O. and Stramaglia, A. (eds.) (1996) *Letteratura di Consumo nel Mondo Greco-Latino*, Cassino.

Pellegrino, C. (1975) *Petronii Arbitri Satyricon*, Rome.
Pelling, C. (1990) *Characterization and Individuality in Greek Literature*, Oxford.
Perutelli, A. (1991) 'Il narratore nel *Satyricon*', *MD* 25: 9–25.
Petersman, H. (1975) 'Textkritische Probleme bei Petron in neuer Sicht', WS 9: 118–34.
(1999) 'Environment, linguistic situation and levels of style in Petronius' *Satyricon*', in Harrison (1999), 105–23.
Petrey, S. (1990) *Speech Acts and Literary Theory*, London.
Petrone, G. (1988) 'Nomen/omen: poetica e funzione dei nomi (Plauto, Seneca, Petronio)', *MD* 20–1: 33–70.
Plass, P. (1995) *The Game of Death in Ancient Rome: Arena Sport and Political Suicide*, Madison, Wis.
Pointon, M. (1990) *Naked Authority: The Body in Western Painting, 1830–1908*, Cambridge.
Poirier, R. (1971) *The Performing Self: Composition and Decomposition in the Languages of Everyday Life*, New York and Oxford.
Pollitt, J. J. (1974) *The Ancient View of Greek Art: Criticism, Theory and Terminology*, New Haven, Conn. and London.
Pontalis, J. B. (ed.) (1972) 'Destins du cannibalisme', *Nouvelle Revue de Psychanalyse* 6.
Powell, A. (ed.) (1992) *Roman Poetry and Propaganda in the Age of Augustus*, Bristol.
Powell, J. U. (1925) *Collectanea Alexandrina: Reliquiae Minores Poetarum Graecorum Aetatis Ptolemaicae, 323–146 A.C., Epicorum, Elegiacorum, Lyricorum, Ethicorum*, Oxford.
Pucci, J. (1998) *The Full-Knowing Reader: Allusion and the Power of the Reader in the Western Literary Tradition*, New Haven, Conn.
Quinn, K. (1979) *Texts and Contexts: Roman Writers and their Audience*, London and Boston, Mass.
Quint, D. (1993) *Epic and Empire: Politics and Generic Form from Virgil to Milton*, Princeton, N.J.
Ramage, E. S., Sigsbee, D. L. and Fredericks, S. C. (1975) *Roman Satirists and their Satire: The Fine Art of Criticism in Ancient Rome*, Park Ridge, N.J.
Rankin, H. D. (1962) 'Saturnalian word play and *apophoreta* in *Satyricon* 56', *C&M* 23: 134–42.
(1966) 'Petronius, Priapus and Priapeum LXVIII', *C&M* 27: 225–42.
(1969) 'Eating people is right: Petronius 141 and a topos', *Hermes* 97: 381–4
(1971) *Petronius the Artist: Essays on the Satyricon and its Author*, The Hague.
Rawson, C. J. (1977, 1978) 'Cannibalism and fiction. Reflections on narrative form and "extreme situations" ', Parts I and II, *Genre* 10: 667–711 and *Genre* 11: 227–313.
Reed Doob, P. (1990) *The Idea of the Labyrinth, from Classical Antiquity through the Middle Ages*, Ithaca, N.Y.
Reeve, M. D. (1983) 'Petronius', in Reynolds (1983), 295–300.
Relihan, J. C. (1984) 'On the origins of Menippean satire as the name of a literary genre', *CPh* 79: 226–29.

Reynolds, L. D. (ed.) (1983) *Texts and Transmission: A Survey of the Latin Classics*, Oxford.
Richardson, N. J. (1983) 'Recognition scenes in the *Odyssey* and ancient literary criticism', *Papers of the Liverpool Latin Seminar* 4: 219–35.
Richlin, A. (1983) *The Garden of Priapus: Sexuality and Aggression in Roman Humor*, New Haven, Conn. and London.
(1997) 'Gender and rhetoric: producing manhood in the schools', in Dominik (1997), 90–110.
Richlin, A. (ed.) (1992) *Pornography and Representation in Greece and Rome*, Oxford and New York.
Ricoeur, P. (1976) *Interpretation Theory: Discourse and the Surplus of Meaning*, Fort Worth, Tex.
(1977) *The Rule of Metaphor*, trans. R. Czerny, Toronto.
(1992) *Oneself as Another*, trans. K. Blamey, Chicago and London.
Rimell, V. (1999) 'Epistolary fictions: authorial identity in Ovid, *Heroides* 15', *PCPhS* 45: 111–35.
(forthcoming) 'The poor man's feast: Juvenal' in Freudenburg (forthcoming).
Rohde, E. (1914) *Der Griechische Roman und seine Vorläufer* (third edition), Leipzig.
Rosati, G. (1983) 'Trimalchione in scena', *Maia* 35: 213–27.
(1999) 'Trimalchio on stage', in Harrison (1999), 85–104.
Rose, J. (1986) *Sexuality in the Field of Vision*, London.
Rose, K. F. C. (1966a) 'Problems of chronology in Lucan's career', *TAPhA* 97: 379–96.
(1966b) 'The Petronian inquisition: an auto-da-fé', *Arion* 5: 275–301.
(1968) 'Petroniana', *RhM* 111: 253–60.
(1971) 'The date and author of the *Satyricon*', *Mnemosyne* Suppl 16, Leiden.
Rose, K. F. C. and Sullivan, J. P. (1968) 'Trimalchio's zodiac dish (Petronius *Sat*.35.1–5)', *CQ* 18: 180–4.
Rudich, V. (1993) *Political Dissidence under Nero: The Price of Dissimulation*, London and New York.
(1997) *Dissidence and Literature under Nero: The Price of Rhetoricisation*, London and New York.
Rudofsky, B. (1972) *The Unfashionable Human Body*, London.
Sanday, P. R. (1986) *Divine Hunger: Cannibalism as a Cultural Construct*, Cambridge.
Sandy, G. N. (1970) 'Petronius and the tradition of the interpolated narrative', *TAPhA* 101: 463–76.
(1974) 'Scaenica Petroniana', *TAPhA* 104: 329–46.
Saylor, C. (1987) 'Funeral games: the significance of games in the *Cena Trimalchionis*', *Latomus* 46: 593–602.
Scarry, E. (1985) *The Body in Pain: The Making and Unmaking of the World*, Oxford.
Schiesaro, A. (1994) 'Seneca's *Thyestes* and the morality of tragic *furor*', in Elsner and Masters (1994), 196–210.
(1997a), 'Passion, reason and knowledge in Seneca's tragedies' in Braund and Gill (1997), 89–111.
(1997b) 'Intertestualità e i suoi disagi', *MD* 38: 75–109.

(forthcoming) *The Pleasure of Passions: Thyestes and the Poetics of Senecan Drama*, Cambridge.
Schlam, C. C. (1992) *The Metamorphoses of Apuleius: On Making an Ass of Oneself*, London.
Schlegor, Y. K. (1970) 'Matrona in Efeso', in Greimas (1970), 591–600.
Schlegor, Y. K. and Zholkovsky, A. (1975) 'Towards a theme – (expression devices) – text model of literary structure', trans. L. M. O'Toole, *Russian Poetics in Translation* 1 : 6–50.
Schmeling, G. (1991) 'The *Satyricon*: the sense of an ending', *RhM* 134: 352–77.
(1994a) '*Quid attinet veritatem per interpretem quaerere? Interpretes* and the *Satyricon*', *Ramus* 23: 144–68.
(1994b) '*Confessor gloriosus*: A role of Encolpius in the *Satyricon*', *WJA* 20: 207–24.
Schmeling, G. and Stuckey, J. H. (1977) *A Bibliography of Petronius*, *Mnemosyne* Suppl. 39.
Schofield, M., Burnyeat, M. and Barnes, J. (eds.) (1980) *Doubt and Dogmatism: Studies in Hellenistic Poetics*, Oxford.
Schor, N. (1987) *Reading in Detail: Aesthetics and the Feminine*, London.
Searle, J. R. (1969) *Speech Acts: An Essay in the Philosophy of Language*, Cambridge.
Sedgwick, W. B. (1925) *The Cena Trimalchionis*, Oxford.
Segal, C. (1983) 'Boundary violation and the landscape of the self in Senecan tragedy', *Antike und Abendland* 29: 172–87.
Sennett, R. (1994) *Flesh and Stone: the Body and the City in Western Civilisation*, London and Boston, Mass.
Shackleton Bailey, D. R. (1982) *Anthologia Latina*, vol. 1, Stuttgart.
(1987) 'On Petronius', *AJPh* 108: 458–64.
Sharrock, A. (1994) *Seduction and Repetition in Ovid's* Ars Amatoria II, Oxford.
(1995) 'The drooping rose: elegiac failure in *Amores* 3.7', *Ramus* 24: 152–80.
Shotter, J. and Gergen, K. J. (eds.) (1989) *Texts of Identity*, London.
Silk, M. S. (1974) *Interaction in Poetic Imagery*, Cambridge.
(1990) 'The people of Aristophanes', in Pelling (1990), 150–73.
(1993) 'Aristophanic paratragedy', in Sommerstein *et al.* (1993), 150–73.
Sinclair, P. (1995) *Tacitus the Sententious Historian: A Sociology of Rhetoric in Annales 1–6*, University Park, Penn.
Slater, N. (1988) 'Against interpretation: Petronius and art criticism', in Boyle (1988), 165–76.
(1990) *Reading Petronius*, Baltimore, Md., and London.
Slater, W. (ed.) (1991) *Dining in a Classical Context*, Ann Arbor, Mich.
Smith, M. S. (1975) *Petronii Arbitri Cena Trimalchionis*, Oxford.
Snell, B. (1953) *The Discovery of the Mind in Greek Philosophy and Literature*, trans. T. G. Rosenmeyer, New York.
Sochatoff, A. F. (1962) 'The purpose of Petronius' *Bellum Civile*: a reexamination', *TAPhA* 93: 229–58.
(1970) 'Imagery in the poems of the *Satyricon*', *CJ* 65: 340–44.

Sommerstein, A. H. *et al.* (eds.) (1993) *Tragedy, Comedy and the Polis*, Bari.
Sontag, S. (1978) *Illness as Metaphor*, New York.
Stallybrass, P. (1990) 'Boundary and transgression: body, text, language', *Stanford French Review* 14: 9–23.
Stallybrass, P. and White, A. (1986) *The Politics and Poetics of Transgression*, London.
Stanford, W. B. (1954) *The Ulysses Theme: A Study in the Adaptability of a Traditional Hero*, Oxford.
Steele, R. B. (1920) 'Literary adaptations and references in Petronius', *CJ* 15: 279–93.
Steiner, D. (1994) *The Tyrant's Writ: Myths and Images of Writing in Ancient Greece*, Princeton, N.J.
Stephens, S. A. and Winkler, J. J. (eds.) (1995) *Ancient Greek Novels: The Fragments*, Princeton, N.J.
Stern, J. P. (1973) *On Realism*, London.
Still, J. and Worton, M. (eds.) (1993) *Textuality and Sexuality: Reading Theories and Practices*, Manchester.
Stübbe, H. (1933) *Die Verseinlagen im Petron*, *Philologus* Suppl. 25, Leipzig.
Suleiman, S. R. (ed.) (1987) *The Female Body in Western Culture: Contemporary Perspectives*, Cambridge, Mass.
Sullivan, J. P. (1967) 'Petronius, artist or moralist?', *Arion* 6: 71–88.
(1968a) *The Satyricon of Petronius: A Literary Study*. Bloomington, Ind., and London.
(1968b) 'Petronius, Seneca and Lucan. A Neronian literary feud?', *TAPhA* 99: 453–67.
(1970) 'Textual notes on Petronius', *CQ* 20: 189.
(1976) 'Interpolations in Petronius', *PCPhS* 22: 90–122.
(1985) *Literature and Politics in the Age of Nero*, Ithaca, N. Y., and London.
(1986) *Petronius: the* Satyricon, *Seneca: the* Apocolocyntosis, London.
Svenbro, J. (1988) *Phrasikleia: Anthropologie de la lecture en Grèce ancienne*, Paris.
Syme, R. (1958) *Tacitus*, Oxford.
Takho-Godi, A. A. (1971) 'Valeur stylistique des thèmes chthoniens dans L'Enéide de Virgile', in Bardon and Verdière (1971), 358–74.
Tanner, T. (1979) *Adultery in the Novel: Contract and Transgression*, Baltimore, Md.
Tarkow, T. A. (1981) 'The scar of Orestes: observations on an Euripidean innovation', *RhM* 124: 143–53.
Tatum, J. (ed.) (1994) *The Search for the Ancient Novel*, Baltimore, Md., and London.
Thompson, D. A. W. (1957) *A Glossary of Greek Fishes*, Oxford.
Tracy, V. A. (1980) '*Aut captantur aut captant*', *Latomus* 39: 399–402.
Tuan, Y. F. (1982) *Segmented Worlds and Self: Group Life and Individual Consciousness*, Minneapolis.
Turner, B. S. (1984) *The Body and Society*, Oxford.
Valdés, M. J. (1991) *A Ricoeur Reader: Reflection and Imagination*, New York and London.

Van Hook, L. (1905) *The Metaphorical Terminology of Greek Rhetoric and Literary Criticism*, Chicago.
Verdière, R. (1967) 'Jeux de mots chez Pétrone', *Giornale Italiano di Filologia* 20: 309–12.
Veyne, P. (1961) 'Vie de Trimalchion', *Annales* 16: 213–47.
(1964) 'Le "Je" dans le *Satyricon*', *REL* 42: 301–4.
Vidal-Naquet, P. (1981) 'Land and sacrifice in the *Odyssey*: A study of religious and mythical meanings', in Gordon (1981), 80–94.
Visser, M. (1991) *The Rituals of Dinner: The Origins, Evolution, Eccentricities and Meaning of Table Manners*, New York.
Voltaire (1972) *Philosophical Dictionary*, trans. P. Gay, New York.
Wallace-Hadrill, A. (1987) 'Time for Augustus: Ovid, Augustus and the *Fasti*', in Whitby and Hardie (1987), 221–30.
Walsh, P. G. (1968) 'Eumolpus, the *Troiae halosis* and the *de bello Civili*', *CPh* 63: 208–12.
(1970) *The Roman Novel: The Satyricon of Petronius and the Metamorphoses of Apuleius*, Cambridge.
(1974) 'Was Petronius a moralist?', *G&R* 21: 181–91.
(1996) *Petronius, The Satyricon*, Oxford.
Warning, R. (1989) *Das Fest, Poetik und Hermeneutik* 12, Munich.
Watt, I. (1976) *The Rise of the Novel: Studies in Defoe, Richardson and Fielding*, London.
Webb, R. (1997) 'Imagination and the arousal of the emotions in Graeco-Roman rhetoric' in Braund and Gill (1997), 112–27.
(1999) 'Ekphrasis ancient and modern: the invention of a genre', *Word and Image* 5.1: 7–18.
Whitby, W. and Hardie, P. (1987) *Homo Viator: Classical Essays for John Bramble*, Bristol.
Wicks, W. (1989) *Picaresque Narrative, Picaresque Fictions: A Theory and Research Guide*, New York.
Wiedemann, T. (1992) *Emperors and Gladiators*, London and New York.
Williams, C. A. (1999) *Roman Homosexuality: Ideologies of Masculinity in Classical Antiquity*, New York and Oxford.
Williams, G. (1978) *Change and Decline: Roman Literature in the Early Empire*, Berkeley, Calif.
Willis, S. (1987) *Marguerite Duras: Writing on the Body*, Urbana, Ill.
Wiltshire, B. (1982) *Role Playing and Identity: The Limits of Theatre as Metaphor*, Bloomington, Ind.
Wimmel, W. (1960) *Kallimachos in Rom. Die Nachfolge seines Apologetischen Dichtens in der Augusteerzeit, Hermes Einzelschriften* 16.
Winkler, J. J. (1985) *Auctor and Actor: A Narratological Reading of Apuleius' Golden Ass*, Berkeley, Calif.
(1990) *The Constraints of Desire: The Anthropology of Sex and Gender in Ancient Greece*, New York and London.
Wirszubski, C. (1950) *Libertas as a Political Ideal at Rome*, Cambridge.

Wiseman, T. P. (1988) 'Satyrs in Rome? The background to Horace's *Ars Poetica*', *JRS* 78: 1–13.
Wolfreys, J. (ed.) (1998) *The Derrida Reader: Writing Performances*, Edinburgh.
Wooton, C. (1976) 'Petronius, the mime and rhetorical education', *Helios* 3: 67–74.
(1984) 'Petronius and "Camp"', *Helios* 11: 133–9.
Worthen, W. B. (1984) *The Idea of the Actor: Drama and the Ethics of Performance*, Princeton, N.J.
Wright, J. (1976) 'Disintegrated assurances: the contemporary American response to the *Satyricon*', *G&R* 23: 32–9.
Wyke, M. (1997) 'Herculean muscle!: the classicizing rhetoric of bodybuilding', *Arion* 4(3): 51–79.
Wyke, M. (ed.) (1998) *Parchments of Gender: Deciphering the Bodies of Antiquity*, Oxford.
Young, K. (1989) 'Narrative embodiments: enclaves of the self in the realm of medicine', in Shotter and Gergen (1989), 152–65.
Zanker, P. (1988) *The Power of Images in the Age of Augustus*, Ann Arbor, Mich.
Zeitlin, F. I. (1971 a) 'Petronius as paradox: anarchy and artistic integrity', *TAPhA* 102: 631–84.
(1971 b) '*Romanus* Petronius: A study of the *Troiae halosis* and the *Bellum civile*', *Latomus* 30: 56–82.
(1990) 'The poetics of eros: nature, art, and imitation in Longus' *Daphnis and Chloe*', in Halperin, Winkler and Zeitlin (1990), 417–64.

Index of passages discussed

Index of subjects

Lightning Source UK Ltd.
Milton Keynes UK
UKOW05f0744301214
243771UK00003B/252/P

9 780521 037013